Foreword

A rubbish dump is perhaps an inauspicious place to make an acquaintance! It was, nonetheless, at the Blairgowrie "Recycling Centre" that Archie McBrain first approached me with the request that I write a short foreword to accompany his book of poems. Having agreed to do so I awaited with interest to read the poetic offerings to be included.

As part of the Blairgowrie and Rattray landscape myself, I am always interested in encouraging the celebration of our little piece of Scotland, and in this instance from the hand of one who has been resident in the area for less than two years. During that time Archie has combined an appreciation of the Blairgowrie district from the Wellmeadow to the silvery Tay with his own quirky view of life and this has produced the humorous pieces contained in this volume.

I am confident that you will be amused by these poems and hope that you will derive the same pleasure from them as I have.

Laurence Blair Oliphant

There You Are

Whistling is a useful skill
A fact which I intend to prove
Whenever there's some time to fill
Standing still or on the move

I use my vacant moments when
I whistle a favourite melody
Re-playing all those tunes again
From my personal memory

Take my advice, I think I know
No iPod needed, 'phones or wires
You just purse your lips and blow
For amusement which never tires

Also take a warning here
It all sounds better in your mind
To other folk your tunes appear
Tuneless, dull and unrefined

Ask my wife about her man
Despite the fact that *I'm* her spouse
My wife is not a whistling fan
But she knows where I am about the house

It's a Hobby

Zack, our cat has a favourite spot
Where he lies in wait, hatching a plot

He sits for ages on the window sill
Observing the birds which are eating their fill

Our bird table provides amusement for Zack
Then temptation sends him on the attack

From the kitchen, down the hall and out the back
Zack runs, but his cat-flap will always *clack*

This scares the birds, they flee the place
Our cat is left with egg on his face

CASTLE FOR SALE

HUMOROUS POEMS FROM BLAIRGOWRIE

Archie McBrain

PODITY
PUBLISHING

CASTLE FOR SALE

Copyright © Archie McBrain 2008

All Rights Reserved

ISBN 978-0-9559641-0-7

First Published 2008 by
Podity Publishing
Second edition published March 2009

www.podity.co.uk

Printed in Great Britain by
www.novelize.co.uk

Fonts: Palatino Linotype, *Monotype Corsiva*, Bradley Hand ITC.

For A

Daisy & Bruce

Handsome Bruce had found a bald patch
On top in the centre of his thatch

This was a bother and a worry
He wanted to marry but was in a hurry

How could the girls be fascinated
By a man who is shiny pated?

Bruce rubbed Vaseline upon it
And roofed it over with a bonnet

He massaged in, raw eggs and beer
Marinated well, from ear to ear

Balding Bruce need not have acted
Someone was already attracted

A lovely girl called Daisy Grey
Fell for Bruce and saved the day

Ketchup & Chips

Near the pub where chips were dropped
Several early birds have stopped

For crows the breakfast is OK
They peck potato at break of day

Soon the pavement's clear once more
Except for ketchup on the floor

A little rain will lick the plate
Where those earlie birdies ate

So mother nature clears the site
For unsteady footsteps in the night

All Too Brief

"Time has wings" like a little bird
Escaping from a net
Should time fly? It's more absurd
The older that you get

"Youth is wasted on the young"
I've often heard it said
The song of life is left unsung
The moment that you're dead

"Die, that's the last thing I'll do"
Oscar was the first to say
Make the most of time or rue
The days you frittered away

Delightful Graffiti

Did you expect to hear that I like graffiti?
Don't worry, that wouldn't be like me

Selfish scrawling, tags on walls
That's not art, it's just… vandalism

But there was this one time
A graffiti quite sublime

Crossing the wooden bridge over the river
Weather so cold it made us shiver

Frosted handrail in late December
Graffiti there, we fondly remember

Traced in frost, a finger tip had writ
"Merry Christmas" then sunshine melted it

Full Flow

The River Ericht rolls and turns
Swollen now by icy burns

Springtime brings a torrent then
From the mountains up the glen

Melt water coursing down from snow
Sphagnum holding rain lets go

Shallows deepen, powerful quick
Speeding water brown and thick

Peaty, swirling, frothy, surging
Heaving, bubbling, onward urging

The rolling river runs and then
Its sudden spate subsides again

Wee Jedi in Kilts

Lads and lassies, tartan and beer
All of local life is here

The Wellmeadow's full, with such a throng
'Tis Braemar night and the force is strong

Two young warriors, contest their skills
Brothers with light sabres, in a battle of wills

Jimmy's the elder but Neil is quick
He delivers a whack with his glowing stick

"You are weak, young Skywalker" says Neil
Half believing his weapon is real

Jimmy comes back with a leap and a twirl
But misses completely and bashes a girl

She's just walking past… when suddenly… splat
Off comes her pink feather trimmed cowboy hat

Neil falls over laughing, Jimmy feels bad
Jenny just thinks they both must be mad

Jimmy says sorry, picks up the headwear
Jenny's not laughing as passers-by stare

Despite all this, she thinks "this boy is cool"
She's not seen the clumsy Jedi at school
Braemar Night works its magic, soon we see
Young love blossom in the heart of Blairgowrie

A Highland Limerick

To wear the kilt there's a certain knack
Smooth at the front and pleats at the back
The sporran is neat
The outfit's complete
Not too tight and not too slack

Another Highland Limerick

A glorious stag near Portree
Got his antlers stuck in a tree
But the Island of Skye
Is no place to die
I'm pleased to say he got free

Yet Another Highland Limerick

Our weather is better than people say
Certainly not *always* raining and grey
It sometimes snows
It sometimes blows
But it's lovely and sunny today

A Final Highland Limerick

Take away the haggis and shortbread
No more of the porridge on which I'm fed
I've had quite enough
Of that clichéd stuff
Just give me McDonald's instead

Accurate Timing

A watchmaker once explained the way
To make my watch keep perfect time
"Remove the seconds hand" he'd say
"Then you'll find its accuracy is fine"

I took his advice and what do you know?
Never again was it fast or slow
Since then my timing has been grand
As I also took off the minute hand

The hour hand slowly trundles round
On its own, the dial displays
But now there's something I have found
Time matters less to me these days

Money Matters

With credit cards, loans and overdraft
A regular income helps and yet
It is so easy to be daft
And slide until you're deep in debt

Your credit rating's shot and then
Your money's never your own again
Being dunned is hardly fun
You'll wish you never had begun

That slippery slope, so hard to beat
Percentage rates you can't defeat
Punitive charges at your expense
Racking up the pounds and pence

Then at last it's off you go
To the Citizens' Advice Bureau
Debt counseling to set you straight
Now you make the creditors wait

Careful planning and strategy
Eventually sets you financially free
Promise to be good and aspire
Never again to get in the mire

****

Some can save while others spend
Money moves, it ebbs and flows
On cold, hard cash, you can depend
So salt some away, because… who knows?

Chocolate Coins

Chocolate money is the very best kind
Of edible currency I can find

The exchange rate is very good
Small change for food

Robins, Mice, Kids & Herons

Springtime surprises ruin my plan:
A family of robins made their nest
Inside my only watering can
Outwith I'll have to do my best

And in my shed some little mice
Have eaten all the seeds I kept
From last year's crops, how nice!
My favourites gone, I could have wept!

My greenhouse, usually just the ticket
Now makes me angry, I confess
Next door's kids were playing cricket
It's all smashed up, it's in a mess

The fish pond was my pride and joy
A closer look, shows what's what
No sign of all my graceful koi
The heron's been and had the lot

So this year, it was all too much for me
To tend my garden, keep fish or plant seeds
I stayed in, watching football on TV
The score was Archie nil, ten to the weeds

On The Perfect Wall

By the back of our cottage, standing seven feet tall
Is our wonderful, perfect garden wall

Built of river boulders, with gaps in between
And four kinds of ferns in shades of green

The stones are mossy, covered in lichen
They're usually shaded by the kitchen

My favourite, it must be seen to be believed
Is a toadflax… of the variety… ivy leaved

It has delicate flowers, snap-dragons so tiny
The leaves are five pointed, rounded and shiny

In drought and flood it clings on and survives
Despite harsh conditions, the toadflax thrives

Setting seed the toadflax does a very clever thing
Reaching up and stretching out like a piece of string

It plants its seeds above itself in a crevice on the wall
And so it can ascend and live where other plants would fall

Rhymes With…

On the way to Perth
You pass a hedge of beech
It is the biggest one on Earth
The top is nearly out of reach
Recorded in the Guinness Book
It is really worth a look
On the right as you tour
Past the sign for Meikleour

Further along the road to Perth
Again on your right
Historic monument of great worth
So far back it's out of sight
Go down the drive and stop
It also has a wee gift shop
Tourists buy a souvenir spoon
At the ancient Palace of Scone

Runner Beans

Seedlings climb the sticks in rows
Sprouting leaves, how do they learn?
To spiral upwards, heaven knows
How they decide which way to turn

Old Age Strikes Again

Is it the pain in my back or the hair in my ears?
Which rewards me for living this many years

"Where are my glasses?" I repeatedly say
Looking for them helps to fill in my day

Am I set in my ways?
It's what everyone says

Is it so wrong to admit to a preference?
It's just that I need a frame of reference

Everything in its place, so I know where they are
Now where did I leave… the keys for the car?

A laugh here and there
Helps me not to care

I'm getting better at handling longevity
With the help of some timely levity

Laugh and your problem's diminished
Cry and you're just about finished

Though every part of me is about to crumble
You'll hear me say "I mustn't grumble"

My Violin

My violin has a tune within
It haunts me night and day
I want it out instead of in
How I wish that I could play

My teacher tries and tries with me
To move the tuneless strings
But so far all there seems to be
Are squeaky, squawky, painful things

My sounds are songs of cats at night
The bow and strings defy
And though I practice, I just might
Never succeed, although I try

My ears and fingers do their best
With the Scales & Arpeggios book
But how I long for a longer rest
Than the quavers and semitones took

My patience has *some* just reward
Though progress is painfully slow
When I try to play, I'm never bored
And at least I can say, I had a go

My fiddle teacher is sweet and kind
She says "the music is strong in you"
Hopefully one day we shall find
The music that's made by the few

Call Me Old Fashioned

Aren't baseball caps daft on British heads?
Do I care what other folk do in their beds?
Too many channels on the TV
Pandering to every talentless wannabe

Call me old fashioned, I won't be offended
I know what I like, others pretended
To move with the times, fit in with the herd
Good taste, bad taste, the distinction is blurred

Holiday Prisoner

Somewhere in the French countryside
A Scottish ladybird is taken for a ride
In our car, she is trapped... on the inside

We watch the vineyards passing by
And fluffy clouds in azure sky
But can't hear the insect's lonely cry

Her *"HELP ME"* Too quiet to hear
Inaudible to the human ear
She sheds a microscopic tear

When her freedom comes one day
She takes the only chance she may
The ladybird unfurls her tiny wings and flies away, away...........

^O^. ... .
                               \
                                .
                               \
                      . . . .

The Golden Boomerang

My friends have gone, it's sad to say
They've mostly died or moved away

There are acquaintances, a few
Saying "Hello Archie, how are you?"

But people tend to pass me by
And no one stops to ask me why

"Are you alone?" or "Do you care?"
Here are some thoughts that I would share

If like-minded folk were to be found
I'd explain myself in words profound

By metaphor and simile
They'd know the meaning of the real me

What makes me laugh or sigh or sing?
What are the joys that life can bring?

To one who thinks, perhaps too much
What are the things a heart can touch?

What are my skills and how could I
Create a rainbow in the sky

Cont∂...

Imagine all you can achieve
If self knowledge gave the strength to leave

To others the deeds you can not do
And so success was all you knew

No fear of failure, doubt or worry
Always calm, not in a hurry

The time to marvel at little things
Like snails and spiders and ants with wings

A love of life of every kind
Respect for all and peace of mind

Now here's a thought, a way of seeing
How I try to learn from every being

The Aborigine can throw
A special stick so well, you know

The boomerang goes out and back
To he who throws with just the knack

So ask yourself which it's better to be
The curved stick or the Aborigine

Both have magic, style and grace
One has a smile, the other a face

Sorry

Brought up to believe good manners are wise
If you tread on my toes, I'll apologize

Supermarket Selection

Near the chocolate Hob-Nobs, where I am
In the biscuit aisle, there's a bit of a jam

Baskets and people crowding in
Around the special offer bin

EIGHT FOR THE PRICE OF TWO is what it says
Surely a mistake amongst the displays

A mistake perhaps, but sure enough
They're loading up with under-priced stuff

"Will eight packets see us through the week?"
I hear a weighty woman shriek

"Get sixteen" her husband replies
With wobbling chins and bulging eyes

Seeing this puts me off, I must admit
I consider the offer and think better of it

Cactusses

There was a cactus and a similar one
In the dessert beneath the sun

So there they were under the sky
A lovely matching pair of cactusses

Fresh Cheese Scones

Flour and milk, cheddar and some butter
Roll out the dough, use a wavy edge cutter

Just out of the oven, too hot to eat
My wife's cheese scones are hard to beat

Dun Roaming

I would refrain
To fly by plane

For safety's sake
A train I'd take

Or better still
I'd walk until

The need to roam
Has brought me home

And then I'd see
On my TV

A travel show
And then I'd know

Where I would really like to go… ideally.

Stoat

Along a lane in broad daylight
Where we drove that sunny day
Out ran a stoat all brown and white
And looked at us in some dismay

We stopped the car, he froze on the tarmac
Neither he nor we could pass
Then like a flash, he ran right back
The stoat was gone amongst the grass

Suddenly he reappeared
Long body whiplash, feet a blur
But stopped again as the middle neared
A panicked streak of teeth and fur

Back again he dashed to hide
Where he had been just before
Then he swallowed all his pride
And scurried back across the floor

With tasseled tail held up high
This final time he kept on going
We thought him funny as he rushed by
What he thought of us… there is no knowing

Spring Cleaning

I have proved, this very Spring
The internet is a wonderful thing

I wanted a mighty Dyson cleaner
But not at new prices, I am meaner

So I searched around on the internet
To see how cheap the thing can get

For a bargain Dyson, so they say
The best place to go is good old eBay

So, on I logged and placed my bid
Setting a maximum of thirty quid

Then while I waited for the auction's end
I checked out Amazon, the reader's friend

I looked for a book to help the wife clean
"Spring Cleaning for Dummies" what can they mean?

Back onto eBay, I'm outbid by a buyer
So I raise my offer higher and higher

contd...

We battle it out till the end of the sale
A frenzy of bidding that leaves me quite pale

Just in the nick of time
The winning bid is mine

A bit of a surprise to me
The final price, plus p&p

It's what auctions are like, everyone knows
I got carried away, that's just how it goes

Then home comes the missus, with another surprise
"You always *wanted* one of these" I can't believe my eyes

"A lovely new Dyson, it's the leading brand"
Now *I'll* do the Spring cleaning with one in each hand

Seriously Though

Now my attempt at a poem that's sensible
I know that I'm usually reprehensible
       Focusing only on the funny stuff
       Hilarity is not nearly enough
Life offers more than this and so should I
I'll write something sensible, here's my try
       Verses improving on the usual whimsy
       Weightier words that don't sound flimsy
I will avoid the temptation to be flippant
Despite the fact that nothing rhymes with flippant
       A poem that's not depending
       On having a twist or a funny ending
So here goes… my serious shot
Look out World, ready or not…

    … Oh blast!

Blairgowrie Meals on Wheels

Morag grits her teeth and sits behind the steering wheel
Her duty to deliver - hot - each and every meal
Riding shotgun, today she has - Agnes. What a team!
Wearing running socks and shoes, she's looking fit and lean

So off they go despite all odds of wind and snow and rain
The Pony Express of the WRVS is ready to ride again
In the town and round about, their route is complicated
The old folk wait anticipating their hunger satiated

Some live alone, remote, lacking company
M-o-W's provide for them a friendly face to see
Human contact, keeping in touch, checking all is well
With friends and family scattered wide, who else is there to tell?

Sadly too, when the Grim Reaper's been
The volunteers may be first on the scene
Happily, today everything's tickety boo
It's Mr Muir's birthday, he's ninety two

Mrs Ogilvy's back from a hospital stay
Mrs Scott has her grandchildren today
Mr Knox is gardening, taking in the sun
Mrs Grant collects garden gnomes, her idea of fun

All deliveries now complete, they're ready to go home
Morag and Agnes return for their own lunch at "The Dome"

Bungee Jumping

Oh what fun it certainly must be
To jump off a bridge attached to a bungee

Freefall followed by elastication
Terrible terror then pure elation

Dangling there, a human yoyo
Proud of yourself for having a go go

When will I try it? Is that what you say?
When hell freezes over, that'll be the day

Random

In a world so organized
Something random should be prized
Treasure unexpected things
Enjoy the delight that this brings

Muddy hoof-marks all rained on
A gateway where the cows have gone
Fragmented reflections of the sky
In cloven pools the clouds pass by

Quite a lot of cards this year
And most feature a reindeer
The rest have robins on them
Out of fashion is Bethlehem

A letter misaddressed to you
Opened quickly before you knew
It was for someone else of course
A bill from a vet about their horse

Bumping into an old friend
The unplanned moment prevents the end
Of elusive friendship, tenuous links
"See you soon" that's what he thinks!

Our National Lottery offers the chance
To those with a ticket bought in advance
Lady Luck smiles, right then and there
The random selection of a millionaire

Common Missblunderstandings

In English … spelling is quite nice
That is to say… it is precise
-o-
A set of rules with exceptions…numerous
Don't really help us understand
How to spell this language, so humorous
Which seems to be utterly unplanned

Historic weirdness, now set in stone
Curious mistakes which went un-deleted
If you're confused you're not alone
Because of what early printers repeated

Portmanteau words can be an irritation
A double-meaning free-for-all
To say nothing of pronunciation
We say nation but also national

'Though homonyms mean different things
They are spelled and sound the same
We love the havoc which this brings
When foreigners play the context game

Yer wot?

English can be strangely phrased
An oxymoron does this best
The clashing senses are amazed
Like a time warp in a string vest
-o-

Nuffink.

Now dictionaries state with authority
The illogical but correct spelling and use of how it all *should* be

113

X Marks the Spot

The desk was old but older still
Hidden within was a pirate's will

A treasure map, on wrinkled parchment
Signed in blood, in the secret compartment

The yellowing, grimy, dusty chart
Depicts an island shaped like a heart

"L'Ile de Coeur" in the Caribbean sea
Marked with a cross where the treasure must be

Pieces of eight and Spanish plunder
Lies buried there, six feet under

By a skull-shaped rock, in the shade of a tree
Yes the map looks genuine, we all agree

So just between us, this is all that I'll say
Guess where we're going for our next holiday!

Near Enough

How many more times
Will I have to find rhymes
For impossible words such as dunderheads?

Sadly for me
The answer will be
A number high up in the hun-der-eds

Aftword

Well... dear reader, you have reached the end.

I hope you enjoyed *'Castle For Sale'* I had fun writing the poems and doing the little drawings.

Poking fun at the serious side of life has become a sort of hobby for me... and you will have spotted my tendency to slip in a measure of philosophy here and there. In the poem 'No Answers' I said that 'philosophizing is inaction' by this I mean that it butters no parsnips but I must admit that I have a fondness for philosophy nonetheless... and buttered parsnips!

Quite a lot of these poems give an insight into my way of thinking, others are entirely misleading, some are deliberately flippant, one or two are perfectly pointless. At my age I apologise for very little, I find this saves a lot of time.

For many years I have written the odd verse but it was my wife's idea to gather together a bouquet of them in this book. She is one of those exceptional people who are loved by all who know them. I am incredibly fortunate to have been married to an angel for nearly fifty years. She is the A to whom *Castle For Sale* is dedicated.

Blairgowrie is lovely... as a place to live... or visit. It is easily the best town in Perthshire and Perthshire is the best county in Scotland, obviously Scotland is the best part of the UK! This is my book... I'll say what I like!

The visitor is probably best able to see what a jewel Blairgowrie is. Fresh eyes are needed to appreciate the wonderful people, beautiful architecture, fine views, fascinating wildlife and verdant, rolling countryside. Many of the local people have lived here their entire lives so it's wallpaper to them. I positively love living in Blairgowrie, perhaps because I'm originally from Dull, a tiny village a few miles to the West... enough said.

Feedback is good, if you would like to comment or ask a question, please feel free. Just go to my publisher's website and e-mail me:

www.podity.co.uk

Thank you:

To my darling wife, for her unending love, support, inspiration and patience!

To Laurence Blair Olliphant, for his kind and generous Foreword.

To Alex Blackburn, for her excellent and timely proof-reading.

To Greg, for his computer expertise and extreme patience, he is totally awesome!

To all at Podity Publishing, for helping a first time author to 'get into print' as painlessly as possible.

To Tim Lunn and all at Novelize Book Print Ltd. for working the magic of print-on-demand.

A Final Word

Now, in a flamboyant show of
unprecedented humility, I leave
the last word to someone whose
insight and eloquence can state
in two sentences, what took
me a whole book of
poems to
say:

**A single event can awaken within us a
stranger totally unknown to us.**

To live is to be slowly born.

Antoine de Saint-Exupery (1900 -1944)

Index

GERMAN

DR.OETKER

HOME

COOKING

COMPILED IN THE TESTING KITCHEN

OF DR. AUGUST OETKER BIELEFELD

PUBLISHER:

CERES-VERLAG RUDOLF-AUGUST OETKER KG BIELEFELD

Printed in Germany by Druckerei Gustav Bentrup, Bielefeld

Ownership, copyright and all other rights reserved in all countries

by Ceres-Verlag Rudolf-August Oetker KG, Bielefeld

© Copyright 1963

Fifth edition 1971

In Germany, the name DR. OETKER is a household word, and even outside that country the name is very familiar to many. But those who have not heard of it may find this brief introduction helpful.

Dr. August Oetker was a chemist, a man tremendously interested in, and knowledgeable about, food in its importance to our health and general well-being. He founded a factory in Bielefeld, in Western Germany, which continues to manufacture many of his own products, such as GUSTIN (corn starch powder), Baking Powder BACKIN, and various Pudding and Blancmange Powders – all bestsellers among German housewives.

In 1911, Dr. Oetker wrote a cookery book incorporating the knowledge and experience he had acquired over the years. The book had an immediate and overwhelming success in his own country. Since then, over twelve million copies have been sold. In Bielefeld a fully qualified research staff, working in a beautifully equipped model testing kitchen, constantly check and revise the original recipes, adding many new ones as kitchen and cooking conditions change with the times. Each new edition of the OETKER cookery book published since 1911 has been brought up-to-date, and because of its continuing usefulness, this book has not only retained but increased its popularity.

Now for the first time we present an English edition of the OETKER cookery book. Many Germans who have settled in the U. S. A., Canada, Australia and other English-speaking countries are familiar with the book through long use. Their children may appreciate this modern English version of an old family friend.

New readers will discover that Oetker methods and recipes are simple, practical and economical; and will find OETKER products easy to use and delicious to eat. Many of the recipes – particularly those in the comprehensive sections on cakes and soups – are full of ideas new to English-speaking housewives, who may enjoy trying out these long-standing German favourites.

We are confident that this first English edition of the OETKER GERMAN HOME COOKING will be as useful and popular as its many predecessors.

DR. AUGUST OETKER BIELEFELD

TABLE OF CONTENTS

INTRODUCTION

HINTS AND ADVICE FOR THE MODERN COOK

HINTS AND ADVICE
FOR THE MODERN COOK

PLANNING THE MENU

1. To be really economical, all menu planning should be done well in advance. A week is a convenient period to plan for.

2. Fix the exact weekly or monthly figure that can be spent on feeding the family.

3. Take into account the age, type of work and standard tastes of the various members of the family, bearing in mind special individual requirements (such as dieting).

4. The food used should be of the best quality. It should contain all the nutritive elements required by the body for health and energy.

5. Learn all you can about the latest developments in the science of nutrition. See that you provide plenty of vitamins in winter when fresh green vegetables are not readily available.

6. Vary your menus as much as possible The more varied they are, the more likely they are to provide a balanced diet. Flavour, colour, health considerations and the way the food is prepared all play a part in the planning of the meal, and individual meals should complement each other in all these respects.

7. Meals should be designed to suit the season. They should be light and refreshing in warm weather, but richer in fat and other energy builders in cooler weather.

8. Choose food which is plentiful, and therefore cheap. Be flexible in your planning and build your menus around the foods available in the stores.

SHOPPING

1. See that you get good food value for your money. Many expensive foods have little or no nutritive value, whilst other, cheaper foods (skim milk or cottage cheese for example) can be made up into many delightful dishes.

2. When shopping for food, bear in mind the purpose for which you are buying. For instance, you will have to buy top quality fruit and vegetables for preserving, but for soups they need not be of such good quality.

3. Always use perishable foods, such as meat or fish, as soon as possible after purchase.

4. Buy food which is in season. It will be cheaper and so give you value for money.

5. Take advantage of any glut of fruit or vegetables and preserve some to use when they are less plentiful and much more expensive.

STORING FOOD

1. Every housewife needs to stock food, even if she has only a small amount of space for the purpose.

Reasons:

a) It saves time. Buy all the food you need for a week, except perishables, in one operation.

b) The larger quantity is often cheaper. Avoid purchasing small quantities of food.

c) By keeping a good supply of food in stock, the housewife will be prepared for emergencies (e. g. unexpected guests).

2. Stocking on a larger scale should only be attempted when suitable storage space and equipment are available.

3. All stocks must be properly stored so that they will not deteriorate. Further information about storing food can be found in the introductions to the various chapters of this book.

4. Keep your larder and food cupboards cool, airy and clean. Any windows should have gauze screens to keep out insects. If you use a basement for storage, it should be cool and dry; the best temperature is about 40° F (4° C).

5. The ideal place for storing perishable food in hot weather is an icebox or refrigerator. If no fly-proof cupboard is available, use gauze covers. Cover them with wet Turkish towels and they will protect even highly perishable foods like meat or sausages, keeping them fresh and cool on the hottest day.

6. If possible, keep vegetables in a basement, either spread out on the floor (beans), buried in moist sand (root vegetables) or wrapped in a wet cloth (asparagus).

7. Items such as cereals, pulses, spices, etc. should be stored in tins or jars to keep them dry. Glass containers are particularly good, because they are easy to check.

PREPARATION OF FOOD

1. Start your preparations in plenty of time but not too early. Vegetables such as potatoes are ruined if they are kept soaking in water and many dishes can be spoiled by being left in the oven too long.

2. Prepare the ingredients economically, throwing away only what is completely unusable. Vegetable stalks and similar parings, bones, gristle and meat trimmings can all be used to make stock for soups and sauces.

3. Never leave food soaking in water for any length of time. Much nutriment may be lost in the liquid.

COOKING

1. Cooking should make food not only delicious to eat, but much easier to digest.

2. To make the most of the nutritive value of food, it must be cooked in the right manner. For instance, you should decide or whether your cut of meat would be best roasted, braised or stewed; whether a cereal needs to be soaked before cooking, and so on.

3. Cooking should not destroy food value. Therefore avoid any prolonged cooking in water as this results in loss of food value.

4. To preserve vitamins, cook food for as short a time as possible, keeping the pot tightly closed. Start at a high temperature then reduce the heat to a minimum.

5. Because heat develops aromatic qualities in food, which stimulate the appetite, take great care with roasting, braising and frying. When food is eaten with a good appetite, the body is able to assimilate the nutritive elements easier.

6. Hot food is easier to digest than cold. Always serve at least one hot meal a day.

7. Always prepare food under hygienic conditions. Hands, cutlery and all kitchen tools and utensils must be scrupulously clean.

SEASONING

1. Carefully season all dishes to taste.

2. Condiments and spices are meant to refine and enhance the flavour of a dish, they themselves must never predominate. Be careful in your choice of spices and sparing in their use.

3. Excessive use of salt, seasoning, condiments, herbs or spices is injurious to health. It dulls the taste buds, irritates the digestive glands and creates thirst, thereby placing an undue burden on the heart and kidneys.

4. Ring the changes on spices and seasonings. Monotonous use of the same seasoning lessens its stimulating effect.

5. In preparing food for children and invalids, take particular care not to over-season.

LEFTOVERS

1. Keep leftovers in a cool place and use them as soon as possible. Be especially careful with left-over fish, meat, mushroom and egg aishes, as they deteriorate rapidly and may cause poisoning.

2. You will find many ideas and recipes in this book which will help you to serve leftovers attractively. There is no need to warm them up and serve them again in the original form.

BASIC COOKING TERMS

Boiling Cooking food in water. Only to be recommended if all the water is later to be used for soups or sauces, as some vitamins and other nutritive substances are boiled out into the cooking water.

Steaming Cooking food in steam. This method helps to preserve food values because the food does not come into direct contact with water. The food is cooked in a steamer over boiling water.

Stewing Cooking food so as to draw out the juices.

Sweating Slow frying in order to extract moisture e.g. from vegetables. If necessary a little stock may be added. All food values are retained by this method.

Braising By this method, food is heated in a little fat until brown. Liquid is then added and the cooking completed with the pot or pan covered. The process brings out aroma and flavour.

Frying Cooking food in fat in a frying pan at a high temperature on top of the stove or range.

Broiling or Grilling Cooking food under the direct heat of a grill in an oven. The process brings out aroma and flavour.

Baking or Roasting Both these terms describe the process of cooking food by means of hot air in an oven, either in an uncovered or a covered pan. In some circumstances, fat may be added. "Baking" is usually applied to cakes, pastry, fish and vegetables; the term "roasting" is used with various cuts of meat, poultry and game.

Deep Frying Cooking food in deep fat. The food floats in very hot fat.

Sautéing Cooking or partly cooking (onions and other vegetables for example) in hot fat. The food may or may not be browned.

Breading (Coating With Egg And Breadcrumbs) The food is dipped first in flour, then in beaten egg or milk and lastly in breadcrumbs.

Roux A mixture of melted fat and flour. The fat is melted, flour added and the whole heated until yellow or brown as required. Liquid is added slowly and the mixture stirred to prevent the formation of lumps. The mixture is then allowed to simmer gently for 5–10 minutes.

QUANTITIES FOR THE FAMILY

The average quantities given below must, of course, be considered in relation to the special needs of each household. Age, type of work, habits and so on must all be taken into account. The following quantities can be used as a general guide for servings per person and per meal.

½ pint (285 ccm)   soup as a first course,
1 pint (570 ccm)   soup as a main course,
⅕ pint (115 ccm)   sauce,
3½–4½ oz. (100–125 g) meat without bones,
4½–5½ oz. (125–150 g) meat with bones,
   9 oz.   (250 g) fish with head,
5½–7 oz. (150–200 g) fish fillet,
7 –9 oz. (200–250 g) vegetable,
   9 oz.   (250 g) potatoes,
   4½ oz.   (125 g) fresh fruit,
   2 oz.   (55 g) dried fruit.

All recipes in this book are sufficient for 4 people (unless stated otherwise). Ingredients are listed in the order in which they are to be used in the recipe.

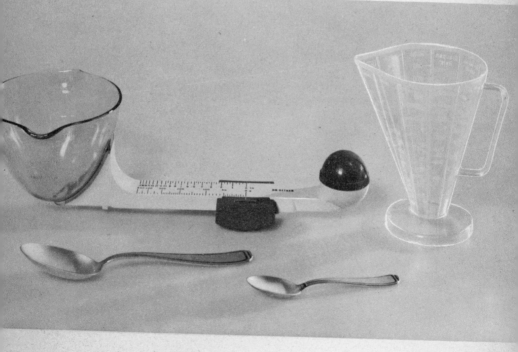

WEIGHTS AND MEASURES

In translating the quantities into English, some rounding off occurs in the equivalent gram and ccm quantities. This has been done to avoid unnecessarily clumsy figures and decimilisation. All the quantities in English have been carefully checked.

All ingredients in this book are given in precise quantities to avoid guess-work, which so often results in waste of food and failure of recipes. Every housewife should learn to be exact in her weighing and measuring, other-wise she will never be successful with her recipes nor economical in her shopping. We hope our chart will make the weighing of small quantities easier, but we must point out that the untrained housewife should always try to weigh ingredients exactly. As she becomes more experienced, she will find herself able to measure the amount she needs with spoons or cups or even with her eye.

1 tbsp. flour, level	⅜ oz.	(10 g)
1 tbsp. GUSTIN (corn starch powder), slightly heaped	⅜ oz.	(10 g)
1 tbsp. breadcrumbs, level	⅜ oz.	(10 g)
1 tbsp. semolina, level	7 drams	(12 g)
1 tbsp. barley, level	7 drams	(12 g)
1 tbsp. salt, level	⅜ oz.	(10 g)
1 tbsp. sugar, level	½ oz.	(15 g)
1 tbsp. sugar, slightly heaped	¾ oz.	(20 g)
1 tbsp. sugar, well heaped	1 oz.	(30 g)
1 tbsp. fat, level	½ oz.	(15 g)
1 tsp. GUSTIN (corn starch powder), slightly heaped	2 drams	(3 g)
1 tsp. salt, level	3 drams	(5 g)
1 tsp. Baking Powder BACKIN, level	2 drams	(3 g)
5 medium-sized apples	1⅛ lb.	(500 g)
6–7 medium-sized potatoes	1⅛ lb.	(500 g)

2¼ lb. = 1000 g (1 kg)

2	pints	= 1125 ccm (1⅛ l)	
1¾	pint	= 1000 ccm (1 l)	
1⅓	pint	= 750 ccm (¾ l)	
1	pint	= 570 ccm	
⅔	pint	= 375 ccm (⅜ l)	
½	pint	= 285 ccm	
¼	pint	= 140 ccm	
16	oz. (1 lb.) =	450 g	
9	oz.	= 250 g	
8	oz.	= 225 g	
7	oz.	= 200 g	

6 oz. =	170 g
5 oz. =	140 g
4 oz. =	115 g
3 oz. =	85 g
2 oz. =	55 g
1½ oz. =	45 g
1 oz. =	30 g (28.35 g)
¾ oz. =	20 g
½ oz. =	15 g
⅜ oz. =	10 g

SOUPS

Soup has in recent years lost the important place it once held on the menu of the average household. This is partly due to a belief that soup spoils the appetite for the main meal by giving a deceptive feeling of repletion. It has also been pointed out that soup dilutes the gastric juices, puts an undue strain on the heart and kidneys, and often has little compensating nutritive value.

But it should be remenbered that these facts are true only in certain circumstances. Properly prepared and appropriately served, soup stimulates the appetite. By increasing the discharge of gastric juices it aids digestion. Soup can in fact still make the perfect prelude to a meal.

Of course the wise housewife uses soup judiciously in her menu planning. She will never serve a rich soup before a heavy meal, hot, filling soup in warm weather, or iced fruit soup when the thermometer is at zero. She will use the cold, refreshing fruit and wine soups in summer, and the heavy, nourishing soups, which can be so comforting after strenuous nervous or physical effort in winter. She will serve clear soup before a heavy meal, a more filling one before a salad or snack. To ensure that soup will aid and not interfere with digestion she will never serve more than about ½ pint (¼ l) per person, unless of course the soup is to be accompanied by dumplings or similar additions and form the main part of the meal.

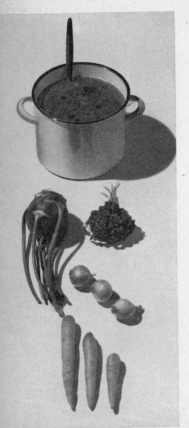

Soup is always based on some main liquid ingredient. The foundation for savoury soups is usually bone, meat, or vegetable stock; for sweet or fruit soups, the foundation is milk, beer, fruit juice, or wine.

Savoury soups may be thick or clear. Rice, dumplings, and similar additions should never be cooked in clear soup, as they make it cloudy. They should be cooked separately in boiling, salted water, rinsed in cold (in the case of cereals and pasta), and then added to the clear soup just before serving.

Thick soups are usually made with flour, Oetker GUSTIN (corn starch powder), semolina, rice, tapioca, noodles, bread, vegetables, and similar thickening agents, so that any further additions in the way of dumplings, meat balls, etc., can be cooked in the soup.

As a general rule, a quart (1⅛ l) of liquid needs 1½ oz. (45 g) flour or Oetker GUSTIN (corn starch powder) to thicken it, or 1½–2 oz. (45–55 g) rice, tapioca, or noodles. Soups which are to be served cold need less of the thickening agent – 1¼ oz. (35 g) flour or Oetker GUSTIN (corn starch powder) for every quart (1⅛ l) of liquid. Flour and GUSTIN should be blended with a little cold liquid before being added to the boiling soup. Rice, semolina, tapioca, etc., can be added direct to the boiling liquid.

Thickening with egg yolk, or the addition of eggs and egg mixtures to soup is dealt with under "Egg Cookery" on page 211 (from rule 5 onwards).

For a stronger flavour, fry the thickening ingredients (flour, semolina, rice, etc.) in a little fat before adding the bulk of the liquid which is to become the soup. Use this method when starting the soup with a roux, browning the flour or not according to taste. A plain basic soup, either white or brown, can be made in this way, according to the following recipes.

16

Stuffed Eggs Recipe See Page 216
Stuffed Tomatoes Recipe See Page 166

A. STOCKS AND BROTHS

1. Wash meat and bones quickly in cold water. Soaking lessens their nutritive value.

2. Bones for stock should be chopped up and put into cold water, then brought to the boil and simmered. To get full value from the bones, a second stock can be obtained by repeating the process.

3. If meat is put into boiling water the cells close up immediately, the meat remains juicy and can be used for other dishes.

4. If meat is to be used solely for broth, it can be cut into small pieces and started off in cold water. Thus the maximum goodness is extracted from meat, bones and marrow.

5. Make sure meat remains covered with water during cooking, otherwise it will be tough.

6. Stock should be brought almost to the boil over high heat and then allowed to simmer gently over low heat.

7. Simmering over a gentle heat in a covered pan does not produce any appreciable evaporation, so no allowance need be made for loss of liquid during cooking.

8. Pot vegetables (carrots, leek, celeriac, parsley root) should be added to the stock for the last hour of cooking and taken out before serving. Finely chopped parsley should be added just before serving, otherwise it loses colour and flavour. An onion fried without fat will brown stock.

General Hints

White Soup

Melt the fat gently over a moderate heat. Add the flour, keeping the roux light in colour. Add the liquid gradually, stirring all the time. Lumps are less likely to form if the liquid is cold or lukewarm and if a whisk is used. With each addition of liquid, bring to the boil. When all the liquid has been added, simmer for about 10 minutes over a low heat before seasoning to taste.

1½ oz. (45 g) butter or margarine
1½ oz. (45 g) plain flour
1 quart (1⅛ l) stock or water
(cold or tepid)

Brown Soup

Melt the fat over a full heat, being careful not to burn. Stir in the flour and cook until a brown roux is formed. Add the liquid gradually, stirring all the time. Lumps are less likely to form if the liquid is cold or lukewarm and if a whisk is used. With each addition of liquid, bring to the boil. When all the liquid has been added, simmer for about 10 minutes over a low heat before seasoning to taste.

1½ oz. (45 g) butter or margarine
2 oz. (55 g) plain flour
1 quart (1⅛ l) stock or water
(cold or tepid)

19

Sauerbraten Recipe See Page 83

Beef Broth

8 oz. (225 g) bones
2¾ pints (1½ l) water
about 1 lb. (450 g) beef
(neck, shin, tail)
salt to taste
pot vegetables (1 leek, 1 small carrot,
1 piece celeriac)
1 onion
a few drops of meat extract or other
seasoning

Wash and chop the bones, cover with the cold water and bring quickly to the boil. Turn down the heat and simmer for 1 hour. Put in the meat and a little salt, bring again to the boil, turn down the heat and simmer for 1½–2 hours. Prepare the pot vegetables (leave whole) and add them with the finely chopped fried onion to the stock for the last hour of cooking. When the broth is done, strain through a fine sieve and season, adding meat extract to taste.

Cooking Time: 2½–3 hours.

This is a clear soup (consommé) and should be served in cups, with white bread or suitable garnish (see page 37). It makes a good basis for a number of other soups with varying garnishes.

Veal Broth

This is made in exactly the same way as Beef Broth (as noted above), but the cooking time is shorter.

Cooking Time: about 1½ hours.

Bone Stock

About 1 lb. (450 g) bones
2¾ pints (1½ l) water
pot vegetables (1 piece celeriac,
1 leek, 1 small carrot)
1 onion
1 tomato

Wash and chop the bones, cover with the cold water and bring quickly to the boil. Turn down the heat and simmer very gently for about 3 hours. After 2 hours simmering, add the prepared pot vegetables (leave whole), the sliced and fried onion, and the washed and quartered tomato. Strain. Use for making thickened or garnished soups. Bone stock is usually cloudy.

Bones contain a gelatinous substance which dissolves slowly and so is difficult to extract. Because of this fact, the same bones can be used at least twice for stock making. Even the bones of boiled or roasted meat are still nutritious and good stock can be made from them.

Cooking Time: approximately 3 hours.

To obtain a more strongly flavoured stock, brown the bones in ¾ oz. (20 g) of fat before adding the water.

Beef Broth with Vermicelli

1 quart (1⅛ l) clear stock
1½–2 oz. (45–55 g) vermicelli
(Italian pasta)
1 tbsp. chopped parsley or chives

Break the vermicelli and sprinkle into the boiling stock. Stir occasionally. Boil gently until done. Serve with the herbs.

Cooking Time: 10–15 minutes.

Sprinkle the washed rice or the tapioca into the boiling stock. Stir occasionally. Boil gently till done. Serve the broth with the herbs.

Cooking Time: rice, about 30 minutes;
tapioca, 15–20 minutes.

Beef Broth with Rice or Tapioca

1 quart (1⅛ l) clear stock
1½–2 oz. (45–55 g) rice or tapioca
1 tbsp. chopped parsley or chives

Wash the rice and sprinkle into the boiling stock. Stir. Add the washed flowerets of cauliflower and the peeled asparagus pieces, simmering gently until done. The vegetables may be cooked in salted water and when done, added to the broth. Make the garnish of "Eierstich" or dumplings according to the recipe and add to the soup.

Cooking Time: about 30 minutes.

Beef Broth with Garnish

1 quart (1⅛ l) clear stock
1½–2 oz. (45–55 g) rice
flowerets of cauliflower and
   asparagus pieces
either "Eierstich" (see page 42)
   or soup dumplings

Beat the egg with the milk or water, salt and nutmeg and pour slowly into the boiling stock, stirring all the time. Bring to the boil. Cover, turn down the heat and simmer till clear (3–4 minutes).

Clear Soup with Egg

1 quart (1⅛ l) clear stock
1 egg
2 tbsp. milk or water
salt to taste
pinch of nutmeg

Combine the flour, milk, egg, salt and nutmeg. Beat well. Add very gradually to the boiling stock, preferably through the holes of a skimming ladle. Sprinkle with the parsley and serve.

Cooking Time: 3 minutes.

Clear Soup with "Einlauf"

1 quart (1⅛ l) clear stock
¾ oz. (20 g) plain flour
1 tbsp. milk
1 egg
salt
pinch of nutmeg
1 tbsp. chopped parsley

Wash and prepare the vegetables. The cauliflower can be broken into small sprigs, the peas shelled, the carrots cut into fancy shapes, the beans and asparagus into short lengths, the tomatoes into pieces. Bring the stock to the boil, add the vegetables and simmer gently over a low heat until done. Season with salt and meat extract, or other seasoning, sprinkle with parsley and serve.

Cooking Time: about 30 minutes.

Garnish with "Eierstich" (see page 42), Semolina Dumplings (see page 43), Marrow Dumplings (see page 44) or Spongy Dumplings (see page 43).

Spring Soup

1 small cauliflower
4 oz. (115 g) fresh peas
2 carrots
2 oz. (55 g) French beans
4 asparagus spears
1–2 tomatoes
1 quart (1⅛ l) clear stock
salt and meat extract, or other
   seasoning, to taste
chopped parsley

Semolina Soup

1 quart (1⅛ l) meat, bone or
vegetable stock
1½–2 oz. (45–55 g) semolina
salt and meat extract, or other
seasoning, to taste
1 tbsp. chopped parsley or chives

Bring the stock to the boil and stir in the semolina. Simmer over a gentle heat until the semolina is done. Season with salt and meat extract or other seasoning, sprinkle with the herbs and serve.

Cooking Time: 10–15 minutes.

Alternatively, the semolina may be stirred into ¾ oz. (20 g) of hot butter or margarine and fried gently till light yellow. Then the stock may be added.

Rice Soup

1 quart (1⅛ l) meat, bone or
vegetable stock
1½–2 oz. (45–55 g) rice
1–2 carrots
salt and meat extract, or other
seasoning, to taste

Bring the stock to the boil, stir in the washed rice and simmer till done. Add the cleaned whole carrots and cook in the stock. Remove the carrots when done, slice them and return them to the stock. Season with salt and meat extract, or other seasoning and serve.

Cooking Time: about 30 minutes.

The rice may be stirred into ¾ oz. (20 g) of hot butter or margarine and fried gently until light yellow. Then the stock may be added and the whole simmered until done.

Barley Soup

1 quart (1⅛ l) meat*), bone or
vegetable stock
1½–2 oz. (45–55 g) barley
cauliflower flowerets
celeriac
salt and meat extract, or other
seasoning, to taste

*) Mutton, salt meat, or gammon
stock are especially recommended
for this soup.

Bring the stock to the boil, add the washed barley and simmer. After half an hour add the cauliflower flowerets and the chopped celeriac. Simmer for a further 30 minutes or so until the vegetables are cooked. Season with salt and meat extract, or other seasoning and serve.

Cooking Time: about 1 hour.

Panades Soup

¾ oz. (20 g) butter or margarine
2 stale bread rolls or white bread
1 quart (1⅛ l) meat, bone or
vegetable stock
1 egg yolk and 2 tbsp. cold water
salt and meat extract, or other
seasoning, to taste

Cut the rolls or the bread into small cubes and fry gently in the butter or margarine until light brown. Add to the boiling stock and cook until soft. Rub the soup through a sieve. Beat the egg yolk with the water and stir into the soup. Season to taste.

Cooking Time: about 15 minutes.

Chop the bones small and brown thoroughly in the fat. Add the chopped onion and the sliced leek, fry for a short time and then add the water. Bring to the boil, turn down the heat and simmer for 2½–3 hours. Add the gravy, strain through a fine sieve and bring to the boil again. Stir in the semolina and simmer for 10–15 minutes. Season to taste.

Cut the roll or bread into cubes and fry in the butter or margarine until light brown. Garnish the soup with the croûtons just before serving.

Cooking Time: about 3 hours.

Alternatively, use a brown roux for thickening instead of the semolina. Stir 2 oz. (55 g) plain flour into 1½ oz. (45 g) butter or margarine and brown well. Stir in the stock. Finish the soup with 1—2 tbsp. of red wine.

Brown Soup

About 1 lb. (450 g) bones leftover from
   roast beef, veal or chicken
¾ oz. (20 g) fat
1 onion
half a leek
2¾ pints (1½ l) water
left-over gravy
1½ oz. (45 g) semolina
salt
1 stale bread roll or white bread
1 tbsp. butter or margarine for frying

Wash the oxtail, dry and separate into joints. Put into a stewpan with the hot fat and the ham leftovers and brown well. Add the sliced onion and the pot vegetables, prepared and finely chopped, and sauté gently with the oxtail for a few minutes. Finally add the water and the spices. Bring to the boil, turn down the heat and simmer gently until the meat is cooked. Strain the stock through a fine sieve and skim off surplus fat. Strip the meat off the bones and cut into neat pieces.

Put the fat into a pan, stir in the flour and brown thoroughly. Pour in the stock, bring to the boil, allow to cook for a while before adding the meat, the lemon juice, the wine and the sugar.

Cooking Time: about 2 hours.

Alternatively, the soup may be thickened instead with 1½ oz. (45 g) Oetker Gustin (corn starch powder).

Oxtail Soup

About ¾ lb. (340 g) oxtail
¾ oz. (20 g) fat
ham leftovers
1 onion
pot vegetables (celeriac, carrot,
   parsley root)
2¾ pints (1½ l) water
spices (4 peppercorns, 2 cloves,
   1 small bay-leaf)
1½ oz. (45 g) fat
2 oz. (55 g) plain flour
salt
1–2 tbsp. lemon juice, red wine or
   Madeira
a little sugar

Melt the 1½ oz. (45 g) fat, stir in the flour and cook gently until pale yellow. Stir in the liquid gradually; turn down the heat and simmer for 10 minutes.

Skin the calf's kidneys and remove the tubes and white tissue. Wash in cold water, then pour hot water over the kidneys and leave them standing for half an hour. Remove from the water, chop finely and cook gently in the fat until done. Add to the soup and allow to boil for a few minutes. Beat the egg yolk in the water and stir into the soup. Season with salt and meat extract, or other seasoning and serve with the parsley.

Cooking Time: 15–20 minutes.

Veal Kidney Soup

1½ oz. (45 g) butter or margarine
1½ oz. (45 g) plain flour
1¾ pint (1 l) meat or bone stock, or
   water
2 calf's kidneys
¾ oz. (20 g) butter or margarine
1 egg yolk and 2 tbsp. cold water
salt and meat extract, or other
   seasoning, to taste
1 tbsp. chopped parsley

Brown Kidney Soup

About 8 oz. (225 g) cow's or pig's
kidneys
1½ oz. (45 g) fat
1 small onion
pot vegetables
2¼ pints (1¼ l) water
2–3 potatoes or 1 oz. (30 g) rice
1–2 heaped tsp. Oetker GUSTIN
(corn starch powder) and 1 tbsp.
cold water
salt
meat extract, or other seasoning,
to taste

Skin the kidneys and remove the tubes and white tissue. Wash in cold water, then pour hot water over them and leave standing for half an hour. Then cut into cubes or slices and fry in the hot fat with the finely chopped onion and the prepared and chopped pot vegetables. Pour on the water, bring to the boil, add the potatoes, peeled and finely diced, (or the rice, well washed) and cook till done. Blend the GUSTIN with the water and thicken the soup with it. Season with salt and meat extract, or other seasoning.

Cooking Time: about 30 minutes.

Chicken Broth

1 boiling fowl of about
2¹/₂ lb. (1¹/₈ kg)
4½ pints (2½ l) water
salt
a few pot vegetables (leek, celeriac,
carrot, parsley root)

Scald, draw and clean the bird. Put into the boiling salted water with the heart, the gizzard (cut a shallow slit across the curve), the neck, the prepared pot vegetables (leave whole). Bring to the boil on full heat and simmer gently until done. Add the liver, but do not allow it to cook longer than a few minutes. Strain the broth through a fine sieve.

Cooking Time: 2–4 hours.

The chicken may be cut into small pieces and served with the soup, or made into Fricassee (see page 111), or browned in the oven and served whole (see page 111).

Chicken Soup, Garnished

1 quart (1⅛ l) chicken stock
2 oz. (55 g) vermicelli or
1¹/₂ oz. (45 g) rice
some cauliflower flowerets
2 or 3 asparagus spears cut
into short lengths
Semolina Dumplings (see page 39)
or White Bread Dumplings
(see page 40)
salt
meat extract, or other seasoning,
to taste
1 tbsp. chopped parsley

Bring the chicken stock quickly to the boil, then sprinkle in the vermicelli or the washed rice. Stir, then simmer gently until done. Wash the cauliflower flowerets, peel the asparagus spears and cut them into short lengths. Add the vegetables and dumplings to the soup, or cook separately in salted water. Season to taste and serve with the parsley.

Cooking Time: vermicelli, 10–15 minutes;
rice, about 30 minutes.

Melt the fat, add the flour and stir until pale yellow. Still stirring, add the chicken stock. Simmer gently for about 10 minutes. Add the almonds and the chicken. The vegetables may be cooked in the soup or separately in salted water. Beat the egg yolk in the milk or cream and add to the soup. Season with salt and meat extract and add the vegetables, if cooked separately.

Cooking Time: 15–20 minutes.

Queen's Soup

1½ oz. (45 g) butter or margarine
1½ oz. (45 g) plain flour
1¾ pint (1 l) chicken stock
8–10 blanched,
    ground almonds (1 bitter)
diced cooked chicken
cauliflower flowerets or asparagus tips
    (prepared)
1 egg yolk and ¼ pint (140 ccm)
    milk or cream
salt and meat extract, or other
    seasoning, to taste

Mock Queen's Soup

Prepare as for Queen's Soup, but use veal stock instead of chicken stock.

Pigeon Broth

Prepare as for Chicken Broth, using, for four servings, 2 old pigeons instead of the boiling fowl. Heart, gizzard and liver can be used for dumplings to garnish the soup (see page 45). Pigeon broth is excellent for invalid or convalescent diet.

Goose or Duck Giblet Soup
(6 – 8 Servings)

Giblets (gizzard and heart) of one
    goose or duck, together with the
    head, neck, wings and feet
4½ pints (2½ l) water
salt
1 onion
pot vegetables
3 oz. (85 g) butter or margarine
3 oz. (85 g) plain flour
2 tbsp. chopped parsley

Clean the giblets, etc., scalding and skinning the feet and cutting off the beak; add to the boiling salted water. Bring to the boil again and simmer gently for about 1 hour. Add the sliced onion and the prepared pot vegetables (leave whole) and cook for a further hour. Strain through a fine sieve.

Melt the fat, stir in the flour and fry until pale yellow. Continue to stir while adding the stock and cook gently for 10 minutes. Remove the meat from the bones, slice or dice the gizzard and heart and add to the soup. Sprinkle with the parsley and serve.

Cooking Time: about 2 hours.

If the duck or goose liver is to be used, Liver Dumplings (see page 45) will make a good garnish. Either cook the dumplings in salted water until done, or allow them to simmer for 10 minutes in the soup.

Game Soup (Leftovers)

Prepare as for Oxtail Soup (see page 23), using, instead of oxtail, left-over bones (chopped small) of any game (partridge, hare, venison, etc.).

Fish Stock (Leftovers)

Head, scraps and bones of
any sea fish
2¼ pints (1¼ l) water
salt
1 onion
pot vegetables
1½ oz. (45 g) butter or margarine
1½ oz. (45 g) plain flour
½ pint (285 ccm) milk
seasoning
lemon juice
1–2 tbsp. chopped chives or dill

Wash the head, scraps and bones, removing the gills from the head. Cover with the water (cold), add the salt, the sliced onion and the prepared pot vegetables (leave whole) and bring quickly to the boil. Simmer for about 1 hour. Strain all the time.

Add the flour to the melted fat and stir through a fine sieve until pale yellow. Gradually stir in the stock and the milk. Bring to the boil, then simmer for about 10 minutes. Add seasoning and lemon juice. Serve with the chives or dill.

Cooking Time: 1–1½ hours.

Suggested garnishes: left-over scraps of fish, Fish Balls (see page 45), Cheese Balls (see page 43), or croûtons.

B. VEGETABLE SOUPS

General Hints

1. Vegetable soups can be made from meat, bone or vegetable stock, or from the liquid leftover after vegetables have been cooked, or from a combination of these.

2. Prepare the vegetables for soup according to the directions given under "Vegetables" see page 143.

3. Fresh vegetables may be cooked simply in boiling liquid, or they may first be fried in hot butter or margarine and then have the boiling liquid added to them. In either case they should be simmered gently until done.

4. Dried vegetables should be soaked in cold water for about 12 hours before cooking. They should then be brought quickly to the boil and simmered gently until done (use the liquid in which they were soaked).

5. Sieving improves the consistency of soup, but is not always necessary.

6. For those on a diet, who are not allowed a white or brown roux made with flour, soups may be thickened with Oetker GUSTIN (corn starch powder), blended with cold water beforehand. Just before serving, a little butter should be added to soups thickened in this way.

Prepare and chop the vegetables. Fry in the hot fat for a minute or two. Add the water (hot) and cook gently for 1 hour. Add the parsley and the celery leaves for the last 5–10 minutes. Rub through a fine sieve. Use in place of meat or bone stock.

Cooking Time: about 1 hour.

Vegetable Stock

About 1¼ lb. (570 g) vegetables
(a piece of celeriac, 1 Kohlrabi,
1 carrot, parsley root, 1 onion,
1 leek, cauliflower flowerets,
asparagus, white cabbage and Savoy
cabbage leaves)
1½ oz. (45 g) butter or margarine,
or 2 tbsp. oil
2¼ pints (1¼ l) water
parsley, celery leaves

Break the cauliflower into flowerets, wash carefully, put into the slightly salted boiling water and cook gently until done. Strain, keeping the liquid.

Melt the fat, stir in the flour and cook until pale yellow. Continue to stir while adding the cauliflower liquid and the milk. Simmer for 10 minutes. Add the cauliflower flowerets. Stir in the egg yolk beaten in the water. Season to taste and serve.

Cooking Time: 30–40 minutes.

Cauliflower Soup

1 medium-sized cauliflower
1¾ pint (1 l) water
1 tsp. salt
1½ oz. (45 g) butter or margarine
1½ oz. (45 g) plain flour
½ pint (285 ccm) milk
1 egg yolk and 2 tbsp. cold water
(optional)

Fry the peas for a few minutes in the hot fat. Sprinkle in the flour and cook together for another 2 or 3 minutes. Continue to stir while adding the boiling water or stock, season with very little salt and bring to the boil. Simmer gently until the peas are quite soft. Season to taste, sprinkle with the parsley and serve. Cook the dumplings or meat balls in the soup or separately in salted water.

Cooking Time: 25–30 minutes.

Fresh Green Pea Soup

8 oz. (225 g) shelled fresh peas
1½ oz. (45 g) butter or margarine
1½ oz. (45 g) plain flour
2¼ pints (1¼ l) water or stock
salt
1 tbsp. chopped parsley
Spongy or Semolina Dumplings
(see page 43) or Meat Balls
(see page 45) to garnish

Trim, wash, and chop or slice the vegetables. Leave peas whole and separate cauliflower into flowerets. Fry for a few minutes in the hot fat, sprinkle in the flour and cook together a little longer. Gradually pour in the stock or water (hot and slightly salted). Bring to the boil, turn down the heat and simmer gently until all the vegetables are cooked. Season with salt and meat extract to taste.

The dumplings or meat balls can be cooked in the soup or separately in salted water.

Cooking Time: about 40 minutes.

Vegetable Soup

About 8 oz. (225 g) prepared vegetables
(cauliflower, shelled green peas,
carrots, Kohlrabi, Brussels sprouts,
asparagus, cabbage)
1½ oz. (45 g) butter or margarine,
or kidney suet
¾ oz. (20 g) plain flour
2¼ pints (1¼ l) stock or water
salt and meat extract, or other
seasoning, to taste
Spongy or Semolina Dumplings
(see page 43) or Meat Balls
(see page 45) to garnish, if desired

Carrot Soup

8 oz. (225 g) carrots
1½ oz. (45 g) butter or margarine
1½ oz. (45 g) rice or tapioca
2¼ pints (1¼ l) water or stock
salt
pinch of sugar
1 tsp. chopped parsley
croûtons

Scrape, wash and grate the carrots. Fry them for a few minutes in the hot fat, then sprinkle in the washed rice or tapioca and cook gently for a further few minutes. Add the water or stock (hot and slightly salted) and simmer gently until the rice or the tapioca is cooked. Season with salt and sugar and serve with the parsley and the croûtons.

Cooking Time: rice, about 30 minutes;
tapioca, about 15 minutes.

Mushroom Soup

12 oz. (340 g) mushrooms
1 small onion
1½ oz. (45 g) butter or margarine
1½ oz. (45 g) plain flour
1¾ pint (1 l) water or stock
salt and meat extract or other seasoning
1 tbsp. chopped parsley

Prepare, wash and chop the mushrooms and fry gently in the fat for a few minutes with the chopped onion. Sprinkle in the flour and cook for a further few minutes. Pour on the water or stock (hot and slightly salted) and simmer for about 15 minutes. Season with salt and with meat extract if water and not stock has been used. Sprinkle with the parsley and serve.

Cooking Time: about 15 minutes.

Leek Soup

8 oz. (225 g) leeks
1 oz. (30 g) bacon, diced
¾ oz. (20 g) plain flour
1¾ pint (1 l) water
2-3 small meat extract cubes
¾ oz. (20 g) Oetker GUSTIN (corn starch powder) and 3 tbsp. milk
salt and meat extract or other seasoning
pinch of grated nutmeg
1 egg yolk and 2 tbsp. cold water (optional)

Fry the bacon, add the washed and finely sliced leeks and cook together for a few minutes. Sprinkle in the flour and cook a little longer. Pour on the water (hot), add the meat extract cubes, and simmer for about 10 minutes. Blend the Gustin with the cold milk and stir into the soup. Bring quickly to the boil. Season the soup with salt, meat extract and nutmeg, and enrich with the egg yolk beaten in the water, if desired.

Cooking Time: about 10 minutes.

Salsify Soup

8 oz. (225 g) salsify
2¼ pints (1¼ l) water
salt
1½ oz. (45 g) butter or margarine
1½ oz. (45 g) plain flour
1 egg yolk and 2 tbsp. cold water (optional)

Wash the salsify and scrape carefully. To keep the sticks white, cover immediately with about 1 quart (1⅛ l) of cold water mixed with 1-2 tbsp. of vinegar and 1 tbsp. of flour. Cut the salsify into pieces about 1 inch (2½ cm) long and cook in the slightly salted boiling water until tender. Strain, keeping the liquid.

Melt the fat, stir in the flour and cook till pale yellow. Continue to stir while adding the salsify liquid gradually. Bring to the boil, turn down the heat and simmer for about 10 minutes. Season the soup with salt and enrich with the egg yolk beaten in the water, if desired. Add the salsify and serve.

Cooking Time: 40-50 minutes.

Celery Soup

8 oz. (225 g) celeriac
2¼ pints (1¼ l) water or stock
salt
1½ oz. (45 g) butter or margarine
1½ oz. (45 g) plain flour
1–2 tbsp. croutôns

Scrub the celeriac thoroughly, pare and cut into small slices or strips. Bring the slightly salted water or stock to the boil, add the celeriac and simmer gently until tender. Rub the pieces of celeriac through a fine sieve, keeping a few by to add to the finished soup. Add the purée to the stock.

Melt the fat, stir in the flour and cook until pale yellow. Continue to stir while adding the celeriac stock. Simmer for about 10 minutes. Season and serve with the croûtons and the pieces of celeriac.

Cooking Time: about 30 minutes.

Asparagus Soup

8 oz. (225 g) soup asparagus
1¾ pint (1 l) water
salt
1½ oz. (45 g) butter or margarine
1½ oz. (45 g) plain flour
½ pint (285 ccm) milk
1 egg yolk and 2 tbsp. cold water
    (optional)

Peel the asparagus, cut into pieces about 1 inch (2½ cm) long and wash. Cook in the boiling slightly salted water until done. Strain, keeping the liquid.

Melt the fat, stir in the flour and cook until pale yellow. Continue to stir while gradually adding the asparagus stock and the milk. Simmer for 10 minutes. Season, and add the egg yolk beaten in the water, if desired. Add the pieces of asparagus to the soup and serve.

Cooking Time: 30—40 minutes.

Fresh Spring Herb Soup

2 tbsp. chopped herbs (dandelion, nettle, sorrel, milfoil, groundivy and chervil)
1½ oz. (45 g) butter or margarine, or 2 tbsp. oil
1½ oz. (45 g) plain flour or rice
2¼ pints (1¼ l) stock or water
salt
1 egg yolk and 2 tbsp. cold water or 2 tbsp. sour cream

Wash the herbs thoroughly, chop finely and fry in the hot fat or in the oil. Add the flour or rice, stirring all the time and cook together for a minute or two. Stir in the stock or water gradually and bring to the boil. Simmer until the flour or rice is cooked. Season, add the egg yolk beaten in the water, or the sour cream and serve.

Cooking Time: flour, about 10 minutes;
                rice, about 30 minutes.

Tomato Soup I

2 oz. (55 g) ham
1 oz. (30 g) butter or margarine
1 onion
1½ oz. (45 g) plain flour
12 oz. (340 g) tomatoes
1⅓ pint (¾ l) stock or water
salt
pinch of sugar
a little lemon juice
1 tbsp. chopped parsley

Dice and gently fry the ham. Add the fat, the chopped onion and the flour and fry together until the flour is pale yellow. Add the washed and finely chopped tomatoes, the stock or water and a little salt. Bring the soup to the boil and simmer gently for 10–15 minutes. Rub through a fine sieve, season with salt, sugar and lemon juice and serve with the parsley.

Cooking Time: 15–20 minutes.

Alternatively, 1–2 tbsp. tomato purée may be used instead of fresh tomatoes. Then use 1¾ pint (1 l) stock or water.

Tomato Soup II

1½ oz. (45 g) butter, margarine
or lard
1 onion
8 oz. (225 g) tomatoes
1¾ pint (1 l) water or stock
salt
1½ oz. (45 g) rice or tapioca
pinch of sugar
a little lemon juice
1 tbsp. chopped parsley

Fry the finely chopped onion in the hot fat and add the washed and sliced tomatoes. Add the hot water or stock and a little salt. Simmer for 10–15 minutes, then rub through a fine sieve and bring to the boil again. Sprinkle in the washed rice or the tapioca, stir, and simmer gently till done. Season with salt, sugar and lemon juice and serve with the parsley.

Cooking Time: 30–45 minutes.

Plain Vegetable Soup

Half a Kohlrabi
half a celeriac
1–2 carrots
1 parsley root
1 leek
2¼ pints (1¼ l) water or stock
salt
1½ oz. (45 g) butter or margarine
¾ oz. (20 g) plain flour
1–2 tbsp. croûtons

Prepare and chop or grate the vegetables and cook in the slightly salted water or stock until done. Rub through a fine sieve.

Melt the fat, stir in the flour and cook until light brown. Continue to stir while adding the vegetable stock gradually. Bring to the boil and simmer for about 10 minutes. Season and serve with the croûtons.

Cooking Time: about 30 minutes.

Potato Soup I

12 oz. (340 g) potatoes
2 oz. (55 g) pot vegetables (1 carrot,
1 leek, some celeriac, parsley root)
salt
2¼ pints (1¼ l) water or stock
1½ oz. (45 g) fat or bacon
1 level tbsp. plain flour
a few drops of meat extract or other
seasoning
chopped parsley or chives

Wash, peel and dice the potatoes and add them, together with the prepared and chopped pot vegetables and the salt to the boiling liquid, and cook till done. Rub through a fine sieve.

Melt the fat, stir in the flour and cook until pale yellow. Gradually pour in the potato stock, stirring all the time. Simmer gently for about 10 minutes. Season, adding meat extract to taste, and serve with the parsley or chives.

Cooking Time: about 30 minutes.

Potato Soup II (Quick Method)

8 oz. (225 g) potatoes
1¾ pint (1 l) bone or vegetable stock
salt
a few drops of meat extract or other
seasoning
chopped chives or parsley

Grate the peeled raw potatoes into the boiling stock. Simmer gently for 10 minutes. Season with salt and meat extract and serve with the herbs.

Cooking Time: about 10 minutes.

Wash the beans and soak for 12–24 hours in the water or stock. Bring to the boil in the same liquid and simmer until the beans are tender. Add the washed, sliced leek about half an hour before the beans are cooked. Rub through a fine sieve. Peel and slice the tomatoes. Fry them in the fat, sprinkle in the flour and cook together for a few minutes, stirring all the time. Add the sieved soup and bring to the boil again. Season, add the herbs and serve.

Cooking Time: about 2 hours.

Lima Bean Soup can be cooked without tomatoes, using the following recipe for Split Pea Soup.

Lima Bean Soup with Tomatoes

6 oz. (170 g) Lima beans
2¾ pints (1½ l) water or stock
half a leek
¾ oz. (20 g) butter or margarine, or kidney suet
6 tomatoes
1 level tbsp. plain flour
salt
thyme
garlic
a few drops of meat extract or other seasoning

Wash the peas and soak for 12–24 hours in the water or stock. Bring to the boil in the same liquid, add the bacon rind and scraps, turn down the heat and simmer gently. After about an hour, add the prepared and finely chopped pot vegetables and continue to simmer until the peas are cooked. Rub through a sieve.

Melt the fat, stir in the chopped onion and fry until pale yellow. Add the flour and gradually pour in the sieved soup, stirring all the time. Bring to the boil, season with salt, a pinch of marjoram and the meat extract, and serve with the herbs and the croûtons.

Cooking Time: about 2 hours.

Split Pea Soup

8 oz. (225 g) split peas
2¾ pints (1½ l) water or stock
bacon rind and scraps
pot vegetables (celeriac, carrot, leek)
¾ oz. (20 g) fat or bacon
1 onion
1 level tbsp. plain flour
salt
marjoram and meat extract or other seasoning
chopped parsley or chives
1–2 tbsp. croûtons

Wash the lentils and soak for 12–24 hours in the water or stock. Bring them to the boil in the same liquid and allow to simmer for ¾ hour. Add the prepared, chopped pot vegetables and the finely sliced onion. Cook until done and rub through a sieve.

Melt the fat, stir in the flour, and cook until pale yellow. Add the sieved soup gradually, stirring all the time. Simmer for about 10 minutes, season with salt and meat extract and serve.

If preferred, about half of the lentils may be kept unsieved and added to the soup before serving.

Cooking Time: about 1½ hours.

Lentil Soup

8 oz. (225 g) lentils
2¾ pints (1½ l) water or stock
pot vegetables (leek, celeriac and carrot)
1 onion
1 oz. (30 g) dripping
1 level tbsp. plain flour
salt and a few drops of meat extract

Rumford Soup

*About 5 oz. (140 g) dried legumes
(peas, beans, lentils)
2¾ pints (1½ l) water or stock
pot vegetables (leek, celeriac and
carrot)
1 onion
1 oz. (30 g) beef or lamb suet, or bacon
1 oz. (30 g) rice or barley
1–2 potatoes (optional)
salt and a few drops of meat extract
1–2 tbsp. croûtons*

Wash the legumes and soak for 12–24 hours in the water or stock. Bring to the boil in the same liquid, turn down the heat and simmer for about an hour. Then add the prepared pot vegetables and the finely chopped onion. Continue to simmer until all the vegetables are tender. Rub through a sieve.

Melt the fat, add the sieved soup, and stir in the washed rice or the barley and the peeled, washed and diced potatoes. Bring to the boil, turn down the heat and simmer gently until done. Season with salt and meat extract and serve with the croûtons.

Cooking Time: 1½–2 hours.

C. SWEET SOUPS

General Hints

1. The basic ingredient of a sweet soup can be milk, water, fruit juice, wine or beer. Most sweet soups, and especially those made of fruit juice, wine or beer, may be served cold and so are very suitable for the summer menu.

2. Thickening agents for sweet soups are usually flour, Oetker GUSTIN (corn starch powder), semolina, oatmeal or other similar cereals. For thickening a quart (1⅛ l) of hot soup, allow about 1½ oz. (45 g) of flour or GUSTIN, or almost 2 oz. (55 g) of ground oatmeal, rice, or tapioca. For cold soups allow 1¼ oz. (35 g) of flour or GUSTIN per quart (1⅛ l), or about 1½ oz. (45 g) of oatmeal, rice, or tapioca. If egg yolks are used for enriching, decrease the amount of thickening agents used by about 3 drams (5 g) per yolk.

3. Milk soups are nourishing and easy to digest, and so are an important item in the diet of children and invalids. They can be served for breakfast or supper.

4. Fruit soups, made from fruit and water or from diluted fruit juice, are thirst-quenching and refreshing. Fresh fruit should be thoroughly washed before cooking; dried fruit soaked for about 12 hours in cold water. Only cook fruit until it is just tender; overcooking results in a considerable loss of vitamins.

5. Never boil soups made from wine or beer, but simmer just below boiling point, so that the alcohol ist not driven off. Farinaceous thickening must be cooked separately in the prescribed amount of water, and the wine or beer added just before serving.

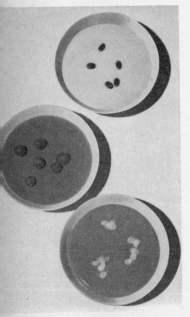

6. Sweet **soups** which are to be served cold should be left to cool in the **saucepan** and stirred occasionally to prevent a skin forming.

7. Little rusks, soup macaroons, snow balls (made of stiffly beaten egg white), semolina or spongy dumplings, or almond rice make good garnishes for sweet soups. Snow balls for garnishing hot soup should be put on the soup and left to stiffen in a covered saucepan or tureen.

Snow balls for cold soups which require stirring while cooling should be left to stiffen in a **covered saucepan of very** hot water.

I. MILK SOUPS

Milk Soup with GUSTIN

Blend the GUSTIN with 4 tbsp. of the milk. Bring the rest of the milk to the boil. Remove from heat, add the GUSTIN mixture, then cook again for a short time, stirring all the time. Add the vanillin sugar, sugar to taste and a little salt. Stir in the butter and serve.

1½ oz. (45 g) Oetker GUSTIN
  (corn starch powder)
1 quart (1⅛ l) milk
1 packet Oetker Vanillin Sugar
1–2 oz. (30–55 g) sugar
salt
a little butter

Milk Soup with Pudding or Blancmange Powder

Blend the pudding powder and about 2 oz. (55 g) of the sugar with 6 tbsp. of the milk. Bring the rest of the milk to the boil, remove from heat, stir in the pudding powder mixture and bring to the boil again for a few seconds, stirring all the time. Season and serve.

If the soup is to be served cold, use an extra 6 tbsp. milk to blend with the pudding powder and boil all the 2¼ pints (1¼ l). If a stronger vanilla flavour is preferred, 3 packets of Oetker Sauce Powder, vanilla flavour may be used instead of 1 packet of Pudding or Blancmange Powder. For a stronger lemon flavour add a few drops of Oetker Baking Essence, lemon flavour.

1 packet Oetker Pudding Powder
  vanilla, almond, cream or lemon
  flavour
2–2½ oz. (55–70 g) sugar
2¼ pints (1¼ l) milk
salt

Caramel Soup

Blend the GUSTIN with 4 tbsp. of the milk. Put the sugar into a pan and melt it, stirring all the time, until it turns light brown. Stir in the remaining milk and bring to the boil. Remove from heat and stir in the GUSTIN mixture. Bring to the boil, and boil for a few seconds, stirring all the time. Add the vanillin sugar, season with salt and sugar to taste and serve.

If the soup is to be served cold, use rather less than 1 oz. of GUSTIN.

1 oz. (30 g) Oetker GUSTIN
  (corn starch powder)
1¾ pint (1 l) milk
2 oz. (55 g) sugar
1 packet Oetker Vanillin Sugar
salt and sugar to season

Snow Milk

1 oz. (30 g) Oetker GUSTIN
(corn starch powder)
2 pints (1⅛ l) milk
¾ oz. (20 g) ground almonds
(1 bitter)
salt
1–2 oz. (30–55 g) sugar
1 egg yolk and 2 tbsp. cold water
1 egg white
2 tsp. sugar
a little grated chocolate

Blend the GUSTIN with 4 tbsp. of the milk. Stir the almonds into the rest of the milk and bring to the boil. Remove from heat, stir in the GUSTIN mixture, bring to the boil and boil for a few seconds, stirring all the time. Season the soup with salt and sugar, and enrich with the egg yolk beaten in the water.

Whisk the egg white stiff and sweeten with the 2 tsp. sugar. Spoon it onto the hot soup so that it forms small balls. Cover the saucepan and leave the balls to stiffen on the soup (about 5 minutes). Sprinkle the balls with grated chocolate and serve.

If the soup is to be served cold, use ¾ oz. (20 g) GUSTIN.

Milk Semolina Soup

1 quart (1⅛ l) milk
a slice of lemon rind
1½ oz. (45 g) semolina
salt
1–2 oz. (30–55 g) sugar

Put the milk and the lemon rind into a pan and bring to the boil. Sprinkle in the semolina, stirring all the time and simmer gently until the semolina is cooked. Season with salt and sugar and serve.

Cooking Time: 10–15 minutes.

Yellow Semolina Soup

1 packet Oetker Sauce Powder,
vanilla flavour
1½ oz. (45 g) semolina
2–2½ oz. (55–70 g) sugar
2¾ pints (1½ l) milk
salt

Blend the sauce powder, the semolina and about 2 oz. (55 g) sugar with 6 tbsp. of the milk. Bring the rest of the milk to the boil, remove from heat and stir in the sauce powder mixture. Return to the heat and boil again for about 2 minutes, stirring all the time. Season the soup with salt and sugar.

If the soup is to be served cold, use only 1 oz. (30 g) semolina.

Cooking Time: about 2 minutes.

1–2 tbsp. washed raisins or currants may be cooked in the soup.

Rice or Tapioca Soup

1¾ pint (1 l) milk
1½–2 oz. (45–55 g) rice or tapioca
1 packet Oetker Vanillin Sugar
salt
1–2 oz. (30–55 g) sugar

Bring the milk to the boil, sprinkle in the washed rice or the tapioca, stir, and leave to cook gently until done. Add the vanillin sugar. Season with salt and sugar and serve.

Cooking Time: for rice, about 30 minutes;
for tapioca, about 10 minutes.

Rolled Oats Soup

1¾ pint (1 l) milk
1½ oz. (45 g) rolled oats
salt
1–2 oz. (30–55 g) sugar (optional)
a little butter

Bring the milk to the boil, sprinkle in the oats and cook gently till done. Season with salt and add sugar if desired. Stir in the butter and serve.

Cooking Time: 10–15 minutes.

Oetker Jelly Powder, "Rote Gruetze", Chocolate Pudding
(prepare according to the directions on the packet)

III. FRUIT SOUPS

Wash and slice the fruit, cover with the cold water, add the lemon rind and cook gently until tender. Rub the fruit (but not the rhubarb) through a sieve and, if cherries are used, leave a few to garnish. Bring the sieved fruit to the boil, remove from heat and stir in the GUSTIN, blended with the water, the semolina or the tapioca. Continue to stir, bring to the boil again and cook gently until done. Season with cinnamon or vanillin sugar, sugar and, if desired, with lemon juice, wine or cider.

Serve hot or cold.

Cooking Time: 10–20 minutes.

Rusks, croûtons, soup macaroons, "Arme Ritter" (see page 254), Almond Rice (see page 41), or Spongy or Semolina Dumplings (see page 41) all make a suitable garnish for this soup.

Fresh Fruit Soup

About 1 lb. (450 g) fresh fruit (apples,
  pears, cherries, plums, gooseberries,
  rhubarb or bilberries)
1¾ pint (1 l) water
a piece of lemon rind
¾ oz. (20 g) Oetker GUSTIN
  (corn starch powder)
  and 2 tbsp. water
  (1 oz. (30 g) for plums or rhubarb)
  or 1 oz. (30 g) semolina or tapioca
  (1½ oz. (45 g) for plums or rhubarb)
a little cinnamon or 1 packet
  Oetker Vanillin Sugar
2–4½ oz. (55–125 g) sugar
a little lemon juice, wine or cider

Wash the fruit well and strip the berries from the stalks. Cover with the water, add the lemon rind and cook till tender. Rub through a fine sieve, bring to the boil again, remove from heat and add the GUSTIN, blended with the water or sprinkle in the tapioca, stirring all the time. Simmer gently till done. Season with lemon juice and sugar. Serve hot or cold.

Cooking Time: about 20 minutes.

8 oz. (225 g) sliced apples or stoned plums may be cooked with the soup.

Elderberry Soup

1 lb. (450 g) dark elderberries
1¾ pint (1 l) water
a piece of lemon rind
¾ oz. (20 g) Oetker GUSTIN
  (corn starch powder)
  and 2 tbsp. cold water
  or 1 oz. (30 g) tapioca
1–2 tbsp. lemon juice
about 3½ oz. (100 g) sugar

Peel the pumpkin, remove the soft middle, dice and cover with the water. Add the cinnamon and lemon rind and bring to the boil. Simmer until tender, then rub through a fine sieve. Bring to the boil again, remove from heat and thicken with the GUSTIN, blended with the water. Add the wine, season with lemon juice and sugar and serve.

Cooking Time: about 30 minutes.

Sliced apples and apple peel may be cooked with the soup before it is sieved.

Pumpkin Soup

About 1½ lb. (680 g) pumpkin
1¾ pint (1 l) water
cinnamon
lemon rind
1 slightly heaped tbsp. (10 g)
  Oetker GUSTIN (corn starch powder)
  and 1 tbsp. cold water
¼ pint (140 ccm) wine
juice of half a lemon
2–2½ oz. (55–70 g) sugar

Stir the sugar into the fruit juice and bring to the boil. Remove from heat, stir in the GUSTIN, blended with the water and, still stirring, sprinkle in the tapioca. Simmer gently for about 10 minutes. Season with lemon juice, if desired. Serve hot or cold.

Cooking Time: about 10 minutes.

Rusks, croûtons, soup macaroons or Snow Balls (see page 41) may be served in the soup.

Fruit Juice Soup

1¾ pint (1 l) diluted fruit juice
sugar to taste
1 slightly heaped tbsp. (10 g)
  Oetker GUSTIN (corn starch powder)
  and 1 tbsp. cold water
1½ oz. (45 g) tapioca
a little lemon juice (optional)

Lemon Soup

1½ oz. (45 g) Oetker GUSTIN
(corn starch powder)
1¾ pint (1 l) water
rind of 1 lemon
juice of 2 lemons
3½ oz. (100 g) sugar
1 egg yolk and 2 tbsp. cold water
1 egg white and 2 tsp. sugar for
Snow Balls (see page 41)

Blend the GUSTIN with 4 tbsp. of the water. Add the lemon rind to the rest of the water and bring quickly to the boil. Remove from heat, stir in the GUSTIN, blended with the water and simmer gently until done. Season with lemon juice and sugar and enrich with the egg yolk beaten in the water. Garnish with the Snow Balls.

If the soup is to be served cold only 1 oz. (30 g) GUSTIN is needed.

Fruit Soup (With Dried Fruit)

4 oz. (115 g) dried fruit
(apples, apricots or prunes)
2¼ pints (1¼ l) water
3 drops Oetker Baking Essence,
lemon flavour
a little cinnamon
¾ oz. (20 g) Oetker GUSTIN
(corn starch powder) and 1 tbsp.
cold water
1 packet Oetker Vanillin Sugar
2–2½ oz. (55–70 g) sugar

Wash the fruit and soak in the water for 12 hours. Add the lemon flavour and the cinnamon and bring to the boil in the same water. Simmer gently until done. Rub through a fine sieve and bring to the boil again. Thicken with the GUSTIN, blended with the water, add the vanillin sugar and season to taste with the sugar.

Cooking Time: about 30 minutes.

IV. WINE AND BEER SOUPS

White Wine Soup

1 pint (570 ccm) water
cinnamon
2–3 drops Oetker Baking Essence,
lemon flavour
1¼ oz. (35 g) Oetker GUSTIN
(corn starch powder)
and 2 tbsp. cold water
1 pint (570 ccm) white wine or cider
about 3 oz. (85 g) sugar
1 egg yolk and 2 tbsp. cold water

Add the cinnamon and lemon flavour to the water and bring to the boil. Remove from heat, stir in the GUSTIN, blended with the water and bring to the boil again. Add the wine. Season with sugar to taste, and reheat but do not boil. Beat the egg yolk in the water and add to the soup.

If the soup is to be served cold, use only 1 oz. (30 g) GUSTIN.

Red Wine Soup

1 pint (570 ccm) water
cinnamon
2 cloves
1½ oz. (45 g) tapioca or rice
1 pint (570 ccm) red wine
2–3 oz. (55–85 g) sugar

Add the cinnamon and cloves to the water and bring to the boil. Sprinkle in the tapioca or the washed rice, stir, and simmer gently till done. Stir in the wine, season with the sugar and reheat without boiling. Serve hot or cold.

Cooking Time: 20–30 minutes.
Garnish with soup macaroons or rusks.

Add the cinnamon to the milk and bring to the boil. Remove from heat, add the sauce powder, blended with the water and bring to the boil again. Add the beer and lemon juice, season to taste with the sugar and reheat without boiling. Beat the egg yolk in the water, add to the soup and whisk for a short time over a low heat. Do not boil. Serve hot or cold.

Garnish with the Snow Balls.

Beer Soup
¾ pint (425 ccm) milk
a piece of cinnamon
2 packets Oetker Sauce Powder,
    vanilla flavour and 3 tbsp. water
1 pint (570 ccm) beer
2½–3½ oz. (70–100 g) sugar
a little lemon juice
1 egg yolk and 1 tbsp. cold water
1 egg white and 2 tsp. sugar for
    Snow Balls (see page 41)

SOUP GARNISHES

1. Garnishes for clear soup must be cooked separately in salted water and should be added to the soup just before serving. For a thick soup they can be cooked in the soup itself. The liquid in which the garnishes have been cooked may be used for other recipes.

2. For clear soups with "Einlauf" make sure the soup is boiling, as the egg mixture must curdle into large flakes the moment it is added. Once the "Einlauf" is in the soup, do not let it go on boiling, but remove it from heat, cover and leave the soup to clear again.

3. To drop dumpling mixture from a spoon easily, dip the spoon into the boiling liquid first. Then dip the spoon into the mixture, fill it and drop the dumpling into the soup. To shape round dumplings, use two wooden spoons dipped in flour.

4. All balls and dumplings (except snow balls) must be put into the boiling liquid in an uncovered saucepan, then left to simmer gently until done.

General Hints

Thoroughly combine the flour, the milk and the egg, making sure the mixture is free from lumps. Add the salt and nutmeg. Then stir very gradually (preferable through the holes of a skimming ladle) into the boiling soup. The mixture should curdle at once into large flakes. Bring to the boil, remove from heat, cover and leave to clear.

Time: about 3 minutes.

"Einlauf" (Egg Garnish)
¾ oz. (20 g) plain flour
1 tbsp. milk
1 egg
pinch of salt
pinch of nutmeg

"Eierstich"

2 eggs
¼ pint (140 ccm) milk
pinch of salt
nutmeg

Beat together the eggs and the milk, add the salt and nutmeg and pour into a greased basin. Cover the basin and put it into hot (not boiling) water. Simmer the water gently until the "Eierstich" is firm. Unmould it, cut into cubes and add to the soup.

Time: about 30 minutes.

The "Eierstich" may be varied by addition of 1 tbsp. finely chopped herbs, finely grated cheese or tomato purée to the eggs.

Soup Noodles

4½ oz. (125 g) plain flour
pinch of salt
1 egg
1 tbsp. water

Sieve the flour onto a pastry board or slab. Make a well in the centre, add the salt, the egg and the water and gradually work in flour from the sides of the well. Still working from the centre, quickly knead together into a smooth dough. Add more flour if the dough seems too sticky. Roll the dough to the desired thickness and put it on a cloth to dry. When it has dried sufficiently, roll it up (it should be neither sticky nor brittle) and cut it into strips. Dry out the strips thoroughly and use as required.

Cooking Time: 15–20 minutes.

"Flädchen" Pancake Strips

(Swabian Speciality)

2½ oz. (70 g) plain flour
salt
1 egg
¼ pint (140 ccm) water
1 tsp. chopped parsley
about 1 oz. (30 g) butter or
margarine for frying

Sieve the flour into a basin, make a well in the centre and add the salt and the egg. Working from the centre, gradually combine the egg and the flour, stirring in the water little by little – the batter must be smooth and free from lumps. Stir in the parsley. Fry very thin pancakes, cut them into strips and add to the soup.

Cheese Crusts

¼ pint (140 ccm) milk
½ egg
about 4 oz. (115 g) thin slices of white
bread
1½ oz. (45 g) breadcrumbs
1½ oz. (45 g) grated cheese
salt
1½ oz. (45 g) fat for frying

Beat the egg in the milk and dip the bread into this mixture, carefully turning the slices over. Remove, and dip into the breadcrumbs, to which the cheese and the salt have been added.

Melt the fat in a frying pan, put in the slices of bread and fry on both sides until brown. Cut into cubes and serve in the soup.

The garnish can be prepared without the grated cheese.

Add the almonds, the flavourings and the butter to the milk and bring to the boil. Stir in the washed rice and simmer gently for about 30 minutes. Press the hot rice into a small greased mould, keep warm for a few minutes, then unmould. May be served with fruit soups instead of dumplings.

Almond Rice

½ pint (285 ccm) milk
1 tbsp. ground almonds or 3 drops
   Oetker Baking Essence,
   bitter almond flavour
2 drops Oetker Baking Essence,
   lemon flavour
pinch of salt
½ oz. (15 g) sugar
1 tsp. butter
2½ oz. (70 g) rice

Whisk the egg whites till they are stiff enough to show and retain the mark made by the blade of a knife. Beat in the sugar by the teaspoonful. Scoop into small balls and place on the boiling soup or water. Cover the saucepan, remove from heat and leave to set for about 5 minutes. Sprinkle with sugar and cinnamon or grated chocolate.

Snow Balls

2 egg whites
2 tsp. sugar
pinch of cinnamon mixed with sugar
   or a little grated chocolate

Add the fat and seasoning to the milk and bring to the boil. Remove from heat, stir in the sieved flour and continue to mix until a heavy lump of dough is formed. Reheat for about 1 minute, then put the hot lump into a basin and stir in the egg. Scoop off small dumplings with a wet spoon and cook till done in boiling salted water or soup.

Cooking Time: about 5 minutes.

Spongy Dumplings

¼ pint (140 ccm) milk
a little butter or margarine
pinch of salt
a little nutmeg
2½ oz. (70 g) plain flour
1 egg

Prepare as for Spongy Dumplings (as noted above). The cheese should be added to the milk.

Cooking Time: about 5 minutes.
Cheese balls are especially good with tomato soup.

Cheese Balls

¼ pint (140 ccm) milk
a little butter or margarine
pinch of salt
1¾ oz. (50 g) grated cheese
2½ oz. (70 g) plain flour
1 egg

Add the fat and seasoning to the milk and bring to the boil. Remove from heat and quickly add the semolina. Stir to a smooth lump and reheat for about 1 minute, stirring all the time. Put the hot lump into a basin and stir in the egg. Scoop out small dumplings with a wet spoon and cook till done in boiling salted water or soup.

Cooking Time: about 5 minutes.

Semolina Dumplings

¼ pint (140 ccm) milk
a little butter or margarine
pinch of salt
nutmeg
2 oz. (55 g) semolina
1 egg

Bread Dumplings

1 oz. (30 g) butter or margarine
1 egg
salt
about 1½ oz. (45 g) breadcrumbs

Cream the fat and add the egg, salt, and as much of the bread-crumbs as will form a smooth dough. Leave to stand for ½ hour before using. Shape into dumplings and simmer till done in boiling salted water or soup.

Cooking Time: about 4 minutes.

"Viennese Nockerln"

1½ oz. (45 g) butter or margarine
1 egg
salt
3 oz. (85 g) plain flour
about 2–3 tbsp. milk

Cream the fat, stir in the egg and salt, and add alternately the sieved flour and the milk. Use only enough milk to make a smooth, soft paste. Scoop off small dumplings and put into boiling salted water. Simmer for about 10 minutes, then add to the soup and serve.

Cooking Time: about 10 minutes.

Mushroom Dumplings

1–2 oz. (30–55 g) mushrooms and
½ oz. (15 g) butter or margarine
for frying
1 oz. (30 g) butter or margarine
1 egg
salt
1 slightly heaped tbsp. (10 g)
Oetker GUSTIN (corn starch powder)
about 1½ oz. (45 g) breadcrumbs

Clean and skin the mushrooms. Fry them in the fat, then chop finely. Cream the fat, add the egg, salt, the GUSTIN and the cooled mushrooms. Add enough breadcrumbs to make a smooth dough. Stand for ½ hour, then shape into small dumplings and cook in boiling salted water or soup till done.

Cooking Time: about 3 minutes.

Herb Dumplings

1–2 tbsp. finely chopped herbs
(parsley, chives, spinach,
chervil, etc.)
1 oz. (30 g) butter or margarine
1 egg
salt
about 1¾ oz. (50 g) breadcrumbs

Make as for Mushroom Dumplings (as noted above), but do not fry the herbs and the spinach.

Cooking Time: about 3 minutes.

Marrow Dumplings

1½ oz. (45 g) fresh bone marrow
1 egg
salt
about 1½ oz. (45 g) breadcrumbs

Melt the marrow, pour through a sieve and cool. Cream the marrow, add the egg, salt and enough breadcrumbs to make a smooth dough. Leave to stand for ½ hour. Shape into small dumplings and cook in boiling salted water or soup till done.

Cooking Time: about 3 minutes.

Dice the bacon, fry and cool it. Cream, add the egg, salt and enough breadcrumbs to make a smooth dough. Leave to stand for about ½ hour, then shape into dumplings and cook in boiling salted water or soup till done.

Cooking Time: about 5 minutes.

Bacon Balls

1½ oz. (45 g) fat bacon
1 egg
pinch of salt
about 1¾ oz. (50 g) breadcrumbs

Cream the fat, mix in the meat, the egg yolk, seasoning and breadcrumbs. Shape into dumplings and cook in boiling salted water or soup till done.

Cooking Time: about 5 minutes.
A particularly good garnish for ragoût and fricassee.

Meat Balls

¾ oz. (20 g) butter or margarine
1¾ oz. (50 g) minced raw meat
1 egg yolk
salt
pepper
¾ oz. (20 g) breadcrumbs

Fish balls are prepared in the same way as Meat Balls (as noted above).

Fish Balls

¾ oz. (20 g) butter or margarine
1¾ oz. (50 g) minced raw fish
1 egg yolk
salt
pepper
¾ oz. (20 g) breadcrumbs

Liver Dumplings

1¾ oz. (50 g) liver
¾ oz. (20 g) fat bacon
1 small onion
1 egg yolk
salt
pepper
about ¾ oz. (20 g) breadcrumbs

Skin and remove the fibre from the liver, finely chop or mince together with the bacon and the onion. Add the remaining ingredients, shape with a teaspoon into dumplings, drop them into boiling salted water or soup and simmer till done.

Cooking Time: about 10 minutes.

Goose liver may also be used for these dumplings.

Cheese Sticks

Pastry:

2 oz. (55 g) plain flour
pinch of salt
2 oz. (55 g) butter or margarine
2 oz. (55 g) grated Gruyère cheese

Egg-Wash:

1 egg yolk mixed with 1 tsp. of milk

For the pastry, sieve the flour onto a pastry board or slab. Make a well in the centre and put into it the salt and the cold fat cut into small pieces. Sprinkle with the cheese and, working from the centre, knead quickly into a smooth dough. Leave to stand in a cool place for a few minutes. Then roll out to about ¼ inch (½ cm) thickness. Cut into strips about ¾ inch (2 cm) wide and 4 inches (10 cm) long. They may be twisted or left straight. Brush with the egg wash and bake on a baking sheet till golden brown. Be careful not to bake too long, as this will make the cheese sticks taste bitter.

Oven: pre-heat for 5 minutes at very hot, bake at moderate.

Baking Time: about 15 minutes.

Salt Sticks

Pastry:

5½ oz. (150 g) plain flour
3½ oz. (100 g) Oetker GUSTIN
(corn starch powder)
2 level tsp. (6 g)
Oetker Baking Powder BACKIN
1 level tsp. salt
1 egg white
4 tbsp. milk
3½ oz. (100 g) margarine

Egg-Wash:

1 egg yolk mixed with 1 tsp. milk

For Sprinkling:

a little salt, some caraway seeds

For the pastry, sieve the flour, the GUSTIN and the BACKIN onto a pastry board or slab. Make a well in the centre and put into it the salt, the egg white and the milk, and combine with some of the flour from the sides of the well until a thick paste is formed. Add the cold fat, cut into pieces, bring in more flour and, working from the centre, knead all the ingredients together into a smooth dough. If necessary, add more flour to prevent the dough getting sticky. Roll out to ¼ inch (½ cm) thickness. Cut strips about ¾ inch (2 cm) wide and 2 inches (10 cm) long. The salt sticks may be twisted or left straight. Brush with the egg wash and sprinkle with salt or caraway seeds. Place on a baking sheet and bake golden brown.

Oven: pre-heat for 5 minutes at very hot, bake at moderate.

Baking Time: about 10 minutes.

SAUCES

Sauces, like soups, are less popular now than they used to be unjustifiably so when the preparation is understood. Originally sauces were only designed to bring out the flavour of the dishes they accompanied, to blend them with the other courses on the menu, and stimulate all the taste organs.

To attain perfection was the aim of the traditional cuisine, and sauces were intended to be "a stimulus to all the taste organs". This still holds good today. But in addition to recognizing their stimulating and digestive value, we also emphasize their importance for health.

Only too often the modern sauce is merely a mixture of water, fat, and flour. Such a sauce deserves to be left out of the meal,

on the grounds that it constitutes a fattening and not particularly nutritious or tasty "extra". But this need not be so. A properly made sauce consists mainly of extracts of meat, fish, poultry and vegetables, and its flavour can be varied by adding the seasonings suitable to the dish it accompanies.

Of course the housewife today can afford neither the time nor the money to make such extracts especially for sauces. But by careful planning she can use the many juices and liquors which result naturally from her everyday cooking of meat and vegetable dishes. These liquors and juices, so often thrown away, she can use in a variety of different sauces which will enrich the meals she serves her family. A good sauce is an economy, not an "extra". It is by far the most effective way of "stretching" a small fish or meat course into a delicious and satisfying meal.

A. HOT SAUCES

General Hints   1. The foundation of a hot sauce is usually a white or brown roux. To this, meat, bone, or vegetable stock is added, the mixture then being simmered for about 10 minutes to get rid of the taste of flour.

2. For the delicately flavoured white sauces, butter or margarine should be used; whereas dripping, lard, or vegetable fat may be used for brown sauces.

3. Sour cream, lemon juice, wine, mustard, horseradish and fine herbs should never be boiled, as this destroys their delicate flavour. Herbs should always be added at the last minute, wine and lemon juice just before serving. Sauces should be seasoned very carefully; it is very easy to destroy the individual flavour of a sauce by too much or inappropriate seasoning.

4. All hot sauces are greatly improved by the addition of a knob of butter just before serving.

5. White sauces can be given "body" by the addition of egg yolk. More is said about this in the chapter on Egg Cookery, from note 5 onwards, page 211.

I. HOT WHITE SAUCES

Melt the fat over a moderate heat. Stir in the flour and cook without browning until it is pale yellow. Gradually stir in the liquid. To avoid lumps, use a whisk and cold liquid. The sauce must be brought to the boil after each addition of liquid. When all the liquid has been added, cook the sauce for about 10 minutes over a low heat before adding the seasoning.

Cooking Time: about 10 minutes.

By using this recipe as a foundation and varying the seasoning the following sauces can be made.

Prepare and slice the mushrooms. Sauté them in the fat until done, then add them to the white sauce. Season with salt and lemon juice, then add the egg yolk, beaten with the water, or stir in a little cream.

Add the dill to the white sauce and simmer for 10 minutes. Season with salt.

Season the white sauce with mustard, salt, vinegar and sugar.

Melt the fat, add the flour and the finely chopped onions and cook till pale yellow. Add the cold stock, stirring all the time. Stir in the caraway seeds. Bring the sauce to the boil and cook for about 10 minutes over a low heat. Rub through a sieve and season with salt and, if desired, with sugar and vinegar.

Cooking Time: about 10 minutes.

White Sauce

This is the basic recipe. Quantities given are for 1 pint (570 ccm).

1½ oz. (45 g) butter or margarine
1½ oz. (45 g) plain flour
1 pint (570 ccm) white stock or water

Mushroom Sauce (Champignon Sauce)

1 pint (570 ccm) White Sauce
  (as noted above)
4 oz. (115 g) mushrooms
½ oz. (15 g) butter or margarine
pinch of salt
a little lemon juice
1 egg yolk and 2 tbsp. cold water,
  or a little cream

Dill Sauce

1 pint (570 ccm) White Sauce
  (as noted above)
1 heaped tbsp. finely chopped dill
salt

White Mustard Sauce

1 pint (570 ccm) White Sauce
  (as noted above)
made mustard to taste
pinch of salt
a little vinegar
pinch of sugar

White Onion Sauce

1½ oz. (45 g) fat
1½ oz. (45 g) plain flour
2–3 onions
1 pint (570 ccm) stock
1 tsp. caraway seeds
pinch of salt
sugar and vinegar to taste

Caper Sauce

1 pint (570 ccm) White Sauce
(see page 49)
1 tbsp. capers
pinch of salt
a little lemon juice
1 egg yolk and 2 tbsp. cold water
(optional)

Add the capers to the white sauce and cook gently for about 10 minutes over a low heat. Season with salt and lemon juice to taste. Enrich the sauce with the egg yolk beaten in the water.

Cheese Sauce

1 pint (570 ccm) White Sauce
(see page 49)
5 oz. (140 g) grated cheese
pinch of salt
a little lemon juice

Add the cheese to the white sauce and season with salt and lemon juice.

Alternatively, 1 pint (570 ccm) of milk instead of 1 pint (570 ccm) of stock can be used to prepare the basic white sauce.

Herb Sauce

1 pint (570 ccm) White Sauce
(see page 49)
2 tbsp. finely chopped herbs
(parsley, chives, dill)
pinch of salt
a little lemon juice

Add the herbs to the white sauce and cook gently for about 10 minutes over a low heat. Season with salt and lemon juice.

Horseradish Sauce

1 pint (570 ccm) White Sauce
(see page 49)
¼ horseradish root
a little milk
pinch of salt
a little lemon juice

Peel and grate the horseradish, mix it with a little milk and add it to the hot sauce. Do not boil. Season with salt and lemon juice.

Alternatively, the basic white sauce may be made with ½ pint (285 ccm) of milk and ½ pint (285 ccm) of stock instead of the full pint of stock.

Parsley Sauce

1 pint (570 ccm) White Sauce
(see page 49)
a little lemon juice
pinch of salt
1–2 tbsp. of cream (optional)
2 tbsp. finely chopped parsley

Season the white sauce with lemon juice, salt and cream. Add the parsley just before serving.

Stir the prepared anchovies or herring into the white sauce and cook gently for about 10 minutes over a low heat. Season with lemon juice and salt, if necessary.

Anchovy or Herring Sauce

1 pint (570 ccm) White Sauce
   (see page 49)
2½–3 oz. (70–85 g) well-soaked
   chopped anchovies or 1 well-soaked
   salt herring, skinned, boned and
   finely chopped
pinch of salt, if necessary
a little lemon juice

Add the chives to the white sauce and cook gently for about 10 minutes over a low heat. Season with salt and lemon juice.

Chive Sauce

1 pint (570 ccm) White Sauce
   (see page 49)
2 tbsp. finely chopped chives
pinch of salt
a little lemon juice

Melt the fat with the gammon, cut into cubes. Add the flour and the finely chopped onions and cook till pale yellow. Slowly stir in the cold or lukewarm stock with the milk or cream. Cook gently for about 10 minutes over a low heat. The sauce may be rubbed through a fine sieve. Season with salt and pepper.

Cooking Time: about 10 minutes.

What is left in the sieve may be used in making pea, bean or lentil soup.

Béchamel Sauce

1½ oz. (45 g) butter or margarine
1½ oz. (45 g) gammon
1½ oz. (45 g) plain flour
2 oz. (55 g) onions
½ pint (285 ccm) white stock
½ pint (285 ccm) milk or cream
salt
pepper

Melt the fat, stir in the flour and cook gently till pale yellow. Gradually add the cold stock, stirring all the time. Add the capers, the sliced mushrooms and the finely chopped anchovies and allow to cook gently for 10 minutes. Then season with salt and lemon juice or wine. Enrich the sauce with the egg yolk beaten in the water. Do not boil.

Cooking Time: about 10 minutes.

Fricassee Sauce

1½ oz. (45 g) butter or margarine
1½ oz. (45 g) plain flour
1 pint (570 ccm) white stock
1 tsp. capers
a few mushrooms (optional)
1–2 well-soaked anchovies (optional)
pinch of salt
1 tbsp. lemon juice or 2–3 tbsp. wine
1–2 egg yolks and 2 tbsp. cold water

Sauce Hollandaise
(Simple Method)

1½ oz. (45 g) butter or margarine
1½ oz. (45 g) plain flour
1 pint (570 ccm) white stock
or ½ pint (285 ccm) white stock
and ½ pint (285 ccm) milk
1–2 tbsp. lemon juice
pinch of salt
1 egg yolk and 2 tbsp. cold water
1 oz. (30 g) butter

Melt the fat, add the flour and cook till pale yellow. Gradually add the cold liquid, stirring all the time, and allow to cook gently for about 10 minutes over a low heat. Season with lemon juice and salt. Enrich the sauce with the egg yolk beaten in the water. Add the butter. Do not boil.

Cooking Time: about 10 minutes.

Sauce Hollandaise

¾ oz. (20 g) plain flour
2 tbsp. water
2 eggs
1 tbsp. lemon juice
½ pint (285 ccm) white stock
2 oz. (55 g) butter
salt
pinch of nutmeg

Mix together the flour and the water until smooth. Add the eggs, the lemon juice and the stock and mix until well combined. Pour into a small saucepan and, whisking all the time, heat very gently until a large bubble forms. Whisk in the butter (cut into small pieces). Season with salt and nutmeg.

Time: about 15 minutes.

Tomato Sauce with Fresh Tomatoes

1 oz. (30 g) butter or margarine
1 oz. (30 g) gammon
1 small onion
¾ lb. (340 g) tomatoes
1½ oz. (45 g) plain flour
1 pint (570 ccm) stock
pinch of salt
a little lemon juice
pinch of sugar

Melt the fat and cook in it the diced gammon. Add the onion, chopped finely, and the tomatoes washed and cut into pieces. Stir in the flour and cook together for a short time. Add the stock, stirring all the time, and cook gently for about 10 minutes over a low heat. Rub through a fine sieve. Bring again to the boil, season to taste with salt, lemon juice and sugar.

Cooking Time: about 10 minutes.

Tomato Sauce with Tomato Purée

1½ oz. (45 g) butter or margarine
1½ oz. (45 g) plain flour
1 pint (570 ccm) white stock
about 1 tbsp. concentrated tomato purée
pinch of salt
a little lemon juice
pinch of sugar

Melt the fat, stir in the flour and cook till pale yellow. Gradually add the cold stock, stirring all the time. Add the tomato purée and cook gently for about 10 minutes over a low heat. Season with salt, lemon juice and sugar.

Cooking Time: about 10 minutes.

Well equipped – Well done !
Please write for catalogue with more than 200 modern
Dr. Oetker Baking– and Kitchen Utensils to
BHG P.O. Box 85 48 Bielefeld BRD

II. HOT BROWN SAUCES

Melt the fat quickly over a full heat. Add the flour, stirring all the time, and cook till fairly brown. Add chopped onion, if desired, but not until the flour is lightly browned or it will become too dark. Stir in the liquid gradually. To prevent lumps forming, use a whisk and cold or lukewarm liquid. Bring the sauce to the boil again every time liquid has been added. When all the liquid has been added, cook the sauce very gently for about 10 minutes over a low heat.

Cooking Time: about 10 minutes.

Brown Sauce

This is the basic recipe. Quantities given are for 1 pint (570 ccm).

$1\frac{1}{2}$ oz. (45 g) fat
(dripping, lard or mixed fat)
2 oz. (55 g) plain flour
1 pint (570 ccm) stock

Dice the gherkin and add to the brown sauce. Simmer for a few minutes. Season to taste with salt, vinegar, pepper and sugar.

Brown Gherkin Sauce

1 pint (570 ccm) Brown Sauce
(as noted above)
1 gherkin (Salzgurke)
salt
a little vinegar
pepper
a little sugar

Add the prepared and chopped mushrooms to the sauce and cook gently for about 10 minutes over a low heat. Season to taste with salt, butter and Madeira.

Cooking Time: about 10 minutes.

Brown Mushroom Sauce

1 pint (570 ccm) Brown Sauce
(as noted above)
4–8 oz. (115–225 g) prepared and
finely chopped mushrooms
(chanterelle, truffle, boletus or other
edible fungi)
salt
1 tbsp. butter
2–3 tbsp. Madeira

Peel the onions, pour boiling water over them and drain. Brown the sugar, stir in some stock, the lemon juice and the salt. Add the onions and stew over a low heat until they look glassy.

Melt the fat. Add the flour, and still stirring, cook until dark brown. Gradually add the cold stock and the onions. Bring to the boil, stirring all the time, and cook for about 10 minutes over a low heat. Season with salt and Burgundy.

Cooking Time: about 10 minutes.

Burgundy Sauce

$1\frac{1}{2}$ oz. (45 g) silver onions
1 level tbsp. sugar
a little stock
a little lemon juice
salt
$1\frac{1}{2}$ oz. (45 g) fat
2 oz. (55 g) plain flour
$\frac{3}{4}$ pint (425 ccm) stock
$\frac{1}{4}$ pint (140 ccm) Burgundy

Potato Dumplings Recipe See Page 176

Madeira Sauce

1½ oz. (45 g) fat
2 oz. (55 g) plain flour
1 onion
1 pint (570 ccm) stock
2 oz. (55 g) gammon
pot vegetables (parsley root,
celeriac, carrot)
2 tomatoes
salt
lemon juice
pinch of sugar
3–4 tbsp. Madeira

Melt the fat and stir in the flour. When it is lightly browned, add the onion, finely chopped. Fry together till dark brown. Gradually add the cold stock, stirring all the time. Dice the gammon, fry it and add to it the prepared and chopped pot vegetables and the washed and sliced tomatoes. When they are hot, add them to the sauce and leave to cook gently for about ½ hour over a low heat. Rub through a sieve. Season with salt, lemon juice, sugar and Madeira.

Cooking Time: about 30 minutes.

Serve with boiled tongue.

Raisin Sauce

¾ oz. (20 g) fat
¾ oz. (20 g) plain flour
1 pint (570 ccm) stock
¾ oz. (20 g) grated gingerbread
2 oz. (55 g) raisins
2 oz. (55 g) currants
a little cinnamon
2 cloves
1 tbsp. vinegar or lemon juice
sugar
salt

Melt the fat, stir in the flour and fry till almost dark brown. Stir in the cold stock a little at a time, add the grated gingerbread, the washed raisins and currants, the cinnamon and the cloves. Cook gently for about 30 minutes over a low heat. Season with the vinegar or lemon juice, sugar and salt.

Cooking Time: about 30 minutes.

The sauce may be varied by the addition of 20 blanched almonds, cut into fine strips, and 1–2 tbsp. of redcurrant jelly.

Serve with boiled tongue or boiled beef.

Brown Mustard Sauce

1½ oz. (45 g) fat
2 oz. (55 g) plain flour
1 small onion
1 pint (570 ccm) stock
made mustard to taste
1 tbsp. vinegar or lemon juice
sugar
salt

Melt the fat, stir in the flour and brown lightly. Add the finely chopped onion. Gradually stir in the cold stock. Cook gently for about 10 minutes over a low heat. Then season with mustard, vinegar or lemon juice, sugar and salt.

Cooking Time: about 10 minutes.

Serve with beef, fish or eggs.

Bacon Sauce

2 oz. (55 g) streaky bacon
2 oz. (55 g) onions
1¾ oz. (50 g) plain flour
1 pint (570 ccm) stock
½ bay-leaf
2 cloves
1–2 tbsp. vinegar
sugar or treacle
pinch of salt

Dice the bacon and the onions. Fry together, stirring all the time until pale yellow. Remove from the pan. Add the flour to the bacon fat and fry until brown. Gradually stir in the cold or luke-warm stock. Add the bay-leaf, cloves, bacon and onions, and cook gently for about 10 minutes over a low heat. Season with vinegar, sugar or treacle, and salt. Remove the bay-leaf and cloves before serving.

Cooking Time: about 10 minutes.

Serve with French beans, potato balls, potatoes boiled in their skins or poached eggs.

B. DRESSINGS AND COLD SAUCES

Salad Dressing I
(Marinade or French Dressing)

Beat the oil, the vinegar and salt together with a fork until thick. Stir in the herbs.

1 finely chopped onion may be added; celery salt, sugar, or honey may be used to vary the flavour. Some salads may be seasoned with lemon juice instead of vinegar. For potato salad, vinegar only should be used.

3 tbsp. salad oil
1–2 tbsp. vinegar
pinch of salt
1 tsp. finely chopped herbs

Salad Dressing II
(Marinade or French Dressing)

Beat the oil, vinegar, salt and sugar thoroughly with a fork until thick. Add the sour cream, the finely chopped onion and the herbs.

For some salads, lemon juice may be substituted for vinegar.

1–2 tbsp. salad oil
1–2 tbsp. vinegar
pinch of salt
a little sugar
2 tbsp. sour cream
1 small onion
1 tsp. finely chopped herbs

Dressing for Raw Vegetables

Beat the oil, the lemon juice or vinegar, and salt thoroughly with a fork until thick. Add the cream, the finely chopped onion and the herbs.

2–3 tbsp. salad oil
2 tbsp. lemon juice or vinegar
pinch of salt
2 tbsp. cream
1 small onion
1 tbsp. finely chopped herbs

Fresh Tomato Dressing

Wash the tomatoes and cut them into small pieces. Rub through a sieve and mix thoroughly with the other ingredients.

8 oz. (225 g) ripe tomatoes
1 tsp. lemon juice
pinch of salt
a little sugar
2–3 tbsp. oil or cream
1 tsp. finely grated onion

Tomato Dressing
(Using Tomato Purée)

Mix the tomato purée thoroughly with the other ingredients.

About 2 oz. (55 g) tomato purée
¼ pint (140 ccm) water
1 tsp. lemon juice
pinch of salt
a little sugar
2–3 tbsp. oil or cream
1 tsp. finely grated onion

Tomato-Horseradish Dressing

8 oz. (225 g) ripe tomatoes
1 tsp. lemon juice
pinch of salt
sugar
2–3 tbsp. oil or cream
1 tsp. finely grated onion
3 tbsp. grated horseradish

Cut the washed tomatoes into small pieces, rub through a sieve and mix thoroughly with the other ingredients.

Apple-Horseradish Dressing

¼ pint (140 ccm) apple wine (cider)
juice of half a lemon
1 tbsp. sugar
salt
2 apples
grated horseradish

Mix together the wine, the lemon juice, the sugar and the salt. Stir in the finely grated apples. Add enough horseradish to give a piquant flavour to the sauce.

Serve with cold meat or fish.

Cream Dressing

½ pint (285 ccm) sour cream
juice of half a lemon
sugar
salt

Whisk together the cream and lemon juice and season to taste with sugar and salt. If the dressing is too heavy, thin it with 2–3 tbsp. of oil or 2 tbsp. of milk.

Dill-Cream Dressing

½ pint (285 ccm) sour cream
juice of half a lemon
1 small onion
1–2 tsp. finely chopped dill
salt

Mix together the cream and lemon juice, add the finely chopped onion and the dill and season with salt to taste.

Fresh Herb and Cream Dressing

½ pint (285 ccm) sour cream
juice of half a lemon
2 hard-boiled eggs
2–3 tbsp. finely chopped herbs
sugar
salt

Mix together the cream and lemon juice, stir in the chopped eggs and the herbs and season with sugar and salt to taste. This dressing is particularly good with boiled beef.

Horseradish-Cream Dressing

¼–½ horseradish root
½ pint (285 ccm) fresh cream
a little lemon juice
salt
sugar

Scrape the horseradish, grate it into a little milk and mix it with the whipped cream. Season to taste with the lemon juice, salt and sugar.

Mix all the ingredients thoroughly together. This dressing is delicious with beetroot salad.

Mustard-Cream Dressing

1/4 pint (140 ccm) fresh cream
made mustard to taste
pinch of salt
sugar
a little lemon juice

Mustard Dressing

Mix the finely chopped eggs with the mustard and the onion. Whisk the cream thickly and stir with the grated apples into the dressing.

3 hard-boiled eggs
made mustard to taste
1 tsp. chopped onion
6 tbsp. sour cream
2 apples

Mayonnaise I

1–2 egg yolks
salt
1/4 pint (140 ccm) salad oil
1 tsp. vinegar or lemon juice

All the ingredients should have the same temperature, preferably lukewarm. If the oil is too cold, stand the bottle in warm water for about 5 minutes. Whisk the egg yolks with a pinch of salt very thoroughly until slightly thick. Then add half of the oil drop by drop whisking or stirring all the time until thick and smooth. Add the seasonings. Lastly stir in the remaining oil.

Should the mayonnaise curdle, it can sometimes be settled again by the addition of about 1 tsp. of cold water, added quickly drop by drop, stirring all the time. Or the curdled mayonnaise can be slowly added to 1 well beaten egg yolk.

To vary the flavour of the mayonnaise, add 1 tsp. of mustard, a little celery salt or some sour or fresh cream.

Mayonnaise II

1 egg yolk
made mustard to taste
salt
1 tsp. sugar
1 tbsp. lemon juice or vinegar
1/4 pint (140 ccm) oil

Put the egg yolk into a basin with the mustard, salt, sugar and lemon juice. Whisk them together until the mixture thickens. Then beat in the oil. If the mayonnaise is prepared in this way it is not necessary to add the oil drop by drop, it can be stirred in a tablespoonful at a time. The seasoning added to the yolk prevents curdling.

To increase the quantity of mayonnaise, mix 1 slightly heaped tbsp. of Oetker GUSTIN with 1/4 pint (140 ccm) water and bring to the boil, stirring all the time. Then add this boiling mixture to the mayonnaise, whisking thoroughly.

Herb Mayonnaise

Using Mayonnaise recipe I or II (as noted above), stir in either 2 tbsp. finely chopped herbs, or the juice of fresh herbs (chervil, tarragon, watercress, chives, etc.).

Horseradish Mayonnaise

Using Mayonnaise recipe I or II (see page 59), add so much grated horseradish as to give a good flavour.

Tomato Purée Mayonnaise

Using Mayonnaise recipe I or II (see page 59), add 1–2 tbsp. of concentrated purée.

Rémoulade Sauce

Yolks of 2 hard-boiled eggs
1 raw egg yolk
salt
¼ pint (140 ccm) oil
2 tbsp. vinegar or lemon juice
made mustard to taste
1 tsp. finely chopped onion
1 tbsp. finely chopped capers
2 small pickled gherkins
1–2 finely chopped, well soaked anchovies
1 tbsp. chopped herbs
salt
pepper
¼ pint (140 ccm) sour cream (optional)

Rub the hard-boiled egg yolks through a fine sieve, then mix them thoroughly with the raw egg yolk and a pinch of salt. Beating all the time, add the oil drop by drop. When half the oil has been used and the mixture is thick and smooth, add the vinegar and mustard. Then add the remaining oil and the other ingredients. The hard-boiled egg whites can be added to the sauce or used as a garnish for salad, brawn, or other cold dish. The anchovies, the finely chopped pickled gherkins and the capers may be omitted.

Cumberland Sauce

Peel of half an orange
4½ oz. (125 g) redcurrant jelly
4 tbsp. red wine
juice of one orange
made mustard to taste
pinch of salt

Remove the pith from the orange peel. Cut into thin shreds and cover with boiling water. Strain. Melt the redcurrant jelly carefully, then add the red wine, orange juice and mustard. Season to taste with salt, then add the orange peel.

This sauce goes well with venison, cold meat and patties.

Devil's Sauce

Yolks of 2 hard-boiled eggs
salt
2 tbsp. salad oil
made mustard to taste
1–2 tbsp. lemon juice
pinch of chopped onion
a little pepper
pinch of sugar
1 tsp. finely chopped tarragon
1 tbsp. grated apple
3 tbsp. red wine

Rub the hard-boiled egg yolks through a fine sieve. Gradually stir in all the other ingredients.

This sauce goes well with brawn and cold roast beef.

C. SWEET SAUCES (Hot and Cold)

Blend the sauce powder and the sugar with the 5 tbsp. milk or water. Bring the ¾ pint (425 ccm) milk to the boil, remove from heat and stir in the prepared sauce powder. Return to the heat and bring again to the boil. Set aside to cool, stirring frequently to prevent a skin forming.

Vanilla Sauce I

1 packet Oetker Sauce Powder,
   vanilla flavour
1 oz. (30 g) sugar
5 tbsp. cold milk or water
¾ pint (425 ccm) milk

Blend the GUSTIN, the vanillin sugar, the sugar and salt with the 5 tbsp. milk or water. Bring the ¾ pint (425 ccm) milk to the boil, remove from heat and add the prepared GUSTIN. Bring to the boil again. Remove from heat and stir in the egg yolk beaten in the water. Set aside to cool, stirring frequently to prevent a skin forming.

Vanilla Sauce II

1 slightly heaped tbsp. (10 g)
   Oetker GUSTIN (corn starch powder)
1 packet Oetker Vanillin Sugar
1 oz. (30 g) sugar
salt
5 tbsp. cold milk or water
¾ pint (425 ccm) milk
1 egg yolk and 2 tbsp. cold water

Put the sugar into a pan and, stirring all the time, cook it gently until it is a light brown colour. Add the ¾ pint (425 ccm) milk to the sugar and bring to the boil. Blend the GUSTIN with the 5 tbsp. milk or water. As soon as the caramel boils, remove from heat, and stir in the prepared GUSTIN. Return to the heat and, still stirring, bring the mixture to the boil again. Beat the egg yolk in the water, remove the sauce from heat and stir in the egg. Add sugar to taste. Set aside to cool, stirring frequently to prevent a skin forming.

The egg yolk may be omitted. If so, use ½ oz. (15 g) Oetker GUSTIN (corn starch powder) instead of the slightly heaped tbsp. (10 g).

Caramel Sauce

2 oz. (55 g) sugar
¾ pint (425 ccm) milk
1 slightly heaped tbsp. (10 g)
   Oetker GUSTIN (corn starch powder)
5 tbsp. cold milk or water
1 egg yolk and 2 tbsp. cold water
sugar to taste

Blend the GUSTIN, the sugar and salt with the 5 tbsp. milk or water. Bring the ¾ pint (425 ccm) milk to the boil, remove from heat and stir in the prepared GUSTIN. Return to heat and bring again to the boil. Beat the egg yolk in the water. Remove the sauce from heat and stir in the egg. Lastly, add the bitter almond flavour. Set aside to cool, stirring frequently to prevent a skin forming.

Almond Sauce

1 slightly heaped tbsp. (10 g)
   Oetker GUSTIN (corn starch powder)
1 oz. (30 g) sugar
pinch of salt
5 tbsp. cold milk or water
¾ pint (425 ccm) milk
1 egg yolk and 2 tbsp. cold water
3–4 drops Oetker Baking Essence,
   bitter almond flavour

Chocolate Sauce

1 packet Oetker Sauce Powder,
vanilla flavour
½ oz. (15 g) cocoa
1½–2 oz. (45–55 g) sugar
1 pint (570 ccm) milk

Blend the sauce powder, the cocoa and 1½ oz. (45 g) sugar with 5 tbsp. of the milk. Bring the remaining milk to the boil, remove from heat, add the prepared sauce powder and bring to the boil again. Add sugar to taste. Set aside to cool, stirring frequently to prevent a skin forming.

Fruit Juice Sauce

2 level tsp. Oetker GUSTIN
(corn starch powder)
¼ pint (140 ccm) water
¼ pint (140 ccm) fruit juice
a little lemon juice
a little sugar, if needed

Blend the GUSTIN with 2 tbsp. of the water. Add the rest of the water to the fruit juice and bring to the boil. Remove from heat and stir in the prepared GUSTIN; return to heat and bring again to the boil. Add the lemon juice and, if necessary, some sugar. Set aside to cool, stirring frequently to prevent a skin forming.

Uncooked Fruit Juice

½ pint (285 ccm) fruit juice
3½–4½ oz. (100–125 g) sugar

Wash and prepare ripe currants, raspberries or cherries and strain through a cloth or fruit press. Add the sugar, stirring until it has all dissolved.

Delicious with pudding, blancmange or rice dishes.

Frothy Wine Sauce

⅜ oz. (10 g) Oetker Sauce Powder,
vanilla flavour
2 oz. (55 g) sugar
1 egg
1 egg yolk
¼ pint (140 ccm) water
¼ pint (140 ccm) wine
1 tbsp. lemon juice

Whisk together the sauce powder, the sugar, the egg and the egg yolk with the water, the wine and the lemon juice. Pour the mixture into a small saucepan and heat very gently. Beat with a wire whisk until a large bubble forms. Then place the pan in a bowl of cold water and continue whisking until the sauce is cold.

Time: about 20 minutes.

Frothy Lemon Sauce

⅜ oz. (10 g) Oetker Sauce Powder,
vanilla flavour
2½ oz. (70 g) sugar
1 egg
1 egg yolk
¼ pint (140 ccm) water
juice of 2 lemons

Whisk together the sauce powder, the sugar, the egg and the egg yolk with the water and the lemon juice. Pour the mixture into a small saucepan and heat very gently. Beat with a wire whisk until a large bubble forms. Then place the pan in a bowl of cold water and continue whisking until the sauce is cold.

Time: about 20 minutes.

MEAT DISHES

Protein provides the main body-building element in our food, the element which cannot be dispensed with, if we are to grow and remain strong and healthy. Butcher's meat averages about 20% protein; poultry and game an even higher proportion; so meat must rank very high as a body-building food. The percentage of fat in meat varies widely with species, grade and cut. Bone marrow has 90% fat, lean beef may have only 4%, fat beef often has 25%, a well-fattened goose may have as much as 45%, whereas venison has only 2–3%. The fat and water content of meat generally depends on the way an animal is fed. Fat meat, which has a higher caloric and nutritive value than lean meat, contains far less water. Carbohydrates are rare in meat, although liver does contain about 2–3% glycogen, an animal starch.

The bones cartilage, skin and sinews of meat are rich in protein-like elements for collagenous substances. They can only be dissolved after long boiling. The best way of extracting them, is to put the bones cartilage etc. into cold water, bring to the boil and simmer steadily for several hours. Bones should be boiled twice. After the second boiling the liquid will jellify when cold, a quality of which we can take advantage when preparing brawn and aspics. Such stock makes an excellent foundation for soups and sauces and its varied uses in preparing meals should not be overlooked. These collagenous substances however are not a substitute for the protein contained in meat from the muscles.

Offal is another important meat food, being as rich in protein and fat and containing more vitamins than meat from the muscles. Blood and liver, too, contain important minerals, notably iron. The food value of offal is not generally appreciated, so it remains cheap and plentiful, a boon to the wise and economical housewife.

In addition to its nutritive value meat contains other important components which are aroma and flavour extracts. These stimulate the appetite and thus the digestive glands of the stomach and the kidneys.

In preparing stock, slow cooking from cold draws the vitamins and flavour into the liquid in which the meat or bones are cooking. The opposite process must be followed if the juices are to be preserved in the meat; that is to say, raw meat shoud always be put into boiling water or hot fat to cook, so that its outer surface may harden instantly, and thus seal in the meat's juices.

For a balanced diet, meat, being rich only in fat and protein, should be eaten in fairly small quantities and supplemented with plenty of potatoes, vegetables, and fruit. This is perhaps just as well, as most meat is expensive. If she is to get full value from what she buys, the housewife must have some knowledge of the various cuts and joints and of the ways in which they can be cooked. She should know that the meat of old animals, being more sinewy, is the best for stocks; that younger animals' meat, being tender and less gristly, needs a shorter cooking time and is easier to digest. She should never soak meat for long, but always wash it quickly, to avoid loss of the natural juices. For the same reason meat should never be left for any length of time on a wooden board or other absorbent surface. Meat from a freshly killed animal is tougher than meat which has been hung for some time. Very soon after killing the muscles of an animal become tough and hard, but if the meat is hung for a day or two the muscles soften again owing to the action of acids formed in the meat.

For a good juicy roast, wash the meat quickly, beat it a little to soften the tissues, and cut away any indigestible skin or sinew. If possible, cover the joint with slices of bacon or lard it, as this will seal in the juices and flavour more effectively. Put the joint into a very hot oven and brown it quickly, thus closing the cells and hardening the surface protein. Turn down the heat to moderate to finish, as prolonged cooking at a high temperature will cause drying and shrinkage. As salt is apt to draw out the natural juices, salt the joint only slightly just before it goes into the oven, or after browning. Turn the meat occasionally, so that it browns and cooks evenly. Always use two spoons to do this, rather than a fork, which would let the juices escape.

Store meat in a cool place, preferably in a refrigerator. A meat cover of wire or gauze will protect meat from flies. A wet cloth will keep the meat cool if no refrigerator is available. Seeping in vinegar or buttermilk is the safest way to preserve meat, but it cannot afterwards be boiled. Stewing, braising or pot-roasting are preferable procedures. A piece of ham or sausage can be kept fresh by greasing the cut surface with lard. If, in spite of all your precautions, you are at some time faced with the problem of trying to save meat which is going bad, scrape it thoroughly and then rinse it in water to which enough hypermanganate of potash has been added to turn the water pale purple. Rinse in fresh water, dry, and use at once.

A. BOILED MEAT

General Hints

1. Large joints should be rolled up and tied with a string, so that the surface area of the meat is as small as possible. This prevents too much meat juice being lost.

2. Before the meat is put in, the water must be boiling, so that the albumen on the surface of the meat will harden instantly and seal in the juices.

3. The temperature of the liquid while the meat is cooking should never go over the simmering point, otherwise the meat will be tough and the stock cloudy. "Boiling" is therefore a somewhat misleading term.

4. The scum produced by simmering is albumen and need not be skimmed.

5. Pot vegetables should never be left to boil for longer than an hour, or their vitamins, flavour and aromatic qualities will be lost.

6. Meat retains its juiciness if it is left in the stock for about 10 minutes before serving.

BUTCHER'S MEAT

Beef   The fore ribs, wing ribs and best chine provide roast beef and rump steak. The choicest cuts – sirloin for roasting and fillet steak for grilling – come from the loin.

The round and the rump provide the best joints for braising and stewing, whereas the best boiling beef, fresh or salted, comes from the brisket. Thin flank, neck, tail, fore shin and clod are used for stock or broth. Shoulder beef is lean and tender. Fresh boiled tongue is served with caper or raisin sauce, salted boiled tongue with horseradish or Madeira sauce.

Veal   Meat of fattened calves is pale pink and tender, if the colour is too strong, the meat may be dry. The best cut for roasting is the loin and best-end, or the tender 'cushion' from the top of the leg. Fillet is best grilled. The breast is usually stuffed or cut up and cooked in a fricassee. The shoulder is excellent for roasts, ragoûts, spiced meat dishes, or goulash. Brains, tongue, and sweetbreads can be boiled or fried or used in fricassee. Because it is easy to digest and has a delicate flavour, veal is much used for invalid dishes.

Pork   Best quality pork comes from young fattened pigs. The meat is rather fat, but very tender. Good pork, like good veal, should be of a pale pink colour, but not too light. Loin and leg are best for either roasting or smoking; spare-rib, too, can be smoked or roasted. Fillet pork is the best cut for grilling, whereas streaky pork from the belly is served boiled with vegetables. Shoulder, neck, and belly are generally used for sausage meat. Ears, snout, and trotters are often salted and served with vegetables and soups, or made into brawn.

Mutton   Good mutton should be a dark brownish-red, lamb a light red. Mutton fat should be white and firm, the meat fine grained. Mutton should be hung from a week to a fortnight if it is to be tasty and juicy. Saddle of mutton is the best joint, either roasted, whole or served as cutlets. Boned shoulder of mutton can be stuffed or cut up and served as ragoût. Leg and breast are usually roasting joints.

HOW TO RENDER FAT

Beef Dripping

After removing the outer skin, soak the fat in cold water for several hours. Mince or cut the fat into very small pieces, then place in a saucepan with milk or water, 2¼ lb. (1 kg) fat to ¼–½ pint (140–285 ccm) of liquid. Bring slowly to the boil, so that all the fat can melt from the skin. Cook in a covered saucepan for about half an hour and then finish with the lid off. Fat will be tasty and fit to keep when the greaves are crisp and yellow. Strain the fat into a warmed earthenware pot, cover with greaseproof paper, and store in a cool place.

Veal Fat

Veal fat is rendered in the same way as beef dripping.

Pork Fat

Pork fat (lard) is made in the same ways as beef dripping, except that no liquid is added when the fat is melted. If it is to be used as a sandwich spread, add slices of apple or chopped onion as soon as the greaves turn yellow.

Mutton Fat and Mixed Fats

Mutton fat is made in the same ways as beef dripping. To get the best results, mix the mutton fat with lard in the proportion of 1⅛ lb. (500 g) mutton fat to 4½ oz. (125 g) lard. Another excellent fat is a mixture of suet, lard, and margarine in the proportion of 2¼ lb. (1 kg) dripping to 2¼ lb. (1 kg) lard and 1⅛ lb. (500 g) margarine. Veal fat, oil, or vegetable fat may be used instead of margarine. Mixed fat is tasty and economical. The fact that no one flavour predominates makes it much more generally useful than fat from one kind of meat only.

In making mixed fat, put the beef suet into a saucepan, then, as soon as all the liquid has been driven off, add the pork fat. If rapeseed oil is to be added to the mixture, boil it first with a peeled raw potato or onion until no more scum rises, then add it to the other fats.

Mixed fat may be used for pea, bean, or lentil soup, for roasting large or small joints, for making roux for soups and sauces, for potato dishes, for such vegetable dishes as sauerkraut, red cabbage, and green cabbage, and for frying pancakes, etc. Mixed fat is especially good for frying as, being almost free from moisture, it will not splutter.

I. LARGE JOINTS, BOILED

Boiled Beef

About 1½ lb. (680 g) beef
(aitchbone, brisket or top ribs)
2¾ pints (1½ l) water
salt
1 onion (fried)
1 oz. (30 g) pot vegetables
(carrot, celeriac, leek)

Quickly wash and dry the joint. Beat it and, if necessary, tie it into a neat shape. This will preserve the juices and make carving easier. If bones are available put them into cold water and boil for about an hour before adding the meat. Put the meat into the boiling salted water, bring back to the boil and simmer for an hour over a low heat. Then add the sliced onion and the pot vegetables, which should be washed but not chopped. When the meat is done, remove from heat and leave it in the hot stock for about 10 minutes. Slice it, pour over some of the hot stock and garnish with parsley and chopped pot vegetables.

Cooking Time: 2–2½ hours.

Serve with stewed vegetables or with Horseradish (see page 50), Tomato (see page 52), Chive (see page 51), Mustard (see page 49) or Anchovy Sauce (see page 51), and boiled potatoes.

Use the stock for soups and sauces.

Boiled Veal

About 1½ lb. (680 g) veal
(middle breast, scrag or shoulder)
2¾ pints (1½ l) water
salt
1 oz. (30 g) pot vegetables
(carrot or leek)

Use the same method as for Boiled Beef (as noted above).

Cooking Time: 1–1½ hours.

Serve the veal with Parsley (see page 50), Caper (see page 50) or Béchamel Sauce (see page 51), and boiled potatoes.

Boiled Pork

About 1½ lb. (680 g) pork
(spare rib from neck end, belly, ribs)
2¾ pints (1½ l) water
salt
1 oz. (30 g) pot vegetables
(carrot, celeriac, leek)

Do not remove the skin from the meat. Use the same method as for Boiled Beef (as noted above).

Cooking Time: 1½ hours.

Serve with Mustard (see page 49), Anchovy (see page 51) or Chive Sauce (see page 51) and boiled potatoes.

Boiled Pickled Meat

About 1½ lb. (680 g) pickled meat
2¾ pints (1½ l) water
1 onion

Over-salted meat should be soaked in cold water for 2–3 hours before boiling. Use the same method as for Boiled Beef (as noted above) but do not salt the water in which the meat is cooked.

Cooking Time: 1½–2 hours.

Pickled ribs of pork (Kasseler Rippespeer, see page 89) are served with sauerkraut and a purée of dried peas. Use the stock for pea, bean or lentil soup.

Use the same method as for Boiled Beef (see page 68).

Cooking Time: 1½–2 hours.

Serve the mutton with mashed potatoes, pickled gherkins and Onion Sauce (see page 49), made with the stock. Dill (see page 49), Chive (see page 51) or Tomato Sauce (see page 52) are also suitable with this dish.

Cut away the root and trim the tongue neatly. Wash it, and scrape it clean. Put into the boiling salted water. Add the celeriac or leek an hour before the tongue is done. The tongue is done if the tip is tender when tested with a fork. Remove it from the stock and skin it while it is still hot. Return it to the hot stock until ready to serve. Cut into finger-thick slices.

Serve the broth in cups.

Cooking Time: 3–4 hours.

Serve with boiled potatoes and Chive (see page 51), Dill (see page 49), Mushroom (see page 49), Tomato (see page 52) or Anchovy Sauce (see page 51).

Use the same method to cook pickled tongue, but soak it in cold water to cover for several hours before cooking and omit the salt in the cooking water. Very good with Horseradish Sauce (see page 50).

Cut away the root, then wash the tongue and scrape it clean. Tie up the washed pot vegetables and put into the boiling salted water with the tongue. The tongue is done if the tip is tender when tested with a fork. Remove it from the stock and skin it while it is still hot. Return it to the hot stock until ready to serve. Cut it into halves or diagonal slices.

Cooking Time: 1–1¾ hours.

Serve with Anchovy (see page 51), Mushroom (see page 49) or Tomato Sauce (see page 52).

Soak the brains in cold water until all the blood has been extracted. Remove skin and veins, and put into the boiling salted water a little vinegar and some fine herbs. Simmer gently without boiling. The brains may be served with brown butter and tomato salad. If they are to be served fried, leave them in the stock to cool before frying.

Cooking Time: 5–6 minutes.

Alternatively, the brains may be used in Fricassee (see page 76) or Ragoût (see page 77).

Boiled Mutton

About 1½ lb. (680 g) mutton
(breast, shoulder or neck)
2¾ pints (1½ l) water
salt
2 oz. (55 g) fried onions
1 tsp. caraway seeds

Boiled Ox Tongue
(10–12 Servings)

1 fresh ox tongue
3½–4½ pints (2–2½ l) water
salt
2 oz. (55 g) celeriac or leek

Boiled Calf's Tongue

1–2 calves' tongues
1¾–2¾ pints (1–1½ l) water
salt
pot vegetables

Boiled Calf's Brain

3 calves' brains
1 pint (570 ccm) water
salt
a little vinegar
fine herbs

Roasting Cuts:
Prime Fore Ribs
(Roastbeef)
Fillet (from sirloin)

Braising Cuts:
Topside
Chuck or Blade
Aitchbone

Boiling Cuts:
Clod
Brisket
Shin
Ribs

BEEF

VEAL

Roasting Cuts:
Blade, Shoulder
Breast (filled)
Rump, Leg
Loin
Best End of Neck
Kidney Chops

Boiling Cuts:
Neck
Breast
Knuckle (stewed)

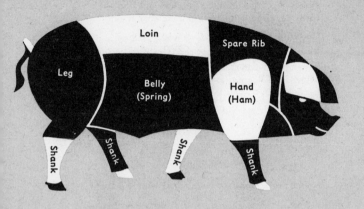

Roasting Cuts:
Loin
Leg
Spare Rib
Hand

Braising Cuts:
Ribs
Spare Rib

Boiling Cuts:
Shank
Belly

PORK

MUTTON

Roasting Cuts:
Loin Chump,
Leg, Saddle

Braising Cuts:
Shoulder
Neck

Boiling Cuts:
Breast

Boiled Sweetbreads

3 sweetbreads
1 pint (570 ccm) water
salt

Soak the sweetbreads for several hours in cold water to blanch them. Then pour over them first hot and then cold water. This makes the sweetbreads coagulate and the veins can be more easily removed. Simmer in salt water until done.

Cooking Time: about 15 minutes.

Serve with Anchovy (see page 51) or Madeira Sauce (see page 56).

Sweetbreads can also be used in Fricassee (see page as noted below) and Ragoût (see page 77).

II. SMALL JOINTS, BOILED

General Hints

1. The water must have reached boiling point when the meat is put in.

2. While cooking, the liquid should simmer gently over a low heat.

3. Use the stock in which the meat has been cooked as the foundation for the sauce with which it is to be served.

4. Serve a white sauce with white meat (Fricassee), and a brown sauce with dark meat (Ragoût).

5. The cooked meat should be simmered in the sauce for about 10 minutes over a low heat before serving.

Fricassee of Veal

About 1 lb. (450 g) veal
1 pint (570 ccm) water
salt
1½ oz. (45 g) butter or margarine
1½ oz. (45 g) plain flour
1 tsp. capers
1 tbsp. lemon juice or wine
1 egg yolk and
2 tbsp. cold water (optional)

Cut the veal into pieces and plunge them into the slightly salted boiling water. Cook for about 30 minutes until tender. Pour off 1 pint (570 ccm) of the stock and leave it to cool. Melt the fat, add the flour and cook until pale yellow. Stir in the cold stock and simmer gently for about 10 minutes over a low heat. Add the capers, season with lemon juice or wine and salt and, if desired, enrich with the egg yolk beaten in the water. Put the veal into the sauce.

Cooking Time: 30–40 minutes.

This fricassee is usually served in a ring of rice, or the rice can be heaped round the dish in the form of a ring (use two spoons to do this neatly).

The fricassee can be garnished with small meat balls, steamed flowerets of cauliflower, asparagus pieces, mushrooms and chopped anchovies.

Cut off the root, then wash the tongue and scrape it clean. Plunge it into the boiling salted water. The tongue is done if the tip is tender when tested with a fork. Remove it from the stock and skin it while still hot. Cut it into diagonal slices. Using 1 pint (570 ccm) of the stock proceed as for Veal Fricassee (see page 76).

Cooking Time: 1–1¾ hours.

Calf's Tongue Fricassee

1–2 calves' tongues
1¾–2¾ pints (1–1½ l) water
salt
1½ oz. (45 g) butter or margarine
1½ oz. (45 g) plain flour
1 tsp. capers
1 tbsp. lemon juice or wine
1 egg yolk and
  2 tbsp. cold water (optional)

Cut the tongue, brains or sweetbread, and the **veal into strips** or cubes. Melt the fat, stir in the flour, and cook until pale yellow. Add the cold stock, stirring all the time, and simmer for 10 minutes over a low heat. Stir in the capers and the finely sliced mushrooms. Season with lemon juice or wine and with salt. Enrich with the egg yolks beaten in the water. Add the meat. Grease 12 shells with butter. Fill with the mixture, sprinkle with the breadcrumbs and the cheese, and dot with pats of butter. Bake in pre-heated oven with full heat until lightly browned.

Time: 11–13 minutes.
Serve with slices of lemon and white bread.

Ragoût Fin in Shells

1 boiled calf's tongue (see page 69)
1 boiled calf's brain or sweetbread
  (see page 76)
8 oz. (225 g) boiled veal (see page 68)
1 pint (570 ccm) stock
1½ oz. (45 g) butter or margarine
2 oz. (55 g) plain flour
1 tsp. capers
2 oz. (55 g) tinned mushrooms
a little lemon juice or wine
salt
1–2 egg yolks and
  2 tbsp. cold water
2 tbsp. breadcrumbs
2 tbsp. grated cheese
1½ oz. (45 g) butter

Cut up the meat, put it into the boiling salted water and cook for about an hour and a half. Pour off 1 pint (570 ccm) of the stock and leave it to cool. To make the sauce, melt the fat, add the flour and cook until yellow. Then add the onion, peeled and chopped. Continue cooking until light brown. Stirring all the time, add 1 pint (570 ccm) of the cold stock and leave to simmer for about 10 minutes over a low heat. Season with salt, pepper, vinegar or lemon juice, and sugar. Add the meat and simmer for about 10 minutes before serving. Lastly add the sliced or finely diced pickled gherkin.

Cooking Time: about 1½ hours.

Beef Ragoût

About 1 lb. (450 g) beef
1 pint (570 ccm) water
salt
1½ oz. (45 g) fat
2 oz. (55 g) plain flour
1 onion
salt
pepper
1 tbsp. vinegar or lemon juice
pinch of sugar
1 pickled gherkin

Veal Ragoût

About 1 lb. (450 g) veal
1 pint (570 ccm) water
salt
1½ oz. (45 g) fat
2 oz. (55 g) plain flour
1 onion
salt
pepper
1 tbsp. lemon juice or wine
2–3 tbsp. red wine
pinch of sugar

Make as for Beef Ragoût (see page 77), but the sauce should be a lighter brown, to accompanying the white meat.

Cooking Time: 30–40 minutes.

Savoury Veal Ragoût
(10 Servings)

2 pints (1⅛ l) water
salt
1 onion
pot vegetables
1¾ lb. (800 g) veal
1 calf's tongue
1 sweetbread
¼–½ lb. (115–225 g) ragoût sausages
(very small sausages)
1 small tin of mushrooms
1 small tin of asparagus
3 oz. (85 g) butter
3 oz. (85 g) plain flour
about 1½ pint (850 ccm) veal stock
made up to 2 pints (1⅛ l) with the
mushroom and asparagus liquid
1–2 egg yolks and
3 tbsp. white wine
about 1 tbsp. lemon juice
salt
about 1½ oz. (45 g) crab meat paste

Bring the water to the boil with the salt, the quartered onion and the prepared and sliced pot vegetables. Put the veal and the cleaned and prepared tongue (the root should be removed) into the boiling liquid and cook until tender. When the veal is done remove from the stock, leave to cool and then cut into cubes about ¾ inch (2 cm) square. When the tongue is done, remove it from stock and pour cold water over it, skin it and cut into slices.

Soak the sweetbread in cold water for several hours. Then pour over it first hot and then cold water. When it is firm, remove the veins. Put the sweetbread into boiling salted water, cook till done and slice. Put the ragoût sausages into boiling salted water. Simmer gently until done, then slice.

To make the sauce, melt the butter, add the flour and cook until pale yellow. Add 2 pints (1⅛ l) of stock, and simmer gently for about 5 minutes. Add the egg yolks beaten in the white wine. Then season with the lemon juice, salt and crab meat paste. Add the meat, the mushrooms and the asparagus pieces to the sauce and simmer gently a little longer over a low heat. Do not boil.

Cooking Time: veal and tongue, about 1¼ hours;
sweetbread, about 20 minutes.

Make as for Beef Ragoût (see page 77). Wash and dry the fruit, cover with cold water and soak overnight. Bring quickly to the boil, then simmer gently for about 20 minutes over a low heat. If apples are used, peel and slice them, and then bring them to the boil in 1 tbsp. of water, stirring all the time. Then simmer them gently for about 5 minutes over a low heat. Add the fruit and the meat to the sauce.

Cooking Time: about 1 hour.

Serve with potatoes in their skins or with potato balls. If preferred, the fruit can be omitted.

(see page 77)

Pork Ragoût

About 1 lb. (450 g) pork
1 pint (570 ccm) water
salt
1½ oz. (45 g) fat
2 oz. (55 g) plain flour
1 onion
1–2 tbsp. lemon juice or vinegar
pinch of sugar
pinch of salt
7 oz. (200 g) dried fruit or
   14 oz. (400 g) fresh apples

Cut off the root, then wash the tongue and scrape it clean. Put into the boiling salted water and, an hour before it is done, add the celeriac or leek. The tongue is done it the tip is tender when tested with a fork. Remove from stock, skin it while still hot and cut into slices.

Using 1¾ pint (1 l) of stock, prepare a brown sauce. Melt the fat, add the flour and cook until medium brown. Add the cold stock, stirring all the time, and simmer for about 10 minutes over a low heat. Season the sauce with red wine or lemon juice, sugar and salt. Add the slices of tongue and about half the meat or bread balls, which should have been cooked separately.

Cooking Time: 3–4 hours.

Serve the ragoût on a round dish, garnished with crescents of puff pastry and the remaining Meat Balls or Bread Dumplings.

The ragoût may be enriched by adding about 8 oz. (225 g) mushrooms.

Tongue Ragoût

(10–12 Servings)

1 ox tongue
3½–4½ pints (2–2½ l) water
salt
2 oz. (55 g) celeriac or leek
3 oz. (85 g) butter or margarine
3½ oz. (100 g) plain flour
1¾ pint (1 l) stock
¼ pint (140 ccm) red wine or
   2–3 tbsp. lemon juice
sugar
salt
Meat Balls or Bread Dumplings
   (see page 45/44)

Slit the kidneys lengthwise, remove the core and wash thoroughly. Cover with boiling water and leave to soak for about half an hour. Remove the kidneys from the water and put them with the onion and the prepared and washed pot vegetables into the boiling salted water and cook until done.

Using 1 pint (570 ccm) kidney stock, prepare a brown sauce. Melt the fat, add the flour and cook until medium brown. Add the cold stock, stirring all the time, then simmer for about 10 minutes over a low heat. Season with lemon juice and salt. Add the sliced kidneys.

Cooking Time: about 30 minutes.

Serve with macaroni or mashed potatoes.

Tomato purée, finely chopped anchovies or a few tbsp. of Madeira may be added to the sauce.

Kidney Ragoût

About 1 lb. (450 g) pig's or lamb's
   kidneys
1 pint (570 ccm) water
salt
1 onion
pot vegetables
1½ oz. (45 g) fat
2 oz. (55 g) plain flour
1 tbsp. lemon juice

Westphalian Pepper-Pot

1 ¾ lb. (800 g) beef (short ribs)
1 pint (570 ccm) water
salt
3 onions
1 tsp. peppercorns
6 cloves
2 bay-leaves
2 tbsp. vinegar or juice of half a lemon
1 ½ oz. (45 g) fat
1 ½ oz. (45 g) plain flour
1 tbsp. capers

Wash the meat. Bring the water to the boil with the chopped onions and the spices, add a little salt, the meat, and simmer gently until done. Remove the bones and cut the meat up into medium-sized cubes. Strain the stock and, if necessary, add water to make up to 1 pint (750 ccm).

To make the sauce, melt the fat, add the flour, and cook until pale yellow. Add the stock, stirring all the time and cook for a short time. Stir in the capers and season to taste with salt and the lemon juice or vinegar. Add the meat.

Cooking Time: about 2½ hours.

Serve with boiled potatoes or potatoes in their skins.

Ragoût of Ox Heart (or Calf's Heart)

About 1 lb. (450 g) ox heart
1 ½ pint (850 ccm) water
salt
1 ½ oz. (45 g) fat
2 oz. (55 g) plain flour
1 onion
1 pint (570 ccm) stock
pepper
1 tbsp. vinegar or lemon juice
pinch of sugar
1 pickled gherkin

Prepare as for Beef Ragoût (see page 77).

Cooking Time: ox heart, about 3½ hours;
calf's heart 1–1¼ hours.

Beef Hash

(Using Left-over Cold Meat)

¾ lb. (340 g) cooked beef
1 ½ oz. (45 g) fat
2 oz. (55 g) plain flour
2 onions
1 pint (570 ccm) stock or water
salt
pepper
made mustard to taste
vinegar to taste

Mince or chop the meat finely. To make the sauce, melt the fat and add the flour, stirring all the time, until pale yellow. Add the finely chopped onions and cook until medium brown. Gradually pour in the stock or water and, beating with a wire whisk, bring to the boil. Simmer for 10 minutes over a low heat. Season the sauce with salt, pepper, mustard and vinegar. Stir in the minced or chopped meat and heat through a few minutes.

Serve with boiled rice or mashed potatoes, and lettuce salad.

Alternatively, diced (pickled) gherkins or mushrooms may be added to the sauce.

Split the kidneys lengthwise, remove the core and wash thoroughly. Cover with boiling water and leave to soak for about half an hour. Cut the heart in half and remove the skin, veins and arteries. Wash thoroughly. Remove the kidneys from the water and put them (or the heart) into the boiling, slightly salted water with the meat and simmer gently until done. If necessary, make the stock up to 2 pints (1 ⅛ l) with water, bring to the boil, sprinkle in the barley groats and simmer gently over a low heat until done. Chop the meat up finely and mix with the groats. Season to taste with salt, pepper, pimento and thyme.

Cooking Time: meat, about 1½ hours;
groats, about 2 hours.

Serve the sausage meat with potatoes in their skins, apple purée, or pickled gherkins.

Work together the minced meat, the roll or bread (from which the water has been squeezed out), the egg white, the finely chopped onion and the finely minced herring into a smooth dough. Season to taste with salt and pepper and shape into balls.

Melt the fat, add the flour and cook until pale yellow. Stir in the cold stock, add the meat balls and simmer gently for 15 minutes over a low heat. Season with capers, lemon juice, salt and enrich with the egg yolk beaten in the water.

Cooking Time: about 15 minutes.

Slice the bread or the rolls very thinly, pour the boiling milk over the slices and leave to soak for an hour. Skin the liver and put it through the mincer with the onion. Stir in the parsley, the eggs, the BACKIN and the bread mixture. Season with the spices and shape into round balls with wet hands. Drop the balls into boiling salted water and simmer gently for 20 minutes.

Time: 20 minutes.

Sausage Meat

2 pig's kidneys or 1 heart
2 pints (1 ⅛ l) water
salt
5 oz. (140 g) pork from the belly
4 oz. (115 g) barley groats
pepper
pimento
thyme

Koenigsberger Klops
(Meat Balls)

14 oz. (400 g) minced beef or pork
1 stale roll or a slice of stale bread
  (soaked in water)
1 egg white
1 onion
½ salted herring (optional)
salt
pepper
1½ oz. (45 g) butter or margarine
1½ oz. (45 g) plain flour
1 pint (570 ccm) stock or water
1 tbsp. capers
1 tsp. lemon juice
1 egg yolk and 2 tbsp. cold water

Liver Balls

14 oz. (400 g) stale white bread
  or rolls
1 pint (570 ccm) boiling milk
9 oz. (250 g) calf's or ox liver
1 medium-sized onion
1 tbsp. chopped parsley
2 eggs
1 level tsp. (3 g) Oetker Baking
  Powder BACKIN
salt
majoram
pepper
grated lemon rind

B. BRAISED MEAT

General Hints

1. Braised meat is meat browned in hot fat in an open saucepan. Liquid is then added and the meat is left to simmer until tender with the saucepan covered. Braising is an excellent method for cooking small joints of less than 2¼ lb. (1 kg), as well as for the tougher cuts of meat.

2. Fry the meat brown in very hot fat in an open saucepan. Just before the meat is brown enough, add the onions, tomatoes or any sliced pot vegetables the recipe requires.

3. When the meat is well browned, season, add about ½ pint (285 ccm) of hot water or stock, and braise in a covered saucepan, simmering gently till done.

4. Before making the gravy, remove the cooked joint from the saucepan and make up the liquid to the amount needed for the accompanying gravy. Turn off the heat. Thicken with GUSTIN, blended in a little cold water. The gravy can be strained through a sieve. It can be improved by the addition of a little cream or tinned milk.

I. LARGE JOINTS, BRAISED

Braised Beef

About 2 lb. (900 g) beef
(aitchbone, top side)
3 oz. (85 g) fat
salt
pot vegetables
1 onion
1 tomato (optional)
½–1 pint (285–570 ccm) water
1–2 tsp. Oetker GUSTIN
(corn starch powder)
1 tbsp. cold water
2 tbsp. sour cream or tinned milk
(optional)

Wash the meat, beat it and, if necessary, tie it up into a neat shape. Heat the fat, put in the joint, and brown it on all sides, leaving the pan uncovered. Salt it, then add the chopped onion, the prepared and chopped pot vegetables and the washed and sliced tomato, and cook for a few minutes before adding the hot water, which should be poured in carefully from the side. Use about ½ pint (285 ccm) of water to start with. Put on the lid and braise the meat gently over a low heat. Turn it from time to time and replace any water which evaporates during the cooking. When the meat is cooked, untie before serving. Strain the liquid in which the meat has been cooked, remove excess fat and thicken it with the GUSTIN, blended with the water, adding a little cream if desired.

Braising Time: a good 2½ hours.

Serve with boiled potatoes, mashed potatoes or macaroni; and vegetables or lettuce salad.

Wash the meat, drain it well, and put it in an earthenware bowl with the onion, skinned and cut into rings, and the spices. Cover it with the vinegar and water and leave to stand for 4–6 days. It should be left in a cool place and turned over daily.

Remove the meat from the marinade and dry it before cooking. Melt the fat and when it is hot, put in the meat. Brown it quickly on all sides in an uncovered pan, then add salt. Carefully pour in about ½ pint (285 ccm) hot water at the side of the pan, add a little gingerbread or crust of bread and leave to simmer gently with the lid on. Turn from time to time, adding water if necessary. When the joint is ready, serve it with the gravy in which it has been cooked, thickened with the GUSTIN, blended with the water.

Braising Time: about 1½ hours.

Potato Dumplings (see page 176) go very well with this dish.

Make as for Braised Pork (see page 84).

Braising Time: 1 hour.

Mushrooms may be added towards the end of the cooking time if desired.

Wash the meat, beat it and, if necessary, tie it up into a neat shape. Heat the fat, put in the meat and brown it on all sides. Salt it, add the prepared and chopped pot vegetables and cook them together for a few minutes. Then carefully pour in down the side of the stewpan about ½ pint (285 ccm) of hot water. Add the juniper berries, if used. Cover and simmer gently. Turn the meat from time to time, adding water if necessary. When the meat is done, untie before serving. Remove excess fat from the gravy, strain it and thicken with the GUSTIN, blended with the water. Stir in the cream or tinned milk if desired.

Braising Time: about 1 hour.

Sauerbraten

(Beef in Marinade)
(Phot. See Page 18)

About 2 lb. (900 g) beef

For the marinade:
1 onion
4 peppercorns
2 cloves
1 small bay-leaf
½ pint (285 ccm) vinegar
⅔ pint (375 ccm) water
For braising:
2 oz. (55 g) fat
salt
½–1 pint (285–570 ccm) water
crust of bread or a little gingerbread
1–2 tsp. Oetker GUSTIN
  (corn starch powder)
1 tbsp. cold water

Braised Mutton

About 2 lb. (900 g) mutton
½–1 pint (285–570 ccm) water
2 oz. (55 g) onions
salt
1–2 tsp. Oetker GUSTIN
  (corn starch powder)
1 tbsp. cold water

Braised Veal

About 2 lb. (900 g) veal
  (leg, breast or shoulder)
3 oz. (85 g) suet from the kidney
salt
pot vegetables
½–1 pint (285–570 ccm) water
some juniper berries (optional)
1–2 tsp. Oetker GUSTIN
  (corn starch powder)
1 tbsp. cold water
1–2 tbsp. sour cream or tinned milk
  (optional)

Braised Pork

About 2 lb. (900 g) pork
2 oz. (55 g) fat (if the pork is lean)
salt
1 onion
pot vegetables
½–1 pint (285–570 ccm) water
1–2 tsp. Oetker GUSTIN
(corn starch powder)
1 tbsp. cold water

Brown the pork in its own (or the 2 oz.) fat, turning it frequently to prevent sticking. Sear it on all sides, salt it and add the chopped onion and the washed pot vegetables. Cook them together for a few minutes. Carefully pour in down the sides of the pan ½ pint (285 ccm) of hot water. Put on the lid and simmer gently over a low heat. Turn the meat from time to time, adding water if necessary. When the meat is done, remove excess fat from the gravy, strain it and thicken it with the GUSTIN, blended with the water.

Braising Time: about 1½ hours.

Tomato salad goes well with braised pork.

II. SMALL CUTS, BRAISED

Beef Rolls

4 thin slices of beef
made mustard
salt
pepper
2 oz. (55 g) fat bacon
2 oz. (55 g) onions
2 oz. (55 g) fat
1 pint (570 ccm) water
1–2 tsp. Oetker GUSTIN
(corn starch powder)
1 tbsp. cold water

Ask the butcher to cut the slices of beef for you. Beat them lightly, brush with the mustard and sprinkle with salt and pepper. Mix together the diced bacon and the chopped onions and spread the mixture onto the beef. Starting at the narrow end, roll up the slices of meat and secure them with a skewer or with thread. Heat the fat and brown the beef rolls well. Add about ½ pint (285 ccm) boiling water very carefully, cover and braise gently until done. Make up any water lost during the cooking, and thicken the gravy with the GUSTIN, blended with the water. Season to taste.

Braising Time: 2–2½ hours.

Alternatively, the sauce may be seasoned with paprika, tomato purée, lemon juice or sour cream.

Haricot beans, cauliflower, salsify and macaroni go well with this dish.

For the stuffing, mince the meat, the roll or bread (squeezed dry) or the potatoes, and the onion and bind with the egg. Season with salt and pepper. Spread the stuffing evenly over the slices of veal, roll up from the narrow end and secure with a skewer or with thread. Brown the rolls well in the hot fat. Carefully add about ½ pint (285 ccm) of hot water, cover and braise gently till done. Thicken the gravy with the GUSTIN, blended with the water. Season to taste.

Braising Time: about 1 hour.

Instead of the forcemeat stuffing, thin bacon rashers with pickled gherkins or tomatoes may be used.

The sauce may be enriched by adding a little sour cream or lemon juice, mushrooms, or finely chopped anchovy.

Veal Rolls I

Forcemeat Stuffing:

5–7 oz. (140–200 g) meat
  (half beef, half pork, or leftovers of
  roasts, venison, or poultry)
1 stale roll or a slice of stale bread
  (soaked in water) or 2–3 boiled
  potatoes
1 onion
1 egg
salt
pepper

Meat:

4 thin slices of veal (leg)
2 oz. (55 g) butter or margarine
½–1 pint (285–570 ccm) water
1–2 tsp. Oetker GUSTIN
  (corn starch powder)
1 tbsp. cold water

Place on each slice of veal 1 slice of gammon, 1 rasher of bacon, and 1 egg. Roll up each slice from the narrow end and fasten with a skewer or thread. Brown well in the hot fat. Carefully add about ½ pint (285 ccm) of hot water, cover and braise gently until done. Thicken the gravy with the GUSTIN, blended with the water, add the sour cream or tinned milk and season with salt. Cut the rolls in half and pour the gravy over them.

Braising Time: about 1 hour.

Serve with mashed potatoes.

Alternatively, finely chopped anchovies or mushrooms may be added to enrich the gravy.

Veal Rolls II

(Swallows' Nests)

4 thin slices of veal
4 slices of gammon
4 rashers of bacon
4 boiled eggs
2 oz. (55 g) butter or margarine
½–1 pint (285–570 ccm) water
1–2 tsp. Oetker GUSTIN
  (corn starch powder)
1 tbsp. cold water
2 tbsp. sour cream or tinned milk
salt

Beat the meat lightly, spread with mustard, season with salt and roll up from the narrow end. Fasten with a skewer or with thread. Brown well in the hot fat. Carefully add about ½ pint (285 ccm) of hot water, cover and braise gently until done over a low heat. Thicken the gravy with the GUSTIN, blended with the water and season to taste.

Braising Time: about 1½ hours.

Pork Rolls

4 thin slices of pork (leg)
made mustard
salt
2 oz. (55 g) fat
1 pint (570 ccm) water
1–2 tsp. Oetker GUSTIN
  (corn starch powder)
1 tbsp. cold water

Goulash

About 1 lb. (450 g) lean beef, veal,
pork or mutton
2 oz. (55 g) fat (pork will need rather
less fat)
1 large onion
1 pint (570 ccm) water
salt
pepper
pinch of paprika
1–2 tsp. Oetker GUSTIN
(corn starch powder)
1 tbsp. cold water

Cut the meat into ¾ inch (2 cm) cubes and brown in the hot fat. Add the finely chopped onion and sauté together a little longer. Pour in the boiling water, season with salt and pepper, cover and braise gently until done. Season to taste with paprika and salt and thicken with the GUSTIN, blended with the water.

Braising Time: beef goulash 1½–2 hours;
pork goulash, about 1 hour;
veal goulash, about 1 hour;
mutton goulash, about 1 hour.

Alternatively, tomato purée or sour cream may be added to the beef goulash. Pork goulash is improved by the addition of 2–3 tbsp. of Madeira, sour cream, or 2 tomatoes, added while cooking. Mutton goulash may be enriched by a few slices of fresh peeled cucumbers (without seeds) or about 4 skinned tomatoes added to it while cooking.

Beef goulash is served with mashed potatoes, rice, or noodles and with a tomato, cucumber or lettuce salad. Veal goulash is served with rice shaped into a ring, or "Spätzle" (see page 245).

Savoury Kidneys

About 1 lb. (450 g) kidneys
2 oz. (55 g) fat
1 onion
½–⅔ pint (285–375 ccm) water
salt
pepper
1–2 tbsp. vinegar
pinch of sugar
1 tsp. Oetker GUSTIN
(corn starch powder)
1 tbsp. cold water

Slit the kidneys, remove the core, wash, scald with hot water and leave to soak for about half an hour. Dry thoroughly, cut up into cubes or slices and brown in the hot fat with the chopped onion. Add the boiling water, salt and pepper. Braise until done, and then season to taste with vinegar, salt and sugar. Thicken the gravy with the GUSTIN, blended with the water.

Cooking Time: 10–15 minutes.

Serve with rice, macaroni or Bread Dumplings (see page 44).

C. ROAST MEAT

I. OVEN-JOINTS

Joints of meat under 2¼ lb. (1 kg) in weight should not be cooked in an oven. It is better and more economical to cook smaller joints on top of the stove. The most suitable kind of meat for roasting is that which is well hung, and from which all skin and sinews have been removed. Game and poultry, too, make good roasts.

Place the joint either onto the greased grill of a roasting pan, or into a greased roasting pan, or into a greased shallow fireproof dish with no lid. The joint may be salted shortly before putting it into the oven, or after browning. If the meat is lean, brush it with oil or melted butter or margarine, or cover it with strips of bacon. No extra fat is needed for the cooking of a fat joint, but if it has a solid layer of fat score this both ways. This will release the fat and prevent surface shrinkhage.

An exellent gravy can be made by removing the bones from the meat and cooking them together with the joint, or by browning them with tomatoes and onions in a saucepan on the stove.

It is, however, advisable to boil the bones in water first and to use the resulting stock with the gravy from the roasting pan to make the sauce required in the recipe.

If the meat has no bones, add onions, tomatoes, and mushrooms, to the joint while roasting. This will improve the flavour. If the joint is small, and needs only a short time in the oven, the vegetables may be added immediately, but if the joint needs longer roasting, it is advisable to add them when the gravy begins to brown, at the same time adding water to prevent the gravy from getting too dark.

Whether or not the meat is put into a cold or hot oven depends on the size and type of joint. Fat meat should start in a cold oven, as this releases the fat more easily. Lean meat which needs less than an hour's roasting and meat which is to be eaten underdone both require a pre-heated oven. When meat is put into a pre-heated oven the albumen on its cut surface hardens quicker and prevents the loss of natural juices.

Meat can be roasted in different ways. It depends on whether the joint is to be turned or not, during roasting. If a joint is to be turned during roasting, put the roasting pan as high as possible in a very hot oven. (Remember the meat may swell, so allow adequate space above it.) Brown the meat quickly first on one side and then on the other. Then put the pan very low in the oven and turn the heat down to very slow. If the joint is not to be turned, place the pan in the middle of a moderately heated oven and let it brown by the normal cooking process.

The time required for roasting depends on the height of the joint. 10 minutes per $\frac{3}{8}$ inch (1 cm) height is needed if the meat is to be well done i. e. that it does not yield to the pressure of the spoon.

Never carve the joint the moment it is done, or far too much juice will run out of the meat. Leave the joint in the hot oven for 10 minutes or so. In the meantime make the gravy, using the stock and the dripping and scrapings from the roasting pan. Strain through a sieve and thicken with the prepared GUSTIN (corn starch powder). Cream or tinned milk may be added to enrich the gravy.

Roastbeef (From Sirloin)

2¼ lb. (1 kg) sirloin
salt
1½ oz. (45 g) butter or margarine
about ½ pint (285 ccm) hot water
1 onion
1 tomato (optional)
1–2 tsp. Oetker GUSTIN
(corn starch powder)
1 tbsp. cold water
4–5 tbsp. sour cream or tinned milk

The meat should be well hung. Remove bones and sinews, score the skin, salt and brush with butter or margarine. Rinse out a roasting pan with water and put the meat, fat side up, onto the greased grill. Place in the middle of the oven.

As soon as the dripping begins to brown, add a little hot water to the pan. About a quarter of an hour before the joint is ready, add the skinned and quartered onion and the washed and sliced tomato.

When the meat is done, turn off the heat. Leave the roast on the grill, and keep it hot while making the gravy. Place the pan on top of the stove. Stir the residue well from the bottom and add enough water to dissolve the meat juices. Scrape the pan well. Strain through a sieve. Thicken with the Gustin, blended with the water and stir in the cream or tinned milk. Serve with the roast.

Oven: pre-heat 15 minutes using high heat, roast with high heat.

Roasting Time: about 45 minutes.

Fillet of Beef

2¼ lb. (1 kg) fillet
salt
1½ oz. (45 g) butter or margarine
some fat bacon rashers
about ½ pint (285 ccm) hot water
1 onion
1 tomato (optional)
1–2 tsp. Oetker GUSTIN
(corn starch powder)
1 tbsp. cold water
4–5 tbsp. sour cream or tinned milk

The meat should be well hung. Remove the skin and sinews. Rub in salt, brush with butter or margarine and spread with bacon rashers. Rinse out a roasting pan with water and place the meat onto the greased grill. Place the roast in the middle of the oven.

As soon as the dripping begins to brown, add a little hot water to the pan. About a quarter of an hour before the joint is done, add the skinned and quartered onion and the washed and sliced tomato.

When the meat is done, turn off the heat. Leave the meat on the grill and keep it hot while making the gravy. Place the pan on top of the stove. Stir the residue well from the bottom and add enough water to dissolve the meat juices. Scrape the pan well. Strain through a sieve. Thicken with the GUSTIN, blended with the water and stir in the cream or tinned milk. Serve with the roast.

Oven: pre-heat 15 minutes using high heat, roast with high heat.

Roasting Time: about 45 minutes.

Remove the fat and skin from the fillets, rub with salt and brush with butter or margarine. Spread with the rashers of bacon. Rinse out a roasting pan with water and place the meat on a greased grill in the middle of the oven.

As soon as the dripping begins to brown, add a little hot water to the pan and, about a quarter of an hour before the joint is done, add the skinned and quartered onion and the washed and sliced tomato.

When the meat is done, turn off the heat. Leave the meat on the grill and keep it hot while making the gravy. Place the pan on top of the stove. Stir the residue well from the bottom and add enough water to dissolve the meat juices. Strain through a sieve. Thicken with the Gustin, blended with the water and stir in the cream or tinned milk. Serve with the roast.

Oven: pre-heat 15 minutes using high heat, roast with high heat.

Roasting Time: 35–40 minutes.

Fillet of Pork

2 fillets of pork weighing
   about 2¼ lb. (1 kg)
salt
1½ oz. (45 g) butter or margarine
a few bacon rashers
about ½ pint (285 ccm) hot water
1 onion
1 tomato (optional)
1–2 tsp. Oetker GUSTIN
   (corn starch powder)
1 tbsp. cold water
4–5 tbsp. sour cream or tinned milk

Remove the bones and score the surface of the fat with a sharp knife, cutting both ways in a criss-cross pattern. Rinse out a roasting pan with water and place the meat fat side up on the greased grill. Place the meat in the middle of the oven.

As soon as the dripping begins to brown, add a little water to the pan. About a quarter of an hour before the meat is done, add the skinned and quartered onion and the washed and sliced tomato.

When the meat is done, turn off the heat. Leave the meat on the grill and keep it hot while making the gravy. Place the pan on top of the stove. Stir the residue well from the bottom and add enough water to dissolve the meat juices. Scrape the pan well. Strain through a sieve. Thicken with the GUSTIN, blended with the water and stir in the cream or tinned milk.

Serve with the roast.

Oven: moderate to hot.

Roasting Time: about 1½ hours.

Kasseler Rippespeer

3¼ lb. (1½ kg) smoked ribs of pork
½ pint (285 ccm) hot water
1 onion
1 tomato
1–2 tsp. Oetker GUSTIN
   (corn starch powder)
1 tbsp. cold water
4–5 tbsp. sour cream or tinned milk

Mock Hare (Phot. See Page 100)

1¾ lb. (800 g) minced meat
(half beef, half pork)
1–2 stale rolls or stale bread
(soaked in water)
1 egg
1 onion
salt
paprika
1 tbsp. breadcrumbs
2 oz. (55 g) butter or margarine
1 oz. (30 g) fat bacon cut in strips
about ½ pint (285 ccm) hot water
1–2 tsp. Oetker GUSTIN
(corn starch powder)
1 tbsp. cold water

Make a mixture of the meat, the rolls or bread (squeezed dry), the egg and the finely diced onion. Add salt and paprika to taste. Form into a loaf and roll in the breadcrumbs. Well grease a roasting pan with butter or margarine and put in the loaf. Spread with bacon rashers, pressing them firmly on the loaf with a knife. Place the loaf in the middle of the oven.

As soon as the fat browns, add a little hot water to the pan. When the meat loaf is done, turn off the heat. Lift the loaf from the roasting pan and keep it hot while making the gravy. Place the pan on top of the stove. Stir the residue well from the bottom and add enough water to dissolve the meat juices. Scrape the pan well. Strain through a sieve. Thicken with the GUSTIN, blended with the water.

Oven: moderate to hot.

Roasting Time: about 1 hour.

Roast Veal

2¼ lb. (1 kg) veal (leg)
salt
1½ oz. (45 g) butter or margarine
a few fat bacon rashers
about ½ pint (285 ccm) hot water
1–2 tsp. Oetker GUSTIN
(corn starch powder)
1 tbsp. cold water
4–5 tbsp. sour cream or tinned milk

Wash the meat, remove the skin, rub with salt and brush with butter or margarine. Spread with the bacon rashers. Rinse out a roasting pan with water and place the meat onto the greased grill in the middle of the oven.

As soon as the dripping begins to brown, add a little hot water to the pan. When the roast is done, turn off the heat. Leave the roast on the grill and keep it hot while making the gravy. Place the pan on top of the stove. Stir the residue well from the bottom and add enough water to dissolve the meat juices. Scrape the pan well. Strain through a sieve. Thicken with the GUSTIN, blended with the water and stir in the cream or tinned milk.

Serve with the roast.

Oven: moderate to hot.

Roasting Time: about 1¾ hours.

Rolled Veal Roast
(With Kidneys)

2¼ lb. (1 kg) veal
(loin with kidneys)
salt
1½ oz. (45 g) butter or margarine
some fat bacon rashers
about ½ pint (285 ccm) hot water
1–2 tsp. Oetker GUSTIN
(corn starch powder)

Remove the bones, rub the inner side of the loin with salt and arrange the kidneys on the meat. Then roll up the meat, tie with thread and salt the outside. Brush with fat and spread with bacon rashers. Rinse out a roasting pan with water and place the meat onto the greased grill. Put the meat in the middle of the oven.

As soon as the dripping begins to brown, pour a little hot water into the pan. When the roast is done, turn off the heat. Leave the roast on the grill and keep it hot while making the gravy.

90

Herrings in Marinade Recipe See Page 125

"Rollmops" (Pickled Herrings) Recipe See Page 126

Place the pan on top of the stove. Stir the residue well from the bottom and add enough water to dissolve the meat juices. Scrape the pan well. Strain through a sieve. Thicken with the GUSTIN, blended with the water and stir in the cream or tinned milk.

Serve with the roast.

Oven: moderate to hot.

Roasting Time: about 1¾ hours.

For the stuffing, mix the forcemeat with the egg and with the roll or bread (squeezed dry), the onion (finely chopped) and the chopped herbs. Season to taste with salt and paprika.

Remove the bones from the meat, salt it on both sides, fill the pocket with the stuffing and sew it up with a coarse needle and thread. Brush the stuffed breast with butter or margarine and spread with the bacon rashers. Rinse out a roasting pan with water and place the meat onto the greased grill. Put the joint in the middle of the oven.

As soon as the dripping begins to brown, pour some hot water into the pan. When the meat is done, turn off the heat. Leave the roast on the grill and keep it hot while making the gravy. Place the pan on top of the stove. Stir the residue well from the bottom and add enough water to dissolve the meat juices Scrape the pan well. Strain through a sieve. Thicken with the GUSTIN, blended with the water and stir in the cream or tinned milk.

Oven: moderate heat.

Roasting Time: about 2¼ hours.

Cut the hearts in two lengthwise. Remove the veins, arteries and blood and wash the hearts carefully. Season with salt and pepper and spread with mustard. Put the fat into a shallow fire-proof dish. Put in the hearts and cover them with the bacon rashers. Put the dish on the middle shelf of the oven. After 30 minutes roasting, add the skinned onion and after a further 15 minutes pour in the water. When the hearts are done, pour off the gravy and thicken with the GUSTIN, blended with the cream or tinned milk. Season to taste.

Oven: moderate to hot.

Roasting Time: about 1 hour.

1 tbsp. cold water
4–5 tbsp. sour cream or tinned milk

Stuffed Breast of Veal

Stuffing:
12 oz. (340 g) forcemeat
   (half beef, half pork)
1 egg
1 stale roll or a slice of stale bread
   (soaked in water)
1 small onion
1 tbsp. chopped herbs
salt
paprika

Meat:
3¼ lb. (1½ kg) breast of veal
salt
1½ oz. (45 g) butter or margarine
a few rashers of fat bacon
about ½ pint (285 ccm) hot water
1–2 tsp. Oetker GUSTIN
   (corn starch powder)
1 tbsp. cold water
4–5 tbsp. sour cream or tinned milk

Calf's Heart

2 calves' hearts
salt
pepper
a little made mustard to taste
2 oz. (55 g) butter or margarine
2 oz. (55 g) fat bacon
1 onion
½ pint (285 ccm) hot water
2 tsp. Oetker GUSTIN
   (corn starch powder)
5 tbsp. sour cream or tinned milk

93

Beef Broth with Vegetables Recipe See Page 129

Roast Spare Rib of Pork

2¼ lb. (1 kg) spare rib of pork
salt
1 onion
1 tomato
½ pint (285 ccm) hot water
1–2 tsp. Oetker GUSTIN
(corn starch powder)
1 tbsp. cold water
2–3 tbsp. sour cream or tinned milk

Rinse out the roasting pan with water. Salt the meat and put it onto the greased grill of the roasting pan. Place the joint in the middle of the oven.

As soon as the dripping begins to brown, add the onion, skinned and quartered, and the tomato, washed and sliced. Pour some water into the pan. When the roast is done, turn off the heat. Leave the roast on the grill and keep it hot while making the gravy. Place the pan on top of the stove. Stir the residue well from the bottom and add enough water to dissolve the meat juices. Scrape the pan well. Strain through a sieve. Thicken with the GUSTIN, blended with the water and stir in the cream or tinned milk.

Oven: moderate to hot.

Roasting Time: about 1¾ hours.

Roast Pork with Crackling

2¼ lb. (1 kg) pork with rind
(leg or hand)
salt
about ½ pint (285 ccm) hot water
1 onion
1 tomato
1–2 tsp. Oetker GUSTIN
(corn starch powder)
1 tbsp. cold water
2–3 tbsp. sour cream or tinned milk

Wash the meat, dry it and salt the under part. Score the rind both ways, making a square pattern. Rinse out a roasting pan with water and put the pork onto the greased grill with the rind on top. Put the roast in the middle of the oven, and as soon as the dripping begins to brown pour some hot water into the pan. About a quarter of an hour before the meat is done, add the onion, skinned and quartered, and the washed and sliced tomato. When the roast is done, turn off the heat. Leave the roast on the grill and keep it hot while making the gravy. Place the pan on top of the stove. Stir the residue well from the bottom and add enough water to dissolve the meat juices. Scrape the pan well. Strain through a sieve. Thicken with the GUSTIN, blended with the water and stir in the cream or the tinned milk.

Oven: moderate to hot.

Roasting Time: about 2 hours.

Stuffed Ribs of Pork

Stuffing:
12 oz. (340 g) apples
8 oz. (225 g) prunes
2 tbsp. breadcrumbs
¾ oz. (20 g) sugar
salt

For the stuffing, peel and slice the apples. The prunes should be soaked for several hours and mixed with the apples, breadcrumbs, sugar and salt. The ribs must be as thin as those used for pickling. Cut them carefully into halves, but do not slice them all the way through. Spread the stuffing onto the lower half and cover with the other, pounding lightly with a mallet. Then sew the two halves together. Sprinkle with salt. Rinse out a roasting pan with water and put the meat onto the greased grill. Put the meat in the middle of the oven and, as soon as the dripping begins to brown, add some hot water to the pan. When the meat is done, turn off the heat. Leave the roast on the grill and keep it hot while making the gravy. Place the pan on top of the stove. Stir the residue well from the bottom and add enough water to dissolve the meat juices. Scrape the pan well. Strain through a sieve. Thicken with the GUSTIN, blended with the water.

Oven: moderate to hot.

Roasting Time: about 2 hours.

Meat:
2¼ lb. (1 kg) ribs of pork
salt
about ½ pint (285 ccm) hot water
1–2 tsp. Oetker GUSTIN
   (corn starch powder)
1 tbsp. cold water

Rinse out a roasting pan with water. Salt the mutton and place it onto the greased grill. Put the meat in the middle of the oven and as soon as the dripping begins to brown, add the skinned and quartered onion and the washed and sliced tomato, together with a little water. When the meat is done, turn off the heat. Leave the roast on the grill and keep it hot while making the gravy. Place the pan on top of the stove. Stir the residue well from the bottom and add enough water to dissolve the meat juices. Scrape the pan well. Strain through a sieve. Thicken with the GUSTIN, blended with the water.

Saddle of Mutton

2¼ lb. (1 kg) saddle of mutton
salt
1 onion
1 tomato
about ½ pint (285 ccm) hot water
1–2 tsp. Oetker GUSTIN
   (corn starch powder)
1 tbsp. cold water

Oven: moderate to hot.

Roasting Time: 1½–1¾ hours.
Alternatively, the meat, after removing the fat, may be soaked for several days in buttermilk, seasoned with juniper berries, then cooked as any lean roast. If sour cream is added, the joint tastes like venison.

II. SMALL CUTS OF MEAT, FRIED

1. Frying is a good way of cooking small cuts of meat. Only meat with tender muscular tissue should be used.

2. The meat may be breaded i.e. with egg and breadcrumbs before cooking, as this helps to seal in the juices.

3. Breaded meat is prepared in the following way: salt the meat, dip first in flour, then in beaten egg and lastly in breadcrumbs.

4. Fry the meat immediately when it is coated, or the egg and breadcrumbs will become soggy and will not brown easily.

5. Meat which is not coated with breadcrumbs is best fried in lard or mixed fat, as butter and margarine brown too quickly and are not suitable for general frying purposes. Butter however, may be added just before the frying in lard or mixed fat is completed.

General Hints

6. The fat must be very hot and the heat full on when the meat is put into the pan, so that it will brown quickly and thus seal in the juices.

7. Never add fat while the meat is still cooking, as this cools the pan.

8. Fried meat should be served as soon as it is done, or it will become tough and unappetising.

9. The fat in which the meat has been fried is often poured over the meat when served.

Or a gravy can be made from the fat in the frying pan by adding stock or water and thickening with GUSTIN, blended with cold water.

a) Frying without Egg and Breadcrumbs

Fillet Beef Steak
(Phot. See Page 110)

1 lb. 5 oz. (600 g) fillet of beef
2 oz. (55 g) butter or margarine
salt
6 tbsp. water
1 onion

Cut the fillet into slices about ¾ inch (2 cm) thick. This thickness will give a good juicy steak. Beat the steaks lightly with a knife, trim into shape and put into very hot fat. Baste continually to keep them juicy. Turn when one side is brown enough, salt and fry the other side. Steaks are best slightly underdone. Serve on a hot dish. Add the water to the frying pan to dissolve the residue and pour over the steaks.

Frying Time: about 8 minutes.

Garnish with browned onion rings or with tomato and lemon slices.

Alternatively, the steaks may be fried in a very hot frying pan without fat. Then brown some butter and pour over the steaks. This is a substitute for grilling.

Fillet of Veal

4 slices of veal fillet
about 1 lb. (450 g)
2 oz. (55 g) butter or margarine
salt
a little water (optional)

Beat the steaks lightly with a knife. Shape them and place in very hot fat. Baste continually to keep them juicy. Turn when one side is brown, salt and fry the other side. Serve on a hot dish. Add a little water to the pan to dissolve the residue. Pour over the steaks.

Frying Time: about 4 minutes.

Rumpsteak

4 rumpsteaks about 1 lb. 5 oz. (600 g)
2 oz. (55 g) butter or margarine
salt
pepper

Beat the steaks lightly with a knife and slash them slightly at the sides. Shape the steaks and place in very hot fat. Baste continually to keep them juicy. When the undersides are browned, turn the steaks, season with salt and pepper and fry them on the other side. Remove to a hot platter. Add the 6 tbsp. hot water to the frying pan to dissolve the residue, then pour over the steaks.

Frying Time: 6–8 minutes.

Serve with the shredded horseradish.

6 tbsp. water
1 oz. (30 g) horseradish

Liver

Wash the liver, skin it and, as far as possible, remove all tubes and membrane. Slice it, salt, dip in flour and fry in the very hot fat. Brown some onion rings at the sides of the pan in which the liver is frying. Turn the liver as soon as the underside is done. Remove to a hot platter and pour over the gravy. Garnish with the onion rings.

Frying Time: 6–8 minutes.

Serve with mashed potatoes, Béchamel-Potatoes (see page 178) or potatoes cooked with apples.

If ox liver is used, it will be more tender if soaked in milk for about half an hour before frying.

About 1 lb. (450 g) calf's or ox liver
salt
¾ oz. (20 g) plain flour
2 oz. (55 g) butter or margarine
2 onions

Fried Kidneys

Split the kidneys lengthwise and cut out white centre and tubes. Wash thoroughly, scald with boiling water and leave to soak for 30 minutes. Slice veal kidneys (pork kidneys may be cooked whole), salt and fry, turning them frequently in the hot fat. Add the water to the frying pan to dissolve the residue. Thicken with the GUSTIN, blended with the water. Season to taste with paprika and lemon juice.

Frying Time: 5–10 minutes.

Serve with mashed potatoes and celeriac salad.

About 1 lb. (450 g) calf's or pig's
   kidneys
salt
2 oz. (55 g) butter or margarine
¼ pint (140 ccm) water
1–2 heaped tsp. Oetker GUSTIN
   (corn starch powder)
1 tbsp. cold water
paprika
lemon juice

Hamburgers

Mix the minced beef with the 2 tbsp. water or the melted butter, season with salt to taste. Shape into flat cakes and cut the surface lightly with crisscross gashes. Fry quickly in the hot butter or margarine. At the same time brown some onion rings at the side of the frying pan. Serve the hamburgers, garnished with onion rings. Add the water to the frying pan to dissolve the residue. Thicken with the GUSTIN, blended with the water and pour over the hamburgers.

Frying Time: about 8 minutes.

Alternatively, 1 stale roll or slice of stale bread, soaked in water and then squeezed dry, or about 1½ oz. (45 g) cold mashed potatoes may be mixed in with the minced beef.

14 oz. (400 g) minced beef
2 tbsp. cold water or
   ¾ oz. (20 g) butter
salt
2 oz. (55 g) butter or margarine
   for frying
2 onions
¼ pint (140 ccm) water
1 tsp. Oetker GUSTIN
   (corn starch powder)
1 tbsp. cold water

Meat Balls, Fried

14 oz. (400 g) minced beef and pork
1 stale roll or slice of stale bread
1 egg
salt
pepper
2 level tbsp. plain flour
2 oz. (55 g) fat
1 slightly heaped tbsp. plain flour for
browning
½ pint (285 ccm) water

Soak the roll or the slice of bread and squeeze it dry, then mix it with minced meat and the egg and add salt and pepper to taste. Shape into oval cakes, dip in the flour and fry in the hot fat. Brown the tbsp. of flour in the fat used for frying, add the water and cook until the gravy is smooth.

Frying Time: about 10 minutes.

Meat Balls
(Using Leftovers)

14 oz. (400 g) cold meat (left-over
from boiled or roast meat)
1 stale roll or a slice of stale bread
1 small onion
1 egg
salt
pepper
2 level tbsp. plain flour
2 oz. (55 g) fat
1 slightly heaped tbsp. plain flour for
browning
½ pint (285 ccm) water

Soak the roll and squeeze it dry. Put the meat, the roll and the onion through the mincer. Stir in the egg and season to taste with salt and pepper. Shape the mixture into flat cakes, dip in the flour and fry in the hot fat. Brown the tbsp. of flour in the fat, add the water and cook until the gravy is smooth.

Frying Time: about 10 minutes.

Fried Sausage

About 1 lb. (450 g) frying sausage
2 oz. (55 g) fat
1 slightly heaped tbsp. plain flour for
browning
½ pint (285 ccm) water

Tie the sausage at both ends, prick with a fork in several places, then scald with hot water to prevent bursting. Fry in the hot fat until an even brown. Then brown the flour in the fat, add the water and cook until the gravy is smooth.

Frying Time: about 10 minutes.

b) Frying with Egg and Breadcrumbs

Cutlets

4 pork or veal cutlets
salt
1 level tbsp. plain flour
1 egg
1½ oz. (45 g) breadcrumbs
2 oz. (55 g) fat
1 slightly heaped tbsp. plain flour for
browning
½ pint (285 ccm) water

Beat the cutlets lightly, salt and dip first in the flour, then in the beaten egg and lastly in the breadcrumbs. Fry on both sides in hot fat until brown. Add the flour to the fat and brown. Add the water and cook until the gravy is smooth.

Frying Time: pork cutlets 10–15 minutes;
veal cutlets 8–10 minutes.

Remove the fat and skin from the cutlets. Beat them lightly, salt and dip first in the flour, then in the beaten egg and lastly in the breadcrumbs. Fry on both sides in the hot fat until brown. Add the flour to the fat and brown. Pour in the water and cook until the gravy is smooth.

Frying Time: 10–15 minutes.
Young French beans are delicious with mutton cutlets.
Mutton cutlets may be prepared like Fillet Beef Steak, without egg and breadcrumbs (see page 96).

Season the meat, dip first in the flour, then in the beaten egg and lastly in the breadcrumbs. Fry in the hot fat on both sides until brown. Add the water and the cream to the fat. Stir well and pour over the veal.

Frying Time: about 10 minutes.
Garnish with slices of lemon, anchovies and capers.

Mutton Cutlets

4 cutlets
salt
1 level tbsp. plain flour
1 egg
1½ oz. (45 g) breadcrumbs
2 oz. (55 g) fat
1 slightly heaped tbsp. plain flour for browning
½ pint (285 ccm) water

Fried Veal Slices
(Wiener Schnitzel)

4 veal escalopes (from rump)
salt
1 level tbsp. plain flour
1 egg
1½ oz. (45 g) breadcrumbs
2 oz. (55 g) fat
¼ pint (140 ccm) water
2–3 tbsp. sour cream

D. MEAT IN ASPIC

Meat bones, cartilage, and sinews contain collagenous substances with which brawns, meat in aspic, and similar cold dishes can be prepared. But these substances can only be extracted after long hours of boiling. So most housewives find it an economy of time, money and labour to use commercially prepared gelatine, which comes to them conveniently measured and packed, and ready for immediate use.

1. Use ¾ pint and 5 tbsp. (500 ccm) of liquid to 1 packet of Oetker powdered Regina Gelatine. One packet is equivalent to six sheets of Regina Gelatine.

2. Mix a little cold water with the powdered gelatine and leave to soak for about 10 minutes. Heat slowly, stirring all the time, until the gelatine is completely dissolved, then add it to the dish which is to set.
Gelatine in sheet form should be soaked in cold water before being added to hot liquid.

3. Liquid containing gelatine will set only if left to stand in a cool place. If the room temperature is more than 73° F (23° C) the gelatine will not set. So prepare any gelatine dish several hours before it is needed – the evening before, if possible – and chill

General Hints

100

Stuffed Cabbage Leaves Recipe See Page 167

Mock Hare Recipe See Page 90

in a refrigerator, a cellar, or, failing these, place it into a bowl of cold water.

4. If a mould is used, rinse out the mould with cold water, before pouring in the liquid containing the gelatine. This will prevent the mixture from sticking to the mould. To unmould, use a knife to loosen the jellied mixture from the sides of the mould and hold the mould for an instant in hot water before turning out.

Aspic (Jelly) for Fish, Meat, Poultry, Eggs and Vegetables

⅔ pint (375 ccm) meat or vegetable stock
6 tbsp. (100 ccm) vinegar or wine
1 egg white
1 egg shell
3 tbsp. cold water
1 packet Oetker Regina Gelatine powdered, white
5 tbsp. cold water

Remove the fat from the cold stock and season to taste with vinegar or wine. Beat together the egg white, the crushed egg shell and the 3 tbsp. water, and add to the stock. Continue beating while heating the mixture almost to boiling point. The egg white will coagulate and clarify the stock. Leave the stock to cool; do not move it until clear. Remove the scum and strain the stock through a clean cloth. Bring the stock back to the boil, then add the gelatine, which should have been soaked for 10 minutes in the 5 tbsp. cold water. Stir until all the gelatine is completely dissolved.

For an attractive effect, decorate the base of the mould which will form the top of the dish when it is turned out. This is done by first pouring in just enough stock to cover the bottom of the moistened mould. When this is set, decorate it with slices of pickled gherkin, tomato and hard-boiled egg. Carefully cover these with a few tablespoonsful of stock and leave to set again. Lastly, add the remaining ingredients and the slightly thickened stock. Chill or leave to set in a cold place.

When the aspic is solid, loosen it from the sides of the mould with a knife, then turn it out onto a plate. If necessary, hold the mould for a second in hot water.

Garnish with parsley, tomatoes, pickled gherkin and quartered hard-boiled eggs.

Pork Cutlets in Aspic
(Phot. See Page 144)

1⅛ lb. (500 g) pork (loin)
1¾ pint (1 l) water
salt
1 onion
pot vegetables
spices (4 peppercorns, 2 cloves, 1 small bay-leaf)
8 tbsp. (125 ccm) vinegar
1 egg white
1 egg shell
3 tbsp. cold water

Put the meat into the boiling salted water. If necessary, remove any scum. After an hour's cooking, add the onion, the prepared pot vegetables, the spices and the vinegar. As soon as the meat is done take it out of the stock and cut it into four equal slices. Cool the stock, remove the fat, and season to taste with salt and vinegar. Beat together the egg white, the crushed egg shell and the 3 tbsp. of cold water. Add to the stock, stirring all the time, until it has almost reached boiling point. The egg white coagulates and clarifies the stock. Leave the stock to cool; do not move it until it is clear. Remove the scum and strain the stock through a clean cloth. Bring about ⅔ pint (375 ccm) of the stock back to the boil, add

1 packet Oetker Regina Gelatine
powdered, white
5 tbsp. cold water
slices of pickled gherkin, tomato
and hard-boiled egg

the gelatine, which should have been soaked for 10 minutes in the water. Stir until all the gelatine is completely dissolved.

Rinse out 4 individual cutlet moulds with cold water, then pour in just enough cold stock to cover the base of each mould. As soon as this has set, garnish with slices of pickled gherkin, tomato and hard-boiled egg. Carefully pour in a few tablespoonsful of stock, and when this has set, put in the cutlets and cover each with about a quarter of the remaining stock, which will by this time have thickened slightly. Leave in a cold place to set. When the aspic is solid, loosen it from the sides of the moulds with a knife, then turn onto plates. If necessary, hold the moulds for a second in hot water.

Brawn
(Phot. See Page 144)

1¾ pint (1 l) water
1 bay-leaf
3–4 peppercorns
a little less than 1 level tbsp. salt
pot vegetables
1 onion
8 oz. (225 g) veal
8 oz. (225 g) pork
8 tbsp. (125 ccm) vinegar
salt and sugar to taste
1 packet Oetker Regina Gelatine
powdered, white
5 tbsp. cold water
a little parsley

Put the spices, the prepared pot vegetables, and the skinned onion into the water and bring to the boil. Add the pork and veal and cook till done. Dice the cold meat and strain the stock. Season about ⅔ pint (375 ccm) of the stock with the vinegar, add salt and sugar to taste and bring back to the boil. Add the gelatine which should have been soaked for 10 minutes in the water. Stir until all the gelatine is completely dissolved. Rinse out a few small moulds or cups with water, fill with meat and stock and leave to cool. When the aspic is solid, loosen it from the sides of the mould with a knife, then turn onto a plate. If necessary, hold the moulds for a second in hot water.

Garnish with the parsley.

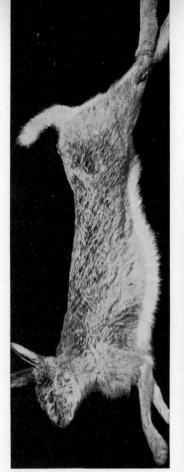

GAME AND POULTRY

Hare

Hare should be hung for several days before cooking.

To skin a hare hang it (back to wall) by two stout hooks through the sinews of the hind legs. Sever the front legs at the joint. Cut through the skin around the hind legs. Make a slit through the pelt inside the legs as far as the tail, and make a short cut on the belly. Pull the skin down off the legs, stripping it inside out over the body and forelegs. Lastly draw the pelt over the head, using a knife for those parts (ears, eyes, etc.) where the pelt is difficult to remove.

Place the hare on a board, slit open the belly, and remove the internal organs except the kidneys, which should be left inside. Reserve the heart, the lungs and the liver (from which the gall-bladder should be carefully removed and then discarded). Chop off the head, the belly skin with the ribs, and the front legs. These can be used, with the liver, heart, and lungs, in the giblets recipe (as noted below) or for Ragoût. Remove all skin from the back and from the hind legs. Cut off the hind legs, as they need a longer cooking time, and gently break the backbone to make cooking and serving easier.

Roast Hare

1 hare (back, legs)
salt
2 oz. (55 g) butter or margarine
about 4 oz. (115 g) fat bacon
¼ pint (140 ccm) sour cream or
5 tbsp. tinned milk
about ½ pint (285 ccm) water
1–2 tsp. Oetker GUSTIN
(corn starch powder)
1 tbsp. cold water

Wash and skin the hare and remove all fat. Rub in some salt. Brush with the fat. Rinse out the roasting pan with water, line with strips of bacon, put in the hare and cover it with more bacon strips. Place in the middle of the oven. The back, which is very tender, should be put in about a quarter of an hour later, to prevent it becoming too dry. 10 minutes before the hare is cooked, pour over the cream or tinned milk. When the hare is done, remove it from the pan and keep it hot while making the gravy. Place the pan on top of the stove. Stir the residue well from the bottom and add enough water to dissolve the juices. Scrape the pan well. Strain through a sieve. Thicken with the GUSTIN, blended with the water.

Oven: moderately hot.

Roasting Time: young hares 1–1¼ hours;
old hares 1½ hours and more.

Hare or Rabbit Giblets

Hare or rabbit giblets (head, split in
half lengthwise, neck, ribs, lungs
and heart)
2 oz. (55 g) fat bacon
1 onion
2 oz. (55 g) plain flour
1 pint (570 ccm) water
salt
pepper
lemon juice or red wine
sugar

Wash the giblets quickly and cut into ¾ inch (2 cm) pieces. Fry the diced bacon, add the small diced onion and the giblets. Dredge with flour and fry until brown. Stir in the water and season with salt and pepper. Simmer gently until the meat is tender. Before serving, season the gravy to taste with lemon juice or red wine, and sugar. The gravy should have a piquant sweet-sour flavour.

Cooking Time: 1¼–1½ hours.

Serve with mashed potatoes.

Alternatively, the giblets may be steeped in buttermilk for several days before cooking. This will improve the flavour and make the meat more tender.

Wash the rabbit gently, skin, and remove all fat. Rub in salt and brush over with fat. Rinse out the roasting pan with water and line with bacon rashers. Place the rabbit on the rashers and cover with more rashers. Place in the middle of the oven. The back, which is very tender, should be put in about a quarter of an hour later to prevent it becoming too dry. 10 minutes before the rabbit is cooked pour over the cream or tinned milk. When the rabbit is done, turn off the heat. Keep the roast hot while making the gravy. Place the pan on top of the stove. Stir the residue well from the bottom and add enough water to dissolve the juices. Scrape the pan well. Strain through a sieve. Thicken with the GUSTIN, blended with the water.

Oven: moderately hot.

Roasting Time: young rabbits 1–1 $\frac{1}{4}$ hours;
old rabbits 1 $\frac{1}{2}$ hours or more.

Roast Rabbit

1 rabbit (back, legs)
salt
2 oz. (55 g) butter or margarine
4 oz. (115 g) fat bacon
$\frac{1}{4}$ pint (140 ccm) sour cream
  or 5 tbsp. tinned milk
$\frac{1}{2}$ pint (285 ccm) water
1–2 tsp. Oetker GUSTIN
  (corn starch powder)
1 tbsp. cold water

Skin the venison, rub with salt and brush with the fat. Rinse out the roasting pan with water, line it with bacon rashers, put in the venison and cover with more bacon rashers. Place in the middle of the oven. As soon as the dripping begins to brown, pour some hot water into the pan, and about 10 minutes before the meat is cooked, pour over the cream or tinned milk. When the roast is done, turn off the heat. Keep the roast hot while making the gravy. Place the pan on top of the stove. Stir the residue well from the bottom and add enough water to dissolve the juices. Scrape the pan well. Strain through a sieve. Thicken with the GUSTIN, blended with the water.

Oven: moderately hot.

Roasting Time: about 2 hours.

Alternatively, the venison, skin being removed, may be soaked for 1–2 days in about 2 pints (1 $\frac{1}{8}$ l) of buttermilk. This will remove the characteristic "game" flavour and make the meat more tender.

Roast Venison
(Red Deer)

2 $\frac{1}{4}$–2 $\frac{3}{4}$ lb. (1–1 $\frac{1}{4}$ kg) loin
salt
1 $\frac{1}{2}$ oz. (45 g) butter or margarine
about 4 oz. (115 g) fat bacon
a little water
$\frac{1}{4}$ pint (140 ccm) sour cream
  or 5 tbsp. tinned milk
1–2 tsp. Oetker GUSTIN
  (corn starch powder)
1 tbsp. cold water

Roast Venison
(Roe Deer)

2¼–3¼ lb. (1–1½ kg) loin
salt
1½ oz. (45 g) butter or margarine
about 3 oz. (85 g) fat bacon
about ½ pint (285 ccm) water
¼ pint (140 ccm) sour cream
or sour milk
1–2 tsp. Oetker GUSTIN
(corn starch powder)
1 tbsp. cold water

Skin the meat, rub with salt and brush with the fat. Rinse out the roasting pan with water, put in the joint and cover it with bacon rashers. Place the meat in the middle of the oven. Add a little hot water into the pan from time to time to prevent the dripping from becoming too brown. About 10 minutes before the meat is cooked, pour over the cream or milk. When the meat is done, turn off the heat. Keep the roast hot while making the gravy. Place the pan on top of the stove. Stir the residue well from the bottom and add enough water to dissolve the juices. Scrape the pan well. Strain through a sieve. Thicken with the GUSTIN, blended with the water.

Oven: moderate to hot.

Roasting Time: 45–60 minutes.

Roast Haunch of Venison
(Roe Deer)

2¼ lb. (1 kg) haunch of venison
salt
1½ oz. (45 g) butter or margarine
about 3 oz. (85 g) fat bacon
½ pint (285 ccm) hot water
¼ pint (140 ccm) sour cream
or sour milk
1–2 tsp. Oetker GUSTIN
(corn starch powder)
1 tbsp. cold water

Skin the haunch, rub with salt and brush with the fat. Rinse out the roasting pan with water, put in the venison, and spread with bacon rashers. Place in the middle of the oven. Add some hot water into the pan from time to time to prevent the dripping from becoming too brown. About 10 minutes before the meat is cooked, pour over the sour cream or milk. When the meat is done, turn off the heat and keep the roast hot while making the gravy. Place the pan on top of the stove. Stir the residue well from the bottom and add enough water to dissolve the juices. Scrape the pan well. Strain through a sieve. Thicken with the GUSTIN, blended with the water.

Oven: moderate to hot.

Roasting Time: about 2 hours.

Braised Shoulder of Venison
(Roe Deer)

About 2 lb. (900 g) shoulder of deer
¾ oz. (20 g) plain flour
1 oz. (30 g) fat bacon
2 oz. (55 g) fat
salt
1 onion
½–1 pint (285–570 ccm) water
1–2 tsp. Oetker GUSTIN
(corn starch powder)
1 tbsp. cold water

Wash the meat quickly, coat with the flour and cover with the bacon rashers. Brown all over in hot fat in an uncovered pan. Sprinkle with salt. Chop the onion and let it cook for a little while in the hot fat. Add some hot water pouring it in carefully down the sides of the pan. About ½ pint (285 ccm) of water is sufficient. Cover the pan and simmer the joint over a low heat. Turn from time to time and make up any loss of water. As soon as the meat is done, strain the gravy, thicken it with the GUSTIN, blended with the water and season to taste.

Braising Time: about 2 hours.

If the meat is steeped for 3–4 days in buttermilk before braising it will be more tender.

Cut the meat into pieces and put into the boiling water, to which the spices and the onion (quartered) have been added. Cover the saucepan and simmer the meat over a low heat until done. Prepare a Brown Sauce (see page 55) with fat, flour and onion, and 1 pint (570 ccm) of the stock in which the meat has been cooked. Season the sauce with salt, vinegar or lemon juice, a little red wine and sugar. Add the meat and leave it simmering in the sauce for a further 10 minutes. Add the diced pickled gherkin and serve.

Cooking Time: 1–2 hours, according to age.

The typical game flavour may be avoided by steeping the meat overnight in about ½ pint (285 ccm) of vinegar, mixed with 1 pint (570 ccm) of water. Then follow the recipe given, but do not use the marinade for cooking the meat. Nor should lemon juice or vinegar be added to the dish.

Venison Ragoût

1⅛ lb. (500 g) red deer or roe deer
1 pint (570 ccm) water
salt
paprika
2 cloves
1 bay-leaf
3–4 peppercorns
1 onion
1½ oz. (45 g) fat
2 oz (55 g) plain flour
1 onion
salt
1 tbsp. vinegar or lemon juice
a little red wine
pinch of sugar
1 pickled gherkin

Roast Wild Boar

Wash the meat, dry it and rub in some salt. Cut diagonal gashes across the fat side in diamond pattern. Grease and rinse out a roasting pan. Put in the meat with the fat side uppermost. Place the roast in the middle of the oven. Add some hot water and red wine into the pan from time to time to prevent the dripping from becoming too brown. About 15 minutes before the meat is done, add the skinned and quartered onions. Remove excess fat and keep the roast hot while making the gravy. Place the pan on top of the stove. Stir the residue well from the bottom and add enough water to dissolve the juices. Scrape the pan well. Strain through a sieve. Season to taste with red wine or redcurrant jelly. Thicken with the GUSTIN, blended with the water and the cream or tinned milk.

3¼ lb. (1½ kg) wild boar's meat
  (loin or fillet from a young wild boar)
salt
½ pint (285 ccm) hot water
½ pint (285 ccm) red wine
2 onions
1–2 tbsp. redcurrant jelly
1–2 tsp. Oetker GUSTIN
  (corn starch powder)
1 tbsp. cold water
2 tbsp. sour cream or tinned milk

Oven: moderate to hot.

Roasting Time: about 2¼ hours.

Poultry

The difference between poultry and game birds is that poultry is sold plucked, the feathers being removed immediately after the bird is killed. Game birds, on the other hand, are sold unplucked, and should be hung before cooking. Whether or not a bird can be roasted depends on its age and quality. Older birds make excellent soup, fricassee, or ragoût. To determine the age of a cock, examine its spur; the older the bird, the longer and harder the spur. Judge the hen bird by the feet. The feet of young birds will have soft smooth skin, that of an old bird will be hard and knobbly. A young goose has a soft yellow beak, and the webs are thin and easily torn.

All poultry should be plucked dry. Grasp the feathers very near the skin and pluck carefully, pulling towards the tail. Be very careful not to tear the skin. Remove all pin feathers with a sharp knife or a pair of tweezers, and singe the hairs by holding the bird over an open flame or candle. Then wash the bird in luke-warm water and wheat bran. This will give a good colour. Rinse in cold water, and wipe.

Cut off the head. Pull back the skin of the neck and cut off the neck bone close to the body. Remove the crop and windpipe. Cut out the vent. Cut through the skin just above the vent, and carefully remove the cavity fat. Take hold of the gizzard and draw out the entrails, being careful not to break the gall-bladder. Cut through the thick muscle of the gizzard, and peel off the rough lining. From a goose, carefully remove the fat from the entrails.

Soak this fat as well as the cavity fat in water. Reserve for frying. Wash the bird under running water and truss. Lay it on its back, press the legs close to the body and, using a coarse needle, draw thick white thread through legs, belly, wings and back. Knot the ends of the string thread. Trussed in this way, the bird will roast and carve easily.

Prepare poultry according to the cooking rules given in the preceding chapter, and to which the following recipes merely refer.

Chicken with Rice

1 boiling fowl weighing
2¼–2¾ lb. (1–1¼ kg)
3½ pints (2 l) water
salt
1 parsley root
1 carrot
9 oz. (250 g) rice
1 small onion
2½ oz. (70 g) butter or margarine
2½ oz. (70 g) plain flour
lemon juice
1 egg yolk and
2 tbsp. cold water

Pluck the fowl, singe, draw and wash. Put it with the prepared gizzard, the heart and the neck into the boiling salted water and simmer over a low heat until tender. After an hour's cooking, add the parsley root and the carrot. As soon as the chicken is done, skim off a little fat and put it into a pan. In it gently sauté the washed rice and the chopped onion. Add about 1¾ pint (1 l) of the hot stock. Leave the rice to cook without stirring until done.

Melt the 2½ oz. (70 g) butter or margarine, stir in the flour and cook until pale yellow. Stirring all the time, add 1½ pint (850 ccm) of cold chicken stock and boil for 10 minutes. Season the gravy with salt and lemon juice, then enrich with the egg yolk beaten with the cold water. Cut up the chicken, put it into a round dish, pour over the gravy and surround with a ring of rice.

Cooking Time: for the chicken, 2–4 hours;
for the rice, about 30 minutes.

108

Stuffed Pancakes Recipe See Page 222

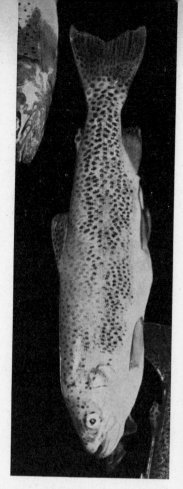

FISH DISHES

Rich in mineral salts, phosphorus, iron, calcium, and iodine, fish is one of our most valuable foods. And there is as much albumen in fish as in butcher's meat. Sea-fish especially, is rich in albumen of high biological quality, easy to digest and extremely nourishing. Most fish contains very little fat. Exceptions are herring, salmon, and eel — which are also rich in vitamins, particularly vitamin A, so necessary to growth and to general well-being. Fish liver oils, such as cod liver oil and halibut liver oil, are of course well known and widely used for their vitamin content.

Modern conditions of refrigerated ships and transport facilities make it possible for us to eat and enjoy fish in perfect condition even in summertime. The summer is in fact the perfect season for many fish; they are then at their tastiest, having recovered from their winter spawning. It should of course be remembered that because of its high water content fish decomposes very quickly, and so must always be prepared as soon as possible after purchase.

It is often said that you can tell fresh fish by its clear eyes and red gills. This is not very helpful nowadays, when so much fish is offered for sale headless, and when it is realised that ice-water pales the gills and dulls the eyes. Moreover, the gills of many fish are not in fact red to start with. Signs of good quality fish are the typical fresh smell, firm flesh, and tight skin. If a fish is fresh, its skin will be elastic and will only retain for a few seconds the mark of a finger's pressure.

Having chosen firm fresh fish, the housewife must prepare and cook it properly if she and her family are to enjoy it to the full. Fish should never be left soaking in water, or its mineral salts will be lost. For the same reason it should never be put into hot or cold water and then boiled, as this extracts too much valuable nourishment. Fish cooked in its own juices retains its delicate flavour and has no need of the excessive seasoning with herbs and spices so often recommended for boiled fish. To make fish firmer and to improve its flavour, sprinkle it with 1–2 tablespoonsful or so of lemon juice after you have cleaned and washed it, and allow a little time for the lemon juice to penetrate before cooking.

With its high albumen content, fish is very easily digested. It is an ideal food for invalids, but because of this, fish is often mistakenly thought to be less nourishing than meat. In fact, $3\frac{1}{2}$ oz. (100 g) of white fish has about the same nutritive value as $2\frac{1}{2}$ oz. (70 g) of lean beef or 3 oz. (85 g) of veal. As fish can be bought so much more cheaply than meat, it is therefore a most economical proposition for the main protein element, not only in the diet of invalids, but in the regular meals of the whole family. Like meat, fish is best eaten with potatoes and vegetables, but a rather larger amount, say, 9 oz. (250 g) of fish, may be allowed per head per meal.

There is an endless variety of ways in which fish can be served – steamed, fried in batter or breadcrumbs, grilled, or baked; as fish balls, or as cutlets; rolled, fricasseed, or minced; as ragoût, or in pies. What a pity it is, then, that fish is still so often served in the old-fashioned and uninteresting boiled way, merely with the addition of a little melted butter. The herring alone seems to have escaped this fate; its versatility seems to be fully appreciated, and it is commonly served smoked (kippers), fried, grilled, soused, and in a marinade. For grilling or frying, the best fish are the lemon and Dover soles, plaice, and flounder. The haddock, hake, cod, and perch can be served in many delicious ways. In fact, if a little skill and imagination are used in its cooking and preparation, fish of all kinds can bring endless variety and interest to our meals.

The bones, head, tail, fins and skin should not be discarded, as they can be used for making stock.

Fish, therefore, can contribute to make our meals nourishing and varied. It must, however, be prepared in the right way, without loss of nutritive substances.

General Hints

1. Always remove the scales from sea fish. Holding the fish up by the tail, scrape it with a knife or with a special fish scaler, working from the tail towards the head.

2. Thin-skinned fish and fish which is to be prepared "au bleu" should not be scaled. The blue comes from the colouring and mucous content of the skin, which therefore must not be damaged. Wash fish of this kind in water or on a wet kitchen board, handling it as little as possible.

3. Fins and tail, especially of larger fish are best removed with scissors.

4. The skin of sole should be removed by loosening it at the tail and then giving it a sudden pull towards the head.

5. To gut fish, slit the belly with a sharp knife, starting from the head towards the vent. Remove the guts, but avoid damaging the gall-bladder.

6. Both the black inner skin and the white leathery skin along the backbone must be removed; so must all the congealed blood.

7. The gills of sea fish should be cut away just under the gill-cover.

8. Fish should be thoroughly washed in cold water, both inside and out, but never leave it soaking in water otherwise valuable nutriments will be lost.

9. Then rub the fish inside and out with salt and sprinkle with lemon juice or vinegar (this will make the fish firmer and minimize the fish odour).

10. Onions, tomatoes and pot vegetables season the fish.

11. To fillet fish, first make a slit in the back near the head, using a sharp knife, and cut as closely as possible along the backbone. Lay the left hand on the fish and draw the knife from head to tail to loosen the flesh from the bones. Remove the skin thus: place one half of the boned fish on a board, skin downwards. Loosen a little of the skin at the tail end and then, holding the knife at a slight angle, work it under the skin; then push it along and so separate the skin from the flesh.

12. If the fish is to be fried, dry it thoroughly before coating it with breadcrumbs. This will make it crisper when cooked. Press the breadcrumbs firmly onto the fish.

13. Fish is thoroughly cooked when the back fin can be easily removed.

A. STEWED FISH

Fish Stewed in Own Juice
(1. In The Saucepan)

2¼ lb. (1 kg) sea or fresh-water fish
(haddock, cod, perch, hake, carp,
trout, tench, pike or perch-pike)
salt
lemon juice or vinegar
a little butter
some margarine or oil

Gut the fish, wash it, rub with salt inside and out and sprinkle with lemon juice or vinegar. Leave to stand for about half an hour. Put it, either whole or in pieces, into a greased saucepan. Cover the saucepan with a well fitting lid and cook slowly over a gentle heat.

Stewing Time: about 35 minutes.

Serve stewed fish with boiled potatoes and melted butter, or with Mustard (see page 49), Tomato (see page 52), Parsley (see page 50) or Horseradish Sauce (see page 50), made with the juice from the cooked fish. Serve Apple-Horseradish Dressing or Horseradish-Cream Dressing (see page 58), with carp; Dill Sauce (see page 49), with tench; Caper (see page 50) or Parsley Sauce (see page 50) with pike.

Fish Stewed in Own Juice
(2. In The Oven)

2¼ lb. (1 kg) fish
salt
lemon juice or vinegar
a little butter or margarine
1 oz. (30 g) bacon rashers

Although any fish may be oven-cooked, it is uneconomical to use this method for fish weighing less than 2¼ lb. (1 kg). Scale the fish, gut it, wash it, salt it inside and out and sprinkle with lemon juice or vinegar. Leave it to stand for about half an hour. Dry it, brush all over with fat and put it into a greased roasting-pan or into a greased fireproof dish. Spread with the bacon and place in the oven on the bottom shelf.

Oven: slow to moderate.

Baking Time: about 40 minutes.

Fish Fricassee

2¼ lb. (1 kg) fish or 1¾ lb. (800 g)
fish fillet
salt
a little lemon juice or vinegar

Fricassee Sauce:

1½ oz. (45 g) butter or margarine
2 oz. (55 g) plain flour
1 pint (570 ccm) water
1 tsp. capers
salt
about 1 tbsp. lemon juice or wine
1–2 egg yolks and
2 tbsp. cold water

A whole fish must first be boned and skinned. Salt the fillets, sprinkle with lemon juice or vinegar, and leave to stand for about half an hour. Dry well and cut into medium-sized pieces. To make the sauce, melt the fat, add the flour and, stirring frequently, cook until it is a light yellow colour. Gradually add the water and cook thoroughly. Add the pieces of fish to the boiling sauce, cover the pan and simmer gently until done. Stir in the capers, season to taste with salt and lemon juice or wine, and enrich with the egg yolk beaten in the water.

Stewing Time: 15–20 minutes.

Serve the fricassee in a ring of rice and decorate with lemon quarters, parsley and tomatoes.

Clean the fish and cut it into convenient sized pieces. Rub with salt and sprinkle with lemon juice or vinegar. Leave to stand for about half an hour, then dry well. Prepare the sauce appropriate to the fish, but use rather more flour than usual i.e. 2 oz. (55 g) instead of 1½ oz. (45 g). This is because the fish when cooking in the sauce will secrete juices which would otherwise make the sauce too thin. Leave the sauce in the pan in which it has been made and add the fish to the boiling sauce. Cover the pan and simmer until done. If the accompanying sauce is seasoned with chopped herbs, add these shortly before serving.

Stewing Time: 20–30 minutes.

If the fish is too small for steaming in the oven, put it into a saucepan, pour over the hot vinegar water, stand it in a draughty place, and then cook on the stove, see Fish Stewed in Own Juice (in the saucepan), see page 118.

Fish Stewed in Sauce

1¾ lb. (800 g) eel and
1 pint (570 ccm) Herb Sauce
(see page 50)
1¾ lb. (800 g) pike and
1 pint (570 ccm) Fricassee Sauce
(see page 51)
1¾ lb. (800 g) carp and
1 pint (570 ccm) Horseradish Sauce
(see page 50)
1¾ lb. (800 g) haddock and
1 pint (570 ccm) Parsley Sauce
(see page 50)
1¾ lb. (800 g) tench and
1 pint (570 ccm) Dill Sauce
(see page 49)
1¾ lb. (800 g) sole and
1 pint (570 ccm) Tomato Sauce
(see page 52)

Fish "au Bleu"
(Steamed In The Oven)

(carp, eel, trout, tench)

2¼ lb. (1 kg) fish
salt
vinegar
a little butter

Do not scale the fish, clean on a wet kitchen board, then salt it on the inside only, as salting on the outside would damage the mucus which produces the blue colour.

Put the fish into the roasting-pan or casserole, pour over it about 1 pint (570 ccm) of boiling water diluted with vinegar and set aside to cool in a draughty place. Lay the fish upright on a fireproof dish (carp should be put onto a peeled raw potato; trout and tench should be tied into a ring). Place the roasting-pan with the vinegar water in the lowest part of the oven and the dish with the fish on the grill of the roasting-pan above it. As soon as the back fin comes away easily, the fish is cooked. About 5 minutes before the cooking is completed, pour a little melted butter carefully over the fish. Never leave fish cooked "au bleu" in the oven once it is done, or it will loose its colour, but serve at once.

Oven: slow.

Time: 40–50 minutes.

Fish Ragoût

2¼ lb. (1 kg) fish or 1¾ lb. (800 g)
fish fillet
salt
lemon juice or vinegar

Sauce:
1½ oz. (45 g) bacon
2½ oz. (70 g) plain flour
1 small onion
1 pint (570 ccm) water
salt
lemon juice or vinegar
sugar
1 pickled gherkin

A whole fish must first be boned and skinned. Then salt the fillets and sprinkle with lemon juice or vinegar. Leave to stand for about half an hour. Dry well and cut into medium-sized pieces.

For the brown sauce, melt the diced bacon, add the flour and cook until medium brown. Add the finely chopped onion while the flour is still yellow. Stirring all the time, gradually add the water and cook for a few minutes. Put the pieces of fish into the boiling sauce and simmer gently until done. Season to taste with salt, lemon juice or vinegar, sugar and lastly, stir in the finely chopped pickled gherkin.

Stewing Time: 15–20 minutes.

Fish Rolls in Tomato Sauce

2¼ lb. (1 kg) fish or 1¾ lb. (800 g)
fish fillet
salt
lemon juice or vinegar
made mustard or anchovy paste

Tomato Sauce:
1½ oz. (45 g) butter or margarine
1 small onion
9–14 oz. (250–400 g) tomatoes
2 oz. (55 g) plain flour
1 pint (570 ccm) water
salt
lemon juice

A whole fish must first be boned and skinned. Then salt the fillets and sprinkle with lemon juice, and leave to stand for about half an hour. Cut the fillets into medium-sized pieces, brush with the mustard or anchovy paste, roll up, and secure with cocktail sticks.

Prepare the tomato sauce. Melt the fat, add the finely chopped onion and the chopped tomatoes, then the flour. Fry, stirring all the time. Gradually add the water and cook briefly. Strain the sauce through a sieve, season to taste and bring back to the boil. Put the fish rolls into the hot sauce and simmer until done.

Stewing Time: 15–20 minutes.

Fish Balls
(Using Leftovers)

1⅛ lb. (500 g) raw or boiled fish
1 stale roll or a slice of white bread
(soaked in water)
a little butter or margarine
1 onion
1 egg
salt

Caper Sauce:
1½ oz. (45 g) butter or margarine
2 oz. (55 g) plain flour
1 pint (570 ccm) water
salt
lemon juice
1 tbsp. capers

Mince the fish and the bread (squeezed dry). Melt the fat and sauté the finely chopped onion and add it together with the egg and salt to the minced fish. Stir until the mixture is smooth and shape into balls.

For the caper sauce, melt the fat, add the flour and cook, stirring all the time, until light yellow. Gradually add the water and cook for a few minutes. Season with salt and lemon juice, then stir in the capers. Bring the sauce to the boil, add the fish balls and simmer till done.

Stewing Time: 15–20 minutes.

Mashed potatoes, rice, all kinds of salad, pickled gherkins and beetroot go well with fish balls.

Alternatively, the balls may be cooked in a Bacon Sauce (see page 56).

B. FRIED FISH

I. FISH FRIED IN A FRYING PAN

Scale the fish, clean it and remove the head, fins and tail.
Dry well, then rub with salt both inside and out, sprinkle with
lemon juice and leave to stand for about half an hour. Coat
with flour, then dip in the beaten egg and lastly, in the breadcrumbs. Fry in hot fat till golden brown. When bubbles appear
on the fried side, the fish is ready.

Frying Time: 6–8 minutes.

Serve with potato salad or boiled potatoes, and lettuce salad.

Fried Small Fish

(Small Haddock, Flounder, Plaice,
Sole, Trout)

2¼ lb. (1 kg) fish
salt
lemon juice or vinegar
¾ oz. (20 g) plain flour
1 egg
3 oz. (85 g) breadcrumbs
3 oz. (85 g) fat for frying

Slit and gut the herring, wash thoroughly and rub off the scales.
Dry, then coat with seasoned flour. Fry in the hot fat.

Frying Time: 6–8 minutes.

Serve with potato salad or potatoes boiled in their skins.

Fried Fresh Herring

(Phot. See Page 180)

2¼ lb. (1 kg) fresh herring
¾ oz. (20 g) plain flour
salt
pepper
3 oz. (85 g) fat for frying
    (or oil, if preferred)

Scale and clean the fish. Cut into steaks (do not skin or bone),
rub with salt and sprinkle with lemon juice. Leave to stand
for about half an hour. Dry the steaks; coat with flour, then
dip in the beaten egg and lastly, in the breadcrumbs. Fry in the
hot fat on both sides till golden brown.

Frying Time: 8–10 minutes.

Fish Steaks

(Cod, Hake, Perch, Haddock)

1¾ lb. (800 g) fish
salt
lemon juice or vinegar
¾ oz. (20 g) plain flour
1 egg
1½ oz. (45 g) breadcrumbs
3 oz. (85 g) fat for frying

Wash the fillet, rub with salt, sprinkle with lemon juice and
leave to stand for about half an hour. Dry, coat with flour, then
dip in beaten egg and lastly, in the breadcrumbs. Fry on both
sides in hot fat till golden brown.

Frying Time: 5–10 minutes.

Serve with potato salad and mayonnaise.

Fried Fillet of Fish

(Hake, Cod, Perch, Dover Sole)

1¾ lb. (800 g) fillet of fish
salt
lemon juice or vinegar
¾ oz. (20 g) plain flour
1 egg
1½ oz. (45 g) breadcrumbs
3 oz. (85 g) fat for frying

Fried Fish Balls
(Using Leftovers)

1⅛ lb. (500 g) cooked fish (leftovers)
1 stale roll or a slice of white bread
(soaked in water)
some butter or margarine
1 onion
1 egg
salt
about 1 oz. (30 g) breadcrumbs
3 oz. (85 g) fat for frying

Flake the fish finely, or mince it with the bread (squeezed dry). Melt the fat and sauté the finely chopped onion and add, with the egg and salt, to the minced fish. Stir until the mixture is smooth and shape into balls. Coat with breadcrumbs and fry in hot fat till golden brown.

Frying Time: 6–8 minutes.

Serve with potato salad or boiled potatoes, and vegetables.

Deep-Fried Fish

1¾ lb. (800 g) fillets of fish
(cod, haddock, sea salmon)
salt
lemon juice or vinegar
4 oz. (115 g) plain flour
1 egg
salt
¼ pint (140 ccm) milk
1 tbsp. oil
melted butter or margarine
fat for deep frying e.g. oil, lard,
cooking fat or dripping

II. FISH, DEEP-FRIED

Wash the fillets, rub with salt, sprinkle with lemon juice, and leave to stand for about half an hour. Dry well and cut into medium-sized pieces.

Prepare the batter. Sieve the flour into a bowl, make a well in the centre and pour in the egg whisked with some of the milk and add the salt. Starting from the middle, gradually stir in the remaining milk, and the oil or melted fat and combine to a smooth batter. Using a fork, dip the fish into the batter and put into the very hot fat. Fry until brown and crisp. Drain well.

Frying Time: about 10 minutes.

Serve with potato salad and mayonnaise.

C. BAKED FISH

Fish au Gratin
(Using Leftovers)

About 1½ lb. (680 g) cooked fish
1 pint (570 ccm) Béchamel, Tomato- or
Cheese Sauce (see page 51/52/50)
2 tbsp. grated cheese
a little butter or margarine

Remove all skin and bones from the fish and put it into a fireproof dish. Pour over one of the suggested sauces. Sprinkle with the cheese and dot with butter. Bake in the oven until golden yellow.

Oven: moderate to hot.

Baking Time: about 30 minutes.

Serve with fried potatoes and lettuce salad.

Fish Pie with Potatoes

About 1½ lb. (680 g) cooked fish
1 lb. 10 oz. (750 g) potatoes boiled in
their skins

White Sauce:

1½ oz. (45 g) butter or margarine

Skin the fish and remove the bones. Boil the potatoes, but do not overcook; skin and slice them.

To make the white sauce, melt the fat, stir in the flour, and cook till pale yellow. Stirring all the time, gradually add the cold water or stock. Bring to the boil, cook for a few minutes and season.

Arrange the fish and the slices of potato in alternate layers in a greased pie-dish or casserole, and finish with a layer of potatoes on the top. Pour over the sauce, sprinkle with the breadcrumbs or the cheese, dot with butter and place low in the oven.

Oven: moderate to hot.

Time: about 40 minutes.

Serve with lettuce, tomato or French bean salad.

Instead of white sauce, Béchamel Sauce (see page 51) or Tomato Sauce with Fresh Tomatoes (see page 52) may be used, or about 1 pint (570 ccm) of sour milk mixed with 2 tbsp. of Oetker GUSTIN (corn starch powder).

1½ oz. (45 g) plain flour
1 pint (570 ccm) water or stock
salt
2 tbsp. breadcrumbs or grated cheese
a little butter

Salt the fillets, rub with lemon juice and leave to stand for about half an hour. Dry with a clean cloth and cut into medium-sized pieces. Roll each piece up, secure with a cocktail stick and place into a greased pie-dish or casserole.

To make the sauce, fry the diced bacon and when almost brown, add the chopped onion and fry until the onion is light brown. Whisk the tinned milk with the lemon juice and add to it the cooled bacon, the diced gherkins and the mustard. Season to taste with sugar, salt and Madeira and stir in the GUSTIN. Pour the sauce over the fish rolls, sprinkle with the cheese and dot with butter. Place the pie-dish or the casserole low in the oven to cook.

Oven: slow to moderate.

Time: about 35 minutes.

Fish Rolls in Savoury Sauce

1¾ lb. (800 g) fillets of fish
salt
lemon juice or vinegar
Savoury Sauce:
2 oz. (55 g) fat bacon
1 onion
1 small tin of evaporated milk
juice of 1 lemon
2–3 pickled gherkins
made mustard
a little sugar
salt
about 2 tbsp. Madeira
1 well heaped tbsp. Oetker GUSTIN
   (corn starch powder)
1 oz. (30 g) grated cheese
1 oz. (30 g) butter

Salt the fillets, rub with lemon juice or vinegar and leave to stand for about half an hour. Dry with a clean cloth and cut up into medium-sized pieces. Roll each piece up and secure with a cocktail stick. Put the rolls into a greased pie-dish or casserole.

To make the sauce, melt the fat, add the flour and stir until light yellow. Gradually add the water, stirring all the time, then leave the sauce to cook over a low heat for about 10 minutes. Add the wine to the sauce, season to taste with salt, lemon juice sugar and mustard and pour over the fish rolls. Place the pie-dish or the casserole low in the oven.

Oven: slow to moderate.

Cooking Time: about 35 minutes.

Fish Rolls in Wine Sauce

1¾ lb. (800 g) fish fillets
salt
a little lemon juice or vinegar
Sauce:
1 oz. (30 g) butter or margarine
1 oz. (30 g) plain flour
½ pint (285 ccm) water
5 tbsp. white wine
salt
lemon juice
sugar and made mustard to taste

Fish Rolls with Mustard-Cream Sauce

About 2 lb. (900 g) fillets of fish
salt
lemon juice or vinegar
a little made mustard

Sauce:

1¼ oz. (35 g) Oetker GUSTIN (corn starch powder)
⅔ pint (375 ccm) milk
¼ pint (140 ccm) fresh cream
salt
lemon juice
a little made mustard
1 oz. (30 g) grated cheese

Wash the fillets quickly, rub with salt and sprinkle with lemon juice or vinegar and leave to stand for about half an hour. Dry well and cut into slices large enough to roll up. Brush with mustard, roll up and secure with cocktail sticks. Place into a greased pie-dish or casserole.

To make the sauce, blend the GUSTIN with 3 tbsp. of the milk. Heat the remaining milk and, when it boils, remove it from the heat and add the prepared GUSTIN. Return to the heat and bring back to the boil. Whisk the cream and add it to the thickened milk. Season the sauce with salt, lemon juice and mustard and pour it over the fish rolls. Sprinkle with the cheese.

Oven: slow to moderate.

Time: about 25 minutes.

Serve with boiled potatoes and lettuce salad.

Fish Pie with Sauerkraut

(Using **Leftovers**)

1½ oz. (45 g) lard
1 onion
1⅛ lb. (500 g) sauerkraut
½ pint (285 ccm) water
about 1½ lb. (680 g) cooked or raw fish

White Sauce:

1½ oz. (45 g) butter or margarine
2 oz. (55 g) plain flour
1 pint (570 ccm) water
salt
2 tbsp. breadcrumbs or grated cheese
a little butter

Sauté the finely chopped onion in the hot fat for a minute or two. Add the sauerkraut (do not wash) and the water and cook until done.

Cooking Time: about 60 minutes.

For the remainder of this recipe, follow the method given for Fish Pie with Potatoes (see page 122) using Sauerkraut instead of potatoes.

Oven: moderate to hot.

Time: about 40 minutes.

Baked Stuffed Fish

2¼ lb. (1 kg) fish fillet
salt
a little lemon juice or vinegar
2½ oz. (70 g) fat bacon
1 onion
a small tin of evaporated milk
juice of 1 lemon
1 pickled gherkin
some chopped parsley
a little made mustard

Cut the fillet into two even sized pieces, wash, rub with salt and lemon juice, and leave to stand for about half an hour. Fry the diced bacon and, just when it begins to brown, add the chopped onion and fry until brown. Whisk the milk with the lemon juice, stir in the cooled bacon and the onion, the diced pickled gherkin and the parsley. Season with mustard and salt, then stir in the GUSTIN. Dry the fish thoroughly and put half into a greased pie-dish or casserole. Cover with stuffing, brush

124

the remaining fish thinly with tomato purée and place on top of the stuffing, purée side up. Sprinkle with the breadcrumbs and the cheese and dot with flakes of butter.

Oven: prepare the oven on full heat, bake at full heat.

Baking Time: about 30 minutes.

2 slightly heaped tbsp. Oetker *GUSTIN* (corn starch powder)
1–2 tbsp. tomato purée
2 tbsp. breadcrumbs
2 oz. (55 g) grated cheese
1 oz. (30 g) butter

Baked Fish Loaf

Wash the fish and mince it with the bread (squeezed dry). Sauté the diced onion in the fat, add to the fish, then stir in the eggs and salt. Shape the mixture into an oblong loaf, coat with the breadcrumbs and cover with the strips of bacon. Rinse out a roasting pan with water, put in the fish loaf, pour over the other 1½ oz. (45 g) butter or margarine, melted and browned, and place in the middle of the oven. About 10 minutes before the loaf is done, pour over the whisked sour cream. To make the sauce, add the water to the pan to dissolve the residue and thicken with the GUSTIN, blended with the water.

Oven: prepare the oven on full heat, bake at full heat.

Baking Time: 25–40 minutes.

1 lb. 10 oz. (750 g) fillet of fish
2 stale rolls or 2 slices of white bread (soaked in water)
1½ oz. (45 g) butter or margarine
1 onion
1–2 eggs
salt
¾ oz. (20 g) breadcrumbs
a few strips of fat bacon
another 1½ oz. (45 g) butter or margarine
4–5 tbsp. sour cream
about ½ pint (285 ccm) water
1–2 tsp. Oetker GUSTIN (corn starch powder)
1 tbsp. cold water

D. FISH IN MARINADE

Herrings in Marinade
(Phot. See Page 91)

Gut the herrings, soak for 12–24 hours, and then wash thoroughly to loosen the scales. Remove the gills, the gillcovers and the black skin. Wash the herrings once more, then arrange in layers with onion rings and spices in a small earthenware jar. Rub the roe through a fine sieve and mix with the vinegar and the sour cream, if desired; then add the cooled, boiled water. Pour the marinade over the herrings and leave covered for 2–3 days.

4–6 salt herrings
2–3 onions
2 small bay-leaves
6–8 peppercorns
⅔ pint (375 ccm) vinegar
a few tbsp. sour cream (optional)
½ pint (285 ccm) water

Fried Herrings in Marinade

Gut the herrings, wash them, cut off their heads and dry them. Rub with salt inside and outside. Coat with flour and fry in hot fat on both sides until golden brown. Arrange in an earthenware jar with the onion rings, mustard seeds and peppercorns. Mix the vinegar with the cooled, boiled water. Pour the marinade over the herrings. They can be served after they have soaked for 4–6 days.

2¼ lb. (1 kg) fresh herrings
salt
¾ oz. (20 g) plain flour
3 oz. (85 g) fat
2 oz. (55 g) onion rings
1 tbsp. mustard seeds
6–8 peppercorns
⅔ pint (375 ccm) vinegar
½ pint (285 ccm) water

"Rollmops"
(Pickled Herrings)
(Phot. See Page 91)

4–6 salt herrings
made mustard
2 small pickled gherkins
2 onions
1 tbsp. capers
6–8 peppercorns
2 small bay-leaves
⅔ pint (375 ccm) vinegar
½ pint (285 ccm) water

Gut and clean the herrings, soak for 12–24 hours, bone and wash. Brush each half with mustard, spread with pickled gherkin slices, finely sliced onions and capers. Roll up carefully and secure with cocktail sticks. Place the rollmops with the peppercorns and bay-leaves in a small earthenware jar. Mix the vinegar with the cooled, boiled water and pour over the rollmops. They can be served after they have soaked for 4–6 days.

Herrings in Sour Cream

4–6 Herrings in Marinade
(see page 125)
½ pint (285 ccm) sour cream
1 small onion
salt
pepper
vinegar or lemon juice

Cut the herrings into small strips. Mix together the cream, the grated onion, the salt and the pepper. Season with vinegar or lemon juice and pour over the herring fillets. Soak for some hours in the marinade before serving.
Some finely sliced or shredded apples may be added.

Fish in Aspic

1⅛ lb. (500 g) fish
(cod, haddock, fresh herrings)
1 pint (570 ccm) water
1 tsp. salt
2–3 Jamaica peppers
1 bay-leaf
pot vegetables
1 onion
8 tbsp. (125 ccm) vinegar
a little more salt, if required
1 egg white
1 egg shell
3 tbsp. cold water
1 packet Oetker Regina Gelatine
powdered, white
5 tbsp. cold water
1 pickled gherkin
1 tomato
1 hard-boiled egg

E. FISH IN ASPIC (JELLY)

Clean the fish. Boil the water, salt, spices, pot vegetables and onion gently for about ¼ hour. Add the fish and leave it to simmer gently for 10–15 minutes. Remove from the saucepan and leave to cool. Strain the stock and remove about ⅔ pint (375 ccm) of it (if there is not enough add some water). Season to taste with vinegar and salt.
If the stock is very cloudy, clarify it in the following way: remove the fat from the cold stock; using a fork, whisk together the egg white, the crushed egg shell and the water. Add to the stock and, beating all the time, heat almost to boiling point. The egg white will coagulate and clarify the stock. Set aside to cool and leave till clear. Remove the scum and strain the stock through a clean cloth. Bring back to the boil and add the gelatine, which has been soaked in the cold water for 10 minutes. Stir until it is completely dissolved.
Rinse out a mould with cold water and pour in enough stock to cover the bottom. When this is set, decorate with pieces of pickled gherkin and tomato and slices of hard-boiled egg. Carefully pour over this a few tablespoonsful of stock. When this has set, arrange on it the diced cold fish and add the remaining stock, which will have begun to thicken slightly. Set aside to chill. As soon as the jelly is firm, loosen it carefully from the sides of the mould with a knife. If necessary, hold the mould for a second in hot water. Turn onto a plate.

EINTOPF —
ONE-DISH MEAL

Eintopf was originally a peasant dish, consisting of meat, vegetables and potatoes, cooked together in one pot over a low heat or in a slow oven. It was, and still is popular because it requires little preparation and is economical both in the use of fuel and ingredients. The long slow cooking process of the Eintopf brings out the full flavour of the meat, which permeates the other ingredients. Thus a little meat goes a long way, and none of its juice is lost, as the liquor is served as an integral part of the dish. The addition of appropriate herbs and seasonings to the basic meat and vegetables brings out the characteristic full hearty Eintopf flavour.

Eintopf is as popular today as ever it was, still providing a cheap, simple, and satisfying meal. From its localised rural beginnings it has grown into a national favourite, a traditional German dish. Eintopf was never intended to appeal to the sophisticated palate of the gourmet. Nevertheless, as some of our less familiar recipes show, Eintopf can provide both subtlety and delicacy of flavour.

A. BOILED EINTOPF DISHES
("All in one pot")

I. THICK SOUPS

Beef Broth with Rice

9–13 oz. (250–375 g) beef
3½–4½ pints (2–2½ l) water
salt
pot vegetables
6–7 oz. (170–200 g) rice
1⅛ lb. (500 g) potatoes
a little meat extract

Wash the meat and put it into the boiling salted water. Leave to simmer. After about an hour and a half, add the pot vegetables, washed and finely chopped, the washed rice and the peeled, washed and diced potatoes. As soon as the meat, rice and potatoes are done, season and add meat extract to taste. The meat may be taken out of the broth and served separately or cut up into pieces and added to the soup.

Cooking Time: about 2 hours.

Asparagus, flowerets of cauliflower, cabbage or Kohlrabi may be added with the rice to the soup.

Beef Broth with Noodles

9–13 oz. (250–375 g) beef
3½–4½ pints (2–2½ l) water
salt
pot vegetables
5½ oz. (150 g) noodles
a little meat extract

Wash the meat and put it into the boiling salted water. Cook gently until done. After about 1 hour and a half, add the pot vegetables, prepared and chopped. Take the meat out of the soup as soon as it is done and add the noodles, leaving them to cook in the soup. Season with salt and meat extract. The meat may be served separately, or cut into small pieces and returned to the soup.

Cooking Time: about 2 hours.

Beef Broth with Barley

9–13 oz. (250–375 g) beef
3½–4½ pints (2–2½ l) water
salt
6–7 oz. (170–200 g) barley
pot vegetables
1⅛ lb. (500 g) potatoes
a little meat extract

Wash the meat and put it into the boiling salted water. Leave to simmer. After about an hour and a half, add the washed barley. When the barley is almost done, add the pot vegetables, prepared and finely chopped, and the potatoes, peeled, washed and finely diced. When done, season the soup with salt and meat extract. The meat may be served separately, or cut into pieces and added to the soup.

Cooking Time: 2½–3 hours.

Mutton may be used instead of beef for this recipe.

Wash the meat and put it into the boiling salted water. Cook gently until done and remove from the soup. Prepare the vegetables, shell the peas, scrape the carrots, peel the Kohlrabi and cut into cubes or thin slices, break the cauliflower into flowerets and clean the Brussels sprouts. Add the prepared, washed vegetables to the boiling soup. At the same time add the potatoes, peeled, washed and diced and the pot vegetables, washed and finely chopped. Simmer until done. Season with salt and meat extract. The meat may be served separately or cut into pieces and returned to the soup.

Cooking Time: about 2½ hours.

If desired, Semolina Dumplings (see page 43) or Spongy Dumplings (see page 43) may be used instead of the potatoes.

Beef Broth with Vegetables
(Phot. See Page 92)

9–12 oz. (250–375 g) beef
3½–4½ pints (2–2½ l) water
salt
1 lb. 10 oz. (750 g) vegetables
   (peas, carrots, Kohlrabi,
   cauliflower, Brussels sprouts)
1⅛ lb. (500 g) potatoes
pot vegetables
a little meat extract

Wash the meat and put it into the boiling salted water. Cook gently until done. Then remove from the soup. During cooking after an hour and a half, add the pot vegetables, prepared and finely chopped and the peeled, washed and diced potatoes. If carrots are used, scrape them, cut them into small cubes or strips and add them to the soup. Season the soup with salt and meat extract. The meat may be served separately, or cut into pieces and added to the soup.

Cooking Time: 2–2½ hours.

Beef Broth with Potatoes

9–13 oz. (250–375 g) beef
3½–4½ pints (2–2½ l) water
salt
pot vegetables
3¼ lb. (1½ kg) potatoes
or 2¼ lb. (1 kg) potatoes and
   1⅛ lb. (500 g) carrots
a little meat extract

Pluck, singe, draw and wash the chicken. Put it into the boiling salted water, together with the heart, the prepared gizzard and the neck. Simmer gently until cooked, then remove from the broth. Add to the broth the pot vegetables, prepared and finely chopped, the washed rice or barley and the potatoes, peeled, washed and diced. Cook together until done. Add the chicken liver but do not leave it in for longer than a minute or two. Add the diced chicken to the soup and season with salt and meat extract.

Cooking Time: with rice, about 3½ hours;
              with barley, about 4 hours.

Chicken Broth with Rice or Barley

1 boiling fowl
3½–4½ pints (2–2½ l) water
salt
pot vegetables
6–7 oz. (170–200 g) rice or barley
1⅛ lb. (500 g) potatoes
meat extract

Goose or Duck Giblet Soup with Rice, Barley, or Potatoes

Goose or duck giblets (head, neck, wings, feet, gizzard and heart of one goose or duck)
3½–4½ pints (2–2½ l) water
salt
1 onion
pot vegetables
6–7 oz. (170–200 g) rice or barley or 2¼ lb. (1 kg) potatoes
meat extract
1 tbsp. finely chopped parsley

Clean the giblets thoroughly, scald and skin the feet and remove the beak and eyes. Put the giblets into the boiling salted water together with the onion and the prepared pot vegetables (leave whole). Cook until done and remove the giblets from the stock. Strain the stock, bring back to the boil and add to it the washed rice or the washed barley or the peeled, washed and diced potatoes. As soon as the rice, barley, or potatoes are done, season the soup with salt and meat extract, add the meat, cut into pieces, and the finely chopped parsley.

Cooking Time: with rice or potatoes, about 2 hours; with barley, about 2½ hours.

Pea Soup with Cured Pork

About 13 oz. (375 g) dried peas
3½–4½ pints (2–2½ l) water
13 oz. (375 g) cured pork (ears, snout, tail or neck)
about 1½ lb. (680 g) potatoes
pot vegetables
salt
marjoram

Wash the peas, then soak them in the water for 12–24 hours. Simmer them gently in the water in which they have been soaked, together with the well-washed meat. When the peas are almost cooked, add the peeled, washed and diced potatoes and the washed, chopped pot vegetables. Simmer until done. Season with salt and a pinch of marjoram. Serve the meat separately or cut into pieces and added to the soup.

Cooking Time: 2–2½ hours.

If desired, about 9 oz. (250 g) of streaky bacon may be used instead of the pork.

Bean Soup with Smoked Sausage (Mettwurst)

About 13 oz. (375 g) Haricot beans
3½–4½ pints (2–2½ l) water
9 oz. (250 g) smoked sausage
about 1½ lb. (680 g) potatoes
pot vegetables
salt

Wash the beans and soak them in the water for 12–24 hours. Add the sausage to the liquid, bring to the boil and simmer gently. Take out the sausage as soon as it is cooked. When the beans are almost done, add the peeled, washed and diced potatoes, the washed and chopped vegetables and the washed savory. Cook until done, then season with salt. The sausage may be served separately or cut up and added to the soup.

Cooking Time: about 1½ hours.

About 7 oz. (200 g) soaked prunes may be added with the potatoes; pork or mutton may be used instead of the smoked sausage.

Lentil Soup

About 13 oz. (375 g) lentils
3½–4½ pints (2–2½ l) water
1⅛ lb. (500 g) pork (ribs)

Wash the lentils and soak them in the water for about 12–24 hours. Then simmer them in the water in which they have been soaked, together with the washed ribs of pork. As soon as the pork is cooked take it out of the soup. When the lentils are almost done, add the peeled, washed and diced potatoes and the washed and chopped pot vegetables. Cook until done, then season with salt. Serve the meat separately, or cut into pieces and added to the soup.

Cooking Time: about 1½ hours.

about 1½ lb. (680 g) potatoes
pot vegetables
salt

Dried Legume Soup without Meat

Wash the legumes and soak them in the water for 12–24 hours. Bring them to the boil in the water in which they have been soaked, cook until tender then rub through a sieve. Melt the fat and add to it the finely chopped onion and the washed and chopped pot vegetables. Stir in the legume purée and the prepared potatoes and, if used, the carrots, peeled and cut into small pieces. Season the soup with salt and meat extract and serve with croûtons made from the roll or bread.

Cooking Time: peas, about 2½ hours;
               Haricot beans, about 1½ hours;
               lentils, about 1 hour.

About 13 oz. (375 g) peas,
   Haricot beans, or lentils
3½–4½ pints (2–2½ l) water
3 oz. (85 g) fat
1 onion
pot vegetables
1 lb 10 oz. (750 g) potatoes
   or 1⅛ lb. (500 g) potatoes
   and 9 oz. (250 g) carrots
salt
meat extract
1 roll or a few slices of stale bread
1 tbsp. butter or margarine

Vegetable Soup

Wash and prepare the vegetables and cut into strips or slices, dividing the cauliflower into flowerets. Cook them for a minute or two in the melted fat. Sprinkle with the flour, add the water, the peeled, washed and diced potatoes and a little salt and cook until done. Season with salt and meat extract and serve, with the parsley.

Cooking Time: about 1 hour.

Meat Balls (see page 45), or Spongy Dumplings (see page 43) or Semolina Dumplings (see page 43), may be added to the soup and simmered till done.

1 lb. 10 oz. (750 g) vegetables
   (new peas, carrots, Kohlrabi,
   cauliflower, savoy cabbage, etc.)
3 oz. (85 g) fat (suet)
¾ oz. (20 g) plain flour
3½ pints (2 l) water
1⅛ lb. (500 g) potatoes
salt
meat extract
1 tbsp. chopped parsley

Pea Soup with Semolina Dumplings

Shell the peas and cook them for a minute or two in the hot fat. Sprinkle with the flour and cook a little longer. Fill up with the water and add a little salt. Add the peeled, washed and diced potatoes. Cook together until done. Add the semolina dumplings and simmer for about 10 minutes. Season with salt and serve sprinkled with the parsley.

Cooking Time: ¾–1 hour.

1 lb. 10 oz. (750 g) new peas,
   with pods 5 lb. (2¼ kg)
4 oz. (115 g) butter or margarine
1½ oz. (45 g) plain flour
3½–4½ pints (2–2½ l) water
salt
1⅛ lb. (500 g) potatoes
Semolina Dumplings (see page 43,
   making twice the quantity)
1 tbsp. finely chopped parsley

Potato Soup

3 oz. (85 g) lard
1 onion
pot vegetables
3½ pints (2 l) water
salt
3¼ lb. (1½ kg) potatoes
meat extract
1 tbsp. finely chopped parsley

Melt the fat, add the finely sliced onion and the prepared and chopped pot vegetables. Cook them together for a minute or two, then add the water and season with salt. Add the peeled, washed and diced potatoes to the boiling water and cook till done. Mash some of the potatoes so that the soup becomes thick; season with salt and meat extract and serve sprinkled with the parsley.

Cooking Time: about 45 minutes.

Westphalian Blind Hen

9–13 oz. (250–375 g) streaky bacon
1⅓ pint (¾ l) water
1⅛ lb. (500 g) French beans
9 oz. (250 g) carrots
2 apples
2 pears
1⅛ lb. (500 g) potatoes
salt

II. VEGETABLE EINTOPF

Bring the water to the boil, add the bacon and cook gently. String, wash and slice the beans, scrape and dice the carrots, peel, core and slice the apples and pears. Peel, wash and dice the potatoes. After the bacon has been cooking for half an hour, add the vegetables, the fruit and the potatoes. As soon as all the ingredients are done, season to taste.

Cooking Time: 1–1½ hours.

Alternatively, Haricot beans may be used in this recipe, but they will lengthen the cooking time. Soak 7 oz. (200 g) Haricot beans tor 12–24 hours in the 1⅓ pint (¾ l) water, then bring to the boil and simmer gently in the water in which they have been soaked. After half an hour's cooking, add the bacon. Only 9 oz. (250 g) of French beans need be used with the Haricots, or they may be left out altogether.

Apples and Potatoes

(Himmel und Erde –
Heaven and Earth)

3¼ lb. (1½ kg) potatoes
⅔ pint (375 ccm) water
salt
1⅛ lb. (500 g) apples
some sugar
a little vinegar
4 oz. (115 g) fat bacon
2 onions

Peel wash, and dice the potatoes, put them into the boiling salted water and cook gently for 15 minutes. Add the peeled apples, cut into quarters, bring back to the boil and cook gently until done. Season with salt, sugar and vinegar. Cut the bacon into cubes and fry, add the sliced onions and brown them; pour over the dish and serve.

Cooking Time: about 45 minutes.

If preferred, pears may be used instead of apples.

Prunes with Potatoes

5 oz. (140 g) Haricot beans
2 pints (1⅛ l) water
5 oz. (140 g) prunes
½ pint (285 ccm) water
1 smoked sausage (Mettwurst)
2¼ lb. (1 kg) potatoes
a little sugar
salt

Wash the Haricot beans and soak them in the 2 pints (1⅛ l) of water for 12–24 hours. Wash the prunes thoroughly and soak them for the same period of time in the ½ pint (285 ccm) of water. Bring the beans to the boil in the water in which they have been soaked, add the sausage and, ¾ of hour before serving, add the peeled, washed and diced potatoes and the soaked prunes. Season to taste with sugar and salt.

Cooking Time: about 2 hours.

Wash the fruit thoroughly and leave it to soak in the 1 pint (570 ccm) of water for 12–24 hours

Wash the meat, bring the other pint (570 ccm) of water to the boil, salt and add the pork. Cook until almost done. Add the soaked dried fruit and cook together until done. Take the meat out of the soup and cut it into cubes. Season with salt, sugar and cinnamon or cloves. Thicken with the GUSTIN, blended with the water and pour the soup over the diced meat and the dumplings, which should be cooked separately in salted water.

Cooking Time: about 1½ hours.

Dried Fruit with Dumplings

(Schlesisches Himmelreich – Silesian Heaven)

9 oz. (250 g) dried fruit
1 pint (570 ccm) water for soaking
9–13 oz. (250–375 g) pork
1 pint (570 ccm) water
salt
1 oz. (30 g) sugar
cinnamon or cloves
1–2 tsp. Oetker GUSTIN
(corn starch powder)
1 tbsp. cold water
Potato Dumplings (see page 176)
or Bread Dumplings (see page 44)

B. STEWED EINTOPF

1. To stew meat, vegetables and potatoes, the lid of the saucepan must fit so closely that no steam can possibly escape during cooking. If steam escapes, the amount of water given in the following recipes will be insufficient.

2. Therefore always start the dish off at a high temperature. Once it has reached boiling point, turn down the heat until it is just sufficient to allow gentle boiling with no loss of steam.

General Hints

Melt the fat quickly over a full heat, add the meat, cut into small pieces, with the bones and brown lightly. Add the sliced onion just before the meat is brown enough, together with the pot vegetables, prepared and chopped, and the finely chopped tomatoes, if used. Cook all these together for a few minutes and season. Add the prepared vegetables and potatoes, cut into small pieces and pour on the water. Bring quickly to the boil in a covered saucepan. As soon as boiling point is reached, lower the heat, cover so that no steam escapes and simmer gently without removing the lid or stirring until the dish is cooked.

If preferred, the meat can be cooked without preliminary browning. Brush the bottom of the pan with fat and fill it with alternate layers of the meat and vegetables. Bring to the boil over a full heat and then simmer gently until done.

Basic Recipe and Method

1½ oz. (45 g) butter,
margarine or lard
9–18 oz. (250–500 g) meat
onion, pot vegetables,
tomatoes (optional)
salt
spices
about 2 lb. (900 g) vegetables
about 1½ lb. (680 g) potatoes
¼–1 pint (140–570 ccm) water

Pickled Bean - Eintopf

1 oz. (30 g) lard
9–13 oz. (250–375 g) pork (neck)
1 onion
1 lb. 10 oz. (750 g) pickled beans
2¼ lb. (1 kg) potatoes
1 pint (570 ccm) water

Use the method given in the Basic Recipe (see page 133).

Stewing Time: about 3 hours.

French Bean - Eintopf

1½ oz. (45 g) lard or margarine
9–13 oz. (250–375 g) beef or pork
(no extra fat is needed if the meat
is fat)
1 onion
2¼ lb. (1 kg) French beans
1 lb. 10 oz. (750 g) potatoes
salt
⅔ pint (375 ccm) water

Use the method given in the Basic Recipe (see page 133).

Stewing Time: about 80 minutes.

Alternatively, 9 oz. (250 g) of chopped tomatoes may be cooked with the meat and onion in the fat. In this case, only ½ pint (285 ccm) of water is needed.

Kale - Eintopf

1½ oz. (45 g) lard
9–13 oz. (250–375 g) pork
(spare rib)
2¼ lb. (1 kg) prepared kale
1 lb. 10 oz. (750 g) potatoes
salt
1 pint (570 ccm) water

Use the method given in the Basic Recipe (see page 133).

Stewing Time: about 2 hours.

Broad Bean - Eintopf

1½ oz. (45 g) lard or margarine
9 oz. (250 g) mutton or lean bacon
(if bacon is used, no extra fat is
necessary)
1 lb. 10 oz. (750 g) shelled broad beans
1 lb. 10 oz. (750 g) potatoes
a little savory
salt
1 pint (570 ccm) water

Use the method given in the Basic Recipe (see page 133).
Stewing Time: about 1½ hours.

Wash the beans and soak them in the water for 12–24 hours. Bring them to the boil in the water in which they have been soaked and leave to simmer for about 1½–2 hours until done. Strain off the water and add the beans to the Carrot-Eintopf which has been made according to the Basic Recipe on page 133. Follow the Basic Recipe on page 133 to finish the dish.

Stewing Time: about 1½ hours.

Carrot - Eintopf

4 oz. (115 g) Haricot beans
1 pint (570 ccm) water
1½ oz. (45 g) lard
1–2 onions
9–13 oz. (250–375 g) beef or belly pork
   (if the latter, leave out the extra fat)
2¼ lb. (1 kg) carrots
1 lb. 10 oz. (750 g) potatoes
salt
½ pint (285 ccm) water
9 oz. (250 g) apples

Use the method given in the Basic Recipe (see page 133).

Stewing Time: about 1 hour.

Turnip - Eintopf

1½ oz. (45 g) lard
9–13 oz. (250–375 g) pork
1–2 onions
2¼ lb. (1 kg) turnips
1 lb. 10 oz. (750 g) potatoes
salt
⅔ pint (375 ccm) water

Use the method given in the Basic Recipe (see page 133).

Stewing Time: 1–1½ hours.

Savoy Cabbage - Eintopf

1½ oz. (45 g) lard or margarine
9–13 oz. (250–375 g) beef
1–2 onions
1 lb. 10 oz. (750 g) savoy cabbage
1 lb. 10 oz. (750 g) potatoes
salt
½ pint (285 ccm) water
   (generously measured)

Use the method given in the Basic Recipe (see page 133).

Stewing Time: 1–1½ hours.

Cabbage - Eintopf

1½ oz. (45 g) lard or margarine
9–13 oz. (250–375 g) beef or mutton
1–2 onions
1 lb. 10 oz. (750 g) cabbage
1 lb. 10 oz. (750 g) potatoes
salt
1 tsp. caraway seeds
about ½ pint (285 ccm) water

Spanish Fricco

1½ oz. (45 g) butter or margarine
13–18 oz. (375–500 g) beef,
pork and veal
2–3 onions
salt
paprika or pepper
3¼ lb. (1½ kg) potatoes
about ¼ pint (140 ccm) water
½ pint (285 ccm) sour cream

Use the method given in the Basic Recipe (see page 133), adding the sour cream 10 minutes before serving.

Stewing Time: 1½–2 hours.

Veal with Asparagus

1½ oz. (45 g) butter or margarine
13–18 oz. (375–500 g) veal
4 oz. (115 g) mushrooms
1⅛ lb. (500 g) asparagus
7 oz. (200 g) rice
salt
1¾ pint (1 l) water

Dice the meat and brown it lightly in the hot fat. Just before it has become brown enough, add the mushrooms, cleaned and sliced. Let them cook together for a few minutes. Peel the asparagus, cut it into short lengths and add it to the meat and mushrooms, together with the washed rice, a little salt and the water. As soon as the boiling point is reached, turn down the heat and leave to simmer gently until done.

Stewing Time: about 50 minutes.

Veal with Tomatoes

1½ oz. (45 g) butter or margarine
13–18 oz. (375–500 g) veal
1⅛ lb. (500 g) tomatoes
2–3 onions
7 oz. (200 g) rice
salt
curry powder
1⅓ pint (750 ccm) water
¼ pint (140 ccm) sour cream

Use the method given in the recipe Veal with Asparagus (as noted above). Cut up the tomatoes and onions and add them to the meat just before it has become sufficiently brown. Add the cream about 10 minutes before serving.

Stewing Time: 40 minutes.

Irish Stew

1½ oz. (45 g) butter or margarine
13–18 oz. (375–500 g) mutton
2–3 onions
salt
pepper
1 tsp. caraway seeds
2¼ lb. (1 kg) cabbage
1⅛ lb. (500 g) potatoes
½ pint (285 ccm) water

Use the method given in the Basic Recipe (see page 133).

Stewing Time: about 1½ hours.

Use the method given in the Basic Recipe (see page **133**).

Stewing Time: about 1½ hours.

Mutton with Beans and Tomatoes

1½ oz. (45 g) fat
13–18 oz. (375–500 g) mutton
1 onion
9 oz. (250 g) tomatoes
salt
1⅛ lb. (500 g) French beans
1⅛ lb. (500 g) potatoes
¼–½ pint (140–285 ccm) water

Use the method given in the Basic Recipe (see page 133).

Stewing Time: about 1½ hours.

Pichelsteiner Meat

3 oz. (85 g) beef marrow or 2 oz. (55 g)
  butter or margarine
13–18 oz. (375–500 g) beef
salt
paprika
½ celeriac
3 carrots
1 parsley root
2¼ lb. (1 kg) potatoes
about ½ pint (285 ccm) water

Use the method given in the Basic Recipe (see page 133).

Stewing Time: about 1¼ hours.

Pichelsteiner with Tomatoes

1½ oz. (45 g) butter or margarine
13–18 oz. (375–500 g) beef and pork
1⅛ lb. (500 g) tomatoes
½ onion
salt
paprika
1⅛ lb. (500 g) carrots
1⅛ lb. (500 g) potatoes
5 tbsp. water

Prepare and chop or slice the vegetables. Cook them in the melted fat for 5–10 minutes, add the peeled, washed and diced potatoes, pour in the water, season with salt and simmer gently until done. Sprinkle with the parsley just before serving.

Stewing Time: 40–60 minutes.

Any variety of vegetable may be used in the recipe.

Vegetarian "Eintopf"

9 oz. (250 g) carrots
9 oz. (250 g) celeriac
1 small cauliflower
9 oz. (250 g) tomatoes
1 onion
2 oz. (55 g) butter or margarine,
  or 3 tbsp. oil
1⅛ lb. (500 g) potatoes
½ pint (285 ccm) water
salt
finely chopped parsley

Beef Goulash with Potatoes

2 oz. (55 g) fat or fat bacon
13–18 oz. (375–500 g) beef
1 onion
9 oz. (250 g) tomatoes
salt
paprika
2¼ lb. (1 kg) potatoes
about ½ pint (285 ccm) water

Use the method given in the Basic Recipe (see page 133).

Stewing Time: about 90 minutes.

Beef Goulash with Rice

2 oz. (55 g) fat or fat bacon
13–18 oz. (375–500 g) beef
1 onion
pot vegetables
9 oz. (250 g) tomatoes (optional)
salt
paprika
2 pints (1⅛ l) water,
if tomatoes are used, only 1½ pint
(850 ccm) of water are needed
6 oz. (170 g) rice

Cut the meat into small ¾ inch cubes (2 cm) and sauté in the melted fat or in the fried diced bacon over a full heat until lightly browned. Add the chopped onion, the prepared and chopped pot vegetables and the sliced tomatoes, and cook together in the fat for a short time. Add the salt, the paprika and the water. Bring to the boil over a full heat, then leave to simmer gently for about 50 minutes over a low heat. Add the washed rice. Bring back to the boil and simmer till done.

Stewing Time: about 90 minutes.

Veal Goulash with Potatoes

2 oz. (55 g) fat or fat bacon
13–18 oz. (375–500 g) veal
1 onion
salt
paprika
2¼ lb. (1 kg) potatoes
¼ pint (140 ccm) water
¼ pint (140 ccm) sour cream

Use the method given in the Basic Recipe (see page 133), adding the sour cream shortly before serving.

Stewing Time: about 1 hour.

Veal Goulash with Rice

2 oz. (55 g) butter or margarine
13–18 oz. (375–500 g) veal
1 onion
9 oz. (250 g) tomatoes (optional)
or 1 tbsp. tomato purée
salt
paprika
2 pints (1⅛ l) water,
if tomatoes are used, only 1½ pint
(850 ccm) of water are needed
6 oz. (170 g) rice

Use the method given in the recipe Veal with Asparagus (see page 136). If tomato purée is used, mix this with water before adding it to the goulash.

Stewing Time: about 1 hour.

Use the method given in the Basic Recipe (see page 133).

Stewing Time: about 1 hour.

Veal Goulash with Vegetables

2 oz. (55 g) butter or margarine
13–18 oz. (375–500 g) veal
1 onion
9 oz. (250 g) tomatoes
salt
1⅛ lb. (500 g) French beans
1⅛ lb. (500 g) potatoes
just under ½ pint (285 ccm) water

Use the method given in the Basic Recipe (see page 133). Add the wine, cider or sour cream just before serving.

Stewing Time: about 1½ hours.

Szegediner Goulash
(Pork with Sauerkraut)

13–18 oz. (375–500 g) pork
1 oz. (30 g) fat (optional)
2 onions
1⅛ lb. (500 g) tomatoes
1⅛ lb. (500 g) sauerkraut
salt
paprika
1⅛ lb. (500 g) potatoes
¼ pint (140 ccm) water
¼ pint (140 ccm) wine,
    cider or sour cream

Use the method given in the recipe Veal with Asparagus (see page 136).

Stewing Time: about 1 hour.

Serbian Rice and Meat

1 oz. (30 g) fat
13–18 oz. (375–500 g) pork
1 onion
1⅛ lb. (500 g) tomatoes
salt
paprika
about 1⅓ pint (¾ l) water
5½ oz. (150 g) rice

Use the method given in the Basic Recipe (see page 133).

Stewing Time: about 1¼ hours.

Viennese Cabbage Stew

1 oz. (30 g) fat
13–18 oz. (375–500 g) pork
1 onion
9 oz. (250 g) pot vegetables
salt
pepper
marjoram
garlic
1 lb. 10 oz. (750 g) cabbage
1⅛ lb. (500 g) potatoes
½ pint (285 ccm) water

Mutton Goulash with Turnips

1 oz. (30 g) fat
13–18 oz. (375–500 g) mutton
1 onion
salt
pepper
1 lb. 10 oz. (750 g) turnips
1 ⅛ lb. (500 g) potatoes
1 pint (570 ccm) water

Use the method given in the Basic Recipe (see page 133).

Stewing Time: about 1 ¼ hours.

Mutton with Salsify

1 oz. (30 g) fat
13–18 oz. (375–500 g) mutton
1 onion
salt
pepper
1 lb. 10 oz. (750 g) salsify
1 ⅛ lb. (500 g) potatoes
1 pint (570 ccm) water

Use the method given in the Basic Recipe (see page 133).

Stewing Time: about 1 ¼ hours.

Mutton Pillaw

1 oz. (30 g) fat
13–18 oz. (375–500 g) mutton
2 onions
a piece of celeriac
9 oz. (250 g) tomatoes
salt
paprika
1 ⅓ pint (¾ l) water
5 ½ oz. (150 g) rice

Use the method given in the recipe Veal with Asparagus (see page 136).

Stewing Time: 1 hour.

C. ONE-COURSE DISHES BAKED IN THE OVEN (Pies and Casseroles)

VEGETABLES

In recent years vegetables have come to be considered one of the most valuable items in our diet by virtue of their many body-building and health-giving properties. Formerly ranked far below meat, eggs, and cereals because of their low calorific value, vegetables are now known to contain vitamins and minerals absolutely vital to good health, and are rightly regarded as an extremely important food.

The high water content of vegetables is alone proof of their low heat-producing value. Most vegetables are 80–85% water, and contain less than 1% fat. Therefore fat must be added to a meal of vegetables in order to make it satisfying. Some vegetables, notably green peas, Brussels sprouts, and green cabbage, contain protein, but the majority of vegetables have very little of this substance. Neither do they have much carbohydrate, although this is found in peas, kale, and Brussels sprouts.

Root vegetables, such as young carrots have the highest sugar content. Cellulose, which forms the chief part of all plants, is a substance extremely conducive to the digestion.

Sunlight develops in the growing vegetable valuable minerals and vitamins, which are then stored in the roots, leaves, tubers and fruits. That is why vegetables should be an essential item in a well-balanced meal. We eat the vegetables, and so absorb this stored goodness. But even the best cooking method will result in some loss of vitamins and minerals. It is therefore essential to include some raw vegetables in the menu. Children have a sound instinct in this respect. They often prefer raw vegetables – peas and carrots particularly – to cooked. They should be encouraged to eat vegetables raw in this way, as they are by this means getting the maximum good from what they are eating.

So include some raw vegetables in the family menu whenever possible. Always include cooked vegetables, and make sure that in the cooking process you destroy as little as possible of the natural goodness of the vegetables. The old-fashioned method of overcooking vegetables in large quantities of water guarenteed that a good 50% of their food value would be lost. Other habits, such as long soaking as a means of cleansing, or scalding to remove overstrong flavour, lessened the vitamin content of the vegetables considerably. Heavy seasoning and smothering in hot sauce before serving was pretty effective in ensuring that most vegetables, by the time they eventually reached the table, had practically no food value whatsoever.

However well they are cooked, vegetables will have much greater mineral and vitamin content if they are fresh than if they are stale. Use vegetables directly after buying. If you grow your own vegetables, do not gather them until you need them. For most of us this perfection is rarely possible. But we can see to it that we buy only fresh vegetables, and that we buy only enough for a single meal at a time. Storing ruins most vegetables, as with their high water content they wilt very readily. This does not of course apply to root vegetables. Some others – white and red cabbage, for example – can be stored without undue wastage.

Wash vegetables quickly, preferably under running water, just before they are to be cooked. Stalks, roots, or other parts should never be thrown away, as they can be used for stocks or sauces. Many vegetables, nutriments and minerals are soluble in water, so avoid soaking vegetables for any length of time, especially after they are cut up, as valuable nutriment, e.g. mineral salts is wasted. The only exception to this rule is cauliflower, which must be soaked in salted water to remove insects and caterpillars which would not be released otherwise.

142

Rice Ring Recipe See Page 241

Boiling vegetables can be even more wasteful than soaking them, because of the great loss of vitamins and mineral salts into the water which is often poured away afterwards.

Unfortunately this habit still prevails in many households today. So use only a little water when cooking vegetables, and use that little, whenever possible, as a basis for a stock or a sauce. If you find the flavour of certain vegetables a little too strong, lessen it not by scalding, but by lifting the lid of the pan for a short time, or by wiping the condensation from the lid fairly frequently during cooking.

The cooking period for all vegetables should be as short as possible. It is advisable to cook them covered. The steam from the water within the vegetables, plus a small addition of fluid, keeps the vegetables from burning if the heat is kept low after the first few minutes of cooking. Asparagus and cauliflower should be cooked in a steamer. This method helps to retain their nutritive value. Vegetables cooked in this way need very little additional seasoning, and their natural flavour is preserved.

A. RAW VEGETABLES

1. Raw vegetables must be washed carefully. Remove any withered or indigestible parts.

General Hints

2. Firm vegetables are best washed under running water. In order to prevent infection, leaf and cabbage-like vegetables should be laid in lukewarm, well salted water for 10 minutes. Rinse well afterwards.

3. Vegetables are cut up roughly or finely according to their nature and their digestibility. Use a knife or a vegetable grater.

4. Grate and prepare the vegetables shortly before the meal.

5. The grated vegetables can be mixed with a simple salad dressing or a cream dressing or a mayonnaise.

6. The taste can be varied in many ways by the addition of herbs, onion, garlic etc.

7. Fresh vegetables should be served attractively. When arranging a plate of varied fresh vegetables, the different tastes and colours should be combined aesthetically.

Cauliflower, Raw

Prepare the cauliflower and wash it thoroughly. Grate it, then mix it with one of the suggested dressings or the mayonnaise. Garnish with tomatoes, lettuce salad or radishes.

1 small cauliflower
Dressing for Raw Vegetables
  (see page 57),
    or Cream Dressing (see page 58)
    or Mayonnaise I (see page 59)

145

Brawn Recipe See Page 102

Pork Cutlet in Aspic Recipe See Page 101

Fresh Peas, Raw

11 oz. (310 g) fresh tender peas,
with pods 2¼ lb. (1 kg)
Dressing for Raw Vegetables
(see page 57)

Shell the peas, wash and drain. Mix with the dressing.

Kohlrabi, Raw

About ¾ lb. (340 g) Kohlrabi, as young
and tender as possible
Dressing for Raw Vegetables
(see page 57)

Peel, wash and grate the Kohlrabi and mix with the dressing.

Young Carrots, Raw

14 oz. (400 g) carrots
Dressing for Raw Vegetables
(see page 57)
or Mayonnaise I (see page 59)

Wash the carrots thoroughly, grate and mix with the dressing or mayonnaise. Stir in a little sugar. If desired, 1 or 2 sour apples, grated, or a grated radish or a chopped pickled gherkin may be added to the sauce.

Green Pepper Salad

About 9 oz. (250 g) green peppers
Salad Dressing:
3 tbsp. salad oil
1–2 tbsp. lemon juice or vinegar
pinch of salt
pinch of sugar
1 onion

Wash the green peppers, remove the stem, the seeds and the white tissue, then cut into thin strips. Whisk together the oil and the lemon juice or vinegar with salt and sugar until the mixture is thick and creamy. Stir in the finely chopped onion and the pepper strips.

Sliced tomatoes may be added to the salad.

Brussels Sprouts, Raw

About ¾ lb. (340 g) Brussels sprouts
Mayonnaise I (see page 59)

Remove the outer leaves, wash the sprouts thoroughly and chop them finely. Mix with the mayonnaise. Sprouts and mayonnaise are delicious mixed with grated raw carrots.

Beetroot, Raw

About ¾ lb. (340 g) beetroot
grated horseradish
1 Chinese radish or sour apple
Dressing for Raw Vegetables
(see page 57)
or Mayonnaise I (see page 59)

Scrub the beetroot thoroughly under running water. Peel, grate and mix with the other ingredients and the dressing or mayonnaise.

Sauerkraut, Raw

About ¾ lb. (340 g) sauerkraut
3 tbsp. oil
2–3 onions
some caraway seeds

The sauerkraut should not be washed. Loosen it with a fork and cut it finely. Heat the oil and pour it over the sauerkraut, then add the grated or finely chopped onions and the caraway seeds.

The sauerkraut may be served with mayonnaise, or with 2 grated raw apples, grated horseradish and sour cream.

Scrub the celeriac thoroughly under running water. Peel, grate and mix with the dressing or mayonnaise. Grated celeriac, mixed with apples, carrots or tomatoes makes a very tasty dish.

Celeriac, Raw

About ¾ lb. (340 g) celeriac
Dressing for Raw Vegetables
   (see page 57)
   or Mayonnaise I (see page 59)

B. BOILED VEGETABLES (Phot. See Page 161)

General Hints

1. Boiling vegetables in water should be avoided, as their flavour and nutritive value will be lost. Steam them, or cook them, first shaking in hot fat (sweating) and then add a little water.

2. If the vegetables must be boiled, use the cooking liquid for soups and sauces as it is full of flavour and vitamins.

3. Salt the water before the vegetables are added, as this makes the water less liable to draw out the goodness from the vegetables.

4. To boil vegetables, bring the prescribed amount of water to the boil on a full heat. Then add the prepared vegetables and close the lid firmly. As soon as the water boils again, turn down the heat so that the vegetables cook in the steam rather than in the water. For this reason the lid should not be removed from the pan during cooking, as the steam would escape and the low heat would not be sufficient to finish the cooking.

5. As soon as the vegetables are done, take them out of the saucepan with a skimming ladle and drain well. If you do not take this precaution the sauce may become too thin.

Cauliflower

1 cauliflower
½–1 pint (285–570) ccm water
1 tsp. salt
3 oz. (85 g) butter or
Sauce Hollandaise:
1½ oz. (45 g) butter or margarine
1½ oz. (45 g) plain flour
1 pint (570 ccm) cooking liquid from
   the cauliflower
1–2 tbsp. lemon juice
pinch of salt
1 egg yolk and 2 tbsp. cold water

Choose a firm white cauliflower, remove the leaves and blemishes and trim, cutting off the hard of the stem. Then wash thoroughly under running water. Soak the cauliflower in cold salted water for about 15 minutes to remove caterpillars and insects. Put the cauliflower head up into the boiling salted water, and cook covered until done. Take 1 pint (570 ccm) of the cooking liquid to make the sauce.

For the sauce, melt the fat, add the flour and heat until pale yellow. Stirring all the time, gradually add the warm cooking liquid and leave to cook for about 10 minutes. Season the sauce with lemon juice and salt. Enrich with the egg yolk beaten in the water.

Cooking Time: 25–30 minutes.

Serve the cauliflower either with the sauce Hollandaise or with melted or brown butter.

Beetroot

2 beetroots, weighing about
2¼ lb. (1 kg)
2 pints (1⅛ l) water
1 tsp. salt

White Sauce:
1½ oz. (45 g) butter or margarine
1½ oz. (45 g) plain flour
1 pint (570 ccm) water or stock
salt
lemon juice

Cut off the roots and the leaves, leaving about 1 inch (2½ cm) of both to prevent loss of juice and colour. Scrub thoroughly under running water. Put into the boiling salted water and cook until tender. Then take the beetroot out of the cooking liquid and pour some cold water over them, so that they can be skinned easily. Peel while still warm and dice or slice.

For the sauce, melt the fat, add the flour and cook until light yellow. Stirring all the time, gradually add the water or stock and simmer for about 10 minutes. Season with salt and lemon juice and pour over the beetroot.

Cooking Time: 1–1½ hours

Chicory

6 heads of chicory
3½ pints (2 l) water
salt

Sauce:
3 oz. (85 g) butter or margarine
1 heaped tbsp. plain flour
¼ pint (140 ccm) water or stock
salt
pepper
pinch of nutmeg
2 tbsp. sour cream (optional)

Remove the outer leaves if necessary and wedge out the stem. Wash and put into the boiling, slightly salted water. Boil gently for 5 minutes, then strain the chicory and cut into thin strips.

For the sauce, melt the fat, add the flour and cook until light brown. Add the water or stock and bring to the boil, stirring all the time. Add the chicory and leave to simmer for about 15 minutes. Season with salt, pepper and nutmeg. If a little sour cream is added before serving it will take away some of the bitter taste.

Time: about 20 minutes.

Salsify

1 lb. 10 oz. (750 g) salsify
1½ pint (850 ccm) water
1 tsp. salt
2 tbsp. vinegar or lemon juice

White Sauce:
1½ oz. (45 g) butter or margarine
1½ oz. (45 g) plain flour
¾ pint (425 ccm) cooking liquid
¼ pint (140 ccm) milk
salt

Scrub the salsify thoroughly under running water. Scrape and wash briefly. Put immediately into cold water, mixed with 1–2 tbsp. vinegar and 1 tbsp. flour. This will keep the sticks white. Bring the 1½ pint (850 ccm) water to the boil with the salt and the 2 tbsp. of vinegar or lemon juice. Add the salsify, cut into pieces. As soon as they are tender, remove them with a skimming ladle. Use about ¾ pint (425 ccm) of the cooking liquid to make the sauce.

For the sauce, melt the fat, add the flour and cook until pale yellow. Stirring all the time, gradually add the warm cooking liquid and the milk and leave to boil for about 10 minutes. Season with salt and add the salsify.

Cooking Time: 50–60 minutes.

Scrub the celeriac carefully under running water, put into the boiling salted water (to which the vinegar has been added) and cook until tender. Remove the celeriac from the water and pour over some cold water to make the peeling easier. Peel while still warm and cut into slices or cubes.

To make the sauce, melt the fat, add the flour and cook until pale yellow. Stirring all the time, gradually add 1 pint (570 ccm) of cold water or stock and leave to cook for about 10 minutes. Season with salt and lemon juice and add the celeriac.

Cooking Time: 1–2 hours.

If preferred, the celeriac may be peeled and diced or cut into slices before cooking. Put the pieces, which should weigh about 1⅛ lb. (500 g) into ½ pint (285 ccm) of boiling salted water with 1 tbsp. of vinegar and cook until tender. Use the cooking liquid for the sauce.

Cooking Time: 20–25 minutes.

Celeriac

2–3 celeriac, weighing about
    2¼ lb. (1 kg)
2 pints (1⅛ l) water
1 tsp. salt
2–3 tbsp. vinegar

White Sauce:

1½ oz. (45 g) butter or margarine
1½ oz. (45 g) plain flour
1 pint (570 ccm) water or stock
salt
a little lemon juice

The asparagus should be white, break easily and be juicy where it is broken. Peel it with downward strokes and remove any coarse parts, taking care not to damage the tips. Cut away the woody ends and cut the stalks into equal lengths. Tie the asparagus sticks into bundles of about eight and put carefully into the boiling water, to which the salt and sugar have been added. Cook until done, then take out carefully with a skimming ladle; lay in a flat dish and untie the bundles. Serve with melted or brown butter in which the breadcrumbs have been fried.

Alternatively, the asparagus may be served with sauce Hollandaise, which is made as follows: melt the fat, add the flour and cook until pale yellow; stirring all the time, gradually add the warm cooking liquid and leave to boil for about 10 minutes. Season with lemon juice and salt and enrich with the egg yolk beaten in the water. Add the butter. Sprinkle the asparagus with chopped parsley and serve the sauce separately.

Cooking Time: asparagus, about 30 minutes;
              sauce Hollandaise, about 10 minutes.

Boiled ham, Fried Veal Slices (Wiener Schnitzel) (see page 99) or Cutlets (see page 98) go very well with asparagus.

Asparagus

2¼ lb. (1 kg) asparagus
1¾ pint (1 l) water
1 tsp. salt
pinch of sugar
3 oz. (85 g) butter
1 tbsp. breadcrumbs

or

Sauce Hollandaise:

1½ oz. (45 g) butter or margarine
1½ oz. (45 g) plain flour
1 pint (570 ccm) cooking liquid
1–2 tbsp. lemon juice
salt
1 egg yolk
2 tbsp. cold water
1 oz. (30 g) butter

Asparagus, Pieces

1¾ lb. (800 g) asparagus
1⅓ pint (¾ l) water
1 tsp. salt
pinch of sugar

White Sauce:

1 oz. (30 g) butter or margarine
¾ oz. (20 g) plain flour
½ pint (285 ccm) cooking liquid
a little lemon juice
salt
1 egg yolk and
1 tbsp. cold water

The asparagus should be white, break easily and be juicy where it is broken. Peel it with downward strokes and remove any coarse parts, taking care not to damage the tips. Cut into pieces about 1½ inch (4 cm) long.

Put the asparagus pieces into the boiling water, to which salt and sugar have been added. Cook until done, then take out carefully with a skimming ladle. Use about ½ pint (285 ccm) of the cooking liquid for the sauce.

For the sauce, melt the fat, add the flour and cook until pale yellow. Stirring all the time, gradually add the warm cooking liquid and leave to boil for about 10 minutes. Season with lemon juice and salt. Enrich with the egg yolk beaten in the water. Put the asparagus pieces into the sauce and serve.

Cooking Time: 30–40 minutes.

C. SWEATED VEGETABLES

General Hints

1. Heat the prepared vegetables in fat, add a little water and cook in a covered saucepan over a low heat until done. Some vegetables, such as spinach, do not require any water.

2. The cooking period for vegetables should be as short as possible, as much of their food value is lost through prolonged cooking.

3. Before serving, add a little Oetker GUSTIN (corn starch powder) to any cooking liquid there may be left in the saucepan.

4. Herbs are a delicious addition, but should never be cooked with the vegetables. They should be added before serving.

Fresh Peas

1 lb. 10 oz. (750 g) peas,
with pods about 4½ lb. (2 kg)
1½ oz. (45 g) butter or margarine
¼ pint (140 ccm) water
salt
sugar
1 tbsp. chopped parsley

Shell the peas, then heat them in the melted fat for a minute or two. Add the water and cook gently until done. Season with salt and sugar and serve with the parsley.

Cooking Time: 15–20 minutes.

Scrape and wash the carrots. If they are young, leave them whole; otherwise cut them into slices or strips. Heat the carrots in the melted fat for a short time, add the water and cook for about 10–15 minutes. Then add the peas and cook until done. Season with salt and sugar, then thicken the cooking liquid with the GUSTIN, blended with the water. Sprinkle with the parsley and serve.

Cooking Time: 20–30 minutes.

Peas and Carrots

1⅛ lb. (500 g) carrots
1½ oz. (45 g) butter or margarine
¼ pint (140 ccm) water
9 oz. (250 g) peas,
    with pods 1 lb. 10 oz. (750 g)
salt
sugar
1 tsp. Oetker GUSTIN
    (corn starch powder)
1 tbsp. cold water
1 tbsp. chopped parsley

Either runner or French beans are suitable for this recipe. String, wash and chop or break the beans.

Melt the fat and fry the finely chopped onion until pale yellow. Add the beans and the savory and heat for a little while. Add the water and cook gently until done. Season with salt and thicken the cooking liquid with the GUSTIN, blended with the water. Serve with the parsley.

Cooking Time: 30–40 minutes.

If desired, about 9 oz. (250 g) of sliced tomatoes may be cooked with the beans for about 10 minutes.

French Beans

1¾ lb. (800 g) beans
1½ oz. (45 g) fat
1 small onion
a sprig of savory
¼ pint (140 ccm) water
salt
1 tsp. Oetker GUSTIN
    (corn starch powder)
1 tbsp. cold water
1 tbsp. chopped parsley

Hull the beans and heat them for a few minutes in the butter or in the diced fried bacon. Add the savory and the water and cook gently until done. Season with salt and thicken with the GUSTIN, blended with the water. Sprinkle with the parsley.

Cooking Time: 30–40 minutes.

Broad Beans

1 lb. 10 oz. (750 g) young broad beans,
    with pods 6½ lb. (3 kg)
1½ oz. (45 g) butter, margarine
    or 2 oz. (55 g) fat bacon
a sprig of savory
¼ pint (140 ccm) water
salt
1–2 tsp. Oetker GUSTIN
    (corn starch powder)
1 tbsp. cold water
1 tbsp. chopped parsley

Kale tastes best when slightly frosted. Strip it from its stalks, then weigh it and wash it thoroughly. Chop it either finely or coarsely. Melt the fat, add the diced onion and fry until pale yellow. Add the kale and cook for a short time. Add the water and the oats. Cook until done and season with salt.

Cooking Time: about 1½ hours.

Kale

1 lb. 10 oz. (750 g) prepared kale
4 oz. (115 g) lard or goose dripping
2 small onions
⅔ pint (375 ccm) water
2 tbsp. oats
salt

Cucumbers

3–4 medium-sized cucumbers,
weighing about 1⅛ lb. (500 g)
1–2 tomatoes
1½ oz. (45 g) butter or margarine,
or 2 oz. (55 g) fat bacon
1 onion
¼ pint (140 ccm) water
salt
1 tbsp. lemon juice
a little sugar
1 slightly heaped tbsp. Oetker GUSTIN
(corn starch powder)
1 tbsp. cold water
1 tbsp. chopped parsley,
dill or chervil

Cut off the ends of the cucumbers and taste to see if they are bitter. If this is the case, continue cutting away until no longer bitter. Then peel the cucumbers and cut into half lengthwise. Remove the seeds with a spoon and cut into 1 inch (2½ cm) pieces. Skin the tomatoes and cut into small pieces.

Melt the fat, or fry the bacon and strain, to remove crisp brown pieces, before adding the cucumber and tomatoes. Cook for a few minutes. Add the water and cook until done. Season with salt, lemon juice and sugar. Thicken the cooking liquid with the GUSTIN, blended with the water. Add the herbs. Sprinkle the dish with the crisp pieces of bacon.

If desired, the cucumbers may be cooked in a Brown Sauce (see page 55), or prepared as Small Turnips (see page 156).

Cooking Time: about 20 minutes.

Chestnuts

2¼ lb. (1 kg) chestnuts
1½ oz. (45 g) butter or margarine
2 heaped tsp. sugar
¼–½ pint (140–285 ccm) water
salt
1 tbsp. lemon juice
1 tsp. Oetker GUSTIN
(corn starch powder)
1 tbsp. cold water

Shell the chestnuts, then scald with boiling water. This will make it easier to remove the inner skin. Keep the chestnuts hot to skin them. Melt the fat, add the sugar and brown. Add the chestnuts and cook for a short time, then add the water and simmer until done. Season with salt and lemon juice. Thicken the cooking liquid with the GUSTIN, blended with the water.

Cooking Time: about 40 minutes.

Alternatively, the GUSTIN may be blended with 2–3 tbsp. of Madeira or red wine.

Kohlrabi

2¼ lb. (1 kg) Kohlrabi
1½ oz. (45 g) butter or margarine
¼ pint (140 ccm) water
salt
1 tsp. Oetker GUSTIN
(corn starch powder)
1 tbsp. cold water
1 tbsp. chopped parsley

Peel the Kohlrabi, wash and cut into slices or strips. Chop up the tender leaves and either prepare them separately like spinach, or cook with the Kohlrabi. Melt the fat, add the sliced vegetable, with or without the leaves, then add the water and simmer until done. Season with salt, thicken the cooking liquid with the GUSTIN, blended with the water and serve, sprinkled with the parsley. If the leaves have been cooked separately, place them in a ring round the vegetable.

Cooking Time: 30–60 minutes.

If preferred, the sliced Kohlrabi may be cooked in 1 pint (570 ccm) of water and then served in a White Sauce (see page 49).

This is an excellent dish, as long as the vegetables are young and fresh. Scrape and wash the carrots, but do not slice. Peel the asparagus carefully, then cut it into pieces. Peel the Kohlrabi and slice. Divide the cauliflower into flowerets and wash the vegetables carefully Melt the fat and cook the vegetables in it for a short time. Add the water and cook until done. Season with salt and sugar. Thicken the cooking liquid with the GUSTIN, blended with the water. Serve the "Leipziger Allerlei" sprinkled with the parsley.

Cooking Time: about 30 minutes.

The vegetables will look much more attractive if they are steamed separately, then tossed in melted butter. A ring of Bread Dumplings (see page 44) makes a delicious garnish.

(see page 44)

"Leipziger Allerlei"

5 oz. (140 g) fresh peas,
with pods 14 oz. (400 g)
5 oz. (140 g) carrots
5 oz. (140 g) asparagus
1 Kohlrabi
1 small cauliflower
1½ oz. (45 g) butter or margarine
¼ pint (140 ccm) water
salt
sugar
1 tsp. Oetker GUSTIN
(corn starch powder)
1 tbsp. cold water
1 tbsp. chopped parsley

Remove the outer leaves, cut the cabbage into 8 sections, remove the hard core and wash. Shred or cut into strips. Fry the diced bacon or melt the lard, add the cabbage and cook for a short time. Add the peeled and finely sliced apples, the water and the caraway seeds. Simmer until done. Season to taste with vinegar, sugar and salt. Thicken the cooking liquid with the GUSTIN, blended with the water.

Cooking Time: about 60 minutes.

Savoury Cabbage

2¼ lb. (1 kg) cabbage
3½ oz. (100 g) fat bacon
or lard
2 apples
½ pint (285 ccm) water
1 tsp. caraway seeds
about 2 tbsp. vinegar
sugar
salt
1 tsp. Oetker GUSTIN
(corn starch powder)
1 tbsp. cold water

Scrape and wash the carrots. Small young carrots may be left whole, others should be diced or cut into strips. Melt the fat, add the carrots and cook for a short time. Add the water and cook the carrots until done. Season with salt and sugar, thicken the cooking liquid with the GUSTIN, blended with the water and serve sprinkled with the parsley.

Cooking Time: young carrots, about 25 minutes;
old carrots, about 60 minutes.

Carrots

1¾ lb. (800 g) carrots
1½ oz. (45 g) butter or margarine,
or fat skimmed from stock
¼ pint (140 ccm) water
salt
sugar
1 tsp. Oetker GUSTIN
(corn starch powder)
1 tbsp. cold water
1 tbsp. chopped parsley

Green Peppers

8 oz. (225 g) green peppers
8 oz. (225 g) tomatoes
8 oz. (225 g) cucumbers
2 oz. (55 g) butter or margarine,
or 3 tbsp. oil
salt
sugar
2 slightly heaped tsp. Oetker GUSTIN
(corn starch powder)
2 tbsp. cold water
about 1 tbsp. vinegar

Wash the peppers, remove the seeds and the white membranes and cut the cases into thin strips. Wash and chop the tomatoes. Peel and slice the cucumber. Melt the fat, add the peppers, tomatoes and cucumbers, season with salt and sugar and simmer in a covered saucepan until done. As soon as the vegetables are cooked, thicken the liquid with the GUSTIN, blended with the water. Season with salt, sugar and vinegar.

Cooking Time: about 30 minutes.

Mushrooms

2¼ lb. (1 kg) mushrooms
1½ oz. (45 g) butter or margarine,
or fat bacon
1 onion
salt
pepper
1–2 tsp. Oetker GUSTIN
(corn starch powder)
1 tbsp. cold water
1 tbsp. chopped parsley

If the mushrooms are very large, remove the lamellae and the cap-skins and wash. Small mushrooms need only be scraped and then washed. Slice the mushrooms vertically to retain their shape and remove all blemishes. Melt the fat, or the diced bacon, and fry the finely chopped onion until pale yellow, then add the mushrooms and cook until done. Season with salt and pepper and thicken the cooking liquid with the GUSTIN, blended with the water.
Serve sprinkled with the parsley.

Cooking Time: 20–30 minutes.

If preferred, the GUSTIN may be blended with 1–2 tbsp. sour cream instead of the water.

Leek

1¾ lb. (800 g) leeks
1½ oz. (45 g) butter or margarine
¼ pint (140 ccm) water or stock
salt
nutmeg
2 tsp. Oetker GUSTIN
(corn starch powder)
1 tbsp. cold water
1 tbsp. chopped parsley

Cut off the roots, the wilted and hard leaves, wash thoroughly and cut into 2 inches (5 cm) lengths. Melt the fat, add the leeks and cook for a few minutes. Add the water and cook until done. Season with salt and nutmeg and thicken the cooking liquid with the GUSTIN, blended with the water.
Serve sprinkled with the parsley.

Cooking Time: about 30 minutes.

Red Cabbage

2¼ lb. (1 kg) red cabbage
4 oz. (115 g) fat, lard or goose
dripping
1 large onion
a bay-leaf

Remove the coarse outer leaves, cut into four sections, remove the hard core, wash and shred finely. Melt the fat, add the diced onion and fry until pale yellow. Add the cabbage and cook for a short time. Add the bay-leaf and cloves, the salt, vinegar, water and the sliced apples. Cook until tender. Season to taste with sugar and salt and thicken the cooking liquid with the GUSTIN, blended with the water.

Cooking Time: 1–1½ hours.

Alternatively, white or red wine may be used instead of water and 1 tbsp. of redcurrant jelly may be cooked with the cabbage.

some cloves (optional)
salt
2 tbsp. vinegar
¼ pint (140 ccm) water
3–4 sour apples
sugar
salt
1 tsp. Oetker GUSTIN
   (corn starch powder)
1 tbsp. cold water

Sauerkraut with Ham Shank

Place the ham shank in a saucepan with the water, bring to the boil and allow to simmer for about 1½ hours. Put the sauerkraut in the cooking liquid under the ham shank. Do not wash the sauerkraut or a lot of its nutritive value will be lost. Bring again to the boil and allow to simmer for another hour over a low heat. Thicken the liquid with the grated potato, bring to the boil and season with salt and sugar.

Cooking Time: about 2½ hours.

Serve with a purée of dried peas or mashed potatoes.

1½ lb. (680 g) ham shank
1 pint (570 ccm) water
1½ lb. (680 g) sauerkraut
1 raw potato
a little salt, if required
a pinch of sugar

Sauerkraut

Do not wash the sauerkraut, or food value will be lost. Melt the fat, fry the chopped onions until pale yellow, then add the sauerkraut and cook for a few minutes. Add the water and cook until done. Thicken the cooking liquid with the grated raw potato and cook briefly. Season with salt and sugar.

Cooking Time: about 1 hour.

Alternatively, 2 apples may be cooked with the sauerkraut, or use ¼ pint (140 ccm) white wine mixed with ¼ pint (140 ccm) water instead of ½ pint (285 ccm) water.

1¾ lb. (800 g) sauerkraut
2 oz. (55 g) lard
2 onions
½ pint (285 ccm) water
1 raw potato
salt
sugar

Spinach

Pick over the spinach carefully and wash well in several waters until it is free from sand and soil. Bring to the boil, without additional water, over a moderate heat. Then cut up, or mince. Melt the fat, fry the chopped onion until pale yellow, add the spinach and a little salt and simmer gently for about 10 minutes. If necessary, thicken with the GUSTIN, blended with the water. If desired, add some tinned milk.

If the spinach is bitter, pour off the cooking liquid and add as much milk as the spinach will absorb.

Cooking Time: about 10 minutes.

2¼ lb. (1 kg) spinach
1½ oz. (45 g) butter or margarine
1 small onion
salt
1 tsp. Oetker GUSTIN
   (corn starch powder)
1 tbsp. cold water
if desired, a little tinned milk

Swiss Chard

Follow the recipe for Spinach (see page 155) for the leaves. The middle ribs may be cooked separately, like asparagus, or cooked in salted water until tender. Serve with melted butter or with Sauce Hollandaise (see page 52) to which 1 tbsp. of grated cheese has been added.

Asparagus
(Cooked In The Oven)

3¼ lb. (1½ kg) asparagus
⅔ pint (375 ccm) water
salt
sugar

Cut off the woody ends of the asparagus, peel carefully and put into a casserole. Add the water, seasoned with salt and sugar, and cover with wet greaseproof paper. Place the casserole low in the oven.

Oven: moderate heat.

Time: about 1 hour.

Turnips

2¼ lb. (1 kg) turnips
2 oz. (55 g) fat,
preferably mutton fat
pinch of sugar (optional)
½ pint (285 ccm) water
salt
1 tsp. Oetker GUSTIN
(corn starch powder)
1 tbsp. cold water

Peel the turnips, cut into pieces about 1½ inch (4 cm) long and as thick as a little finger. Melt the fat, brown the sugar in it, add the turnips and cook for a short time. Add the water and cook until tender. Season with salt and thicken with the GUSTIN, blended with the water.

Cooking Time: 1–1½ hours.

Brussels Sprouts

1¾ lb. (800 g) Brussels sprouts
1½ oz. (45 g) butter or margarine
¼ pint (140 ccm) water
salt
nutmeg
1 tsp. Oetker GUSTIN
(corn starch powder)
1 tbsp. cold water

Remove all discoloured and wilted leaves, cut off tough part of stalk and wash. Melt the fat, add the sprouts and cook for a short time. Add the water and simmer until done. Season with salt and nutmeg and thicken the cooking liquid with the GUSTIN, blended with the water.

Cooking Time: about 30 minutes.

If preferred, the sprouts may be steamed or cooked in salted water until tender and then tossed in melted butter before serving.

Small Turnips
(Teltower Rübchen)

1¾ lb. (800 g) small turnips
1½ oz. (45 g) butter or margarine
pinch of sugar
¼ pint (140 ccm) water
salt
1 tsp. Oetker GUSTIN
(corn starch powder)
1 tbsp. cold water

Carefully scrape and wash the turnips. Brown the sugar in the melted fat, add the whole turnips and cook for a short time. Add the water and cook the turnips until tender. Season with salt before serving and thicken with the GUSTIN, blended with the water.

Cooking Time: about 1 hour.

Wash the tomatoes, dry with a cloth, cut a shallow cross in the skin and place in a flat saucepan in which the fat has been melted. Sweat gently, season with salt, sprinkle with the parsley and serve.

Cooking Time: 10–20 minutes.

Tomatoes

About 1½ lb. (680 g) tomatoes
1½ oz. (45 g) butter or margarine
salt
1 tbsp. chopped parsley

Remove the coarse and discoloured outer leaves, divide into 8 sections and cut out the stem. Wash the cabbage and cut up coarsely. Melt the fat and fry the chopped onion until pale yellow. Add the cabbage and the caraway seeds and cook for a short time. Add the water and cook until the cabbage is tender. Season with salt and thicken with the GUSTIN, blended with the water.

Cooking Time: young cabbage, about 50 minutes; old cabbage 60–90 minutes.

Cabbage

2¼ lb. (1 kg) cabbage
3 oz. (85 g) fat, mutton fat or
   dripping
1 onion
1 tsp. caraway seeds
¼ pint (140 ccm) water
salt
1 tsp. Oetker GUSTIN
   (corn starch powder)
1 tbsp. cold water

Remove the coarse and discoloured outer leaves, divide into 8 sections and cut out the stem. Wash and cut into small pieces. Melt the fat, fry the chopped onion until pale yellow, add the cabbage and cook for a short time. Add the water and cook the cabbage until done. Season with salt and thicken the cooking liquid with the GUSTIN, blended with the water.

Serve sprinkled with the parsley.

Cooking Time: young cabbage, about 45 minutes; old cabbage 50–90 minutes.

Savoy Cabbage

2¼ lb. (1 kg) Savoy cabbage
3 oz. (85 g) fat
1 onion
¼ pint (140 ccm) water
salt
1 tsp. Oetker GUSTIN
   (corn starch powder)
1 tbsp. cold water
1 tbsp. chopped parsley

Peel and wash the onions and if they are large, slice them; leave small onions whole. Melt the fat, brown the sugar, add the onions and cook for a few minutes. Add the water and cook until tender. Season to taste with lemon juice and salt. Thicken the cooking liquid with the GUSTIN, blended with the water.

Serve sprinkled with the herbs.

Cooking Time: 20–30 minutes.

If preferred, 3–4 halved tomatoes may be added 10 minutes before the onions are cooked.

Onions

1¾ lb. (800 g) onions
1½ oz. (45 g) butter or margarine
pinch of sugar
¼ pint (140 ccm) water
a little lemon juice
salt
1 tsp. Oetker GUSTIN
   (corn starch powder)
1 tbsp. cold water
1–2 tbsp. chopped herbs

D. FRIED VEGETABLES

General Hints

1. Fried vegetable dishes add variety to our menus and are a welcome change, especially in a vegetarian diet.

2. The fried vegetable dish, with its many additional ingredients, can provide substantial nourishment, at the same time offering an attractive means of using up vegetable leftovers.

3 But as many vegetables are not improved by re-heating, it is advisable not to serve such dishes too often.

Vegetables, Deep-Fried in Batter

1⅛ lb. (500 g) vegetables
(salsify, carrots, cauliflower,
Brussels sprouts, Kohlrabi, celeriac,
or firm tomatoes)

Batter:
3 oz. (85 g) plain flour
1 egg
salt
6 tbsp. milk
1 tsp. oil or melted butter
fat for deep-frying

Peel and wash the salsify and cut it into pieces about 2 inches (5 cm) long. Put them into water mixed with vinegar and flour – 2¾ pints (1½ l) water, 1–2 tbsp. vinegar, 1 tbsp. flour — and leave them until they are to be cooked. Peel and slice the Kohlrabi, the celeriac and the washed tomatoes. Break the cauliflower into flowerets, remove the discoloured leaves from the Brussels sprouts and cut off the stalks. Cook the vegetables, except the tomatoes, until almost tender.

For the batter, sieve the flour into a bowl, make a well in the centre and pour in the egg, mixed with a little of the milk and the salt. Working from the middle, blend the egg mixture with the flour, then gradually add the remaining milk and the oil or the melted fat. Continue mixing until the batter is smooth and free from lumps. Drain the vegetables well and, using a fork, dip them into the batter. Heat the fat gently until a very faint blue haze rises. Lower the coated vegetables gently into the fat, which should be deep enough to cover the food generously and cook over a medium heat until golden brown and crisp. Remove from the fat and drain well on a sieve.

Time: about 10 minutes, boiling;
2–5 minutes, deep-frying.

Serve with Mayonnaise (see page 59) or with Rémoulade Sauce (see page 60); very good with lettuce salad or cold roast beef.

Vegetable Croquettes I

1⅛ lb. (500 g) vegetables (cabbage,
Savoy cabbage, Kohlrabi or celeriac)
1 onion
a little butter or margarine
1–2 eggs
2 oz. (55 g) breadcrumbs or
crushed oats
salt
chopped herbs
1½ oz. (45 g) breadcrumbs
2 oz. (55 g) fat for frying

Prepare the vegetables, steam and chop finely or mince. Sauté the finely chopped onion in the butter or margarine and add, with the eggs and the breadcrumbs (crushed oats), to the vegetable mixture. Season with salt and chopped herbs and form into rissoles. Coat in the breadcrumbs and try in the hot fat until golden brown.

Frying Time: 5–10 minutes.

Chop the vegetables finely or rub through a sieve. Mix with the mashed potatoes, the eggs, the salt, the finely chopped onion and as much of the breadcrumbs as will make a smooth mixture. Form into rissoles, coat in the breadcrumbs, and fry in the hot fat.

Frying Time: 10–12 minutes.

Vegetable Croquettes II

(Leftovers)

1 plate of vegetable leftovers
3–4 boiled mashed potatoes
1–2 eggs
salt
1 small onion
1½ oz. (45 g) breadcrumbs
3 oz. (85 g) fat for frying

Prepare the mushrooms; if they are very large, skin them and remove the lamellae, small mushrooms only need scraping. Soak the bread in water, then squeeze out all the liquid. Wash the mushrooms, chop finely and sauté for a short time in the butter or margarine with the finely diced onion. Add the eggs and the bread and season to taste with salt and marjoram. If the mixture is too soft, add some more breadcrumbs. Shape into rissoles, coat in the breadcrumbs and fry in the hot fat till brown and crisp.

Frying Time: 10–12 minutes.

Mushroom Croquettes

8 oz. (225 g) mushrooms
1 oz. (30 g) butter or margarine
1 small onion
1–2 eggs
4 stale rolls or slices of bread
salt
marjoram
about 1½ oz. (45 g) breadcrumbs
about 2 oz. (55 g) fat for frying

Blend the GUSTIN with the cream and bring to the boil on a full heat, stirring all the time. Remove from heat, add the grated cheese and season to taste with salt and paprika.

Toast the white bread and spread with butter. Add the asparagus, cut into pieces, and the diced ham to the cheese-mixture. Mix together.

Spread the slices of bread with this mixture. Place high in the oven.

Oven: very hot.

Baking Time: about 10 minutes.

Toast with Asparagus au Gratin

½ oz. (15 g) Oetker GUSTIN
   (corn starch powder)
¼ pint (140 ccm) fresh cream
2½ oz. (70 g) cheese
salt
paprika
6 slices of white bread about ¾ inch
   (1½ cm) thick
a little butter
4½ oz. (125 g) asparagus, cooked
2½ oz. (70 g) ham, boiled

Vegetable au Gratin

About 1½ lb. (680 g) vegetables
Béchamel Sauce:
1½ oz. (45 g) butter or margarine
2 oz (55 g) gammon
2 oz. (55 g) onions
1½ oz. (45 g) plain flour
½ pint (285 ccm) vegetable stock
½ pint (285 ccm) milk or cream
salt
pepper
2 tbsp. breadcrumbs or grated cheese
a little butter

Use any vegetables available or leftovers. Particularly suitable are cauliflower, Brussels sprouts, asparagus, salsify and Savoy cabbage. Steam the vegetables or boil in salted water until almost tender. Put the vegetables into a greased pie-dish.

For the sauce, melt the butter with the diced gammon, stir in the flour and the finely chopped onions and cook until pale yellow. Stirring all the time, gradually add the lukewarm vegetable stock and the milk or cream, and cook for 10 minutes. Rub the sauce through a fine sieve, then season to taste with salt and pepper. Pour the sauce over the vegetables, sprinkle with the breadcrumbs or cheese and dot with small knobs of butter. Bake in the oven till done.

Oven: moderate heat.

Baking Time: about 25 minutes.

Tomato Sauce (see page 52) or Sauce Hollandaise (see page 52) may be used instead of Béchamel Sauce. If Sauce Hollandaise is used, omit the lemon juice. If desired, Meat or Fish Balls (see page 45), leftovers of gammon, fish, slices of hard-boiled eggs or sliced tomatoes may be added to the dish before baking.

Vegetable Pie

About 1½ lb. (680 g) vegetables
1½ oz. (45 g) butter or margarine
2–3 egg yolks
3 stale rolls or slices of bread
salt
chopped herbs
2–3 egg whites
2 tbsp. breadcrumbs or grated cheese
a little butter

A variety of vegetable is suitable for this dish, though asparagus, celeriac and carrots are especially good. Soak the bread in water, then squeeze out all the liquid. Clean the vegetables, steam and chop finely. Cream the butter or margarine, add the egg yolks, the bread and the vegetables. Season to taste with salt and herbs. Fold in the egg whites, beaten stiff. Fill the mixture into a greased pie-dish, sprinkle with the breadcrumbs or cheese and dot with knobs of butter. Bake in the oven.

Oven: moderate heat.

Baking Time: about 45 minutes.

E. STUFFED VEGETABLES

General Hints

1. Stuffed vegetables make a pleasant change in the daily menu. They may also be used as a delicious and decorative extra to other meat or vegetable dishes.

2. Particularly suitable for stuffing are root vegetables (Kohlrabi, celeriac, potatoes, etc.), vegetables which can be scooped out, such as tomatoes or cucumbers, and the large leaves of Savoy or white cabbage.

160

3. Vegetables may be steamed a little before stuffing, or they may be stuffed raw.

4. Choose vegetables of the same size, so that they all take about the same time to cook.

5. The stuffings need not always be meat; other stuffings are equally delicious and make a welcome change. Some suggestions for such stuffings are offered in the following recipes.

6. Stuffed vegetables, with the exception of stuffed cabbage, should be stewed or braised. They should be browned quickly over a strong heat and then cooked gently at a lower temperature, with just enough water to keep the pan from burning.

Stuffings

1. Meat Stuffing

Soak the bread in water. Mince together the meat, the bacon (if used), the bread (well squeezed) or the potatoes and the onion. Stir in the egg, then season to taste with salt and pepper.

If you are a little short of meat, add to the mixture an extra slice of bread, or finely chopped vegetable leftovers (scooped out centres of celeriac or Kohlrabi).

7–9 oz. (200–250 g) minced beef or pork (or leftovers of any roast meat, venison or poultry)
1–2 oz. (30–55 g) bacon, if the meat is lean
1 stale roll or slice of bread, or 2–3 grated boiled potatoes
1 onion
1 egg
salt
pepper

2. Mushroom Stuffing

Skin and remove the lamellae of very large mushrooms (small ones need only be scraped) and wash them thoroughly. Chop the mushrooms finely and then sauté in the melted fat, together with the finely diced onion. Stir in the beaten egg, seasoning to taste, the parsley and sufficient breadcrumbs to form a smooth paste.

9 oz. (250 g) mushrooms (champignons, boletus, chanterelles)
1 oz. (30 g) butter or margarine
1 onion
1 egg
salt
pepper
chopped parsley
breadcrumbs

3. Breadcrumb Stuffing

Rub the crust from the outside of the rolls or bread, cut it into cubes and pour over it the hot water or milk. When sufficiently soaked, stir in the melted fat and the finely chopped onion. Put into a saucepan and heat until a compact mass forms. Cool, then stir in the egg and the herbs, and season to taste with salt and nutmeg.

2 tbsp. of grated cheese or 1 tbsp. of tomato purée may be added to vary the flavour.

3 stale rolls or slices of bread
just under ½ pint (250 ccm) water or milk
1 oz. (30 g) butter or margarine
1 small onion
1 egg
1 tbsp. chopped herbs
salt
nutmeg

163

Oetker Chocolate Flana (prepare according to the directions on the packet)
Portuguese Cream Recipe See Page 276

4. Rice Stuffing

1 pint (570 ccm) water or stock
salt
a little butter
5 oz. (140 g) rice
curry powder

Bring the liquid with the salt and the butter to the boil. Add the washed rice and cook over a low heat until liquid is absorbed. Season with a pinch of curry powder.

Cooking Time: about 20 minutes.

Alternatively, the rice may be seasoned with grated cheese or tomato purée.

Stuffed Cucumbers
(Phot. See Page 336)

2 large or 4 small cucumbers
salt
a little vinegar
Meat, Mushroom,
or Breadcrumb Stuffing
(see page 163)
3 oz. (85 g) fat bacon
1 small onion
½ pint (285 ccm) water
vinegar
sugar
salt
1 tbsp. Oetker GUSTIN
(corn starch powder)
1 tbsp. of cold water

Peel the cucumbers, cut them in halves lengthwise, scoop out the seeds and rub with salt and vinegar. Fill with one of the suggested stuffings, then tie the two halves together. Cut the bacon into small cubes and brown with the sliced onion. Put in the stuffed cucumbers, add very little water and simmer until tender. Season the liquid with vinegar, sugar and salt and thicken it with the GUSTIN, blended with the water.

Cooking Time: 30–40 minutes.

About 10 minutes before the end of cooking time, about 9 oz. (250 g) of chopped tomatoes may be added. Before serving, rub the sauce through a sieve.

Stuffed Potatoes

12 large potatoes
Meat or Mushroom Stuffing
(see page 163)
3 oz. (85 g) fat
½–1 pint (285–570 ccm) water
salt
1 tbsp. Oetker GUSTIN
(corn starch powder)
2 tbsp. sour milk or sour cream

Choose very large potatoes. Peel and wash them, remove a portion of the top for a lid and carefully scoop out the centres (reserve centres for soup). Fill each potato with stuffing, replace the lid and tie firmly. Heat the fat in a shallow saucepan, put in the potatoes and brown slightly. Add boiling water as required and simmer until done. Season the liquid with salt and thicken with the GUSTIN, blended with the sour milk or cream.

Cooking Time: about 30 minutes.

Stuffed with a meat stuffing, the potatoes may be served with young vegetables; stuffed with a mushroom stuffing, they are delicious with salad. Tomato (see page 52), Caper (see page 50), or Anchovy Sauce (see page 51) are very good with stuffed potatoes.

Peel the Kohlrabi and remove the woody parts. Remove a portion of the top for a lid and carefully scoop out the centre (reserve centres for soup). Fill each with stuffing, replace the lid and tie firmly. Line a shallow saucepan with the bacon or ham slices, put in the Kohlrabi and brown slightly. Add the boiling water as required and simmer until done. Season the liquid with salt and thicken with the GUSTIN, blended with the sour milk or cream.

Cooking Time: about 1 hour.

Tomato (see page 52) or Parsley Sauce (see page 50) are very good with stuffed Kohlrabi.

Stuffed Kohlrabi
(Phot. See Page 336)

8 large Kohlrabi
Meat or Rice Stuffing
(see page 163/164)
3 oz. (85 g) fat bacon or slices of ham
½–1 pint (285–570 ccm) water
salt
1 tbsp. Oetker GUSTIN
(corn starch powder)
2 tbsp. sour milk or sour cream

Wash and dry the peppers. Cut off the tops below the stems and remove the seeds and the white tissues Salt the water, bring it to the boil and add the washed rice. Cook gently until the grain is tender. Leave the rice to cool, then mix with the meat, the finely chopped onion and the egg. Season with salt and pepper, then fill the pepper cases. Remove the stems from the tops and put the tops back onto the peppers as lids.

Melt the fat, add the finely chopped onion and the chopped tomatoes and sauté for a little while. Add the ⅔ pint (375 ccm) water and leave to simmer for a short time. Rub through a fine sieve, bring again to the boil and thicken with the GUSTIN, blended with the ¼ pint (140 ccm) water. Season to taste with salt, lemon juice and sugar. Carefully put the stuffed peppers into the tomato sauce, heat again and simmer until done.

Cooking Time: about 45 minutes.

Stuffed Green Peppers

6 green peppers
½ pint (285 ccm) water
salt
2½ oz. (70 g) rice
13 oz. (375 g) minced beef and pork
1 onion
1 egg
pepper
1 oz. (30 g) butter or margarine
1 small onion
7 oz. (200 g) tomatoes
⅔ pint (375 ccm) water
1¼ oz. (35 g) Oetker GUSTIN
(corn starch powder)
¼ pint (140 ccm) water
salt
a little lemon juice
pinch of sugar

Scrub the celeriacs under running water until clean, then steam or boil them until they are half cooked. Peel, cut off the tops with a sharp knife and carefully cut out the centres (reserve for soup). Fill with the stuffing, put back the tops and tie down if necessary. Line a shallow saucepan with the bacon or ham slices and place the celeriacs side by side in the pan and brown slightly. Add boiling water as required and simmer until done. Season the liquid with salt and thicken it with the GUSTIN, blended with the sour milk or cream.

Cooking Time: about 1 hour.

Stuffed Celeriacs

8 small celeriacs
Meat or Rice Stuffing
(see page 163/164)
3 oz. (85 g) fat, bacon slices or slices of ham
½–1 pint (285–570 ccm) water
salt
1 tbsp. Oetker GUSTIN
(corn starch powder)
2 tbsp. sour milk or sour cream

Stuffed Tomatoes
(Phot. See Page 17)

8–10 large firm tomatoes
any one of the stuffings described on
page 163/164
3 oz. (85 g) butter or margarine
1 slightly heaped tbsp. plain flour
½ pint (285 ccm) water
salt

Wash the tomatoes and dry well with a cloth. Cut off the tops with a sharp knife and scoop out the pulp (reserve for the sauce). Fill with stuffing and put back the tops. Put the tomatoes side by side in a shallow saucepan and sauté gently into the hot fat. Remove the tomatoes from the saucepan, stir in the flour and cook until pale yellow. Stirring all the time, add the boiling water and the strained pulp. Cook for a short time, season with salt and pour over the stuffed tomatoes.

Cooking Time: about 20 minutes.

Stuffed Onions

4–8 large onions
Meat or Bread Stuffing (see page 163)
3 oz. (85 g) butter or margarine
1 level tbsp. sugar
½–1 pint (285–570 ccm) water
1 tbsp. lemon juice
sugar
salt
1–2 tsp. Oetker GUSTIN
(corn starch powder)
1 tbsp. cold water

Peel the onions, scoop out the centres and fill with the stuffing. Brown the sugar in the fat, add the water and place the onions side by side in the pan. Cook until tender. Season the cooking liquid with the lemon juice and with sugar and salt to taste and thicken it with the GUSTIN, blended with the water. 2 tbsp. of Madeira may be added to the sauce.

Cooking Time: about 30 minutes.

Stuffed Head of Cabbage

1 head of cabbage or Savoy cabbage
any one of the stuffings described on
page 163/164
Caper Sauce:
1½ oz. (45 g) butter or margarine
1½ oz. (45 g) plain flour
1 pint (570 ccm) water
1 tbsp. capers
salt
lemon juice

Remove the leaves from the stalk of the cabbage, then pare down the ribs so that the leaves are fairly flat. Put the leaves into boiling salted water and cook until about half done. Grease a basin or mould and line it with the large outer leaves. Fill it with alternate layers of stuffing and cabbage leaves. Cover the top with 1 or 2 large leaves. Cover with a lid and place in a steamer or saucepan containing boiling water to come half-way up the sides of the basin. Cook until done.

The leaves may be cooked in a napkin instead of a basin or mould. Grease the centre of the napkin and cover it with alternate layers of leaves and stuffing. Cross over the corners of the napkin and tie securely. Suspend from a wooden spoon placed across a saucepan containing boiling water. Cook until done.

Cooking Time: about 1 hour.

For the sauce, melt the fat, add the flour and cook until pale yellow. Stirring all the time, gradually add the water and leave to simmer for about 10 minutes. Add the capers, season to taste with salt and lemon juice and serve with the stuffed cabbage.

Alternatively, Tomato (see page 52) or Anchovy Sauce (see page 51) may be served with the cabbage instead of the caper sauce.

Remove the leaves from the stalk of the cabbage, then pare down the ribs so that the leaves are fairly flat. Put the leaves into boiling salted water and cook until half done. Lay 2 or 3 large leaves together, spread with stuffing and roll up. Tie them with thread (previously boiled) or secure with skewers. Heat the fat or the diced bacon, put in the cabbage rolls and brown slightly on all sides. Add water as required and a little gravy, if available. Thicken the cooking liquid with the GUSTIN, blended with the water, season to taste, and pour over the cabbage rolls.

Cooking Time: about 45 minutes.

Alternatively, about 9 oz. (250 g) tomatoes may be added the last 10 minutes of the cooking time. Then rub the liquid through a sieve before it is thickened. This tomato variation is particularly good with cabbage leaves filled with Rice Stuffing (see page 164).

Stuffed Cabbage Leaves
1 head of cabbage or Savoy cabbage
Meat or Rice Stuffing
  (see page 163/164)
3 oz. (85 g) fat or fat bacon
½–1 pint (285–570 ccm) water
left-over gravy
1 tbsp. Oetker GUSTIN
  (corn starch powder)
1 tbsp. cold water
salt

F. DRIED VEGETABLES (Pulse)

Pulse are the dried seeds of peas, beans and lentils. They are very rich in starch and protein, containing about 23–26% of the latter, far more than any other vegetables. In some of them – peas, for instance – there is more protein than in beef although the protein in beef is of a higher biological quality. Pulse are rich, too, in starch, containing almost as much as cereals. Except for the soya bean, pulse contain very little fat, but they do supply phosphorous, sulphur, and the nerve-building lecithin. Pulse are therefore an extremely nourishing food, and their low price makes them a very useful addition to the menu.

If they are to be delicious as well as nourishing, pulse must be properly prepared and cooked. Their coarse texture makes them indigestible, so they must be soaked for at least 12 hours before cooking. Soft water should be used for soaking instead of hard, because it contains less calcium salts which prevent the pulse from becoming soft. If no soft water is available, use boiled water. Cook pulse in the water in which they have been soaked, bringing them to the boil, then simmering until tender, because the starch they contain takes much longer to swell than the starch of cereals. Sieve the pulse when they are cooked, to break down their coarse skins. Pulse will be more digestible if sauerkraut, vinegar, or lemon juice is added to them. Cook pulse with plenty of pot herbs and onions, or potatoes and tomatoes; additions such as these will make up for the lack of minerals and vitamins in the pulse themselves.

General Hints

1. Pick over and thoroughly wash the pulse, then soak them for 12–24 hours before cooking.

2. Soft water is best for soaking, but if not available, use boiled water.

3. Cook the pulse in the liquid in which they have been soaked. Start them off at a high temperature, then turn down the heat and cook gently until tender.

4. It is advisable to rub the pulse through a sieve as the coarse skin is somewhat indigestible.

Purée of Dried Peas

13 oz. (375 g) dried peas
1⅓ pint (¾ l) water
pot vegetables
salt
2 oz. (55 g) diced fat bacon, or 1½ oz. (45 g) butter, or margarine
1 onion

Pick over the peas and wash them thoroughly, then soak them in the water for 12–24 hours. Bring them to the boil in the liquid in which they have been soaked and cook until tender. When the peas have been cooking for about 1½ hours, add the prepared pot vegetables, (leave whole and remove later). When the peas are done, rub through a sieve, then re-heat and whip until frothy. Season to taste and garnish with the sliced onion, fried in the bacon or fat.

Cooking Time: about 2 hours.

Serve with sauerkraut and rib of pork, or pickled meat.

Haricot Beans

11 oz. (300 g) Haricot beans
1⅓ pint (¾ l) water
pot vegetables
2 oz. (55 g) fat bacon or lard
1 onion
¾ oz. (20 g) plain flour
salt
finely chopped parsley

Pick over the beans and wash them thoroughly, then soak them in the water for 12–24 hours. Bring them to the boil in the liquid in which they have been soaked, and cook until tender. Add the prepared pot vegetables (leave whole and remove later), when the beans have been cooking for about 1½ hours. Fry the diced bacon, or melt the lard, then add the finely diced onion; stir in the flour and cook until pale yellow. Add the beans and cook for a little while. Season with salt and serve with the parsley.

Cooking Time: about 2 hours.

Alternatively, season with 1–2 tbsp. of vinegar or lemon juice or add some tomato purée.

Savoury Lentils

13 oz. (375 g) lentils
1⅓ pint (¾ l) water
pot vegetables
2 oz. (55 g) fat bacon or lard
1 onion
¾ oz. (20 g) plain flour
2–3 tbsp. vinegar or lemon juice
salt
sugar

Pick over the lentils and wash them thoroughly, then soak them in the water for 12–24 hours Bring them to the boil in the liquid in which they have been soaked, add the prepared pot vegetables (leave whole and remove later), and cook until tender. Fry the finely diced bacon, or melt the lard, add the finely chopped onion, stir in the flour and brown slightly. Add the lentils and cook for a little while. Season with vinegar or lemon juice, and with salt and sugar.

Cooking Time: 35–40 minutes.

Serve with Frankfurter Sausages.

POTATO DISHES

The potato was first introduced into Europe from South America in the sixteenth century. Since that time it has become more and more widely known and used, and today it is about the most familiar and popular vegetable in the Western world. Cheap and nutritious, with a pleasant, satisfying flavour, the potato is easy to digest, and can be cooked and served in countless different ways, all equally nourishing and delicious.

Except for fat, the potato offers a complete food in itself, containing everything the body needs – as much as 21% starch, as well as protein, minerals, and vitamins. Much of these valuable substances can very easily be lost, however, if the potato is not prepared and cooked in the right way. If potatoes are peeled before cooking, as much as 30% is wasted. They should not be left to soak once they are peeled, as water extracts valuable salts and vitamins. Potatoes should be cooked in their skins. This not only eliminates waste, but helps to retain their nutritive value. Peeled potatoes cooked in unsalted water lose most of the substances essential to nutrition.

The best way to prepare and cook potatoes is to wash them thoroughly and then cook them in their skins, a special steamer or wire basket being ideal for this purpose.

Potatoes prepared in this way have the best flavour and retain all their goodness. Potatoes should be peeled while still hot, and then mashed or sliced. Attractive recipes for preparing a variety of dishes will be found in the following chapter.

Potatoes are an economical vegetable because they can be bought in bulk in the autumn, when they are at their cheapest, and then stored to last through the winter. Always store in a dry and airy place, preferably in one of the special potato containers which has a small opening at the base from which the potatoes may be taken out. This type of container is excellent because it keeps the potatoes moving and so prevents early sprouting. Sort out the potatoes carefully before storing, removing any with blemishes. Rotten or rotting potatoes may infect all the others stored with them. The longer the potatoes are stored, the more they will sprout, and sprouting means they are losing their nutritive value. Within six months of storing as much as 30% of their goodness can be lost in this way, because the process of growth, that is the sprouting, develops in the potato the poisonous substance, solanin. So always remove all sprouts as soon as they appear.

Frost is an enemy of the stored potato. The best storage temperature is from 36°–43° F (2°–6° C). Potatoes which are stored for some time at freezing point tend to develop sugar to an unpleasant degree. The potato cannot absorb this excess sugar, and therefore develops a very strong sweet taste. This taste can be considerably lessened, however, if the potatoes are stored for a while in a temperature of 68°–86° F (20°–30° C).

In late spring avoid unnecessary raking and turning over of the potatoes, as this leads to the development of black spots, loss of taste, and general deterioration in quality.

General Hints 1. Choose potatoes of the same size, so that they will all be done at about the same time.

2. Wash or scrub the potatoes thoroughly to make sure that no dirt penetrates the skin while cooking.

3. It is advisable to steam potatoes rather than to cook them in water. To preserve all their food value, cook them in their skins.

4. To avoid unnecessary waste, peel potatoes thinly.

5. Potatoes quickly become discoloured, so put them in water as soon as they are peeled; but avoid leaving them in water too long before cooking, especially if they are sliced.

6. New potatoes should be put into boiling water; old potatoes are best started in cold water, as this helps the starch to swell slowly.

7. As soon as the potatoes are done, drain them, then leave them to stand for a short time in the uncovered pan over a good heat, shaking them frequently. This will dry them and make them mealy.

A. BOILED AND STEAMED POTATOES

Potatoes in Their Skins

Choose potatoes of the same size, scrub and wash them thoroughly in cold water. Put them into the cold water to which the salt and the caraway seeds have been added and cook until done. Drain and leave to stand for a short time in the uncovered pan over a good heat, shaking them frequently to allow the steam to escape.

2¼ lb. (1 kg) potatoes
2 pints (1⅛ l) water
salt
1 tsp. caraway seeds (optional)

Cooking Time: 20–30 minutes.

Boiled Potatoes

Wash the potatoes and peel them thinly, removing sprouts and blemishes. Then put them in cold water and wash them again. Cut large potatoes into halves or quarters. Peeled potatoes are best steamed, but if boiled in water, use just enough water to cover them, then add the salt and bring to the boil. When they are cooked, drain and leave to stand for a short time in the uncovered pan over a good heat, shaking them frequently to allow the steam to escape. Do not throw away the cooking liquid, but use it for soup or stock.

2¼ lb. (1 kg) potatoes
salt

Cooking Time: about 20 minutes.

Potatoes Boiled in Stock

Peel and wash the potatoes, cut them into cubes and cook in the stock until done. Before serving, season with salt, butter and parsley according to taste.

2¼ lb. (1 kg) potatoes
1 pint (570 ccm) meat or vegetable stock
salt
a knob of butter
1 tbsp. chopped parsley

Cooking Time: about 20 minutes.
Serve with fish, gammon or boiled meat.
Carrots, cut into strips, may be boiled with the potatoes, if desired.

Parsley Potatoes
(Phot. See Page 183)

2¼ lb. (1 kg) potatoes
2 oz. (55 g) butter or margarine
salt
1–2 tbsp. chopped parsley

Choose small potatoes of the same size and boil them in their skins. Peel while still hot, toss well in melted fat and season with salt and the parsley.

New potatoes are excellent cooked in this way.

Cooking Time: 25–30 minutes.

Potatoes with Caraway Seeds
(Dr. Bircher-Benner Recipe)

2¼ lb. (1 kg) small potatoes
caraway seeds
salt
a little melted butter or oil

B. FRIED AND SAUTÉ POTATOES

Wash the potatoes thoroughly, but do not peel. Halve them, dip the cut side in caraway seeds and salt, then place on a greased baking sheet. Brush with melted butter or oil and bake in the oven until done.

Oven: moderate heat.

Time: 30–40 minutes.

These potatoes are delicious with cottage cheese.

Sauté Potatoes

2¼ lb. (1 kg) potatoes
2 oz. (55 g) fat
salt

Choose small potatoes — about the size of plums — and wash them thoroughly. Then boil them in their skins. Peel them as soon as they are done, season with salt and sauté in the hot fat in a frying-pan until evenly browned.

Boiling Time: about 20 minutes.

Frying Time: about 10 minutes.

Sprinkled with a little sugar, these potatoes are a good accompaniment to kale.

Fried Potatoes I

2¼ lb. (1 kg) potatoes
4 oz. (115 g) fat
1 onion
salt

Wash the potatoes thoroughly and boil in their skins. Peel them as soon as they are done. When cold, slice, then fry with the finely chopped onion in the hot fat until browned. Sprinkle with salt.

Boiling Time: 20–30 minutes.

Frying Time: about 10 minutes.
Left-over potatoes may be prepared in this way.

If preferred, some sliced cooking apples or sliced tomatoes may be added, or 2–3 tbsp. sour cream or grated cheese.

Peel the raw potatoes, wash them and cut into slices or strips. Sprinkle with salt, put into a pan with the fried diced bacon or the melted fat, sauté for a while covered, then remove the lid and fry until browned.

Frying Time: 20–30 minutes.

Fried Potatoes II

2¼ lb. (1 kg) potatoes
3 oz. (85 g) fat bacon or other fat
salt

Wash the potatoes thoroughly and boil them in their skins. Peel as soon as they are done, leave to cool and cut into slices. Fry the diced bacon, add the potatoes and cook until browned. Beat the eggs in the milk, add a little salt, the diced gammon and the chives. Pour this over the potatoes, stir, and serve as soon as the egg mixture is firm.

Boiling Time: 20–30 minutes.

Frying Time: about 10 minutes.

Serve with lettuce salad, tomato salad or pickled gherkins.

Peasant's Breakfast

1 lb. 10 oz. (750 g) potatoes
3 oz. (85 g) fat bacon
3 eggs
3 tbsp. milk
salt
5 oz. (140 g) gammon
some finely chopped chives (optional)

Finely dice the meat and the onions. Brown lightly in the hot fat. Peel, wash and slice the potatoes, season with salt and cook until browned. Serve sprinkled with chopped parsley.

Frying Time: about 20 minutes.

Tyrolese Potatoes

3 oz. (85 g) fat
½ lb. (225 g) boiled or roast beef
1–2 onions
2¼ lb. (1 kg) potatoes, boiled in their skins
salt
a little parsley

Wash the potatoes thoroughly and boil in their skins. Peel as soon as they are done, leave to cool, then cut into slices. Fry the diced bacon with the finely chopped onion, add the potatoes and cook until well browned. Beat together the milk, the flour and the eggs, add a little salt and the herbs. Pour this over the potatoes and, without stirring, allow the egg mixture to become firm. As soon as the bottom is brown and the top firm, slip the omelette onto a plate.

Boiling Time: 20–30 minutes.

Frying Time: 10–15 minutes.

Serve with lettuce salad, vegetable marrow, pickled gherkins or beetroot.

Potato Omelette

1⅛ lb. (500 g) potatoes
2 oz. (55 g) fat bacon
1 onion
¼ pint (140 ccm) milk
1 level tbsp. plain flour
2 eggs
salt
finely chopped parsley and chives

Pommes Frites

1 lb. 10 oz. (750 g) potatoes
fat for frying (dripping or vegetable oil)
salt

Peel the potatoes, wash them and cut into lengthwise strips ¼ inch (½ cm) thick. Dry well in a linen cloth, then drop into the hot fat. Deep fry until half done. Fry only a small quantity at a time, otherwise you will reduce the temperature of the fat. As soon as the tips become yellow, take the potatoes out of the fat with a skimming ladle and put them into a colander or on absorbant paper to drain. When they are cool, return them to the hot fat and cook until brown and crisp. Sprinkle with fine salt and serve at once.

Frying Time: 2 minutes for the first frying;
about 3 minutes for the second.

Potato Chips

1⅛ lb. (500 g) potatoes
cooking fat (vegetable oil)
salt

Peel the potatoes, wash them, cut them in halves and slice very thinly. Dry well in a linen cloth, then drop them into deep hot fat. Fry until half done. Fry only a small quantity at a time. As soon as they become yellow, take the chips out of the fat with a skimming ladle and put them to drain into a colander. Allow to cool, then return them to the hot fat and fry until brown and crisp. Leave them to get quite cold, sprinkle them with fine salt and serve with liqueur or wine.

Frying Time: 2 minutes for the first frying;
about 3 minutes for the second.

Stuffed Potatoes

Recipe see page 164.

C. MASHED AND CREAMED POTATOES

Potato Snow

Rub steamed potatoes through a sieve and serve at once, dotted with knobs of butter.

Mashed Potatoes

2¼ lb. (1 kg) potatoes
salt
½ pint (285 ccm) milk
2 oz. (55 g) butter or margarine
salt
1 oz. (30 g) butter for frying
1 onion or 1 tbsp. breadcrumbs

Peel and wash the potatoes and boil in salted water. Drain and while still hot, mash the potatoes with a potato masher or rub through a sieve. Add the hot milk and the fat. Return the saucepan to the heat and whip the potatoes until they are white and creamy. Season with salt. Pile into a plate and serve, garnished with fried onion rings or fried breadcrumbs.

Cooking Time: 20–30 minutes.

Steam or boil the peeled and washed potatoes, then drain. Rub at once through a sieve and leave to cool. Cream the fat, then gradually add the egg yolks, the potatoes, the salt and the nutmeg. Whip the egg whites very stiffly and fold into the potato mixture. Fill into a well greased ring baking tin and bake in the oven. Turn out, when done, onto a flat round plate and pour a meat or mushroom ragoût into the centre.

Oven: slow to moderate.

Time: 30–40 minutes.

Potato Ring

1 lb. 10 oz. (750 g) potatoes
2 oz. (55 g) butter or margarine
2–3 egg yolks
salt
nutmeg
2–3 egg whites
1 oz. (30 g) butter or margarine
  for greasing

Steam or boil the peeled and washed potatoes, and drain. Rub the potatoes at once through a sieve and leave to cool. Cream the fat and gradually add the egg, the mashed potatoes, the flour, salt and nutmeg. Shape the mixture into rolls about 2 inches (5 cm) long, dip in the beaten egg and coat with breadcrumbs. Fry at once in deep hot fat until golden brown.

Alternatively, the potatoes may be shaped into balls or rings.

Cooking Time: 20–30 minutes.

Frying Time: 2–3 minutes.

Potato croquettes go well with a roast and vegetables; they also make an attractive garnish.

Alternatively, shape the potato mixture into flat cakes and fry in shallow fat in a frying pan.

Potato Croquettes

1 lb. 10 oz. (750 g) boiled potatoes
1 oz. (30 g) butter or margarine
1 egg
3–3½ oz. (85–100 g) plain flour
salt
nutmeg
fat for deep-frying

For Coating:
1 egg
breadcrumbs

Steam or boil the peeled and washed potatoes, then drain. Rub the potatoes at once through a sieve and leave to cool. Cream the fat, gradually add the egg yolks, the mashed potatoes, the cheese, salt and nutmeg. Whip the egg whites very stiffly and fold into the mixture. Grease a pudding basin, sprinkle it with breadcrumbs. Fill the basin about three-quarters full. Stand the basin in a steamer over boiling water or in a pan containing boiling water to come half-way up the sides of the basin and cook the pudding until done. Turn it out onto a flat dish and pour the brown butter over it.

Cooking Time: about 1 hour.

Serve with fresh peas, with Braised Beef (see page 82) or Sauerbraten (see page 83). As a dish in itself, the potato pudding may be served with Tomato (see page 52) or Anchovy Sauce (see page 51) and lettuce salad.

The same mixture may be cooked in the oven. Put it into a greased pie-dish, sprinkle with grated cheese and dot with knobs of butter and bake until done.

Potato Pudding

1 lb. 10 oz. (750 g) potatoes
2½ oz. (70 g) butter or margarine
2–3 egg yolks
4 oz. (115 g) grated cheese
salt
nutmeg
2–3 egg whites
1 oz. (30 g) butter or margarine
  for greasing
breadcrumbs
a little brown butter

D. POTATO DOUGH

Potato Dumplings
(Phot. See Page 54)

About 2¾ lb. (1¼ kg) potatoes
3 level tsp. salt
9 oz. (250 g) Oetker GUSTIN
(corn starch powder)
½ pint (285 ccm) milk
1 level tsp. (3 g) Oetker Baking Powder
BACKIN
1 stale roll or slice of bread
butter or margarine

Wash the potatoes and boil until done. Skin at once, then rub through a sieve. Taking 2¼ lb. (1 kg) of the mashed potatoes, stir into them the salt, the GUSTIN and the boiling milk. This dough will be rather soft at first, but will become firmer as it cools. When it is lukewarm, stir in the BACKIN. Dice the roll or slice of bread and fry it golden brown in the hot fat. With floured hands, shape the potato dough into dumplings, press into each ball a few croûtons, then drop the dumplings, a small quantity at a time, into boiling salted water. Simmer until done.

Cooking Time: 20–25 minutes.

Serve with fat joints, stewed dried fruit, or with Tomato (see page 52), Herb (see page 50), or Onion Sauce (see page 49).

Thuringian Dumplings

3¼ lb. (1½ kg) peeled raw potatoes
½ pint (285 ccm) milk
salt
2 oz. (55 g) butter or margarine
5 oz. (140 g) semolina
1 stale roll or slice of bread
a little butter or margarine

Grate the potatoes into a bowl of water, put them into a cloth and squeeze out as much liquid as possible. Bring the milk, salt, and the fat to the boil, stir in the semolina, and stir all the time until a solid mass has formed. Cook this for about a minute, then remove from heat and stir into the grated pressed potatoes. With floured hands, shape the mixture into balls about the size of your fist. Press into each ball some croûtons, then drop the balls into boiling salted water and simmer until done.

Cooking Time: 12–15 minutes.

Serve with fat joints or with sauerkraut.

Dumplings Made with Boiled and Raw Potatoes Mixed

1 lb. 10 oz. (750 g) potatoes
1⅛ lb. (500 g) large raw (peeled) potatoes
1 egg
2¼ oz. (65 g) plain flour
1 tsp. salt

The day before you need the dumplings, wash and boil the 1 lb. 10 oz. (750 g) of potatoes. Peel while still hot and mash. Then leave them to cool. The next day, rub them through a fine sieve. Grate the raw potatoes, put them into a cloth and squeeze out as much liquid as possible. Combine the cooked mashed with the raw grated potatoes and knead into them the egg, the flour and the salt. With floured hands shape the mixture into dumplings about the size of your fist. Drop into boiling salted water and simmer until done.

Cooking Time: about 20 minutes.

Wash the potatoes, boil them in their skins, peel while still hot, then slice.

To make the sauce, melt the fat, add the flour and cook until pale yellow. Gradually stir in the water or stock, the milk and the chives and lastly the hot sliced potatoes. Simmer gently for about 10 minutes. Season to taste with salt and lemon juice.

Parsley (see page 50) or Dill Sauce (see page 49) may be used instead of Chive Sauce.

Potatoes with Chives
2¼ lb. (1 kg) potatoes

Chive Sauce:

1 oz. (30 g) butter or margarine
1¼ oz. (35 g) plain flour
½ pint (285 ccm) water or stock
½ pint (285 ccm) milk
2 tbsp. finely chopped chives
salt
lemon juice

Wash the potatoes, boil them in their skins, peel while still hot, then slice

To make the sauce, heat the fat, stir in the flour and cook until pale yellow. Gradually stir in the water or stock, add the sliced potatoes and simmer gently for about 10 minutes. Season to taste with mustard, salt, vinegar and sugar.

Mustard Potatoes
2¼ lb. (1 kg) potatoes

Mustard Sauce:

1 oz. (30 g) butter or margarine
1¼ oz. (35 g) plain flour
1 pint (570 ccm) water or stock
made mustard
salt
vinegar
sugar

F. POTATO PIES

For general hints on making of pies, see page 256.

Wash the potatoes, boil them in their skins, peel while still hot, then slice. Dice the gammon and the ham and arrange in alternate layers with the sliced potatoes in a well greased pie-dish. The top layer should be potatoes.

To make the sauce, heat the fat, stir in the flour and cook until pale yellow. Gradually stir in the stock or water and the milk and simmer gently for about 10 minutes. Season the sauce and pour it over the potatoes. Sprinkle with the breadcrumbs or the cheese, dot with butter and bake in the oven.

Oven: moderate to hot.

Baking Time: about 40 minutes.

Potato Pie with Ham
2¼ lb. (1 kg) potatoes
3 oz. (85 g) gammon
3 oz. (85 g) boiled ham

White Sauce:

1½ oz. (45 g) butter or margarine
1½ oz. (45 g) plain flour
½ pint (285 ccm) stock or water
½ pint (285 ccm) milk
salt
2 tbsp. breadcrumbs or grated cheese
a little butter

181

Fried Fresh Herrings Recipe See Page 121

Potato Pie with Eggs

2¼ lb. (1 kg) potatoes
2-3 hard-boiled eggs
a little finely chopped chives
some grated cheese

White Sauce:

1½ oz. (45 g) butter or margarine
1½ oz. (45 g) plain flour
½ pint (285 ccm) stock or water
½ pint (285 ccm) milk
salt
2 tbsp. breadcrumbs or grated cheese
a little butter

This pie is made in exactly the same way as Potato Pie with Ham (see page 181). Alternate the layers of sliced potato with layers of hard-boiled egg instead of ham. Sprinkle the top of the pie with chives and cheese.

Oven: moderate to hot.

Baking Time: about 40 minutes.

Potato Pie with Herring

2¼ lb. (1 kg) potatoes
3 finely chopped soaked salt herrings

White Sauce:

1½ oz. (45 g) butter or margarine
1½ oz. (45 g) plain flour
½ pint (285 ccm) stock or water
½ pint (285 ccm) milk
salt
2 tbsp. breadcrumbs or grated cheese
a little butter

Make in the same way as Potato Pie with Ham (see page 181), using herring instead of ham.

Oven: moderate to hot.

Baking Time: about 40 minutes

Potato Pie with Mushrooms

2¼ lb. (1 kg) potatoes
9 oz. (250 g) mushrooms
1-2 onions
1½ oz. (45 g) fat bacon
9 oz. (250 g) tomatoes (optional)

White Sauce:

1½ oz. (45 g) butter or margarine
1½ oz. (45 g) plain flour
½ pint (285 ccm) stock or water
½ pint (285 ccm) milk
salt
2 tbsp. breadcrumbs or grated cheese
a little butter

Prepare the mushrooms, cut into slices and sauté in the diced bacon together with the finely chopped onions. Then proceed as Potato Pie with Ham (see page 181). The tomatoes should be sliced and arranged on top of the mushrooms.

Oven: moderate to hot.

Baking Time: about 40 minutes.

Parsley Potatoes Recipe See Page 172

Princess Potatoes

1 lb. 10 oz. (750 g) potatoes
3 well soaked salt herrings
5 oz. (140 g) boiled ham
2–3 hard-boiled eggs
⅔ pint (375 ccm) sour cream or milk,
if milk is used, thicken it with
1 slightly heaped tbsp. Oetker GUSTIN
(corn starch powder)
2 eggs
2 tbsp. breadcrumbs or grated cheese
a little butter

Wash the potatoes, boil them in their skins, peel while still hot, then slice. Bone and skin the soaked herrings and slice them. Dice the ham, slice the eggs and arrange in alternate layers with the sliced potatoes and the herrings in a well-greased pie-dish. The top layer should be potatoes. Beat the eggs with the cream or with the milk, blended with the GUSTIN and pour this over the pie. Sprinkle with the breadcrumbs or the cheese, dot with butter and bake in the oven.

Oven: moderate to hot.

Baking Time: about 40 minutes.

Rechauffée Pie

9 oz. (250 g) left-over meat or ham
1 onion
a little butter or margarine
about 1½ lb. (680 g) left-over boiled
potatoes
1–2 eggs
¾ oz. (20 g) Oetker GUSTIN
(corn starch powder)
salt
½ pint (285 ccm) milk
2 tbsp. breadcrumbs or grated cheese
a little butter

Mince or finely chop the meat or ham. Heat the fat and in it sauté the finely chopped onion. Stir in the meat. Mash or sieve the potatoes. Arrange the minced meat and mashed potatoes (add salt if the potatoes are boiled in their skins) in alternate layers in a well-greased pie-dish. The top layer should be potatoes. Beat together the eggs, the GUSTIN, salt and the milk and pour this mixture over the pie. Sprinkle with the breadcrumbs or the cheese, dot with butter and bake in the oven.

Oven: moderate to hot.

Baking Time: about 40 minutes.

If you have left-over vegetables — cauliflower, asparagus, tomatoes, etc. — they can be used instead of meat.

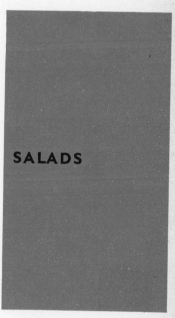

SALADS

"Salad" is the name not only given to the uncooked green leaves of the "salad" plants (lettuce, watercress, endive, chicory, and so on), but also to mixtures of some salad dressing and raw or cooked vegetables, fruits and meat. Salads play a large part in the menu, and, if attractively garnished, they are a treat to the eye as well as to the palate. Most salads are served cold, and their naturally delicious flavour is enhanced by the addition of suitable sauces and dressings.

Making up a salad gives the housewife an opportunity of adding interest and variety to her menus, and an opportunity, too, of using up leftovers in a delicious and attractive way. She can use herbs and spices, every kind of vegetable, garnish, sauce, and dressing, and exercise her ingenuity to the full in concocting new and exciting mixtures.

Salads supply in a delicious form those minerals and vitamins so vitally necessary to a balanced and healthy diet. The raw vegetables supply that daily ration of uncooked food so full of natural nourishment and goodness. If the housewife is serving a meal without cooked vegetables, she should always try to balance this deficiency by adding lettuce or some similar uncooked vegetable salad with the meal. In hot weather, of course, salads of cooked vegetables are especially welcome; they are cool and refreshing, and many of their ingredients (especially their herbs) make them very easy to digest.

Salad making is always important, and salads should be carefully prepared and seasoned. Lettuce and vegetables should be well picked over and all discoloured and wilted parts removed. Wash thoroughly, preferably under running water, to remove sand and soil. To be quite sure that vegetables which are to be eaten raw are clean, soak them for 10 minutes or so in cold salted water. Be sure they are quite dry before adding the dressing. Dry them thoroughly by shaking them in a colander, or in a wire lettuce-basket, or drying them between cloths.

Never press or squeeze lettuce leaves to dry them, as this will damage them and cause bruising. If you are using cooked vegetables in your salad, steam them; or else cook them in as little water as possible, then use this cooking water in a sauce or dressing. The right dressing is very important if your salad is to be a success. The addition of an inappropriate dressing can be ruinous, destroying not only the salad's flavour, but also much of its food value. Excessive and monotonous seasoning with salt, pepper, vinegar, and sugar is a common failing in the preparation of salads. Salad vegetables have a delicious natural flavour, but it is delicate, and can easily be spoilt. The dressing should bring out this natural flavour, and enhance it, so must be used judiciously and with restraint. Use salt, pepper, oil, vinegar and sugar sparingly, and add whenever possible such natural flavourings as horseradish, tomato juice, or lemon juice. Try using celery salt instead of ordinary salt occasionally. And make full use of the wonderful variety of herbs – parsley, chives, dill, chervil, estragon, pimpernel, fennel, tarragon, thyme, marjoram, borage, and so on. These can add subtlety and flavour to the simplest basic ingredients.

It is worth while paying attention, too, to the appearance of your salad. If it is served, to please the eye as well as the palate, it will be certain to be a success both with your family and your guests.

1. Wash all raw salad vegetables carefully and drain them well. If the vegetables are wet they will not take oil and the flavour of the dressing will be spoilt.

2. Never leave cut up salad vegetables to soak; many of their valuable mineral salts are soluble in water.

3. When making salad, touch the leaves as little as possible; they are delicate and bruise easily. Shake dry in a clean cloth or wire salad basket.

4. Add the dressing to the salad just before serving; dressing mixed in too soon makes the salad limp. Mix green salad with 1 tbsp. of oil before adding the rest of the dressing.

5. Salads made from meat or the more solid vegetables should be left to marinate in their dressing or mayonnaise for several hours before serving.

General Hints

A. GREEN SALADS

Remove the outer leaves and loosen the others without bruising them. Tear the large leaves if small pieces are needed, but leave the heart whole. Wash carefully in plenty of water. Put in a colander to drain or, better still, shake dry in a wire salad basket or cloth. Dress with one of the salad dressings just before serving.

Lettuce salad may also be served with Cream Dressing (see page 58) or Mayonnaise (see page 59).

Lettuce Salad
2 heads of lettuce
Salad Dressing I or II (see page 57)

Cut off the coarse outer leaves and the roots. Wash the rest carefully, hold in a bundle and slice thinly, like noodles. Taste the endive and if you find it bitter, soak it for about half an hour in lukewarm water. Mix the salad with one of the salad dressings and serve.

Endive Salad
1 or 2 heads of endive
Salad Dressing II (see page 57) or Cream Dressing (see page 58), using half the given quantity

Lambs' Lettuce
(Corn Salad, Valerianella)

7 oz. (200 g) of lamb's lettuce
Salad Dressing I or II (see page 57)

Cut off the roots, carefully remove the wilted outer leaves and wash thoroughly. Drain well and, just before serving, dress with one of the salad dressings. Lamb's lettuce is a suitable garnish for Potato (see page 191/192) or Celeriac Salad (see page 191).

Watercress
7 oz. (200 g) watercress
Salad Dressing I (see page 57)

Pick over the watercress and wash thoroughly in plenty of water. Do not bruise the leaves. Drain well and mix with the salad dressing just before serving.

B. VEGETABLE SALADS

I. SALADS MADE FROM RAW VEGETABLES

Cucumber Salad

1 large cucumber
Salad Dressing I or II (see page 57)

Peel the cucumber, starting at the tip and working towards the stalk. Cutt off a slice, taste it, and if you find it bitter, continue cutting away until no longer bitter. Cut into fine slices. Mix with one of the salad dressings and, if necessary, add a little salt. Serve at once.

If the cucumber is salted after it has been sliced and then left to stand, it will not only become indigestible, but the salt will draw out the water from the cucumber. If this water is poured away, valuable minerals will be lost.

The cucumber is also delicious served with a Cream Dressing (see page 58) using half the given quantity, mixed with some finely chopped dill.

Radish Salad

3–4 bunches of radishes
Salad Dressing I (see page 57)

Cut off the roots and leaves of the radishes, wash thoroughly and slice or shred very finely. Mix with the salad dressing and leave to stand for a short time before serving.

Chinese Radish

2–3 Chinese radishes
sugar
Salad Dressing I or II (see page 57)

Peel the radishes, shred or slice them and then mix with one of the suggested salad dressings. Leave to stand for an hour or so before serving.

Red Cabbage Salad

1 lb. (450 g) red cabbage
Salad Dressing I or II (see page 57)
1 apple

Remove the outer leaves and discoloured parts of the cabbage. Halve it, cut out the core, then wash it thoroughly and shred very finely. Pound with a potato masher until it looks glassy. This makes the cabbage more digestible and tender. Make one of the suggested salad dressings without herbs, mix it with the cabbage and add the finely shredded apple.

Sorrel Salad

5 oz. (140 g) sorrel
Salad Dressing II (see page 57)

Pick over the sorrel carefully, wash it thoroughly, drain it and mix with the salad dressing, prepared without vinegar or lemon juice.

Press out as much moisture as possible from the sauerkraut, then chop it finely. Loosen it with a fork, mix with the oil and season to taste with vinegar, salt and sugar. Sprinkle the capers over the top just before serving.

Alternatively, sauerkraut may be mixed with Cream Dressing (see page 58), Fresh Tomato Dressing (see page 57), or Mayonnaise (see page 59).

Pick over the spinach carefully, remove all roots and tough stalks, then wash it at least five or six times. Drain it well, mix it with the salad dressing and leave it to stand for about half an hour before serving.

Spinach may also be mixed with Mayonnaise (see page 59), or with Fresh Tomato Dressing (see page 57).

Wash the tomatoes, dry and slice with a tomato cutter. Salt slightly and mix with the finely chopped onion and the salad dressing. It is best to slice the tomatoes directly into the salad bowl, adding a spoonful of the finely chopped onion and the salad dressing over each layer of tomatoes.

Remove the outer leaves and the discoloured parts of the cabbage. Halve it, remove the hard core, wash it and shred or grate finely. Pound the cabbage with a potato masher until it looks glassy. This makes the cabbage more tender and digestible Mix in one of the suggested salad dressings and leave to stand for several hours before serving.

II. SALADS MADE WITH BOILED OR STEAMED VEGETABLES

The asparagus should look white, break easily and be juicy where it is broken. Peel the asparagus, starting near the tip and working downwards. Be very careful not to damage the tips. Cut it into pieces about 2 inches (5 cm) long, wash, put into boiling salted water and cook until tender. Take it out of the water with a skimming ladle and mix with the salad dressing while still warm. Leave to stand for a short time, then season to taste.

Cooking Time: 30–40 minutes.

Garnish with slices of tomatoes and hard-boiled eggs.

Alternatively, the asparagus may be mixed with Mayonnaise (see page 59) and served as a tilling for scooped out tomatoes.

Sauerkraut Salad

About 1 lb. (450 g) sauerkraut
3 tbsp. salad oil
a little vinegar (optional)
salt
sugar
1 tbsp. capers

Spinach Salad

5–6 oz. (140–170 g) spinach
Salad Dressing II (see page 57)

Tomato Salad

1 lb. (450 g) firm tomatoes
salt
1 onion
Salad Dressing I (see page 57)

Cabbage Salad

1 lb. (450 g) cabbage
Salad Dressing I or II (see page 57)

Asparagus Salad

1 lb. (450 g) asparagus
Salad Dressing I (see page 57)

Cauliflower Salad

1 cauliflower
Salad Dressing I or II (see page 57)

Choose a firm white cauliflower, remove the leaves, cut away any blemishes and cut off the core. Wash under running water, then soak a little in cold salted water to remove insects and caterpillars. Put into boiling salted water and cook until tender. Break into flowerets and mix with one of the suggested salad dressings. Leave to stand for a little while, season and serve.

Cooking Time: 25–30 minutes.

Cauliflower may also be served piled in the middle of a dish. Pour some Mayonnaise (see page 59) over the cauliflower, and surround with a ring of lettuce or tomato salad.

French Bean Salad

1 lb. (450 g) French beans
Salad Dressing I (see page 57)
1 onion

String the beans, wash them and cut into pieces about 1½ inch (4 cm) long. Put into boiling salted water or a steamer and cook until done. Mix with the salad dressing and the finely chopped onion while they are still hot. Leave to stand for a while, season to taste and serve. If preferred, the salad dressing may be thinned with 2–3 tbsp. of cooking liquid, or with sour cream. Parsley, dill or savory are suitable herbs.

Cooking Time: about 30 minutes.

There is a yellow variety of French bean found in some areas which is especially delicious as a salad vegetable. Prepare as for ordinary French beans, but with Fresh Tomato Dressing (see page 57), which is a particularly good accompaniment for this type of bean.

Chicory Salad

4 heads of chicory
2¾ pints (1½ l) water
salt

Dressing:
2 tbsp. oil
juice of half a lemon
salt
pepper
1 tsp. sugar
2 tbsp. cream
1 small onion

Remove the discoloured outer leaves and wedge out the stalk. Wash, then put into boiling, slightly salted water and cook gently for about 10 minutes. Drain and cut into thin strips.

Cooking Time: about 10 minutes.

For the dressing, beat together with a fork the oil, lemon juice, salt, pepper and sugar. Add the cream and the chopped onion, then mix with the chicory.

Carrot Salad

1 lb. (450 g) carrots
Salad Dressing II (see page 57) or
Cream Dressing (see page 58)
1 tsp. chopped parsley

Scrape the carrots, wash and steam or cook in boiling salted water until tender. Slice finely or cut into strips, then mix with one of the suggested dressings and the chopped parsley. Season to taste.

Cooking Time: for young carrots, about 25 minutes;
for old carrots, about 1 hour.

Cut off the roots and the leaves leaving about 1 inch (2½ cm) to prevent loss of colour and juice. Scrub thoroughly under running water, put into the boiling salted water and cook until tender. Take the beetroot out of the water and pour cold water over it. This will make peeling easier. Peel while still warm, slice and mix with the finely chopped onion, the horseradish and the diluted vinegar. Season to taste with salt, sugar and the caraway seeds, if desired. Leave to stand for 2–3 days.

Cooking Time: 1–1½ hours.

Mustard Cream Dressing (see page 59) is also delicious with beetroot salad.

(see page 59)

Beetroot Salad

1 lb. (450 g) beetroot
2 pints (1⅛ l) water
1 tsp. salt
1 small onion
1 tsp. finely diced horseradish
¼ pint (140 ccm) vinegar (diluted)
salt
sugar
½ tsp. caraway seeds (optional)

Scrub the celeriac carefully under running water. Add the salt and vinegar to the water and bring it to the boil. Put in the celeriac and cook until tender. Remove and pour cold water over it. This will make peeling easier. Peel while still warm, slice and mix with the salad dressing.

Cooking Time: 1–2 hours.

Garnish with finely chopped beetroot or serve with Mayonnaise (see page 59).

Celeriac Salad

1–2 celeriacs
2 pints (1⅛ l) water
1 tsp. salt
2–3 tbsp. vinegar
Salad Dressing I (see page 57)

Remove the coarse outer leaves, cut into halves or quarters, remove the core and wash thoroughly. Then shred the cabbage finely. Dice the bacon and fry. Add the shredded cabbage and cook for a short time. Add the salted water and simmer until the cabbage is half done. While still warm, mix the cabbage with the salad dressing. Add grated apple to red cabbage.

Cooking Time: 20–30 minutes.

White or Red Cabbage Salad

1 lb. (450 g) cabbage
¾ oz. (20 g) fat bacon
a little salted water
Salad Dressing I (see page 57)
1 apple (if red cabbage is used)

Wash the potatoes, boil them in their skins and peel as soon as they are done. Cut the potatoes into fine slices while they are still warm and pour over them the warm stock or water. Mix with the finely chopped onion and the salad dressing. Leave to stand for 1–2 hours.

Cooking Time: 20–30 minutes.

Garnish with parsley, lettuce, sliced beetroot or cucumber.

Alternatively, the potato salad may be mixed with Cream Dressing (see page 58) or with Mayonnaise II (see page 59).

Potato Salad I

1 lb. 10 oz. (750 g) medium-sized potatoes
¼ pint (140 ccm) stock or water
1 onion
Salad Dressing I (see page 57)

Potato Salad II

1 lb. 10 oz. (750 g) medium-sized
potatoes
¼ pint (140 ccm) stock or water
1 onion
1½ oz. (45 g) fat bacon
pepper
salt
vinegar

Wash the potatoes, boil them in their skins and peel as soon as they are done. Cut the potatoes into fine slices while they are still warm and pour over them the warm stock or water. Add the finely chopped onion. Dice the bacon and cook until pale yellow. Pour this over the potatoes and season to taste with pepper, salt and vinegar. Serve warm.

Cooking Time: 20–30 minutes.

Macaroni Salad

7 oz. (200 g) macaroni
3½ pints (2 l) water
salt
Herb Mayonnaise (see page 59) or
Tomato Purée Mayonnaise
(see page 60)

Break the macaroni into finger-length pieces and sprinkle into boiling salted water. Stir them now and then at the start of the cooking, or they will stick to the bottom of the pan and burn. When cooked, pour into a colander to drain and pour cold water over it.

Cooking Time: about 20 minutes.

Mix the macaroni with one of the suggested mayonnaise and garnish with sliced tomatoes or slices of hard-boiled eggs.

III. MIXED SALADS

Half- and Half Salads
(Raw and Cooked Vegetables Mixed)

Salads made of raw and cooked vegetables mixed together are delicious and very wholesome. The following are suggested as good mixtures:

1. Asparagus Salad with Tomatoes.
2. Cauliflower Salad with Tomatoes.
3. French Bean Salad with Tomatoes.
4. French Bean Salad with Cucumbers.
5. French Bean Salad with Cucumbers and Tomatoes.
6. Celeriac Salad with Tomatoes.
7. Celeriac Salad with Raw Apples.
8. Red Cabbage Salad with Beetroot and Grated Horseradish.
9. Potato Salad with Cucumbers.
10. Potato Salad with Radish or Grated Chinese Radish.
11. Potato Salad with Tomatoes.
12. Potato Salad with Tomatoes and Cucumbers.

Prepare the various salads according to the recipes already given. Raw fruit and vegetables should be added just before serving.

Prepare the vegetables and steam separately until done. Mix them all together with the herbs and the mayonnaise. Garnish with endive or serve as a filling for scooped out tomatoes.

Alternatively, the vegetables may be mixed with Rémoulade Sauce (see page 60).

Vegetable Salad

5 oz. (140 g) asparagus
5 oz. (140 g) small carrots
5 oz. (140 g) peas (without pods)
5 oz. (140 g) French beans, a few mushrooms (optional)
1 tsp. finely chopped herbs
Mayonnaise (see page 59)

Wash the potatoes, the beetroot and the celeriac, and steam separately. Pour cold water over each vegetable when cooked, and peel. Dice the potatoes, the beetroot and the celeriac, the pickled gherkins and the peeled, cored apple. Mix them all together in a salad bowl with the herbs and the mayonnaise.

Salad Medley

5 oz. (140 g) potatoes
5 oz. (140 g) beetroot
5 oz. (140 g) celeriac
1–2 pickled gherkins
1 small apple
1 tsp. finely chopped herbs
Mayonnaise (see page 59)

Peel the onions, slice them and cook in 1 pint (570 ccm) of water containing 1 tbsp. of vinegar and 1 tsp. of salt until they look glassy. Leave to cool, then arrange in layers alternately with the sliced tomatoes (sprinkled with a little salt) and with the boned and diced salt herrings and the chopped parsley. They look best in a glass salad bowl. Pour over the mayonnaise, then leave to stand in a cool place until ready to serve.

If preferred, 2 or 3 sliced hard-boiled eggs may be used instead of the herrings.

Tomato and Onion Salad

9 oz. (250 g) onions
1⅛ lb. (500 g) tomatoes
salt
2 soaked salt herrings
chopped parsley
Mayonnaise (see page 59)

Wash the potatoes, scrub the celeriac under running water and steam or boil separately. Pour cold water over them when cooked, and peel. Dice finely the potatoes, the celeriac, the peeled, cored apples and the pickled gherkins. Add the nuts and put the salad into a bowl.

For the dressing beat together the oil, lemon juice or vinegar, and the salt with a fork until thick and creamy. Stir in the herbs, then add this sauce to the salad. Leave to stand for a little before adding the mayonnaise.

Waldorf Salad

9 oz. (250 g) potatoes
9 oz. (250 g) celeriac
9 oz. (250 g) apples
1–2 pickled gherkins
1 tbsp. chopped nuts

Salad Dressing:
3 tbsp. salad oil
1–2 tbsp. lemon juice or vinegar
salt
1 tsp. finely chopped herbs
Mayonnaise (see page 59)

C. EGG, MEAT, AND FISH SALADS

Egg Salad
(Phot. See Page 213)

4 tbsp. oil
2 tbsp. vinegar
made mustard
salt
1 tbsp. finely chopped chives
4–6 hard-boiled eggs
tomatoes
cooked celeriac or pickled gherkins

Beat together the oil, the vinegar, mustard and salt with a fork until thick and creamy. Stir in the chives. Carefully slice the eggs, the tomatoes and the celeriac or pickled gherkins and arrange them in alternate layers in a salad bowl. Pour over the dressing and leave to stand for several hours.

If preferred, 1 tsp. of tomato purée added to the salad dressing may be used instead of the tomatoes.

Mixed Salad

5 oz. (140 g) boiled ham
3 oz. (85 g) gammon
14 oz. (400 g) cooked celeriac
2 medium-sized apples
2–3 small pickled gherkins
1 tsp. chopped herbs
Mayonnaise I (see page 59)

Finely dice the ham and the gammon, the celeriac, the peeled, cored apples and the pickled gherkins. Mix them all with the herbs and the mayonnaise. Leave to stand for several hours before serving.

Meat Salad

9 oz. (250 g) white boiled meat
9 oz. (250 g) apples
2 hard-boiled eggs
1–2 pickled gherkins
1 tsp. capers
Mayonnaise I (see page 59), using one and a half times the given quantity
1 tsp. finely chopped herbs

Cut the meat, the peeled and cored apples, the eggs, and the pickled gherkins into thin strips. Mix them in a salad bowl with the capers, the mayonnaise and the herbs. Boiled potatoes, celeriac, or beetroot may be added to the salad, if desired.

Chicken Salad
(Phot. See Page 213)

Any other poultry may be used instead of chicken

9 oz. (250 g) chicken meat, boiled or roasted
9 oz. (250 g) boiled vegetables (asparagus, young peas, or celeriac)
1 tsp. finely chopped herbs
Mayonnaise, (see page 59) or Tomato Purée Mayonnaise (see page 60)

Cut the meat and the celeriac into oblong strips, and the asparagus into pieces about 1¼ inch (3 cm) long. Add the herbs and the mayonnaise and mix well.

Serve in scallop shells or on small glass dishes, garnished with lettuce leaves and radishes.

Sprinkle the washed rice into the boiling salted water and leave to simmer for about 25 minutes. As soon as it is cooked, drain it and rinse with cold water.

Cut the meat up into small cubes, and peel and dice the oranges.

For the mayonnaise, put the egg yolk, mustard, salt, sugar and vinegar into a bowl and beat until creamy. Stir in the oil gradually, 1 or 2 tbsp. at a time. Blend the GUSTIN with the ¼ pint (140 ccm) of water containing the orange juice, then bring it to the boil, stirring all the time. While it is still hot, beat it into the mayonnaise. Add the beef, the oranges and the cold rice. Season with salt, sugar, lemon juice and curry powder. Stir well together and serve.

Japanese Salad

½ pint (285 ccm) water
salt
2½ oz. (70 g) rice
9 oz. (250 g) roast or boiled beef
2 oranges

Mayonnaise:

1 egg yolk
made mustard
salt
1 tsp. sugar
1 tbsp. vinegar
¼ pint (140 ccm) oil
juice of 1 orange, made up with water to ¼ pint (140 ccm)
1 slightly heaped tbsp. (10 g) Oetker GUSTIN (corn starch powder)
salt
sugar
lemon juice and curry powder

Flake the fish. Beat together the oil, the lemon juice or vinegar, salt, and the mustard until thick and creamy. Stir in the finely chopped onion and the herbs. Mix the salad dressing with the flaked fish, then leave to stand for a while before serving.

If preferred, tomatoes, celeriac, or pickled gherkins may be added to the salad. Instead of the sauce given in the recipe Rémoulade Sauce (see page 60), Mustard Dressing (see page 59), or Tomato-Horseradish Dressing (see page 58) may be used.

Fish Salad

About 1½ lb. (680 g) cooked fish

Salad Dressing:

3 tbsp. salad oil
1–2 tbsp. lemon juice or vinegar
salt
made mustard
1 onion
1 tsp. finely chopped herbs

Flake the fish and mix with the peeled and diced oranges and the diced pickled gherkins. Stir in the mayonnaise.

Fish Salad with Oranges

9 oz. (250 g) cooked fish
2 medium-sized oranges
1 pickled gherkin
Mayonnaise II (see page 59), using half the quantity, but add GUSTIN

Herring Salad I

2–3 soaked salt herrings
1⅛ lb. (500 g) potatoes, boiled
in their skins
2 sour apples
1 pickled gherkin

Salad Dressing:
3 tbsp. salad oil
1–2 tbsp. vinegar
salt
made mustard
1 onion
1 tsp. finely chopped herbs

Skin and bone the herrings and cut them into small cubes. Dice the peeled potatoes, the peeled, cored apples and the pickled gherkin. Put all these ingredients into a bowl.

For the dressing, beat together the oil, vinegar, salt and mustard with a fork until thick and creamy, then stir in the finely chopped onion and the herbs. Mix this dressing with the other ingredients, then leave to stand for a time in a cool place before serving.

Herring Salad II

2–3 soaked salt herrings
9 oz. (250 g) roast veal
2 pickled gherkins
1–2 apples
1 boiled beetroot
2 potatoes, boiled in their skins
2 oz. (55 g) hazelnuts or walnuts
1 tbsp. cranberry sauce
a little hot stock
1 tsp. finely chopped herbs
Mayonnaise (see page 59)

Dice the skinned and boned herrings, the veal, the pickled gherkins, the peeled and cored apples, the skinned beetroot and the peeled potatoes. Put into a bowl. Add the chopped nuts, the cranberry sauce, the stock and the herbs. Stir in the mayonnaise, garnish with capers, sliced hard-boiled eggs, pickled gherkins and beetroot.

Italian Salad
(Phot. See Page 213)

5 oz. (140 g) left-over meat or
boiled ham
5 oz. (140 g) apples
5 oz. (140 g) pickled gherkins
5 oz. (140 g) potatoes, boiled in their
skins
4 oz. (115 g) boiled carrots and
celeriac
2 soaked anchovies
1 tsp. capers
1 onion
1 tsp. finely chopped herbs
Mayonnaise (see page 59)

Cut the meat or ham into strips, the peeled and cored apples, the pickled gherkins, the peeled potatoes, the carrots and the celeriac. Put into a bowl. Chop the anchovies and add them to the mixture, together with the capers, the finely chopped onion, the herbs and the mayonnaise. Garnish with sliced pickled gherkins, tomatoes and hard-boiled eggs.

Rémoulade Sauce (see page 60) makes a delicious change from mayonnaise with this salad.

FRUIT DISHES

Fruit plays a large part in keeping us healthy. Quite apart from the fact that it is rich in vitamins and minerals, its glucose and acid content make it indispensable to our daily diet. Since lack of vitamins and minerals is particularly harmful to growing children, fruit should always be given to them from infancy right through to adolescence, so that their blood and bones will be strong and healthy. Berries and citrus fruits are richest in vitamins. Since the caloric value of our native fruit is low, and because it is almost completely lacking in fat and protein, it should never from the only item in the diet.

For the invalid, fruit is especially beneficial. Its high fluid content helps to irrigate the body, whereas its cellulose aids and regulates the digestion. Prunes and figs (taken early in the day, on an empty

197

stomach) are well known as a laxative; dried bilberries are equally good as a remedy for diarrhoea. All who suffer from irregularities of the digestion should eat fruit regularly, as this is the most natural as well as the most efficient way of keeping themselves fit.

Raw fruit is the best fruit, from the point of view of health. Cooked, well stirred fruit, is more digestible, as cooking breaks down the coarse fibres; fruit in the form of juice is easiest to digest. Never drink water after eating raw fruit, as pectin (the setting agent in jams and jellies), swells in the stomach as the digestive process starts. It goes without saying that all fruit eaten raw should be scrupulously clean. It should also be eaten as fresh as possible because the high water content of most fruits does not permit it to be kept for long. Only apples and certain kinds of pears, if properly stored, can be kept almost throughout an entire winter. They should be stored in special racks, in an airy, frost-free cellar or similar cool place; leave sufficient space between each fruit. If any fruit gets bad, it should be removed and discarded before it can infect its neighbours.

Fruit, properly and carefully preserved or bottled, will not only ensure a minimum loss of vitamins and minerals, but will also give us an adequate supply of this essential food throughout the winter and on into the spring.

General Hints

1. Always wash fruit quickly; if it is firm (apples, pears, plums, etc.), it should be washed under running water, drained in a colander, or dried well with a cloth.

2. Dried fruit should be washed in lukewarm water to remove the dirt. It should then be soaked for 12–24 hours in cold water.

3. Fruit should not be stoned or peeled until it has been washed.

4. Never leave fresh fruit soaking too long in water. To prevent apples and pears turning brown after peeling, cover them with a damp cloth.

5. Juicy fruit may be stewed in its own juice without the addition of any water.

6. If water is required for cooking, make a syrup by heating together sugar and water until the sugar is dissolved. Then add the fruit. This helps the fruit to keep its appearance and flavour.

7. To avoid wasting sugar, sweeten fruit purée after it has been rubbed through a sieve.

8. Added flavourings, such as lemon and orange peel, vanilla pods etc., should be removed before serving.

A. RAW FRUIT

Wash the fruit (except raspberries), remove the stalks, and dry in a cloth or colander. Arrange in a glass bowl in alternate layers with the sugar. Leave to stand in a cool place. Garnish with whipped cream or serve whipped cream separately.

Sugared Fruit

About 1½ lb. (680 g) strawberries, raspberries, red or black currants, or blackberries
sugar to taste

Carefully wash, remove the stalks and sugar a mixture of soft fruits (strawberries, raspberries, red or black currants, or blackberries). Pour over fresh cream or milk flavoured with Oetker Vanillin Sugar just before serving.

Raw Fruit with Cream or Milk

Whisk fresh cottage cheese with milk or cream, sugar and vanillin sugar until the mixture is light and frothy. Stir in fresh sugared raspberries, red or black currants, blackberries or sliced strawberries. Serve in a mound, decorated with berries, reserved for the purpose.

Raw Fruit with Cottage Cheese

Carefully wash the fruit, (except raspberries), skin the bananas, stone the peaches and mash with a fork. Add the lemon juice and beat until frothy. Prepare the gelatine according to the directions on the packet and stir it into the fruit mixture. Lastly fold in the whipped cream and season to taste with sugar. Fill into glasses and garnish with fruit or jelly.

Fruit Snow

13 oz. (375 g) fruit
juice of half a lemon
2 heaped tsp. Oetker "Regina" Gelatine, powdered white
3 tbsp. cold water
½ pint (285 ccm) cream
sugar to taste

For this delicious dish, choose only the best and freshest fruit and clean it carefully. Oranges should be free of white pith and pips; dried figs, currants and raisins should be washed and soaked before being added to the salad. Cut the fruit into slices and arrange in alternate layers with the sugar. Pour a little lemon juice, wine, or fresh fruit juice over the salad and garnish with almonds, nuts and raisins. Puffed rice, corn flakes, rusks, or macaroons are delicious with fruit salad. Serve with fresh cream or vanilla sauce, prepared with Oetker Sauce Powder, vanilla flavour.

Fruit Salad

The following fruit combinations are especially delicious and refreshing:

1. Apples, oranges, sugar, lemon juice, nuts.
2. Apples, oranges, bananas, sugar, nuts.
3. Apples, figs, sugar, lemon juice.
4. Apples, oranges, tomatoes, sugar, lemon juice.
5. Apples, oranges, bananas, pineapple, sugar and wine.
6. Apples, oranges, pears, pineapple, bananas, sugar, fruit juice.
7. Oranges, bananas, sugar, lemon juice.
8. Plums, pears, peaches, sugar, lemon juice.

Muesli
(After Dr. Bircher-Benner)

4 tbsp. rolled oats
12 tbsp. water
juice of 2 lemons
4 tbsp. fresh cream or milk
1 lb. 5 oz. (600 g) apples
a little sugar or honey
4 tbsp. ground hazelnuts or almonds

Soak the oats in the water for several hours. Shortly before serving, add the lemon juice and the cream or milk. Wash the apples (do not peel or core) and grate them with a glass grater, if available, onto the oats, stirring frequently. The lemon juice will keep the mixture white. Season to taste with sugar or honey, and sprinkle with the hazelnuts or almonds.

Muesli is a most nourishing fruit dish. It is especially suitable for breakfast or supper, eaten with wholemeal bread buttered and spread with honey.

The dish may be varied in many ways. Rye, wheat, or rice flakes may be used instead of the oats; crushed berries can be used instead of apples. In winter, Muesli may be prepared with dried fruit, allowing about 3½ oz. (100 g) per person. Wash and soak the fruit for 12 hours, then mince or chop finely before adding to the other ingredients.

B. STEWED FRUIT (In Own Juice)

Stewed Apricots

1 lb. 5 oz. (600 g) apricots
3–3½ oz. (85–100 g) sugar

Dip the fruit briefly into boiling water, skin and stone. Break up some of the stones and add the kernels to the fruit. Sprinkle with 3 oz. (85 g) of sugar and leave to stand until sufficient juice has accumulated. Bring the fruit to the boil and simmer gently until tender. Leave to cool, then add more sugar, if necessary.

Stewed Bananas

4 bananas
1½ oz. (45 g) butter
sugar
cinnamon

Peel the bananas, cut in half lengthways and stew in the butter until golden brown. Sprinkle with sugar and cinnamon and serve warm.

Stewed Strawberries

1⅛ lb. (500 g) strawberries
2–3 oz. (55–85 g) sugar

Wash the strawberries carefully and remove stalks and hulls. Sprinkle with 2 oz. (55 g) of sugar and leave to stand until sufficient juice has accumulated Bring them to the boil and simmer gently until tender. Leave to cool and add more sugar, if necessary.

Stewed Bilberries or Blueberries

1⅛ lb. (500 g) bilberries
3–3½ oz. (85–100 g) sugar
a piece of cinnamon or lemon rind

Pick over the berries and wash them. Sprinkle with 3 oz. (85 g) of sugar and leave to stand until sufficient juice has accumulated. Bring to the boil with the cinnamon or lemon rind and simmer gently until tender. Leave to cool and add more sugar, if necessary.

Pick over the raspberries carefully and remove stalks and hulls. Sprinkle with 2 oz. (55 g) sugar and leave to stand until sufficient juice has accumulated. Bring the fruit to the boil and simmer gently until tender. Leave to cool and add more sugar, if necessary.

Wash the bunches carefully, use a fork to strip the fruit from the stalks and sprinkle with 3½ oz. (100 g) sugar and leave to stand until sufficient juice has accumulated. Bring the fruit to the boil and simmer gently until tender. Leave to cool and add more sugar, if necessary.

Dip the fruit briefly into boiling water, skin and remove the stones. Break up some of the stones and add the kernels to the fruit. Sprinkle with 2 oz. (55 g) sugar and leave to stand until sufficient juice has accumulated. Bring to the boil and simmer gently until done. Leave to cool and add more sugar, if necessary.

Wash the rhubarb thoroughly and cut it into pieces about 1 inch (2½ cm) long (do not skin). Sprinkle with 3½ oz. (100 g) sugar and leave to stand until sufficient juice has been extracted. Add the vanillin sugar or orange peel, bring to the boil and simmer gently until done. Cook very carefully, so that the rhubarb pieces remain whole. Leave to cool and add more sugar, if necessary. Serve with a sauce, made with Oetker Sauce Powder, vanilla flavour.

Wash the cherries, stone them and sprinkle with 4½ oz. (125 g) sugar and leave to stand until sufficient juice has accumulated. Bring to the boil and simmer gently until tender. Leave to cool and add more sugar, if necessary.

Wash the cherries, stone them and sprinkle with 2 oz. (55 g) sugar and leave to stand until sufficient juice has accumulated. Bring to the boil and simmer gently until done. Leave to cool, then add the vanillin sugar and more sugar, if necessary.

Stewed Raspberries

1⅛ lb. (500 g) raspberries
2–3 oz. (55–85 g) sugar

Stewed Black or Red Currants

1⅛ lb. (500 g) black or red currants
3½–4½ oz. (100–125 g) sugar

Stewed Peaches

1 lb. 5 oz. (600 g) peaches
2–3 oz. (55–85 g) sugar

Stewed Rhubarb

1⅛ lb. (500 g) rhubarb
3½–4½ oz. (100–125 g) sugar
1 packet Oetker Vanillin Sugar or a little orange peel

Stewed Sour Cherries

1⅛ lb. (500 g) sour cherries
4½–5½ oz. (125–150 g) sugar

Stewed Sweet Cherries

1⅛ lb. (500 g) cherries
2–3 oz. (55–85 g) sugar
1 tsp. Oetker Vanillin Sugar

C. STEWED FRUIT

Stewed Apples

1⅛ lb. (500 g) apples
½ pint (285 ccm) water
2–3½ oz. (55–100 g) sugar
1 tbsp. lemon juice or white wine

Wash the apples, peel thinly, core and cut into quarters or eighths. Bring the water to the boil with 2 oz. (55 g) sugar, add the apples and simmer gently with the lid on the pan. Shake frequently and cook until the apples are soft and transparent. Remove the apples, then reduce the liquid by cooking a little longer with the lid off. Season with the lemon juice or wine and add more sugar, if necessary. Then pour the juice over the apples and serve.

Apple Purée

1 lb. 10 oz. (750 g) apples
4 tbsp. water
2–3½ oz. (55–100 g) sugar

Wash the apples and cut them up small. Bring them to the boil with the water in a covered pan and simmer gently until soft. Rub through a sieve and season to taste with sugar. Fill into a glass bowl. Level the surface with a knife and then press in a design. Garnish with little dots of jelly or swelled dried currants.

Stuffed Apples

1 lb. 10 oz. (750 g) apples
½ pint (285 ccm) water
½ pint (285 ccm) wine
3½ oz. (100 g) sugar
lemon peel or cinnamon

Choose apples of the same size. Peel smoothly and remove the core with a corer, leaving the apples whole. Boil the water and wine with the sugar and the lemon peel or cinnamon, then add the apples to the boiling liquid, placing them side by side in the pan. As soon as the apples are soft on one side turn them and cook in an uncovered pan until they are transparent. Remove the apples from the cooking liquid very carefully and set aside to cool. When they are cold, fill the centres with jam or jelly. Reduce the syrup by boiling a little longer and pour it over the apples.

Cooking Time: about 10 minutes.

Stewed Pears

1⅛ lb. (500 g) pears
½ pint (285 ccm) water
about 2 oz. (55 g) sugar
a little lemon peel or 1 packet Oetker Vanillin Sugar

Wash the pears, peel and halve them and remove the core. Bring the water to the boil with 1½ oz. (45 g) sugar and the lemon peel or vanillin sugar. Put the pears into the boiling liquid and cook until soft. Leave to cool, then add more sugar, if necessary.

Stewed Blackberries

1⅛ lb. (500 g) blackberries
¼ pint (140 ccm) water
3–3½ oz. (85–100 g) sugar

Pick over and wash the berries carefully. Add the sugar to the water and bring to the boil. Add the berries, then simmer gently until done. Leave to cool and add more sugar, if necessary.

Peel the marrow and scoop out the seeds. Cut with a garnishing knife into evenly sized pieces. Bring the water to the boil with 2 oz. (55 g) sugar, the lemon juice and the vinegar. Add the marrow, and cook until transparent. Leave to cool and add more sugar, if necessary.

Stewed Marrow

1⅛ lb. (500 g) marrow
½ pint (285 ccm) water
2–3 oz. (55–85 g) sugar
a little lemon peel
4–5 tbsp. vinegar

Wash the plums and remove the stalks. Do not stone. Bring the sugar and the water to the boil, add the plums and cook gently until tender. Leave to cool and add more sugar, if necessary.

Stewed Mirabelle Plums
(Small Yellow Plums)

1⅛ lb. (500 g) plums
2 oz. (55 g) sugar
¼ pint (140 ccm) water

Wash, halve and stone the plums. Bring the water to the boil with 2 oz. (55 g) sugar. Add the plums and spices and simmer gently until tender. Leave to cool and add more sugar, if necessary.

Stewed Plums

1⅛ lb. (500 g) plums
¼ pint (140 ccm) water
2–3 oz. (55–85 g) sugar
a piece of cinnamon
a few cloves to taste

Rub the quinces thoroughly with a cloth, peel, cut into quarters or eighths and core. Cover with water and cook gently until tender, adding 6 oz. (170 g) of the sugar a little before the end of the cooking time. Reduce the syrup by cooking a little longer, if necessary, and add more sugar.

Stewed Quinces

1⅛ lb. (500 g) quinces
a little water
6–7 oz. (170–200 g) sugar

Wash the greengages and prick them several times with a needle. Do not stone. Bring the water to the boil with 3 oz. (85 g) of the sugar, add the greengages and simmer gently until done. Leave to cool and add more sugar, if necessary.

Stewed Greengages

1⅛ lb. (500 g) greengages
¼ pint (140 ccm) water
3–3½ oz. (85–100 g) sugar

Top and tail the gooseberries with kitchen scissors, then wash. Bring the water to the boil with 3½ oz. (100 g) sugar, add the gooseberries and cook gently until tender. Do not stir the fruit. Leave to cool and add more sugar, if necessary.

Stewed Gooseberries

1⅛ lb. (500 g) half-ripe gooseberries
¼ pint (140 ccm) water
3½–5½ oz. (100–150 g) sugar

Wash the tomatoes and prick them several times with a needle. This prevents the skin breaking during cooking. Bring the water to the boil with the sugar and spices, add the tomatoes and simmer gently until tender.

Cooking Time: about 40 minutes.

Stewed Tomatoes

1⅛ lb. (500 g) firm green tomatoes
½ pint (285 ccm) water
9 oz. (250 g) sugar
a piece of ginger root
a little lemon rind

Dried Apple Rings

5 oz. (140 g) dried apple rings
1 pint (570 ccm) water
a little lemon or orange peel
2 oz. (55 g) sugar

Wash the apple rings thoroughly and soak in the water for 12–24 hours. Cook them in the liquid in which they have been soaked, together with the lemon or orange peel and the sugar until tender. Season to taste with red wine, if desired.

Cooking Time: about 15 minutes.

Dried Apricots

5 oz. (140 g) dried apricots
1 pint (570 ccm) water
2 oz. (55 g) sugar
1 slightly heaped tsp. Oetker GUSTIN
(corn starch powder)
a little cold water

Wash the apricots thoroughly and soak in the water for 12–24 hours. Cook them in the liquid in which they have been soaked, together with the sugar until tender. Thicken the juice with the GUSTIN, blended with the water.

Cooking Time: about 15 minutes.

Prunes

9 oz. (250 g) prunes
1 pint (570 ccm) water
1 oz. (30 g) sugar
a piece of cinnamon
1 heaped tsp. Oetker GUSTIN
(corn starch powder)
a little cold water

Wash the prunes thoroughly and soak in the water for 12–24 hours. Cook them in the liquid in which they have been soaked together with the sugar and cinnamon until tender. Thicken the juice with the GUSTIN, blended with the water.

Cooking Time: about 15 minutes.

Dried Fruit for Dumplings

9 oz. (250 g) dried mixed fruit
1⅓ pint (¾ l) water
a little lemon peel
a little cinnamon
2 oz. (55 g) sugar
3 heaped tsp. Oetker GUSTIN
(corn starch powder)
a little cold water

Wash the dried fruit thoroughly, then soak in the water for 12–24 hours. Bring to the boil in the liquid in which they have been soaked with the spices and the sugar and simmer over a low heat until tender. Thicken the juice with the GUSTIN, blended with the water.

Cooking Time: about 20 minutes.

D. BAKED FRUIT

Wash the apples, do not peel and core them very carefully without cutting through the stem end. Place the apples in a shallow greased baking-dish or on individual greased dishes. Fill each centre with butter, sugar and vanillin sugar and bake in the oven until done. Pour a little wine over them before serving, if desired.

Oven: moderate heat.

Time: 30–45 minutes.

Alternatively, the apples may be filled with redcurrant jelly and placed on slices of white bread.

Baked Apples

8 apples
1 oz. (30 g) butter
a little sugar
1 packet Oetker Vanillin Sugar

Wash the plums, but do not stone them. Put them into a greased baking-dish and mix with the sugar. Bake in the oven.

Oven: slow to moderate.

Time: about 25 minutes.

Baked Roman Plums
(Blue Plums)

1⅛ lb. (500 g) blue plums
2 oz. (55 g) sugar

Wash the apples and peel them carefully, using a garnishing knife, if available. Core them and put them into the boiling sugared water. Cook them gently until done, but do not allow them to lose their shape. Remove them carefully from the syrup and place them on a greased shallow fireproof dish. Leave the syrup to boil a little longer, then pour over the apples. Fill the centres with a little fruit jelly. Beat the egg whites until stiff, then whisk in the sugar. Spread evenly over the apples and bake in the oven.

Oven: moderate heat.

Time: 10–15 minutes.

Apple Meringues

4 medium-sized apples
½ pint (285 ccm) water
3–3½ oz. (85–100 g) sugar
a little fruit jelly
1–2 egg whites
1 tbsp. sugar

Wash, peel and core the apples and cut into ½ inch (1 cm) rings. To make the batter, sieve the flour with the BACKIN into a bowl, make a well in the centre and add the sugar and the egg. Starting from the middle, carefully mix the egg into the flour, gradually adding the milk, until the batter is smooth and of a good dropping consistency. Dip the apple rings into the batter and put into the very hot fat. Fry until golden brown on both sides, remove from the fat, sprinkle with sugar and serve as a dessert.

Time: 1–2 minutes.

Many other fruits — rhubarb or bananas in slices, slices of pineapples, peach or apricot halves — all make delicious fritters, prepared in the same way as apple fritters.

Apple Fritters
(Phot. See Page 250)

1 lb. 10 oz. (750 g) cooking apples

Batter:

9 oz. (250 g) plain flour
3 level tsp. (9 g) Oetker Baking
    Powder BACKIN
1 oz. (30 g) sugar
1 egg
about ½ pint (285 ccm) milk
fat for deep-frying

For Sprinkling:

2 oz. (55 g) sugar

E. FRUIT PUDDINGS OR PIES

General Hints See general hints given for the baking of pies on page 256.

Apple Layer Pudding

1⅛ lb. (500 g) apples
2 eggs
4½ oz. (125 g) sugar
4 drops Oetker Baking Essence, lemon flavour
4½ oz. (125 g) plain flour
2 level tsp. (6 g) Oetker Baking Powder BACKIN

Wash, peel, core and slice the apples. Beat the eggs and the sugar until frothy, add the baking essence and fold in the sieved flour mixed with the BACKIN. Fill the mixture alternately with the apples into a greased pie-dish. The top layer should not be apples. Bake in the oven until golden brown.

Oven: slow to moderate.

Time: about 30 minutes.

Stoned cherries, bilberries, or stoned plums may be used instead of apples.

Cherry Pudding

9 oz. (250 g) left-over cake, white bread, rusks or stale roll
⅔ pint (375 ccm) milk, but only ¼ pint (140 ccm) of milk is needed if cake crumbs are used
3 eggs
1 oz. (30 g) butter or margarine
3–3½ oz. (85–100 g) sugar
1 packet Oetker Vanillin Sugar
1 heaped tsp. plain flour
1 level tsp. (3 g) Oetker Baking Powder BACKIN
14 oz. (400 g) sweet or sour cherries

Grate the cake, bread or rusks and mix with the milk and the eggs. Allow to soak for about 10 minutes. Then add to it the melted fat, the sugar, the vanillin sugar and the flour sieved with the BACKIN. Fold in the washed and stoned cherries. Put the mixture into a greased pie-dish and bake until golden brown.

Oven: moderate heat.

Time: 35–45 minutes.

Cherry Semolina Pudding

2 oz. (55 g) butter or margarine
4½ oz. (125 g) sugar
1 packet Oetker Vanillin Sugar
3–4 drops Oetker Baking Essence, bitter almond flavour
2 eggs
5½ oz. (150 g) semolina
4½ oz. (125 g) plain flour
3 level tsp. (9 g) Oetker Baking Powder BACKIN
½ pint (285 ccm) milk
1⅛ lb. (500 g) dark sweet cherries, or sour cherries

Cream the fat, then gradually add the sugar, the vanillin sugar, the baking essence, the eggs and the semolina. Sieve the flour with the BACKIN and stir this into the mixture alternately with the milk. Fold in the washed, stoned cherries, place into a greased pie-dish and bake in the oven until done.

Oven: slow to moderate.

Time: 50–60 minutes.

Any other fruit may be used instead of cherries.

Snow-Capped Fruit Pudding

3½ oz. (100 g) rusks
about ½ pint (285 ccm) milk
5 drops Oetker rum flavour
about 1⅛ lb. (500 g) mixed stewed
fruit
1 pint (570 ccm) milk
1 packet Oetker Pudding Powder,
vanilla flavour
2 oz. (55 g) sugar
6 tbsp. water or milk
1 egg yolk
1 egg white
2 tsp. sugar

Mix the rum flavour with the ½ pint (285 ccm) of milk and bring to the boil. Soak the rusks in this hot milk. Pour the stewed fruit into a well greased pie-dish and arrange the rusks in a layer on top of the fruit.

Make up the pudding mixture according to the instructions given on the packet, using the egg yolk, and pour this on top of the rusks. Beat the egg white until stiff and whisk in the sugar. Spread evenly on top of the pudding and bake in the oven.

Oven: slow to moderate.

Time: about 20 minutes.

Rhubarb Pudding with Cream

11 oz. (310 g) rhubarb
3½ oz. (100 g) sugar
4½ oz. (125 g) rusks
2 oz. (55 g) butter
3 eggs
1 oz. (30 g) sugar
1 packet Oetker Vanillin Sugar
1½ oz. (45 g) Oetker GUSTIN
(corn starch powder)
1 level tsp. (3 g) Oetker Baking Powder
BACKIN
6–7 tbsp. fresh or sour cream

Wash the rhubarb and cut it into 1½ inch (4 cm) pieces. Do not skin. Sprinkle with the 3½ oz. (100 g) sugar and leave to stand until sufficient juice has accumulated. Bring to the boil and simmer gently until soft. Set aside to cool. Spread both sides of the rusks with butter and line the bottom of a greased pie-dish with them. Pour over the cold rhubarb and lastly add the egg mixture, which should be prepared as follows. Whisk the egg yolks, the sugar and vanillin sugar together until frothy. Beat the egg white until stiff and put this onto the egg mixture. Sieve the GUSTIN together with the BACKIN onto this and carefully fold into the egg mixture. Then, gradually add the cream. Pour this on top of the rhubarb. Bake in the oven until golden brown.

Oven: slow to moderate.

Time: 20–25 minutes.

EGG COOKERY

By its very nature the egg contains in itself all food required by a growing organism. Rich in protein, fat, minerals, and almost all the vitamins, the egg is one of our most valuable foods. Starch is the only nutritive substance in which it is deficient.

The protein and fat in one medium-sized egg correspond to a cup of milk, or 1½ oz. (45 g) of good fat meat. The yolk is the richest part of the egg; it has a lower water content than the white, is one-third fat, and contains a higher percentage (11–12%) than any other food of lecithin, which is particularly valuable to the brain and the nerves. The yolk contains all the vitamins, with the exception of vitamin C, whereas the white has hardly any; the white, too, has less than half the minerals of the yolk, which is also especially rich in phosphorous and calcium. These important body-building properties of the yolk make the egg a food especially suitable for children and invalids.

In the yolk, too, lies the flavour of the egg. This, like the colour of the yolk, depends on how the hen has been fed. Grain fed hens produce eggs with pale yolks, yolks of a reddish-yellow come from hens on free range, whereas those of a rich yellow indicate that the hens have eaten green food. Incidentally, milk and butter are also of a much stronger, and richer colour when the cows have had green fodder.

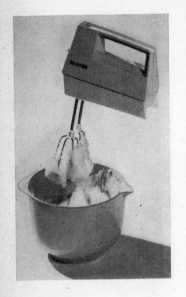

Apart from its nutritive value, the egg serves many very useful culinary purposes. We use it for thickening and at the same time, enriching, such dishes as soups, sauces, and pastes (macaroni, spaghetti, etc.). The white of the egg gives lightness to cakes and desserts. The whisking of the white breaks down the delicate cell tissues, drawing in air, which produces tiny air-filled bubbles. Egg white, too, is used to clarify clear soups and stocks. It binds together all the opaque substances, leaving the liquid clear. It is therefore indispensable for the preparation of jellies and aspics.

A freshly laid egg is germ-free. But its shell, which is made of calcium, is porous, and bacteria penetrate with the air through the fine pores, causing the egg to deteriorate, and to lose weight and flavour. Eggs readily absorb odours and should not be kept near strong smelling foods. So always store eggs for immediate consumption in a cool, airy place.

Since washing destroys the natural protective qualities of the shell, and allows bacteria to penetrate, it is advisable to wash eggs only just before they are to be used.

To preserve eggs for several months, use water-glass, lime, or one of the special egg preservatives. Chopped straw and bran are not recommended, because the eggs absorb the characteristic musty smell of these preserving agents. Lime water has the disadvantages of transferring its chalky flavour to the eggs, and of making the whites of eggs very difficult to whisk. A 10% solution of water-glass is the most satisfactory method. Eggs lose nothing of their flavour, and the whites can be beaten as easily as fresh ones. Allow about 1¾ pint (1 l) of water-glass to 16 pints (9 l) of water; this is enough to preserve about 200 eggs.

A fresh egg is clear when held up against a strong light, and shows a small air bubble. In a vessel containing a 10% salt solution, a fresh egg will sink to the bottom. If it floats, it is stale. Eggs laid in the spring have the best flavour, and should be preserved at that time of the year.

1. Before cooking, clean the egg thoroughly with water; remove any clinging dirt particles by rubbing with salt or washing with water.

2. Break each egg separately into a cup to test its freshness.

3. Beat the egg well before stirring it into a dish, so that the egg yolk and the egg white will be evenly mixed.

4. If the egg yolk only is used, mix it well with 1 tbsp. of water before adding it to the dish.

5. It is best to use the egg yolk alone for thickening soups and sauces. Add 2 tbsp. of cold water to the yolk and whisk thoroughly with a fork. Slowly add some of the hot liquid, stirring all the time; then add this mixture to the soup or sauce, which should be off the heat when this is done. Be especially careful if you use a whole egg for thickening; once the egg has been added to the soup or sauce, it should not be allowed to boil again, or it will curdle. A dish which has been thickened with whole egg should be reheated with the greatest care. It is better to keep it hot in a saucepan containing hot water or in a double boiler. (See page 269 — How to keep desserts firm.)

6. If the white is to be whisked, separate it very carefully from the yolk, making sure that no yolk is left in the white. One or two egg whites can easily be beaten in a flat plate, using a fork. If more than 2 eggs are used, beat them in a bowl, using a rotary beater or wire egg whisk. Beat until very stiff. They must not run out when the basin is tipped to one side or even upside down. Use immediately after beating, as whisked egg white liquifies if left standing.

7. Fold in beaten egg white lightly; never stir.

8. Left-over egg yolk will keep for 1–2 days if covered with water.

A. RAW EGGS

Beaten Egg

1 egg
pinch of salt or sugar

Beat the whole egg well with a pinch of salt or a little sugar. If desired, whisk in 1 tsp. of brandy or 1 tbsp. lemon juice. This makes an excellent tonic for invalids and convalescents.

Alternatively, the egg white may be beaten to a stiff froth and then the egg yolk and flavourings stirred in.

Egg in Clear Soup

1 egg
1 cup of meat or vegetable stock

Remove the fat from the stock and gradually add the well-beaten egg.

Egg with Milk

1 egg or 2 egg yolks
1 tbsp. sugar
1 glass of hot milk

Beat the sugar into the egg or egg yolks, then add the hot milk by degrees. This is a good remedy to relieve coughs or hoarseness.

Egg with Wine

1 egg or 2 egg yolks
2 tbsp. sugar
1 glass of red or white wine

Beat the egg or egg yolks with the sugar until frothy, then slowly add the wine.

B. BOILED EGGS

Boiled Eggs

The eggs must be fresh and clean. If several eggs are to be boiled at the same time, put them in a wire basket. Lower into the boiling water so that all the eggs start to cook at the same time. Use plenty of water, so that when the eggs are put in, they will not reduce the temperature of the water. Warm very cold eggs beforehand in warm water, or they will crack when put into boiling water. As soon as the eggs are done, put them in cold water for a very short time. This makes it easier to remove the shells.

Cooking Time: for soft-boiled eggs 3–4 minutes;
for medium-boiled eggs 4–5 minutes;
for hard-boiled eggs 8–10 minutes.

Poached Eggs

1¾ pint (1 l) water
salt
2 tbsp. vinegar
4–6 eggs

Add the salt and the vinegar to the water and bring it to the boil. Break each egg into a saucer, then slip it gently into the boiling water. Do not cook more than 4–6 eggs at one time. As soon as the whites are firm, remove them with a perforated spoon (a skimming ladle) and dip for an instant into cold water. Trim the edges of the eggs.

Cooking Time: 3–4 minutes.

Serve poached eggs as a garnish for clear soups, on toast as hors d'œuvre, or with a sauce as a main course.

Italian Salad Recipe See Page 196 · Egg Salad Recipe See Page 194
Chicken Salad Recipe See Page 194

Boil fresh eggs until they are hard. Crack the shell slightly, then put the eggs into brine which must be strong enough to float them. Leave the eggs in the brine for at least 24 hours. Eggs can be preserved in brine for 6–8 days.

Cooking Time: 10 minutes.

Eggs in Brine

Boiled as well as poached eggs are suitable for the sauces here suggested. Poached eggs should be left whole, boiled eggs cut into halves or quarters. Put the eggs into a shallow serving dish, pour over the warm sauce and garnish. Serve with fried potatoes and lettuce salad, as a main course.

As an alternative put layers of freshly boiled, sliced potatoes with thick slices of egg into a fireproof dish, pour on the sauce and leave for a while over steam.

Serve with lettuce salad.

Eggs in Hot Sauce

4–8 eggs
1 pint (570 ccm) Béchamel Sauce
   (see page 51)
4–8 eggs
1 pint (570 ccm) Tomato Sauce
   (see page 52)
4–8 eggs
1 pint (570 ccm) Mushroom Sauce
   (see page 49)
4–8 eggs
1 pint (570 ccm) Mustard Sauce
   (see page 49)
4–8 eggs·
1 pint (570 ccm) Bacon Sauce
   (see page 56)

Boil or poach the eggs, place on pieces of toast or in scooped out tomato halves or on lettuce leaves. Pour over one of the suggested sauces.

Eggs in Cold Sauce

6–8 eggs
recipe for Mustard Dressing
   (see page 59)
6–8 eggs
recipe for Mayonnaise
   (see page 59)
6–8 eggs
recipe for Rémoulade Sauce
   (see page 60)
6–8 eggs
recipe for Devil's Sauce
   (see page 60)

215

Pigeons Recipe See Page 111

Egg Fricassee

6–8 eggs
cooked asparagus tips

Fricassee Sauce:

1½ oz. (45 g) butter or margarine
1½ oz. (45 g) plain flour
1 pint (570 ccm) stock
1 tsp. capers
a few mushrooms (optional)
1–2 anchovies,
well soaked in water (optional)
salt
1 tbsp. lemon juice or 2–3 tbsp. wine
1–2 egg yolks
2 tbsp. cold water

Small Bread Balls:

1 oz. (30 g) butter or margarine
1 egg
salt
about 1½ oz. (45 g) breadcrumbs

For the sauce, melt the fat, stir in the flour and cook until pale yellow. Gradually add the cold stock and boil the sauce gently for about 10 minutes. Add the capers, the finely sliced mushrooms and the finely chopped anchovies. Leave to simmer in the sauce for about 10 minutes before adding the salt and the lemon juice or wine. Beat the egg yolks with the cold water and add to the sauce.

When the sauce is ready, shell and slice the hard-boiled eggs and add them with the cooked asparagus tips to the fricassee sauce.

For the bread balls, cream the fat, add the egg, salt, and sufficient breadcrumbs to make a smooth dough. Set aside for about half an hour, then shape into small balls. Boil in salted water until done and serve in the fricassee.

Cooking Time: for the bread balls, about 3 minutes.

If preferred, the fricassee may be served in shells, sprinkled with grated cheese and browned in the oven.

Stuffed Eggs
(Phot. See Page 17)

Halve hard-boiled eggs lengthwise, or, cut off the top. Carefully scoop out the yolk and rub through a fine sieve. Add to it some salad oil, lemon juice, mustard and salt and mix to a smooth paste. Stuff the eggs or egg halves generously with the mixture and serve on lettuce leaves, garnished with anchovies or sliced pickled gherkins.

Serve with Mayonnaise, if desired.

The egg yolk stuffing may be enriched by the addition of finely sliced, sautéd mushrooms, tomato purée, finely chopped green herbs, finely chopped anchovies, or finely minced ham. Season with salt, if necessary, and stuff into the eggs.

Egg Salad
Recipe see page 194.

C. SCRAMBLED EGGS

Egg Custard
Recipe see page 42.

Mince the ham finely and mix with the cheese. A mixture of different left-over cheeses may be used. Grease four cups or small moulds well with melted fat and break one egg into each. Spread with the ham mixture, cover the moulds and put them into hot, but not boiling water. As soon as the mixture is set, turn out the moulds onto a shallow plate.

Time: about 30 minutes.

Serve with lettuce salad and Tomato Sauce (see page 52) or with Fricassee Sauce (see page 51).

Moulded Eggs with Ham

2 oz. (55 g) boiled ham
1½ oz. (45 g) grated cheese
a little butter or margarine to grease
     the moulds
4 eggs

Beat the eggs with the milk and the lemon juice and mix with the minced leftovers, the capers and the finely chopped anchovy. Season to taste and fill into well greased moulds. Cover the moulds and put into hot, but not boiling water. When the mixture is set, turn out onto slices of toast.

Time: about 20 minutes.

Eggs on Toast
(Leftovers)

4 eggs
¼ pint (140 ccm) milk
1 tsp. lemon juice
9 oz. (250 g) left-over chicken, veal,
     calf's brain, fish or ham
1 tsp. capers
1 soaked anchovy
a little butter or margarine to grease
     the moulds

Beat the eggs, the milk and salt well together and pour them into the heated fat. As soon as the mixture begins to set, stir it with a spoon to prevent it from sticking to the bottom of the pan. Keep over a low heat until no liquid egg is left. Scrambled eggs should be soft and flaky, but not dry.

Time: about 5 minutes.

Serve with fried potatoes, asparagus, mushrooms, ham or bloaters.

Scrambled eggs may be cooked without fat, like egg custard, in a double-boiler or in a basin over hot water (recommended for those on a diet).

Scrambled Eggs

1 oz. (30 g) butter or margarine
4 eggs
4 tbsp. milk
pinch of salt

Beat the eggs, the flour, the salt and the water well together. Pour into the heated fat, and when it begins to set, stir it with a spoon to prevent it from sticking to the bottom of the pan. Keep over a low heat until no liquid egg is left. Scrambled eggs should be soft and flaky but not dry.

Time: about 5 minutes.

Scrambled Eggs
(Economical Method)

3 eggs
¾ oz. (20 g) plain flour
1 tsp. salt
⅓ pint (200 ccm) water
1 oz. (30 g) butter or margarine

Scrambled Eggs with Ham

4 eggs
4 tbsp. milk
pinch of salt
2 oz. (55 g) ham
1 oz. (30 g) butter or margarine

Beat together the eggs, the milk and salt. Add the finely diced ham. Melt the fat and pour in the egg mixture. As soon as it begins to set, stir it with a spoon to prevent it from sticking to the bottom of the pan. Keep over a low heat until no liquid egg is left. Scrambled eggs should be soft and flaky but not dry.

Time: about 5 minutes.

Alternatively, 2 oz. (55 g) finely chopped Salami can be used instead of the ham.

Scrambled Eggs with Bacon

2 oz. (55 g) bacon
4 eggs
4 tbsp. milk
pinch of salt

Dice the bacon finely and fry gently until pale yellow. Beat together the eggs, the milk and the salt and pour over the bacon. As soon as the mixture begins to set, stir with a spoon to prevent it from sticking to the bottom of the pan. Keep over a low heat until no liquid egg is left. Scrambled eggs should be soft and flaky but not dry.

Time: about 5 minutes.

Scrambled Eggs with Cheese or Chives

4 eggs
4 tbsp. milk
pinch of salt
1 tbsp. grated cheese or finely chopped chives
1 oz. (30 g) butter or margarine

Beat together the eggs, the milk and salt, then add the cheese or the chives. Heat the fat and pour in the egg mixture. When it begins to set, stir it with a spoon to prevent it from sticking to the bottom of the pan. Keep over a low heat until no liquid egg is left. Scrambled eggs should be soft and flaky but not dry.

Time: about 5 minutes.

Scrambled Eggs with Asparagus or Bloaters

4 eggs
4 tbsp. milk
pinch of salt
1 oz. (30 g) butter or margarine
3½ oz. (100 g) cooked asparagus pieces or 2 skinned and boned bloaters, cut into strips

Beat together the eggs, the milk and salt. Melt the fat in a pan, add the asparagus pieces or the bloater strips, then pour in the egg mixture. As soon as the mixture begins to set, stir it with a spoon to prevent it from sticking to the bottom of the pan. Keep over a low heat until no liquid egg is left. Scrambled eggs should be soft and flaky but not dry.

Time: about 5 minutes.

Scrambled Eggs with Tomatoes

4 eggs
4 tbsp. milk
pinch of salt
1 oz. (30 g) butter or margarine
2–3 tomatoes

Beat together the eggs, the milk and salt. Melt the fat and pour in the egg mixture. Slice the washed tomatoes and add them to the eggs, when they are half cooked. Stir the mixture with a spoon to prevent it from sticking to the bottom of the pan. Keep over a low heat until no liquid egg is left. Scrambled eggs should be soft and flaky but not dry.

Time: about 5 minutes.

D. FRIED EGGS

Heat the fat in a frying-pan, break the eggs carefully and slide them side by side into the fat. Sprinkle with fine salt and cook very gently until set.

A fireproof dish of porcelain or glass is excellent for frying eggs, as they can then be served in the cooking dish. Fried eggs which are to be served on spinach, on slices of bread, or on tomatoes, should be trimmed with a round pastry cutter or the top of a glass.

Time: about 5 minutes.

The eggs may be broken into a plate and cooked until set over boiling water (recommended for those on a diet).

Fried Eggs

1 oz. (30 g) butter or margarine
4–6 eggs
salt

Put thin slices of bacon or ham into a frying-pan and fry lightly. Break the eggs side by side on top of the bacon or ham, sprinkle with fine salt and cook until set.

Frying Time: about 6 minutes.

Bacon or Ham and Eggs

1–1½ oz. (30–45 g) bacon or ham
4–6 eggs
salt

Melt the fat in a frying-pan, add the washed and sliced tomatoes, then the eggs. Sprinkle with fine salt and cook until the eggs are set.

Frying Time: about 5 minutes.

Fried Eggs with Tomatoes

1 oz. (30 g) butter or margarine
2–3 firm tomatoes
4–6 eggs
salt

E. OMELETTES AND PANCAKES

Beat together the eggs, salt and milk. Heat the fat in a frying-pan, but be careful not to brown it. Pour in the egg mixture and let it set very slowly over a low heat. The underside of the omelette should be golden brown, but it should still be creamy on top. Fold the omelette over, starting at the handle end of the pan and slide it gently onto a warm oblong dish. Sprinkle with icing sugar, if it is to be a dessert and serve at once.

Time: about 10 minutes.

Alternatively, 1 tbsp. of finely chopped herbs (chervil, parsley, chives, spinach, tarragon), or ¾ oz. (20 g) grated cheese may be added to the egg mixture for a savoury omelette.

Omelette

3 eggs
salt
1 tbsp. milk
about 1 oz. (30 g) butter or margarine

Stuffed Omelette

3 eggs
salt
1 tbsp. milk
about 1 oz. (30 g) butter or margarine

Savoury Stuffing:
sautéd finely sliced mushrooms,
asparagus pieces, peas, minced roast
or poultry leftovers;
or

Sweet Stuffing:
jelly or jam

Beat together the eggs, salt and milk. Melt the fat in a frying-pan, but do not brown it. Pour in the egg mixture. Allow to set very slowly over a low heat. The underside of the omelette should be golden brown, but it should still be creamy on top. Cover half of the top of the omelette with the desired stuffing and fold over the other half.

Choose a savoury stuffing if the omelette is to be the main course or an hors d'oeuvre; a jam or jelly stuffing, if it is to be a dessert.

Omelette Soufflé

3 egg yolks
rind and juice of half a lemon
1 oz. (30 g) sugar
3 egg whites
1 heaped tsp. Oetker GUSTIN
(corn starch powder)
about 1 oz. (30 g) butter or margarine

Stuffing:
stewed cranberries or any jam
(optional)
a little icing sugar for dusting

Beat together the egg yolks, the grated lemon peel, the lemon juice and the sugar until frothy. Whisk the egg whites until stiff and put on top of the egg yolk mixture. Sprinkle with the GUSTIN and fold into the egg yolk mixture. Use a fairly large frying-pan, melt the fat and pour in the mixture. Cover with a lid. Cook very slowly on a low heat until the underside is golden brown. Fold in half, dust with icing sugar and serve.

If stuffed with cranberries or jam, it makes a delicious dessert.

(Two omelettes can also be made from this quantity.)

Pancakes I

9 oz. (250 g) plain flour
1 level tsp. (3 g) Oetker Baking Powder
BACKIN
2–3 egg yolks
1 tsp. salt
¾ pint and 5 tbsp. (500 ccm) milk
2–3 egg whites
about 4 oz. (115 g) fat for frying

Sieve the flour and the BACKIN into a bowl. Beat together the egg yolks, the salt and a little of the milk. Make a well in the middle of the flour and pour in the egg mixture. Starting from the middle, combine the egg mixture with the flour. Gradually add the remaining milk and stir until smooth and free from lumps. Whisk the egg whites until stiff and fold lightly into the batter. Heat a little fat in a frying-pan, pour in some of the batter and fry on both sides until brown. Put a little fat on the uncooked side of the pancakes before turning. As the pancakes are cooked, slide them onto a warmed plate and sprinkle with sugar.

Frying Time: 25–30 minutes.

Serve with stewed fruit or salad.

Sieve the flour, the sauce powder and the BACKIN into a bowl. Beat together the egg yolks, a little of the milk, the salt and the sugar. Make a well in the middle of the flour and pour in the egg mixture. Starting from the middle, combine the egg mixture with the flour; gradually add the remaining milk and stir until smooth and free from lumps. Whisk the egg whites until stiff and fold them lightly into the batter. Heat a little fat in a frying-pan, pour in a little of the batter and fry on both sides until golden brown. Put a little fat on the uncooked side of the pancake before turning. As the pancakes are cooked, slide them onto a warmed plate and sprinkle with a little sugar.

Time: 25–30 minutes.

Serve with stewed fruit or salad.

Pancakes II
(Golden Yellow)

½ lb. (225 g) plain flour
1 packet Oetker Sauce Powder,
   vanilla flavour
2 level tsp. (6 g) Oetker Baking Powder
   BACKIN
2–3 egg yolks
1 tsp. salt
sugar
¾ pint and 5 tbsp. (500 ccm) milk
2–3 egg whites
about 4 oz. (115 g) fat for frying

Sieve the flour and the BACKIN into a bowl. Beat together the egg yolks, the salt and a little of the milk. Make a well in the middle of the flour and pour in the egg mixture. Starting from the middle, combine the egg mixture with the flour, gradually add the remaining milk and stir until smooth and free from lumps. Whisk the egg whites until stiff and fold them lightly into the batter. Heat some thin rashers of bacon or thin slices of ham in a frying-pan until browned. Pour over a little batter and fry on both sides until golden brown.

Serve with lettuce salad.

Pancakes with Bacon or Ham

9 oz. (250 g) plain flour
1 level tsp. (3 g) Oetker Baking Powder
   BACKIN
2–3 egg yolks
1 tsp. salt
¾ pint and 5 tbsp. (500 ccm) milk
2–3 egg whites
about 4 oz. (115 g) streaky bacon
   or ham
about 4 oz. (115 g) fat for frying

Sieve the flour and the BACKIN into a bowl. Beat together the egg yolks, the salt and a little of the milk. Make a well in the middle of the flour and pour in the egg mixture. Starting from the middle, combine the egg mixture with the flour, gradually add the remaining milk and stir until smooth and free from lumps. Then stir in the herbs. Whisk the egg whites until stiff and lightly fold them into the batter. Heat a little fat in a frying-pan, pour in a small quantity of batter and cook both sides golden brown. Put a little fat on the uncooked side of the pancake before turning. As the pancakes are cooked, slide them onto a warmed plate.

Serve with Mushroom (see page 49) or Tomato Sauce (see page 52), or as an accompaniment to vegetables.

If preferred, 1½ oz. (45 g) of grated cheese may be added to the batter instead of the herbs.

Green Pancakes

9 oz. (250 g) plain flour
1 level tsp. (3 g) Oetker Baking Powder
   BACKIN
2–3 egg yolks
1 tsp. salt
¾ pint and 5 tbsp. (500 ccm) milk
2–3 tbsp. finely chopped herbs
2–3 egg whites
about 4 oz. (115 g) fat for frying

Potato Pancakes

9 oz. (250 g) plain flour
1 level tsp. (3 g) Oetker Baking Powder
BACKIN
2–3 egg yolks
1 tsp. salt
¾ pint and 5 tbsp. (500 ccm) milk
1–2 tbsp. chopped chives
2–3 egg whites
about 1 lb. (450 g) potatoes
(boiled in their skins, peeled and sliced)
about 4 oz. (115 g) fat for frying

Sieve the flour and the BACKIN into a bowl. Beat together the egg yolks, the salt and a little of the milk. Make a well in the middle of the flour and pour in the egg mixture. Starting from the middle, combine the egg mixture with the flour. Gradually add the remaining milk and stir until smooth and free from lumps. Then stir in the chives. Whisk the egg whites until stiff and fold them lightly into the batter. Heat a little fat in a frying-pan. Pour in a thin layer of batter, put potato slices on top and fry on both sides golden brown. Put a little fat on the uncooked side of the pancake before turning. As the pancakes are cooked, slide them onto a warmed plate.

Serve with lettuce salad.

These pancakes are even more delicious if about 4 oz. (115 g) of diced ham is added. Sprinkle the ham over the sliced potatoes.

Stuffed Pancakes
(Savoury)
(Phot. See Page 109)

Batter:
9 oz. (250 g) plain flour
1 level tsp. (3 g) Oetker Baking Powder
BACKIN
2–3 egg yolks
1 tsp. salt
¾ pint and 5 tbsp. (500 ccm) milk
2–3 egg whites
about 4 oz. (115 g) fat for frying

Vegetable Stuffing:
about 1 lb. (450 g) vegetables –
asparagus, young peas, salsify,
mushrooms and tomatoes
salt
some fat
a little plain flour
or

Meat or Fish Stuffing:
leftovers of roast, ham, poultry or fish
a little gravy or stock and plain flour
lemon juice
finely chopped parsley
a few drops Worcester sauce or similar
savoury sauce

For the batter, sieve the flour and the BACKIN into a bowl. Beat together the egg yolks, the salt and a little of the milk. Make a well in the middle of the flour and pour in the egg mixture. Starting from the middle, combine the egg mixture with the flour. Gradually add the remaining milk and stir until smooth and free from lumps. Whisk the egg whites until stiff and fold them lightly into the batter.

Heat a little fat in a frying-pan, pour in a thin layer of batter and fry on both sides until golden brown. Put a little fat on the uncooked side of the pancake before turning. Spread the stuffing on half of each pancake, then fold over, or, alternatively, put the pancakes onto a warmed plate, spread with stuffing and top with another pancake and so on These pancakes may also be cut into sections, coated in egg and breadcrumbs, then fried in butter.

For the vegetable stuffing, cook the vegetables in a little water, season with salt, add some fat and thicken with a little flour, blended with cold water.

For the meat or fish stuffing, finely chop the leftovers, and moisten them with a little left-over gravy or stock, thickened with flour, mixed with cold water. Season to taste with lemon juice, parsley and a few drops of Worcester sauce, if desired.

For the batter, sieve together the flour, the BACKIN and the sauce powder into a bowl. Beat together the egg yolks, salt, sugar and a little of the milk. Make a well in the middle of the flour and pour in the egg mixture. Starting from the middle, combine the egg mixture with the flour. Gradually add the remaining milk and stir until smooth and free from lumps. Whisk the egg whites until stiff and fold them lightly into the batter.

Heat some fat in a frying-pan and pour in a thin layer of batter. Fry on both sides until golden brown. Put a little fat on the uncooked side of the pancake before turning.

For the stuffing, rub the cottage cheese through a fine sieve. Stir in the eggs and the washed currants and season with sugar to taste. Spread some stuffing on half of the hot pancake and fold over.

Stuffed Pancakes
(Sweet)

Batter:

3½ oz. (100 g) plain flour
½ packet Oetker Sauce Powder, vanilla flavour
1 level tsp. (3 g) Oetker Baking Powder BACKIN
1–2 egg yolks
½ tsp. salt
a little sugar
about ⅓ pint (200 ccm) milk
1–2 egg whites
about 3 oz. (85 g) fat for frying

Stuffing:

11 oz. (300 g) cottage cheese
1–2 eggs
2 oz. (55 g) currants
about 1½ oz. (45 g) sugar

For the batter, sieve together the flour, the BACKIN and the sauce powder into a bowl. Beat together the egg yolks, the salt, sugar and a little of the milk. Make a well in the middle of the flour and pour in the egg mixture. Starting from the middle, combine the egg mixture with the flour. Gradually add the remaining milk and stir until smooth and free from lumps. Whisk the egg whites until stiff and fold gently into the batter.

Pancakes with Apples: melt a little fat in a frying-pan and pour in a thin layer of batter. As the pancake begins to set, put in some peeled, sliced apples. Fry on both sides until golden brown. Sprinkle with sugar and serve.

Pancakes with Cherries or Plums: melt a little fat in a frying-pan and pour in a thin layer of batter. As the pancake begins to set, put some of the stoned fruit on top of it, pour over some more batter and fry on both sides until golden brown. Do not turn the pancake over until it is quite set on top. Sprinkle with sugar and serve.

Pancakes with Bilberries or Red or Black Currants: melt a little fat in a frying-pan, pour in a thin layer of batter and fry on one side until golden yellow, turn, and put bilberries or red currants on top. Cover the pan with a lid and stew the fruit slowly. When ready, sprinkle with sugar and serve.

This delicious dessert may also be served cold, with coffee.

Pancakes with Fruit

Batter:

½ lb. (225 g) plain flour
1 packet Oetker Sauce Powder, vanilla flavour
2 level tsp. (6 g) Oetker Baking Powder BACKIN
2–3 egg yolks
1 tsp. salt
a little sugar
¾ pint and 5 tbsp. (500 ccm) milk
2–3 egg whites
about 4 oz. (115 g) fat for frying

Fruit:

about 2¼ lb. (1 kg) apples, cherries, plums, bilberries, or red or black currants
sugar to sprinkle

"Pfitzauf"

3 oz. (85 g) plain flour
2 oz. (55 g) Oetker GUSTIN
(corn starch powder)
3 eggs
pinch of salt
½ pint (285 ccm) milk
1 oz. (30 g) melted butter or margarine

Sieve together the flour and the GUSTIN into a bowl. Beat together the eggs, salt and a little of the milk. Make a well in the middle of the flour and pour in the egg mixture. Starting from the middle, combine the egg mixture with the flour. Gradually add the remaining milk and the melted fat and stir until smooth and free from lumps. Grease some patty tins and half fill each with batter.

Oven: slow to moderate.

Baking Time: about 35 minutes.

Serve with soup made of pears or prunes.

F. SOUFFLÉS AND OTHER EGG DISHES

Baked Omelette Soufflé

4 egg yolks
3½ oz. (100 g) sugar
4 egg whites
¾ oz. (20 g) Oetker GUSTIN
(corn starch powder)
a little icing sugar

Whisk the egg yolks and the sugar until frothy. Beat the whites until stiff and fold them together with the GUSTIN lightly into the egg yolks. Pile the mixture into a well-buttered oval fireproof dish and bake in the oven. When done, sprinkle the soufflé with sugar and serve at once.

Oven: slow to moderate.

Baking Time: 30–35 minutes.

Lemon Soufflé

4 egg yolks
grated rind of 1 lemon
3½ oz. (100 g) sugar
juice of 1 lemon
4 egg whites
¾ oz. (20 g) Oetker GUSTIN
(corn starch powder)
a little icing sugar

Whisk together the egg yolks, the lemon rind and the sugar until frothy. Gradually add the lemon juice. Beat the whites until stiff and fold them together with the GUSTIN lightly into the egg mixture. Pile the mixture into a buttered oval fireproof dish and bake in the oven. When done, sprinkle with sugar and serve at once.

Oven: slow to moderate.

Baking Time: 30–35 minutes.

225

Peach Ring Recipe See Page 271
Cold Tea with Lemon Juice Recipe See Page 263

Apple, Apricot or Strawberry Soufflé

4 egg yolks
3½ oz. (100 g) sugar
1⅛ lb. (500 g) apples, apricots
or strawberries
¾ oz. (20 g) Oetker GUSTIN
(corn starch powder)
4 egg whites
a little icing sugar

Whisk together the egg yolks and the sugar until frothy. Wash, peel and grate the apples, or wash and stone the apricots and rub them through a sieve, or wash the strawberries and rub them through a sieve. Add the GUSTIN to the fruit and stir into the egg mixture. Beat the egg whites until stiff and fold into the mixture. Pile into a well buttered oval fireproof dish and bake in the oven. When done, sprinkle with icing sugar and serve at once.

Oven: slow to moderate.

Baking Time: 25–35 minutes.

Eggs au Gratin

4–8 eggs

Béchamel Sauce:
1½ oz. (45 g) butter or margarine
1½ oz. (45 g) ham
1½ oz. (45 g) plain flour
2 oz. (55 g) onions
½ pint (285 ccm) water or stock
½ pint (285 ccm) milk or cream
salt
pepper
a little grated cheese
a little butter

Boil the eggs until hard (about 10 minutes). Slice or halve them and put into a greased pie-dish.

To make the sauce, melt the fat with the diced ham, add the finely chopped onions and the flour and cook until pale yellow. Gradually stir in the cold water or stock and the cold milk or cream and leave simmering for 10 minutes. Strain the sauce through a fine sieve and season to taste with salt and pepper. Pour the sauce over the eggs, sprinkle with cheese and dot with butter. Bake until golden brown.

Oven: moderate heat.

Time: about 25 minutes.

Serve with lettuce salad and fried potatoes.

Alternatively, Tomato (see page 52), Mushroom (see page 49), Mustard (see page 49), or Bacon Sauce (see page 56), may be used instead of Béchamel Sauce.

Patties or Egg Pies
(Using Leftovers)

4 tbsp. mashed potatoes
4 eggs
4 tbsp. vegetable or meat leftovers
(roast meat, ham, venison
or poultry)
a little sour cream or milk
salt
a little lemon juice (optional)
2 tbsp. grated cheese
1 tbsp. butter or margarine

Grease some small patty tins with melted butter. Put a thin layer of mashed potatoes on the bottom of each tin, then carefully crack a raw egg on top of each. Chop up the leftovers, blend with the sour cream or milk, season to taste and spread over the eggs. Sprinkle with the cheese, dot with butter, put in the oven and bake until golden brown.

Oven: moderate heat.

Baking Time: about 20 minutes.

MILK AND COTTAGE CHEESE DISHES

As a food milk stands in a class by itself containing practically everything the body needs. $1\frac{3}{4}$ pint (1 l) of cow's milk contains about $1\frac{1}{4}$ oz. (35 g) protein, about $1-1\frac{1}{4}$ oz. (30–35 g) of fat and $1\frac{1}{2}$ oz. (45 g) of milk sugar (carbohydrate) plus all the important minerals and vitamins. Milk is the perfect food for infants being dual-purpose both body-building and protective. Liquid, milk cannot be the only food for an adult but it can constitute an extremely valuable element in his diet.

The protein in milk is of high quality and can be completely absorbed by the body. Milk should be added to vegetables to compensate for the protein they lack and thus providing a well-balanced meal. The fat is suspended in the milk in the form of fine particles (emulsion) and gives the milk its creamy colour.

When milk is left to stand, the fat collects at the top as cream which can then be skimmed off and whipped or churned to obtain butter. Milk sugar gives the milk its sweetness. Certain air-borne bacteria break down the sugar into lactic acid. This in its turn produces the protein known as casein, which is the basis of cheese. Milk contains all the minerals the body needs especially calcium and phosphorous, as well as haloid compounds, essential to the growth and formation of bones. All the vitamins (A, B, C and D), are found in milk, the quantity and proportion depending on how the animals are fed, the way they are kept and, of course on their breed and age.

Different breeds of cattle produce milk offering the various nutriments in differing proportions. Goat's milk for instance has a higher fat content than cow's milk, whereas ass's milk contains more milk sugar and fat but less protein.

Fresh whole milk, as the cow gives it, has a creamy yellow colour, a good smell and taste and leaves no sediment. One drop placed on a finger nail should not run; placed in water, the drop should sink because of its weight.

Dried milk either whole or skimmed is milk with the water removed, and is obtained by a special spraying process. Dried milk can be mixed with water and used exactly like as fresh milk.

Buttermilk is the name given to the liquid that remains after churning. It still contains a slight amount of fat, plus most of the proteins, milk sugar and minerals. Buttermilk is very easy to digest and is most useful in the making of soups containing bread or cereals, and as an addition to sauces, meat and desserts. It makes a delicious and refreshing drink either on its own or mixed with fruit juice. It can be the basic ingredient of inexpensive and nutritious sweets.

Yoghurt (Koumiss, Kefir) is fermented milk and has as much food value as buttermilk. It is made by adding yeast to the milk, a substance which ferments the milk sugar.

Curdled milk is formed by the action of air-borne bacteria which turn milk sugar into lactic acid and cause the milk to congeal. Because of its high content of lactic acid and protein, it is an digestible and wholesome food. Whisked to a froth, it is a delicious accompaniment to brown bread and potatoes. Curdled milk is especially suitable for invalids.

Cottage cheese is a semi-solid, unripened cheese made from soured milk heated until the whey separates from the curd. This is then left to drain in a cloth or bag until it is firm to the touch. Cottage cheese has more than 20% protein and contains all the food value of milk except cream. Because it is highly nutritious and palatable, it may be used as the main part of the meal or in salads, desserts and cooked dishes.

Scrupulous cleanliness is essential when milk is being used, for in spite of the great care taken in the production and distribution of milk it is never completely free from bacteria. Boiling milk before use is a wise precaution — an essential one when milk is not sold in bottles. Bring the milk briefly to the boil three times; this destroys the harmful germs, whereas the vitamins remain intact. Most housewives today buy their milk bottled and pasteurized. Pasteurized milk is obtained by a method of partial sterilization. The milk is heated to a temperature of 158° F (70° C). This process destroys pathogenic organisms and undesirable bacteria. But even this milk may become contaminated if it is not stored properly. Always keep milk in a cool place, well-covered from dust and flies. Warmth will encourage the development of harmful bacteria, so be very careful with milk in warm weather. If possible store milk in a refrigerator.

General Hints

1. Fresh milk should be scalded as soon as possible after purchase unless it is to be used at once.

2. Scald milk quickly or you will destroy its vitamins.

3. Stir the milk frequently after scalding or a skin will form.

4. Cool the milk as quickly as possible after scalding and keep it in a cool place.

5. Never keep milk uncovered; never mix new milk with old.

6. Saucepans and jugs in which milk is cooked and stored should never be used for anything else.

7. Saucepans should be thoroughly washed every day and rinsed out with cold water before using as milk burns easily.

MILK DISHES

COTTAGE CHEESE DISHES

How to Make Cottage Cheese

Allow uncooked milk to sour in a warm, not hot place until the whey separates from the curd. Drain the curd in a muslin bag until it is firm and dry to the touch.

A quicker way to make cottage cheese is to heat soured milk, before the whey separates from the curd, to a temperature of 100° F (38 °C). Stirring all the time while heating, then drain well.

It is not possible to calculate the exact amount of cottage cheese obtained, as this depends on the quality of the milk.

A. COTTAGE CHEESE SANDWICH SPREADS

White Cottage Cheese

8 oz. (225 g) cottage cheese
3–4 tbsp. milk or cream
pinch of salt

Rub the cottage cheese through a fine sieve, then mix with the milk or cream. Season to taste and stir until creamy.

Cottage Cheese with Herbs or Caraway Seeds

8 oz. (225 g) cottage cheese
3–4 tbsp. milk or cream
pinch of salt
1–2 tbsp. finely chopped chives or mixed herbs, or 1 tbsp. caraway seeds

Rub the cottage cheese through a fine sieve, then mix with the milk or cream. Season to taste with salt and stir until creamy. Lastly, add the chives or caraway seeds.

If preferred, grated onion, shredded beetroot, chopped shrimps, finely chopped smoked fish, or finely diced ham leftovers may be added to the cheese instead of caraway seeds.

Cottage Cheese with Carrots

8 oz. (225 g) cottage cheese
3–4 tbsp. milk or cream
5 oz. (140 g) carrots
pinch of salt
1 tsp. finely chopped chives

Rub the cottage cheese through a fine sieve, then mix it with the milk or cream and the prepared and grated carrots. Season to taste and stir until creamy. Lastly, add the chives.

Cottage Cheese with Paprika

8 oz. (225 g) cottage cheese
3–4 tbsp. milk or cream
salt
pinch of paprika

Rub the cottage cheese through a fine sieve, mix it with the milk or cream, season to taste with salt and paprika and stir until creamy.

230

Gentleman's Cake Recipe See Page 304

CEREALS

We need a considerable amount of carbohydrate in our diet, as it is our main source of energy. This need can most easily be met by cereals and the starchy foods made from them. These foods are about 70% starch, the amount of protein they contain varying according to the degree of refinement of grain achieved during milling. Whole grain and brown flour are richer in protein because of their germ, husk and bran coating; but they are less digestible and cannot be fully used by the body.

Cereals are low in fat gently content, averaging about 2%, except for oats, which has 6–8% fat and related substances (lecithin). The food value of oats is therefore considerable, and makes it especially valuable in the diet of children and invalids.

237

In Great Britain, America and Scandinavia, oats take their place on the daily menu in the form of the breakfast helping of porridge.

The principal minerals found in cereals are phosphor as potassium and calcium, indispensable bone and nerve builders. But these minerals, just like most of the cereal vitamins (mainly vitamin B), are found only in the outer coating and germ, so that in refined cereals, like bleached white flour or polished rice, minerals and vitamins are practically non-existent. Nevertheless, the various processes of polishing, hulling, grinding, flaking, rolling, roasting, boiling and so on, to which cereals are subjected by modern methods of preparation do render them more digestible, which compensates for the loss of minerals and vitamins to some extent. These processes enable the gastric juices to convert the starch in the cereal, which is not soluble in water, into sugar, which is soluble, and easily absorbed into the body.

Some distinction should be made between bread foods and cooked cereals. Rye and wheat belong to the first group, whereas the second includes oats, barley, rice, maize (Indian or Sweet Corn), buckwheat and millet. Hulled whole grains, like green wheat or groats, should be soaked for some time before cooking as their starch granules take longer to swell. Thinly rolled flakes only of course need a short time to cook; and specially prepared corn flakes need no preparation at all and are served as they are. Finely ground cereals can be stirred into the boiling liquid without preliminary preparation e. g. dry semolina should be sprinkled in direct; flour and corn flour should first be blended with a little cold liquid.

The cereal "green wheat" deserves special mention. It comes from a kind of wheat (spelt), is harvested while still unripe and dried by a particular process which gives it its distinctive taste and smell. Green wheat comes in the form of whole grain, groats or meal and so can be used for many culinary purposes.

Cereals can be prepared in countless ways. After soaking in milk or water they may be sweetened for serving with fruit, or salted and served with vegetables, meat or eggs.

As a breakfast food, cereals may appear as gruel or porridge, or be flaked, puffed, shredded and so on. For lunch or supper we eat cereals in the form of desserts, dumplings, "pasta", pancakes and soufflés. Whichever way they are prepared, they are nourishing and filling.

It is not advisable to store cereals in large quantities. They should be kept in a cool place, tightly covered, and should be watched, especially in summer, for rancidity and insect infestation. The best way to store cereals is to hang them in small bags in a dry, airy room. All flour should be sifted before use and, if possible, sifted occasionally during storage.

A. CREAMED CEREALS AND
HOT BOILED PUDDINGS

General Hints

1. Cereals swell as they absorb moisture. A slow even heat is best for making a creamed cereal (rice, millet, semolina, etc.).

2. For cereal puddings cooked in a saucepan on top of the stove, bring the mixture quickly to the boil at a high temperature, then turn down the heat as slow as possible and simmer gently. Keep closely covered to prevent steam escaping.

3. Soak the coarsely ground cereals, like green wheat, barley or groats for several hours before use and they will not need so much cooking.

4. Either whole or skimmed milk can be used in a hot cereal pudding.

5. Boiled cereal foods make good breakfast and supper dishes. Because they are so easy to digest they are especially suitable for children and invalids.

Rice Pudding
(Creamed Rice)

1¾ pint (1 l) milk
a knob of butter or margarine
1 tsp. salt
lemon rind
7 oz. (200 g) rice
2 well heaped tbsp. (50 g) sugar
½ tsp. cinnamon

Bring to the boil the milk, the fat, the salt and the lemon rind. Add the washed rice and simmer gently until tender.

Cooking Time: about 40 minutes.
Serve sprinkled with sugar and cinnamon.

Alternatively, boil the rice with 1 oz. (30 g) sugar, then pour it into a mould, rinsed out with cold water and leave to cool. Turn out and serve with fresh fruit juice, stewed or fresh fruit or sugared berries. Sprinkle the cold rice with Oetker vanillin sugar instead of cinnamon.

Creamed Oats

5 oz. (140 g) oats
2 pints (1⅛ l) milk
a little salt
lemon rind
a knob of butter or margarine

Put the oats into a saucepan and stir in the milk and salt. Add the lemon rind and the fat and bring to the boil, stirring frequently. Simmer gently until tender.

Cooking Time: 5–10 minutes.
Serve with fresh cream or fruit juice.

Creamed Millet

1¾ pint (1 l) milk
a knob of butter or margarine
a little salt
lemon rind
7 oz. (200 g) millet
2 well heaped tbsp. (50 g) sugar
½ tsp. cinnamon

Put the fat, salt and lemon rind into a pan with the milk and bring to the boil. Add the washed millet and leave to simmer until tender.

Cooking Time: about 45 minutes.
Serve heaped on a dish, sprinkled with sugar and cinnamon.

Creamed Semolina or Tapioca

2 pints (1⅛ l) milk
a knob of butter or margarine
a little salt
lemon rind
5 oz. (140 g) semolina or tapioca

Bring the milk with the fat, the salt and the lemon rind to the boil. Sprinkle in the semolina or tapioca and simmer gently until tender.

Cooking Time: 10–15 minutes.

Serve with fruit juice or stewed fruit.

Creamed Groats

5 oz. (140 g) groats
2 pints (1⅛ l) milk or water
a little salt
1 oz. (30 g) butter or margarine

Soak the groats for several hours in cold water. Add the salt to the milk or water and bring to the boil. Stir in the groats and simmer gently until tender. Add the fat just before serving.

Cooking Time: about 30 minutes.

Serve with fresh cream or milk, fruit juice, or stewed fruit.

Creamed Buckwheat Groats

5 oz. (140 g) buckwheat groats
2 pints (1⅛ l) milk or water
a little salt
1 oz. (30 g) butter or margarine

Soak the buckwheat groats for several hours in cold water. Add the salt to the milk or water and bring to the boil. Stir in the buckwheat groats and leave to simmer gently until tender. Add the fat just before serving.

Cooking Time: about 30 minutes.

Serve with milk.

Boiled Rice

1¾ pint (1 l) stock
a little salt
paprika or onion
9 oz. (250 g) rice

Add the salt and the paprika or onion to the stock and bring to the boil. Add the washed rice and leave to simmer gently until tender. Do not stir, as this makes the rice grains disintegrate. Fill lightly into a bowl and serve instead of potatoes with boiled or roast meat.

Cooking Time: about 25 minutes.

If water is used instead of the stock, add 1 heaped tbsp. butter.

Tomato Rice

1¾ pint (1 l) stock
a little salt
paprika or onion
9 oz. (250 g) rice
9 oz. (250 g) tomatoes and a knob of butter or margarine,
or 1–2 tbsp. tomato purée

Salt the stock and add the paprika or onion. Bring to the boil. Add the washed rice and simmer gently until tender. Do not stir or the rice grains will disintegrate. Wash and slice the tomatoes, then fry them in the fat. Rub through a fine sieve and stir into the rice. 1–2 tbsp. of tomato purée may be used instead of the tomatoes.

Cooking Time: about 35 minutes.

Mix Boiled Rice (see page 240) with 1 tsp. curry powder.

Rice Ring (Phot. See Page 143)

Add the salt and the paprika or onion to the stock and bring to the boil. Add the washed rice and simmer until tender. Do not stir or the rice grains will disintegrate. Rinse out a ring mould with cold water and fill with the cooked rice. Put in the oven for about 15 minutes or into gently boiling water. Turn out onto a warmed plate, fill the centre with fricassee, ragoût, or vegetables (preferably mushrooms) and serve.

1¾ pint (1 l) stock
a little salt
paprika or onion
9 oz. (250 g) rice

Cooking Time: for the rice, about 35 minutes;
(for the ring, about 15 minutes).

Oven: slow to moderate.

Risotto

Rub the rice on a dry cloth; do not wash. Melt the fat, add the finely diced onion and the rice and fry pale yellow. Fill up with the boiling, slightly salted stock and simmer until done. Do not stir or the rice grains will disintegrate. Fill lightly into a bowl and serve sprinkled with chopped herbs.

9 oz. (250 g) rice
1 oz. (30 g) butter or margarine
1 small onion
1¾ pint (1 l) stock
pinch of salt
chives or parsley

Cooking Time: about 30 minutes.
Barley may be used instead of rice.

Rice with Apples

Put the salt, the sugar, the fat and the baking essence into a pan with the water and bring to the boil. Sprinkle in the washed rice, add the peeled, cored and sliced apples and simmer gently until done. Add sugar to taste and serve with sugar and cinnamon.

1¾ pint (1 l) water
a little salt
about 2 oz. (55 g) sugar
a knob of butter or margarine
2 drops Oetker Baking Essence,
    lemon flavour
7 oz. (200 g) rice
1⅛ lb. (500 g) apples

Cooking Time: about 40 minutes.
The rice and the apples may be cooked separately and filled into a bowl in alternate layers. Instead of rice, millet or barley may be used.

For Sprinkling:
2 well heaped tbsp. (50 g) sugar
½ tsp. cinnamon

Rice with Oranges

Put the salt, the sugar, the fat and the grated orange rind into a pan with the water and bring to the boil. Sprinkle in the washed rice and simmer until tender. In the meantime, peel the oranges and cut them into small pieces, add the sugar and leave standing for a while. Mix the cooked rice with the sugared oranges, sprinkle with sugar and serve.

1¾ pint (1 l) water
a little salt
3 well heaped tbsp. (75 g) sugar
a knob of butter or margarine
orange rind
7 oz. (200 g) rice
3 oranges
1 well heaped tbsp. sugar
a little sugar for sprinkling

Cooking Time: about 40 minutes.

Rice with Cherries

1¾ pint (1 l) water
a little salt
2 well heaped tbsp. (50 g) sugar
a knob of butter or margarine
2 drops Oetker Baking Essence,
lemon flavour
7 oz. (200 g) rice
1⅛ lb. (500 g) cherries

For Sprinkling:
2 well heaped tbsp. (50 g) sugar
½ tsp. cinnamon

Put the salt, the sugar, the fat and the baking essence into a pan with the water and bring to the boil. Wash the rice and wash and stone the cherries, then add both to the boiling water. Simmer gently until done.

Cooking Time: about 40 minutes.

Serve sprinkled with sugar and cinnamon.

Rice with Rhubarb

1¾ pint (1 l) water
a little salt
5½ oz. (150 g) sugar
a knob of butter or margarine
2 drops Oetker Baking Essence,
lemon flavour
9 oz. (250 g) rice
1⅛ lb. (500 g) rhubarb

For Sprinkling:
2 well heaped tbsp. (50 g) sugar
½ tsp. cinnamon

Put the salt, the sugar, the fat and the baking essence into a pan with the water and bring to the boil. Sprinkle in the washed rice and add the washed and sliced rhubarb (the skin should be left on). Simmer gently until tender.

Cooking Time: about 40 minutes.

Serve sprinkled with sugar and cinnamon.

Millet or barley may be used instead of rice.

Rice with Dried Fruit

7 oz. (200 g) dried apricots,
peaches, or apple rings
1 pint (570 ccm) water
1⅓ pint (¾ l) water
a little salt
2–3½ oz. (55–100 g) sugar
a knob of butter or margarine
2 drops Oetker Baking Essence,
lemon flavour
7 oz. (200 g) rice
a little sugar for sprinkling

Wash the dried fruit and soak it for 12–24 hours in the 1 pint (570 ccm) of water. Put the salt, 2 oz. (55 g) sugar, the fat and the baking essence into a pan with the 1⅓ pint (¾ l) water, and bring to the boil. Wash the rice and add it to the boiling water with the fruit and the liquid in which it has been soaked. Simmer gently until tender. Sweeten with sugar to taste, sprinkle with more sugar and serve decorated with a few pieces of fruit set aside for this purpose.

Cooking Time: about 40 minutes.

Barley may be used instead of rice.

If prunes are used, boil them separately and serve arranged round the rice with the juice poured over.

242

B. PASTA

(Spaghetti, Macaroni, Noodles, etc.)

General Hints

1. Pasta or starch foods, must be quite dry when sprinkled into boiling water.

2. Allow a good quantity of water, so that the pasta has room to swell during cooking.

3. Stir fairly often with a wooden spoon to make sure no pasta sticks to the bottom of the pan.

4. Put the pasta into boiling water, bring again to the boil, then leave to cook over a low heat until tender.

5. As soon as the pasta is done, put into a sieve or colander, rinse and drain.

Home-Made Noodles

For recipe I, sift ⅔ of the flour into a bowl and make a well in the middle. Add the salt and vinegar, then gradually pour the water into the centre of the flour and stir. Knead in the remaining flour until a rather stiff dough is formed. Add more flour if the dough seems sticky.

Recipe I:
1½ lb. (680 g) plain flour
1 heaped tsp. salt
1 tbsp. vinegar
½ pint (285 ccm) water

For recipe II, sift the flour onto a pastry board. Make a well in the middle. Beat the eggs in the water with the salt and pour into the well. Draw in some flour from the sides of the well and work to a smooth paste. Starting in the centre, knead all the ingredients into a stiff dough. Add more flour if the dough seems sticky.

Recipe II:
9 oz. (250 g) plain flour
½ tsp. salt
2 eggs
2–3 tbsp. water (2, if the eggs are large, 3, if they are small)

For Method I or II, take a piece of the dough, roll it out very thinly. Repeat until the dough is used. Spread the rolled out dough on a clean cloth to dry. When no longer sticky, but not dry or brittle, roll up like a pancake, cut into thin strips, spread out and leave to dry again.

Noodles with Milk

Put the salt and the fat into a pan with the milk and bring to the boil. Add the noodles and simmer gently until tender. Soak the sultanas. Serve the noodles mixed with the sugar and the sultanas or sprinkled with sugar and cinnamon.

1¾ pint (1 l) milk
a little salt
a knob of butter or margarine
9 oz. (250 g) noodles
2 well heaped tbsp. (50 g) sugar
2 oz. (55 g) sultanas or ½ tsp. cinnamon

Cooking Time: about 30 minutes.

The noodles may be served with breadcrumbs and stewed dried fruit instead of the sugar and sultanas.

Noodles with Apples

2¾ pints (1½ l) water
a little salt
9 oz. (250 g) noodles
1⅛ lb. (500 g) apples
4 tbsp. water
2 well heaped tbsp. (50 g) sugar
2 drops Oetker Baking Essence,
lemon flavour

For Sprinkling:
2 well heaped tbsp. (50 g) sugar
½ tsp. cinnamon

Add the salt to the water and bring to the boil. Break the noodles into small pieces, put them into the boiling water and simmer gently until done. Peel, core and slice the apples, add to them the 4 tbsp. water, the sugar, and the baking essence and stew until done. Mix the drained noodles with the butter, stir in the apples and sprinkle with sugar and cinnamon.

Cooking Time: for the noodles, about 30 minutes.

Fresh plums may be used instead of apples.

Boiled Noodles

2¾ pints (1½ l) water
a little salt
9 oz. (250 g) noodles
1 tbsp. butter or margarine

Add the salt to the water and bring to the boil. Sprinkle in the noodles and simmer gently until done. Drain and rinse with cold water. Toss the noodles in the melted fat before serving.

Cooking Time: about 30 minutes.

Alternatively, grated cheese or tomato purée may be stirred into the noodles before serving, or they may be sprinkled with brown butter and breadcrumbs.

Macaroni

2¾ pints (1½ l) water
a little salt
7-9 oz. (200-250 g) macaroni
1-2 oz. (30-55 g) butter
2 level tbsp. grated cheese
pepper or paprika (optional)

Add the salt to the water and bring to the boil. Break the macaroni into fingerlength pieces, put into the boiling water and simmer gently until done. Drain and rinse with cold water. Toss the noodles in the melted fat, add the cheese and, if desired, sprinkle with pepper or paprika and serve.

Cooking Time: about 30 minutes.

1-2 tbsp. of tomato purée may be used instead of the cheese.

Ravioli

Dough:
9 oz. (250 g) plain flour
2 eggs
½ tsp. salt
3-4 tbsp. water (3, if the eggs are
large, 4, if they are small)

Stuffing I:
4½ oz. (125 g) ham or cold
roast meat
1 egg yolk
2 tbsp. grated cheese
1-2 tbsp. milk
or

For the dough, sift the flour onto a pastry board and make a well in the middle. Beat the eggs with the salt and the water, pour into the well and starting from the centre, work to a stiff paste with some of the flour. Then quickly work all the ingredients together into a smooth dough; if it is sticky, use a little more flour.

For the stuffing I, add the egg yolk to the diced ham or meat and the cheese. Stir in enough milk to make a smooth paste.

Roll out the dough (not all at once, but a small piece at a time) to the thickness of a knife. Cut it into small pieces about 3 inches (7½ cm) square. Put about 1 tbsp. of stuffing I or II into the centre of each square, brush the edges of the dough with whisked egg white and fold over into a triangle. Press the edges firmly together.

Put the ravioli into boiling salted water and cook gently until done. Remove with a skimming ladle onto a hot plate. Pour over with hot brown butter and serve with lettuce salad or stewed fruit.

Cooking Time: about 20 minutes.

Stuffing II:
spinach, mushrooms or tomatoes, slightly sautéed, then chopped

For Brushing:
1 egg white
1 tbsp. butter for browning

"Dampfnudeln"

Sift together the flour and the BACKIN into a bowl. Make a well in the middle and put into it the salt, the sugar, the vanillin sugar and the eggs. Starting from the middle, mix these ingredients with the flour. Gradually stir in the milk, taking care to avoid lumps. Melt some fat in a roasting-pan (the roasting-pan must have a tight-fitting lid). Pour in enough milk to reach about ½ inch (1 cm) up the sides of the pan. Bring to the boil. Using 2 tablespoons, shape the dough into the boiling milk. Close the pan tightly and simmer gently until done. Serve poured over with browned butter and stewed fruit.

Cooking Time: about 20 minutes.
Left-over "Dampfnudeln" may be cut into slices and fried in hot butter.

¾ lb. (340 g) plain flour
1 packet Oetker Baking Powder BACKIN
a little salt
1 well heaped tbsp. sugar
1 packet Oetker Vanillin Sugar
2 eggs
⅓ pint (200 ccm) milk
1 tbsp. butter for browning

"Spätzle"

Sift the flour into a bowl. Make a well in the middle and pour in the eggs, beaten up with the salt. Starting from the middle, mix the eggs into the flour, then gradually add the liquid, taking care to avoid lumps. Beat the dough with a wooden spoon until it shows bubbles. Press the dough through a colander or top of a steamer into boiling salted water. Alternatively, put the dough onto a plate and cut shreds of the dough with a knife from the side of the plate into the water. Toss in browned butter or serve with browned breadcrumbs.

Cooking Time: 5–8 minutes.
If desired, 7 oz. (200 g) boiled and finely chopped spinach or 5 oz. (140 g) grated cheese may be added to the dough.

1⅛ lb. (500 g) plain flour
a little salt
2 eggs
⅔ pint (375 ccm) water or milk
1 tbsp. butter for browning

Fried "Spätzle"

Prepare and cook the "Spätzle" as in the recipe noted above. Pour cold water over them when they are done and fry in the hot fat until pale yellow, turning them frequently. Serve with stewed fruit, salad or meat.

1⅛ lb. (500 g) plain flour
a little salt
2 eggs
⅔ pint (375 ccm) water or milk
2–3 oz. (55–85 g) butter or margarine for frying

C. DUMPLINGS

General Hints

1. For a firm, well-shaped dumpling, knead the ingredients thoroughly and work until the dough is perfectly smooth.

2. Season the dough before shaping it into dumplings.

3. To make sure the dough is of the right consistency, make one sample dumpling. If the dough is too stiff, lighten it by adding some cooked ingredients, such as cooked meat or potatoes, semolina pudding, breadcrumbs, etc. If the dumplings breaks, bind it with raw ingredients, such as fresh egg, raw potatoes, semolina or flour.

4. Shape the dumplings with a spoon, dipped in boiling water.

5. Another way of shaping dumplings is to make a long roll of the dough and put it onto a floured board. Then cut it into even slices and shape the dumplings with your hands, which should first be dipped in flour.

6. Leave the dumplings on the floured board until they are to be cooked.

7. Put the dumplings to cook into boiling, slightly salted water.

8. Do not put too many dumplings into the pan, as they swell during cooking.

9. Dumplings should be simmered gently until done; violent boiling will spoil them. Never cook the dumplings in a pan with the lid on, as the steam will make them fall apart.

10. There is one exception to the previous hint — yeast dumplings, which are best steamed.

11. To test whether a dumpling is done, tear it apart with two forks; the centre should be flaky and dry.

12. When they are ready, take the dumplings out of the pan with a perforated spoon or ladle and leave to drain well before serving.

Flour Dumplings

1½ oz. (45 g) butter or margarine
3 eggs
a little salt
14 oz. (400 g) plain flour
1 level tsp. (3 g) Oetker Baking Powder BACKIN
¼ pint (140 ccm) milk
1 oz. (30 g) butter for frying
2 level tbsp. breadcrumbs

Cream the fat, add the eggs and the salt, then add alternately the milk and the flour, sieved together with the BACKIN. Beat the dough well with a wooden spoon until it is light and bubbly. Dip a tablespoon into hot water and scoop out the dumplings; cook them in boiling salted water over a moderate heat. Serve with the fried brown breadcrumbs and either stewed dried fruit or meat.

Cooking Time: about 10 minutes

For the dumpling, cream the fat, then gradually add the sugar, the eggs and the seasoning. Sift together the flour and the BACKIN and add to the mixture alternately with the milk. Shape the dough into one big dumpling and put this on top of the boiling dried fruit.

To prepare the dried fruit, wash it and soak for 12–24 hours in the 1⅓ pint (¾ l) water, bring to the boil in the water in which it has soaked, and add sugar to taste. Cook the dumpling for 1¼ hours in a covered pan, then uncovered for another quarter of an hour.

Cooking Time: 1½ hours.

Large Flour Dumpling with Baking Powder

Dumpling:
2 oz. (55 g) butter or margarine
3 well heaped tbsp. (75 g) sugar
3 eggs
a little salt
3 drops Oetker Baking Essence, lemon flavour
1⅛ lb. (500 g) plain flour
1 packet Oetker Baking Powder BACKIN
barely ½ pint (250 ccm) milk

Dried Fruit:
(e.g. dried apple rings, apricots, prunes)
8 oz. (225 g) mixed dried fruit
1⅓ pint (¾ l) water
3 slightly heaped tbsp. (60 g) sugar

Dumplings with Yeast

Mix the yeast with the 1 tsp. sugar and 5 tbsp. of the milk, which should be lukewarm. Sift into a bowl ⅔ of the flour, make a well in the middle, pour in the yeast and sprinkle flour about ¼ inch (½ cm) thick on top. Put the other ingredients — the sugar, the eggs, the fat (warm and melted) and the seasoning around the bowl, but not touching the yeast. As soon as the flour on top of the yeast shows cracks, mix the yeast with the flour and the other ingredients, working from the centre. Gradually add the remaining milk. Beat the dough with a wooden spoon until it is light and bubbly. Knead in the remaining flour. If the dough is sticky, knead in a little more flour. Set aside the dough in a warm place for about an hour to prove. Knead again and shape into dumplings. Leave these for a short time to rise a little more. Finally, drop the dumplings into boiling salted water and cook until done. They are better cooked in a steamer. If no steamer is available, tie a clean white cloth across the top of the saucepan (which should have boiling water underneath). Put the dumplings on the cloth, close down the lid and cook until done.

Cooking Time: about 10 minutes.

When the dumplings are cooked, remove them from the pan and tear them a little at the top with two forks, to allow the steam to escape. Pour brown butter over the dumplings, or sprinkle with vanillin sugar and serve with stewed dried fruit or apple purée.

Alternatively, the dough may be placed as one large dumpling on top of boiling dried fruit and cooked until done. Served this way, the dish is called "Fat Michael".

1 oz. (30 g) fresh yeast
1 tsp. sugar
barely ½ pint (250 ccm) milk
1⅛ lb. (500 g) plain flour
1 oz. (30 g) sugar
1–2 eggs
1 oz. (30 g) butter or margarine
1 tsp. salt
3 drops Oetker Baking Essence, lemon flavour
1 oz. (30 g) butter or margarine for browning, or 1 packet Oetker Vanillin Sugar

Semolina Dumplings

1⅓ pint (¾ l) milk
¾ oz. (20 g) butter or margarine
1 tsp. salt
3 drops Oetker Baking Essence, lemon flavour or
2 drops Oetker Baking Essence, bitter almond flavour
9 oz. (250 g) semolina
2 eggs
2 tbsp. butter for frying
¾ oz. (20 g) breadcrumbs

Bring the milk, the fat and the seasonings to the boil. Remove the pan from the heat, slowly sprinkle in the semolina and stir constantly until the mixture forms a compact mass. Put back on the stove and heat for another minute, stirring all the time. Quickly put the hot lump of dough into a bowl and work in the eggs, one after the other. As soon as the mixture has cooled, shape it into evenly sized dumplings and cook in boiling salted water over a moderate heat until done. Serve sprinkled with the fried breadcrumbs, with stewed fruit or braised meat.

Cooking Time: about 10 minutes.

If the dumplings are to be served with meat, omit the baking essence and flavour instead with chopped chives or parsley.

Bread Dumplings with Bacon (Semmelknödel)

9 oz. (250 g) stale rolls or slices of bread
⅔ pint (⅜ l) boiling milk
2 oz. (55 g) fat bacon
1 onion
3½ oz. (100 g) Oetker GUSTIN (corn starch powder)
2 eggs
1–2 tsp. finely chopped herbs
2 level tsp. (6 g) Oetker Baking Powder BACKIN

Cut the rolls or the bread into very thin slices, pour over them the boiling milk and leave to soak for an hour.

Fry the finely diced bacon and onion together, leave to cool and then stir into the soaked bread and add the GUSTIN. Heat this mixture until it forms a smooth compact mass. Leave to cool, then stir in the eggs one after another. Add the BACKIN and season to taste with salt.

With wet hands, shape the dough into evenly sized dumplings. Put the dumplings into boiling salted water and simmer over a moderate heat for about 20 minutes.

Bread Dumplings (Semmelknödel)

11 oz. (310 g) stale rolls or slices of bread
2 oz. (55 g) butter or lard
¾ pint and 5 tbsp. (500 ccm) boiling milk
2 eggs
1 level tsp. (3 g) Oetker Baking Powder BACKIN
a little salt

Cut the rolls into very thin slices, pour over them the hot melted fat and the boiling milk and leave to soak for about an hour. Beat in the eggs and the BACKIN, then season to taste with salt. With wet hands, shape the mixture into evenly sized dumplings. Put the dumplings into boiling salted water and bring to the boil, then simmer over a moderate heat until done. Pour browned butter over the dumplings.

Cooking Time: about 20 minutes.

They are delicious with fruit sauces or with white meat (veal or chicken).

Iced Coffee Recipe See Page 266

Cream the fat. Gradually add to it the eggs, the rolls (from which all moisture has been squeezed), the salt and the milk alternately with the sifted flour. Peel and cut the apples into small pieces and add these into the mixture. Dip a spoon into hot water and scoop out dumplings. Put the dumplings into boiling salted water and cook over a moderate heat until done. Sprinkle with sugar and cinnamon.

Cooking Time: about 15 minutes.

Apple Dumplings

2 oz. (55 g) butter or margarine
2 eggs
2 soaked rolls or slices of bread
a little salt
9 oz. (250 g) plain flour
3 tbsp. milk
1⅛ lb. (500 g) apples
sugar and cinnamon for sprinkling

Stone the cherries, add the sugar and stew them in their own juice. Leave to cool. Stir in the melted fat, a little salt, the eggs, the baking essence, the flour and enough breadcrumbs to make a firm dough. Shape into dumplings. Put these into slightly salted boiling water and cook over a moderate heat until done.

Cooking Time: about 8 minutes.

Sprinkle with sugar and serve with Frothy Wine Sauce (see page 62).

Cherry Dumplings

1⅛ lb. (500 g) cherries
3 slightly heaped tbsp. (60 g) sugar
1½ oz. (45 g) butter or margarine
a little salt
2 drops Oetker Baking Essence, lemon flavour
3 eggs
2 oz. (55 g) plain flour
about 7 oz. (200 g) breadcrumbs
sugar for sprinkling

D. FRIED CEREAL DISHES

General Hints

1. It is essential to use the right cooking fat and to fry at the correct temperature if your fried cereal dishes are to be a success.

2. Neither butter nor margarine is suitable for frying as they tend to burn very easily.

3. Oil, lard, vegetable fat or mixed cooking fat are recommended (see page 67).

4. The fat must be hot when the food is put into it. Hot fat immediately forms a crust round the food and prevents excessive fat absorption.

5. When the food is cooked on one side, turn it and cook the other. Remove it as soon as it is well browned.

6. The thicker the slice, the longer it will take to cook. Therefore thick slices must be cooked at a moderate heat to ensure that they are cooked through.

251

Apple Fritters Recipe See Page 205
Semolina Slices Recipe See Page 252

Semolina Slices
(Phot. See Page 252)

1 pint (570 ccm) milk
1 oz. (30 g) butter or margarine
¾ oz. (20 g) sugar
a little salt
2 bitter almonds
6 oz. (170 g) semolina
1–2 eggs
1½ oz. (45 g) breadcrumbs
2–3 oz. (55–85 g) fat for frying

Add the fat, the sugar, salt and the chopped almonds to the milk and bring to the boil. Remove the pan from the heat and slowly stir in the semolina. Return to the heat and simmer gently until done. Stir the eggs into the hot mixture, then fill into an oblong cake tin lined with wetted paper. Leave to cool. Remove from tin and cut into slices; coat these with breadcrumbs and fry in hot fat in a frying-pan until golden brown on both sides.

Cooking Time: about 10 minutes.

Serve with stewed apricots.

Oatmeal Slices

1 pint (570 ccm) milk
1 oz. (30 g) butter or margarine
1 slightly heaped tbsp. (20 g) sugar
a little salt
2 bitter almonds
7 oz. (200 g) rolled oats
1–2 eggs
1½ oz. (45 g) breadcrumbs
2–3 oz. (55–85 g) fat for frying

Prepare as for Semolina Slices (as noted above).

Rice Slices

1 pint (570 ccm) milk
1 oz. (30 g) butter or margarine
a little salt
3 drops Oetker Baking Essence, lemon flavour
1 slightly heaped tbsp. (20 g) sugar
4 oz. (115 g) rice
2 oz. (55 g) sultanas
1–2 eggs
1½ oz. (45 g) breadcrumbs
2–3 oz. (55–85 g) fat for frying

Put the milk, the fat, the salt, the baking essence and the sugar into a pan and bring to the boil. Sprinkle in the washed rice and the washed sultanas. Simmer very gently until done. Stir the eggs into the hot mixture, then put it into an oblong cake tin lined with wetted paper. Leave to cool. Remove from tin and cut into slices, coat these with breadcrumbs and fry in hot fat in a frying-pan until light-brown.

Cooking Time: about 40 minutes.

Excellent with stewed cranberries.

This is a useful way of using up leftover creamed rice, apple rice or rice pudding.

Prepare as for Semolina Slices (see page 252).

When the tapioca is cooked, stir in the sauce powder, blended with the water and bring again briefly to the boil.

(see page 252)

Tapioca Slices

1 pint (570 ccm) milk
1 oz. (30 g) butter or margarine
1 slightly heaped tbsp. (20 g) sugar
a little salt
2 bitter almonds
5 oz. (140 g) tapioca
1 packet Oetker Sauce Powder, vanilla flavour
2 tbsp. cold water
1–2 eggs
1½ oz. (45 g) breadcrumbs
2–3 oz. (55–85 g) fat for frying

Beat the eggs and the sugar until creamy and add the seasoning. Sift together the BACKIN and the flour and add to the egg mixture by the tablespoonful alternately with the milk. Lastly fold in the washed currants. Pour a spoonful of the batter into the hot fat and fry over a slow heat until brown on both sides. Sprinkle with sugar and serve with coffee or stewed fruit as a dessert or as a supper-dish.

Fried Currant Cakes

2 eggs
2 slightly heaped tbsp. (40 g) sugar
1 level tsp. salt
2–3 drops Oetker Baking Essence, lemon flavour
9 oz. (250 g) plain flour
3 level tsp. (9 g) Oetker Baking Powder BACKIN
barely ½ pint (250 ccm) milk
2 oz. (55 g) currants
3–4 oz. (85–115 g) fat for frying

Add the salt to the stock and bring to the boil. Sprinkle in the oats and stir until done. Fry the onion, finely chopped, in the hot fat and add this to the oats, then stir in the beaten eggs and the parsley. Line an oblong cake tin with wetted paper and fill with the mixture. Allow to cool. Remove from the tin and cut it into slices. Coat the slices in breadcrumbs and fry in the fat.

Cooking Time: about 5 minutes.

Serve with Tomato or Herb Sauce (see page 52/50) and Lettuce Salad (see page 187). These cakes may be served instead of meat with vegetables or potato salad.

Alternatively, 2–3 tbsp. finely chopped herbs, 3½ oz. (100 g) grated vegetables (celeriac), tomato purée or grated cheese may be added instead of the chopped parsley.

(see page 52/50) ... (see page 187)

Fried Oatmeal Cakes

¾ pint and 5 tbsp. (500 ccm) stock or water
a little salt
9 oz. (250 g) rolled oats
a knob of butter or margarine
1 onion
1–2 eggs
1–2 tbsp. chopped parsley
1½ oz. (45 g) breadcrumbs
2–3 oz. (55–85 g) fat for frying

Prepare as for Oatmeal Cakes (as noted above), using 9 oz. (250 g) barley instead of the oats.

Cooking Time: about 1 hour.

Barley Cakes

Rice Cakes

Prepare as for Oatmeal Cakes (see page 253), using **9 oz. (250 g)** rice. Wash it and sprinkle it into the boiling, salted stock.

Cooking Time: about 35 minutes.

Poor Knights
(Arme Ritter)

½–1 pint (285–570 ccm) milk
1–2 eggs
1 slightly heaped tbsp. (20 g) sugar
2–3 drops Oetker Baking Essence,
lemon flavour
a little salt
12 small slices of white bread
6 level tbsp. (60 g) breadcrumbs
3–4 oz. (85–115 g) fat for frying
2 oz. (55 g) sugar
½ tsp. cinnamon

Beat together the milk, the eggs, the sugar, the baking essence and the salt. Pour the mixture over the slices of white bread. Leave to soak for a short time but do not let the slices get too soft. Coat with breadcrumbs and fry in hot fat. Sprinkle with sugar and cinnamon and serve with Frothy Wine Sauce (see page 62) or Frothy Lemon Sauce (see page 62).

Carthusian Dumplings

8 stale rolls
1 pint (570 ccm) milk
1–2 eggs
1 slightly heaped tbsp. (20 g) sugar
salt
2 drops Oetker Baking Essence,
bitter almond flavour
about 4½ oz. (125 g) fat for frying
2 oz. (55 g) sugar
½ tsp. cinnamon

Grate the crust off the stale rolls, then cut them into halves or quarters. Beat together the milk, the eggs, the sugar, the salt and the baking essence, then pour over the cut rolls. Turn the pieces now and again so that they absorb the liquid. Add a little more milk, if necessary. Coat with the grated crust and fry in plenty of hot fat until golden brown. Sprinkle with sugar and cinnamon and serve with Frothy Wine Sauce (see page 62) or Frothy Lemon Sauce (see page 62).

Beggar's Apple

7 oz. (200 g) breadcrumbs from brown bread
1 oz. (30 g) sugar
2 drops Oetker Baking Essence,
lemon flavour
1⅛ lb. (500 g) apples
1 tbsp. water
2 well heaped tbsp. (50 g) sugar
1 heaped tbsp. currants
1 heaped tbsp. almonds (chopped)
2 oz. (55 g) fat for frying

Mix the bread with the sugar and the baking essence. Stew the peeled, sliced apples in the water with the sugar, the washed and drained currants and the almonds. Heat the fat, then add to it about half of the breadcrumb mixture, pressing well down, then add the stewed apple mixture as a middle layer and top with the remaining breadcrumbs. Fry on both sides over a very low heat and sprinkle with sugar.

Frying Time: about 20 minutes.

Sift the flour into a bowl and make a well in the middle. Beat the egg yolks with a little of the milk, the salt, the sugar and the vanillin sugar, and pour the mixture into the well. Starting from the middle, blend the yolk mixture and the flour. Gradually add the milk, taking care to avoid lumps. Whisk the egg whites until stiff and fold carefully into the mixture.

Heat the fat in a frying-pan and pour in about ⅜ inch (1 cm) of the batter. Fry until the underside is light yellow then tear into small pieces with two forks. Brown the pieces well, turning frequently. Repeat until the batter is used up.

Serve sprinkled with sugar.

Time: about 5 minutes.

Flour "Schmarren"
(South German Dish)

9 oz. (250 g) plain flour
3–5 egg yolks
a little salt
1 slightly heaped tbsp. (20 g) sugar
1 packet Oetker Vanillin Sugar
¾ pint and 5 tbsp. (500 ccm) milk
3–5 egg whites
2½ oz. (70 g) butter or margarine for frying
a little sugar for sprinkling

Peel and dice the apples, stew in the butter, then leave to cool. Sift the flour into a bowl, make a well in the middle and pour in the egg yolks beaten with a little of the milk, the salt, the sugar and the vanillin sugar. Starting from the middle, stir the egg yolks into the flour and gradually add the milk, stirring all the time, to avoid lumps. Stir the cold apples into the batter. Whisk the egg whites until stiff and fold them carefully into the batter. Heat the fat in a frying-pan and pour in enough batter to cover the bottom of the pan to a depth of about ⅜ inch (1 cm). Fry the underside light yellow, then tear into small pieces with two forks. Brown the pieces well, turning frequently. Repeat until the batter is used up.

Serve sprinkled with sugar.

Frying Time: about 10 minutes.

Apple "Schmarren"

5 ripe apples
a knob of butter
9 oz. (250 g) plain flour
3–5 egg yolks
a little salt
1 slightly heaped tbsp. (20 g) sugar
1 packet Oetker Vanillin Sugar
¾ pint and 5 tbsp. (500 ccm) milk
3–5 egg whites
2½ oz. (70 g) butter or margarine
a little sugar for sprinkling

Sift the flour into a bowl and make a well in the centre. Beat the egg yolks with a little of the milk or cream, the salt and the baking essence and pour the mixture into the well. Starting from the middle, stir the egg yolks into the flour, then gradually add the remaining milk or cream, stirring all the time, to avoid lumps. Wash and drain the currants and add them to the batter, together with the almonds. Lastly, whisk the egg whites until stiff and fold carefully into the batter.

Heat the fat in a frying-pan and pour in batter to about ⅜ inch (1 cm) thickness. Fry the underside light yellow, then tear into small pieces with two forks. Brown the pieces well, turning them frequently.

Serve sprinkled with sugar.

Frying Time: 8–10 minutes.

Emperor's "Schmarren"

4 oz. (115 g) plain flour
4 egg yolks
a little salt
2 drops Oetker Baking Essence, lemon flavour
½ pint (285 ccm) milk or cream
3 oz. (85 g) currants
3 oz. (85 g) almonds (ground)
4 egg whites
3 oz. (85 g) butter for frying
a little sugar for sprinkling

E. SOUFFLÉS AND BAKED PUDDINGS

General Hints

1. For soufflés, which are made with beaten egg whites, and for puddings, use a fireproof glass, porcelain, or earthenware baking-dish.

2. Grease the dish well before filling.

3. When making a soufflé, fill the baking-dish only threequarters full to allow mixture to rise.

4. Sprinkle the top of the dish with breadcrumbs or grated cheese and dot with butter.

5. Clean the edges of the dish carefully after filling; scraps of the mixture left around the edges will burn.

6. Place the dish fairly low in the oven.

7. If most of the ingredients are pre-cooked, a good moderate heat is the best for cooking.

8. When making a soufflé or a dish with raw ingredients, a moderate oven is needed. An egg or cake mixture needs a slow oven.

9. Serve the soufflé or pudding in the dish in which it has been cooked.

Semolina Soufflé

1 pint (570 ccm) milk
a little salt
5 oz. (140 g) semolina
1½ oz. (45 g) butter or margarine
2–3 oz. (55–85 g) sugar
2–3 egg yolks
3–4 drops Oetker Baking Essence, lemon flavour
2 level tsp. (6 g) Oetker Baking Powder BACKIN
2–3 egg whites
2 tbsp. breadcrumbs
a knob of butter

Add the salt to the milk and bring to the boil. Take the saucepan off the heat and slowly stir in the semolina; return to heat and cook gently until done. Cream the fat, then gradually add the sugar, the egg yolks, the baking essence, the BACKIN and the cooled semolina. Lastly fold in the stiffly beaten whites. Well grease a pie-dish, fill it with the mixture, sprinkle with breadcrumbs and dot with butter. Put in the oven and bake.

Oven: moderate heat.

Time: about 35 minutes.

Serve with fruit juice, fruit sauce or stewed fruit. Alternatively, 1⅛ lb. (500 g) fresh fruit (stoned cherries, apricots or plums), or 4½ oz. (125 g) soaked dried fruit or jam may be added in alternate layers with the semolina. Or, the soufflé may be cooked in a greased mould placed in a steamer or double-boiler. When done, turn out onto a hot plate.

Oatmeal Soufflé

Make as for Semolina Soufflé (as noted above), using 5 oz. (140 g) rolled oats instead of semolina.

Make as for Semolina Soufflé (see page 256), using 5 oz. (140 g) barley instead of semolina.

Barley Soufflé

Make as for Semolina Soufflé (see page 256), using 5 oz. (140 g) rice instead of semolina. If desired, about 2 oz. (55 g) washed and drained raisins or currants may be added before the whisked egg whites are folded in. This mixture can well be cooked in a mould.

Rice Soufflé

Make as for Semolina Soufflé (see page 256), using 5 oz. (140 g) vermicelli instead of semolina. Crush the vermicelli before adding to the milk. Season with Oetker rum flavour.

Vermicelli Soufflé

Bread Soufflé

4–5 stale rolls
⅔ pint (375 ccm) milk
1½ oz. (45 g) butter or margarine
2–3 oz. (55–85 g) sugar
2–3 egg yolks
3–4 drops Oetker Baking Essence,
    lemon flavour
a little salt
1 level tsp. (3 g) Oetker Baking Powder
    BACKIN
2–3 egg whites
2 tbsp. breadcrumbs
a knob of butter

Dice the rolls and pour over them the boiling milk. Leave to soak for some time, then stir to a smooth paste. Cream the fat and gradually add the sugar, the egg yolks, the baking essence, the salt, the BACKIN and the soaked bread. Whisk the egg whites until stiff and fold them carefully into the mixture. Fill into a well-greased pie-dish. Sprinkle with breadcrumbs and dot with butter. Bake in the oven.

Oven: moderately hot.

Time: about 40 minutes.

Serve with Frothy Wine Sauce (see page 62) or Frothy Lemon Sauce (see page 62).

Baked Macaroni with Ham

2¾ pints (1½ l) water
salt
9 oz. (250 g) macaroni
5–9 oz. (140–250 g) boiled ham
2 oz. (55 g) grated cheese
2 eggs
½ pint (285 ccm) milk or sour cream
pinch of salt
2 tbsp. breadcrumbs or grated cheese
a knob of butter

Add the salt to the water and bring to the boil. Break the macaroni into fingerlength pieces and sprinkle into the water. Simmer gently until done. Drain in a sieve and rinse with cold water. Leave to cool.

Cooking Time: about 30 minutes.

Put alternate layers of cold macaroni and the finely diced ham mixed with the cheese into a greased pie-dish, finishing with a layer of macaroni. Beat the eggs with the milk or cream, season with salt and pour over the mixture. Sprinkle with breadcrumbs or cheese and dot with knobs of butter.

Oven: moderately hot.

Time: about 40 minutes.

Serve with lettuce salad.

Alternatively, half-cooked mushrooms or sliced raw tomatoes may be taken instead of the ham, or Tomato Sauce (see page 52) may be poured over instead of the egg mixture.

Macaroni Soufflé

2¾ pints (1½ l) water
salt
9 oz. (250 g) macaroni or spaghetti
5 oz. (140 g) grated cheese

White Sauce:

1½ oz. (45 g) butter or margarine
1½ oz. (45 g) plain flour
1 pint (570 ccm) stock or sour milk
1–2 egg yolks
1–2 egg whites
2 tbsp. breadcrumbs
a knob of butter

Add the salt to the water, and bring to the boil. Break the macaroni or spaghetti into fingerlength pieces and sprinkle into the water. Simmer gently until done. Drain in a sieve and rinse with cold water.

Cooking Time: about 30 minutes.

Grease a pie-dish and fill it with alternate layers of macaroni and grated cheese, finishing with a layer of macaroni.

To make the sauce, melt the fat, add the flour and cook until pale yellow, stirring all the time. Gradually stir in the cold stock or the sour milk and bring quickly to the boil. Add the egg yolks, then carefully fold in the stiffly beaten egg whites. Pour the sauce over the macaroni and cheese, sprinkle with breadcrumbs and dot with butter.

Oven: moderately hot.

Time: about 40 minutes.

Baked Rice with Ham

1¾ pint (1 l) stock
salt
paprika or onion
9 oz. (250 g) rice
5–9 oz. (140–250 g) boiled ham
2 oz. (55 g) grated cheese
2 eggs
½ pint (285 ccm) milk or sour cream
pinch of salt
2 tbsp. breadcrumbs or grated cheese
a knob of butter

Add the paprika or onion to the salted stock and bring to the boil. Sprinkle in the washed rice and leave to simmer gently until done. Do not stir during cooking as this makes the grains disintegrate. Set aside to cool.

Cooking Time: about 35 minutes.

Grease a baking-dish and put into it alternate layers of cold rice and of finely diced ham, mixed with the cheese, finishing with a layer of rice. Beat together the eggs, the milk or cream and the salt and pour the mixture over the rice. Sprinkle with breadcrumbs or cheese and dot with butter.

Oven: moderately hot.

Time: about 40 minutes.

Serve with lettuce salad.

BEVERAGES

Beverages supply the liquid our bodies need; thirst-quenching, stimulating, warming, nourishing or healing, all these varieties of drink play a part in helping to keep us healthy.

Some beverages of course, such as tea, coffee, beer and wine contain substances (tannin, caffeine, alcohol) harmful to the heart and nerves, should be drunk in moderation. Children should drink milk or cocoa; in place of alcoholic drinks they can be given unfermented grape juice or other fruit juices.

A. HOT BEVERAGES

General Hints

1. Always use a good brand of coffee, tea or cocoa. The good brand makes the best brew and is therefore the most economical.

2. Store coffee, tea and cocoa in airtight containers in a cool place or the aroma will soon be lost. Buy in small quantities. Grind coffee just before making.

3. Keep special equipment for tea and coffee making.

4. Heat the tea or coffee pot thoroughly with some hot water from the kettle just before it boils. Pour this away.

5. Always use water freshly drawn from the cold tap. Soft (but not softened) water usually makes better tea and coffee than hard water.

6. Allow tea and coffee to stand for 3–5 minutes before serving. To keep hot while infusing, stand pot in hot water.

Coffee

2 oz. (55 g) coffee beans
2 pints (1⅛ l) water

Grind the beans, but not too finely or the coffee will taste bitter. Rinse out a porcelain or earthenware container with hot water, put in the ground coffee and, as soon as the water boils, pour it onto the coffee and stir. Allow to stand for 4–6 minutes, then strain into a warmed coffee pot. A tiny pinch of salt improves the flavour. Add a little chicory if desired. Serve with hot milk or cream and sugar.

Viennese Coffee: use a filter coffee pot. Put the ground coffee into a filter paper or drip filter and pour over it freshly boiling water in small quantities. The water must be kept at boiling point. Place the coffee pot in hot water during the dripping process.

Very good coffee can also be made by using one of the many different types of coffee-maker – vacuum coffee pot, electric, percolator and so on.

Mocha Coffee

2–3 oz. (55–85 g) mocha coffee
1¾ pint (1 l) water
sugar to taste

Mocha is very strong coffee, very finely ground. Mocha (mocha turc) is made by mixing the coffee with cold water and sugar, bringing to the boil and leaving to stand for 5 minutes.

Chinese Tea

2–3 tsp. tea
1¾ pint (1 l) water

Rinse out an earthenware container with hot water and put in the tea. Pour in at first ½ pint (285 ccm) of boiling water and leave to stand for 2 minutes. Pour in the remaining boiling water. Allow to stand for a minute or two. Strain into a warmed teapot.

Serve with sugar, lemon juice, rum, cream or milk.

German herb tea is a combination of different herbs and parts of various plants such as the leaves of strawberry, raspberry, blackberry, bilberry, cherry and rose; and the blossoms of heather, thyme, sweet woodruff, etc. Pour the boiling water over the herbs. Allow to stand for about 5 minutes, then strain.

German Herb Tea

2 tbsp. mixed herbs
1¾ pint (1 l) water

Pour cold water over the peel, bring to the boil and boil for 10–15 minutes. Strain and sweeten with sugar or honey.

Apple Peel Tea

¾ oz. (20 g) dried apple peel
1¾ pint (1 l) water

Pour cold water over the seeds and bring to the boil. Leave simmering gently for ¾–1 hour, then strain.

Rose Hip Tea

¾ oz. (20 g) rose hips seeds
1¾ pint (1 l) water

Pour the boiling water over the leaves and allow to stand for 5–10 minutes. Strain.

Mint Tea

½ oz. (15 g) dried mint leaves
2 pints (1⅛ l) water

Camomile Tea
Blackberry Tea
Lime Blossom Tea
Elderberry Blossom Tea

} Prepare in the same way as Mint Tea.

Mix the boiling water with the cocoa and the sugar. Pour into the boiling milk, bring again to the boil and serve. Cocoa may be made with water or equal parts of milk and water.

Cocoa

1–1½ oz. (30–45 g) cocoa
2 well heaped tbsp. (50 g) sugar
½ pint (285 ccm) water
1⅓ pint (¾ l) milk

Break the chocolate into small pieces, put it into a pan, add the water and bring slowly to the boil. Stir until well blended and smooth. Add the milk and, still stirring, bring again to the boil. Sweeten with sugar to taste.

Water may be used instead of milk, but more chocolate will be needed. Or add 1 tbsp. Oetker GUSTIN (corn starch powder), blended with a little cold water. This improves the consistency of the drink.

Chocolate

3½ oz. (100 g) plain chocolate
4 tbsp. cold water
about 1¾ pint (1 l) milk
a little sugar

Gluehwein
(Mulled Wine)

½ pint (285 ccm) water
a piece of cinnamon
4 cloves
a piece of lemon rind
2–3 oz. (55–85 g) sugar
1 pint (570 ccm) red wine

Mix the water with the spices and boil gently for about 5 minutes. Add the sugar and let it dissolve. Add the red wine and heat it almost to boiling point. Remove the spices before serving; put a slice of lemon into each glass, if desired.

The water may be omitted and the drink made with 1⅓ pint (¾ l) of red wine. Proceed as above.

Grog

1 pint (570 ccm) water
1–3½ oz. (30–100 g) sugar
½ pint (285 ccm) rum or arrack

Bring the water with the sugar to the boil and mix with the rum or arrack.

Red Wine Punch

1 pint (570 ccm) strong tea
3–5½ oz. (85–150 g) sugar
½ pint (285 ccm) red wine
¼ pint (140 ccm) arrack or rum
juice of 1 lemon

Strain the hot tea, pour onto the sugar, add the red wine, the arrack or rum and the lemon juice, then heat until almost boiling.

B. COLD BEVERAGES

General Hints

1. Prepare and serve cold drinks as cold as possible (preferably chilled or with ice in summer).

2. Whisk all the ingredients well together.

3. Sugar syrup gives a better result than undissolved sugar. Use 1⅛ lb. (500 g) sugar to ½ pint (285 ccm) water, bring slowly to the boil, boil till clear, then allow to cool.

4. If possible, add a few ice cubes to cold drinks.

5. Serve cold drinks (except Wine Cup) in tall glasses with straws.

6. Mixed drinks containing sour or buttermilk have food value as well as being refreshing.

Orangeade I

5–7 oranges
½ lemon
1¾ pint (1 l) water
3–3½ oz. (85–100 g) sugar

Squeeze the juice of the oranges and the half lemon and strain through a fine sieve. Mix with very cold water and sugar. Put a slice of orange into each glass, when serving.

Blend the sauce powder and the sugar with the 5 tbsp. of water. Bring the ¾ pint (425 ccm) water to the boil in an enamel saucepan. Remove from heat, add the prepared sauce powder and, stirring all the time, bring to the boil again. Set aside to cool, stirring frequently to prevent a skin forming. Mix with the soda-water just before serving.

Orangeade II

1 packet Oetker Sauce Powder,
   orange flavour
4½ oz. (125 g) sugar
5 tbsp. cold water
¾ pint (425 ccm) water
1 pint (570 ccm) soda-water

Peel the oranges and cut them into thin slices. Sprinkle with sugar. When nicely soaked, add the apple juice and finally the soda-water.

Orange Drink

3–4 oranges
a little sugar
1⅓ pint (¾ l) apple juice
1 pint (570 ccm) soda-water

Grate the outer rind into the other ingredients and mix well. The citric acid may first be dissolved in a little lukewarm water. Stir until the sugar is dissolved. Pour the mixture into little bottles and cork. 2 tbsp. of this essence mixed with a glass of water makes a very refreshing drink.

Orange or Lemon Essence

The rind of 6 oranges or lemons
1¾ pint (1 l) water
3¼ lb. (1½ kg) sugar
1 oz. (30 g) citric acid crystals

Mix the fruit juice with the water, season with lemon juice to taste or put a thin slice of lemon into each glass.
Alternatively, soda-water may be used instead of water.

Fruit Drink

½ pint (285 ccm) fruit juice
   (raspberry, red currant, cherry
   or elderberry)
1⅓ pint (¾ l) water
some lemon juice

Squeeze the juice from fresh strawberries, raspberries, blackberries, bilberries or grapes, dilute with water or soda-water and sweeten to taste.

Fruit Juice

Squeeze the juice from the lemons and strain through a fine sieve. Mix with the chilled water and the sugar. Put a thin slice of lemon into each glass and serve.
Prepared with hot water and sweetened with honey, lemonade is very good for colds.

Lemonade

3–4 lemons
1¾ pint (1 l) water
2–3 oz. (55–85 g) sugar

Squeeze the juice from the lemons and strain through a fine sieve. Mix with the chilled tea and add sugar to taste.

Cold Tea with Lemon Juice
(Phot. See Page 225)

1–2 lemons
1¾ pint (1 l) cold tea
about 2 tbsp. sugar

Bowle (Wine Cup)

1⅛ lb. (500 g) strawberries, peaches
or pineapple
3½–5½ oz. (100–150 g) sugar
2 bottles white wine
1–2 pints (570–1125 ccm) soda-water

Wash and stem the strawberries, wash and stone the peaches or peel the pineapple. Slice the fruit into a deep bowl or tureen alternately with layers of sugar. Pour over ½ pint (285 ccm) of wine. Set aside, well covered for 1–2 hours to chill, preferably in a refrigerator. Then add the rest of the wine and the soda-water. Serve very cold.

To make a non alcoholic drink fruit juice may be used instead of white wine.

Orange Milk

1¾ pint (1 l) milk
about 1½ oz. (45 g) sugar
juice of 6 oranges

Mix the milk and the sugar well together. Strain the juice through a fine sieve and add to the milk, stirring all the time. Sweeten to taste with sugar.

Strawberry Milk

9 oz. (250 g) strawberries
1⅓ pint (¾ l) milk
2 well heaped tbsp. (50 g) sugar
juice of ½ lemon

Wash and stem the strawberries and rub them through a fine sieve. Slowly mix in the milk, which should be very cold, add the lemon juice and sweeten with sugar to taste.

Lemon Milk

1¾ pint (1 l) milk
2–3 well heaped tbsp. (50–75 g) sugar
juice of 4 lemons

Mix together the milk and 2 well heaped tbsp. (50 g) sugar. Squeeze the juice from the lemons and strain through a fine sieve. Gradually whisk in the milk and add more sugar, if desired.

Egg and Milk
(Recommended for those on a Diet)

1 egg yolk
1 tsp. sugar
1 tsp. lemon juice
½ pint (285 ccm) boiling milk
1 tbsp. brandy
1 egg white

Beat together the yolk, the sugar and the lemon juice until creamy. Gradually add the milk and whisk until the mixture cools. When quite cold, add the brandy and fold in the stiffly beaten egg white. The brandy may be omitted.

Almond Milk

2–3 oz. (55–85 g) sweet almonds
3–4 bitter almonds
1¾ pint (1 l) milk
2–3 well heaped tbsp. (50–75 g) sugar

Scald the almonds and leave to soak in boiling water. After a while, drain and skin. Dry them and grind finely. Pour cold or boiling milk over them, and leave to chill in the refrigerator for several hours. Strain through a sieve, sweeten to taste with sugar and serve.

Gustin-Pudding with Fruit Recipe See Page 270

Fruit Milk Shake

1⅓ pint (¾ l) milk
½ pint (285 ccm) fruit juice
about 2 oz. (55 g) sugar

Whisk the milk and fruit juice well together and sweeten to taste with sugar. Allow the drink to chill, then serve. Soda-water may be added, if desired.

Iced Coffee (Phot. See Page 249)

1½ oz. (45 g) coffee beans
1⅓ pint (¾ l) water
½ pint (285 ccm) Vanilla Ice
(see page 260)
¼-½ pint (140–285 ccm) cream

Grind the beans, pour over the boiling water and stir frequently. Leave to stand for 4–6 minutes. Strain and put aside to chill. Fill glasses about two-third full with the chilled coffee. Add a dip of vanilla ice and top with whipped cream.

Iced Chocolate

4 oz. (115 g) chocolate
¼ pint (140 ccm) water
1 pint (570 ccm) milk
¼ pint (140 ccm) fresh cream
½ pint (285 ccm) Vanilla Ice
(see page 260)
¼-½ pint (140–285 ccm) cream

Break the chocolate into little pieces and heat slowly with the water until it becomes a smooth paste. Gradually add the milk, then the cream. Bring almost to the boil. Remove from the heat and leave to cool. When lukewarm, place in the icebox or refrigerator and leave to chill. Fill glasses two-thirds full with the chilled chocolate, add a dip of vanilla ice and top with whipped cream.

DESSERTS
AND SWEETS

The dessert or sweet course provides a wholesome and attractive conclusion to a meal, appealing both to the palate and to the eye. Desserts made with pudding powder are not only delicious, but are simple and quick to make. Oetker Pudding Powders are among the very best available, and owe their undoubted popularity to the fact that they are made with the best possible raw materials under hygienic conditions, and then packed and sent out in the familiar conveniently measured portions. At the Oetker factory raw materials, as well as the finished product, are under the permanent supervision of experienced chemists.

The basic ingredients in these pudding powders are corn and potato starches or mixtures of food starch and wheat semolina, combined with various flavourings, and different fruit extracts.

Many of the powders too, contain gelatine, tapioca, cocoa, chocolate and sugar.

A pudding dessert is made with milk, water, sugar, and often with butter and eggs as well, so that it contains in itself (being served, as it so often is, with fruit, or fruit juice), most of the valuable nutritive substances, such as carbohydrates, in the form of food staches, semolina, tapioca and sugar, also proteins, fats, minerals and vitamins. It also stimulates the digestion and adds considerably to the meal's nutritive value.

Mothers who have difficulty with their children's appetites should include Oetker puddings in their meals. Children will eat more readily, and at the same time will take in their nourishment in a way that they will enjoy. These puddings are especially valuable to young children when taken as an evening meal as they are easily digested and will provide them with wholesome and sub-staining nourishment. Even adults will find in them a welcome and delicious change, and because of the many attractive ways in which they can be served, they will be a treat both to the eye and the palate.

Oetker Sweet and Dessert Products

1. Pudding or Blancmange Powder:

A variety of flavours – almond, cream, vanilla, caramel, raspberry, strawberry, and lemon flavour,

Mandella Pudding or Blancmange Powder, vanilla flavour with chopped almonds,

"Rote Gruetze" Pudding or Blancmange Powder, raspberry flavour,

Pudding or Blancmange Powder, chocolate flavour,

GALA Pudding or Blancmange Powder, chocolate flavour,

Pudding or Blancmange Powder, chocolate flavour with chopped almonds.

2. Sauce Powder:

Sauce Powder, vanilla flavour,

Sauce Powder, chocolate flavour.

3. Corn Starch Powder:

GUSTIN.

4. Powdered Gelatine:

REGINA-Gelatine, white and red.

A. PUDDINGS

1. Use Oetker Pudding Powders according to the instructions on the packet.

2. Blend Oetker Pudding Powder or GUSTIN (corn starch powder) with sugar and any cold liquid before adding to boiling liquid. Use a fork to blend, as this ensures an even texture. Take the saucepan with the hot liquid off the heat before stirring in the cold mixture so that no lumps will form. Return to the heat and boil again for a second or two.

3. The egg yolk may be blended with the pudding powder and then heated. If it is to be an extra enrichment, blend the egg yolk with a little cold liquid and gradually stir it into the hot mixture after it has been removed from heat.

4. Whisk the egg white stiff and fold into the hot mixture as soon as it comes off the boil.

5. If the sweet is to be turned out when cold, rinse out the dish or mould with cold water and pour in the pudding as soon as it comes off the boil. Before unmoulding it, brush the top with a little cold water. This will make it easy to slide the pudding into the middle of the plate.

How to keep Desserts firm, and how to maintain the proper consistency in soups and sauces, thickened with Corn Starch Powder!

Occasionally puddings, soups and sauces thickened with corn starch powder lose their consistency. The quality of the corn starch powder is not to blame for this. Cooked starch can only be liquified by a starch disintegrating substance (enzyme). This substance is destroyed at a temperature of over 176° F (80° C) and shows no reaction under 50° F (10° C). It is most effective at 86–176° F (30–75° C). Since food that is thickened with starch is generally cooked, it cannot contain, after the cooking process has been completed, any starch disintegrating substance. If, however a dish liquifies after cooking, this substance must have been introduced later with some other ingredients — perhaps through the addition of raw yolk or white of egg, unpasteurized milk or chopped walnuts, all of which contain, in their uncooked state, this starch disintegrating substance. So it is important to make sure that the temperature of a dish thickened with corn starch powder does not drop to below 173° F (78° C) when raw egg, milk or nuts are added. These ingredients contain starch disintegrating substances.

If large quantities of egg white are to be folded into a cooked pudding mixture, it should be reheated after the white has been added. If you want to cool a dish quickly by adding cold milk, make sure it is cold boiled milk or the dish may liquify.

A cooked food that has been thickened with corn starch powder should never be stirred with the same spoon that was used for tasting while the food was being cooked. If saliva comes into contact with the food it will, under favourable conditions, act on the cooked starch and cause it to liquify.

Pudding with Caramel Topping

Pudding:

1 packet Oetker Pudding Powder, vanilla or cream flavour
1½ oz. (45 g) sugar
1–2 eggs
1 pint (570 ccm) milk

Topping:

3 oz. (85 g) sugar

For the pudding, blend the pudding powder, the sugar and the egg yolks with 6 tbsp. of the milk; whisk the egg whites until stiff. Bring the rest of the milk to the boil, remove from heat and stir in the pudding powder mixture. Bring again to the boil and cook for a second or two. Remove from heat and fold in the whisked egg white while the mixture is still hot.

For the topping, heat the sugar in an iron frying-pan, stirring all the time. When it is light brown, pour it into 4 or 5 small cups or moulds previously rinsed out with hot water. Turn each cup around to spread the caramel as thinly as possible over its base and sides. Pour the hot pudding into the cups. Leave to cool for several hours. Do not attempt to cool by putting the cups into cold water, as this would prevent the caramel from unmoulding. Turn out each cup onto a small plate just before serving. If turned out too soon, the pudding may break.

Pudding with Caramel or Chocolate Sauce

Pudding:

1 packet Oetker Pudding Powder, vanilla, almond or cream flavour
1½ oz. (45 g) sugar
1–2 eggs
1 pint (570 ccm) milk

Caramel Sauce:

2 well heaped tbsp. (50 g) sugar
¾ pint (425 ccm) milk
1 packet Oetker Sauce Powder, vanilla flavour
5 tbsp. cold milk or water
a little sugar

Chocolate Sauce:

¾ pint (425 ccm) milk
1 packet Oetker Sauce Powder, vanilla flavour
½ oz. (15 g) cocoa
2 well heaped tbsp. (50 g) sugar
6 tbsp. cold milk or water

For the pudding, blend the pudding powder with the sugar, the egg yolks and 6 tbsp. of the milk. Whisk the whites until stiff. Bring the rest of the milk to the boil, remove from heat and stir in the pudding powder mixture. Bring again to the boil and cook for a second or two. Remove from heat and fold in the whisked egg whites while the pudding is still hot.

For the caramel sauce, heat the sugar until it is light brown, stirring all the time. Quickly add the ¾ pint (425 ccm) of milk and bring to the boil. Meanwhile blend the sauce powder with the milk or water. Remove the caramel milk from heat and stir in the prepared sauce powder. Bring again to the boil. Set aside to cool. Stir the sauce frequently while it is cooling to prevent a skin forming. Add more sugar, if necessary.

For the chocolate sauce, bring the ¾ pint (425 ccm) of milk to the boil. Meanwhile blend the sauce powder, the cocoa and the sugar with the 6 tbsp. of milk or water. Remove the milk from heat, stir in the prepared sauce powder and bring again to the boil. Set aside to cool. Stir the sauce frequently while it is cooling to prevent a skin forming.

GUSTIN-Pudding with Fruit
(Phot. See Page 265)

1½ oz. (45 g) Oetker GUSTIN (corn starch powder)
2 well heaped tbsp. (50 g) sugar

Blend the GUSTIN, the sugar, the vanillin sugar and the egg yolk with the 6 tbsp. cold milk or water. Bring the pint (570 ccm) of milk to the boil, remove from heat and stir in the GUSTIN mixture. Bring again to the boil. Whisk the egg white until stiff and fold into the pudding while it is still hot.

Pour the fruit into a glass dish and pour the hot pudding over it. When cold, decorate with fruit.

1 packet Oetker Vanillin Sugar
1 egg yolk
6 tbsp. milk or water
1 pint (570 ccm) milk
1 egg white
any fresh or preserved fruit – apricots, apples, pears, cherries, plums, or fruit salad

Caramel Pudding

Blend the pudding powder with the egg yolks and 5 tbsp. of the milk. Whisk the egg whites until stiff. Stirring all the time, heat the sugar until it is light brown. Add the remaining milk quickly and bring to the boil. Remove from heat and stir in the prepared pudding powder. Bring again to the boil. Fold in the egg white while the pudding is still hot.

Serve with sauce, made with Oetker Sauce Powder, vanilla flavour.

1 packet Oetker Pudding Powder, vanilla flavour
1–2 eggs
1 pint (570 ccm) milk
3½ oz. (100 g) sugar

Semolina Pudding

Blend the sauce powder, the semolina, the sugar and the egg yolks with the 6 tbsp. cold milk or water. Whisk the egg whites until stiff. Bring the 1 pint (570 ccm) milk to the boil, remove from heat and stir in the prepared sauce powder. Return to heat and boil for 2 minutes. Remove from heat again and fold in the whisked egg white. Rinse out a dish or mould with cold water and pour in the pudding.

Serve with stewed fruit (cherries or apricots) or fruit juice.

1 packet Oetker Sauce Powder, vanilla flavour
1¼ oz. (35 g) semolina
2 well heaped tbsp. (50 g) sugar
1–2 egg yolks
6 tbsp. milk or water
1–2 egg whites
1 pint (570 ccm) milk

Peach Ring (Phot. See Page 225)

If the peaches are fresh, halve them carefully and cook in the ⅔ pint (375 ccm) of water with the sugar until tender. Carefully take out of the cooking liquid. Skin and drain (preserved peaches should be drained as well). Add the wine to ½ pint (285 ccm) of the cooking liquid (or syrup). If necessary sweeten the preserving liquid with sugar. Blend the GUSTIN and the egg yolks with the 6 tbsp. cold water. Whisk the egg whites until stiff. Bring to the boil the mixture of wine and liquid, remove from heat and stir in the prepared GUSTIN. Bring again to the boil and remove from heat. Fold in the egg whites, then return to heat for a very short time.

Oil a ring mould and carefully arrange in it the peach halves with the round side down. Pour in the hot mixture. Turn out when firm, using a knife to loosen the pudding from the sides of the mould.

Plums, pears, apricots or other fruit may be substituted for the peaches.

1⅛ lb. (500 g) peaches, fresh or preserved
⅔ pint (375 ccm) water
6 oz. (170 g) sugar if fresh fruit is used
¾ pint (425 ccm) white wine or cider
2½ oz. (70 g) Oetker GUSTIN (corn starch powder)
3 egg yolks
6 tbsp. water
3 egg whites

Tutti Frutti

About 1 lb. (450 g) fresh or stewed fruit
about 3 oz. (85 g) biscuits
1 packet Oetker Pudding Powder, vanilla or almond flavour
1½ oz. (45 g) sugar
1 pint (570 ccm) milk

Put the fruit into a large glass bowl or several small custard glasses and cover with a layer of biscuits. Blend the pudding powder and the sugar with 6 tbsp. of the milk. Bring the rest of the milk to the boil, remove from heat and stir in the prepared pudding mixture. Return to heat and bring again to the boil. Pour the pudding over the biscuits.

"Rote Gruetze"
(Phot. See Page 302)

1½ oz. (45 g) Oetker GUSTIN (corn starch powder)
6 tbsp. water
1 pint (570 ccm) fruit juice diluted with water (any fruit juice may be used)
sugar to taste

Blend the GUSTIN with the water. Sweeten the fruit juice to taste and bring to the boil. Remove from heat and stir in the prepared GUSTIN. Bring again to the boil. Rinse out small glass bowls with cold water and pour in the mixture. Turn out when cold. This dish may also be served in a large glass bowl.

Serve with sauce, made with Oetker Sauce Powder, vanilla flavour.

Apple "Gruetze"

1⅛ lb. (500 g) apples
⅔ pint (375 ccm) water
3½ oz. (100 g) sugar
1 packet Oetker "Rote Gruetze"
¼ pint (140 ccm) wine

Peel and slice the apples (reserve some slices to decorate) and cook with the sugar and water until almost tender. Take the apples out of the cooking syrup. Blend the "Rote Gruetze" with the wine, stir it into the syrup and bring again to the boil. Stir in the apple slices. Rinse out a mould with cold water, then pour in the mixture. Instead of a mould, individual glasses or a glass bowl may be used. Decorate with apple slices.

Serve with sauce, made with Oetker Sauce Powder, vanilla flavour.

Queen's Rice

1 pint (570 ccm) milk
pinch of salt
1 packet Oetker Vanillin Sugar
2–3 drops Oetker Baking Essence, lemon flavour
4 oz. (115 g) rice
½ packet Oetker Pudding Powder, vanilla flavour
about 1½ oz. (45 g) sugar
3 tbsp. water
½ pint (285 ccm) milk

Bring the pint (570 ccm) of milk to the boil with salt, the vanillin sugar and the lemon essence. Add the washed rice and simmer gently for about ½ hour (the grains should remain flaky).

Blend the pudding powder with the sugar and the 3 tbsp. water. Bring the ½ pint (285 ccm) of milk to the boil, remove from heat and stir in the prepared pudding powder. Bring again to the boil. Mix the pudding mixture with the rice, pour into a glass bowl and leave to cool.

Serve with fruit juice.

Mix the water with half of the wine and bring almost to boiling point. In the meantime, mix the pudding powder with the rest of the wine, the sugar and the egg yolks. Remove the water and wine mixture from the heat just as it is about to boil and stir in the prepared pudding powder. Bring again to the boil and cook for a second or two. Whisk the egg whites until stiff and fold into the wine mixture while it is still hot. Carefully pour into a glass bowl and leave to cool.

Wine Sweet

½ pint (285 ccm) water
⅔ pint (375 ccm) white wine or cider
1 packet Oetker Pudding Powder,
   vanilla flavour
3½ oz. (100 g) sugar
1–2 eggs

B. GELATINE DESSERTS

General Hints

1. The contents of 1 packet Oetker REGINA Gelatine, powdered, is enough to set ¾ pint and 5 tbsp. (500 ccm) of liquid and is the equivalent of 6 sheets of gelatine.

2. Blend the powdered gelatine with a little cold water and set aside to soak for about 10 minutes. Then heat gently over a low heat until it is completely dissolved, stirring all the time. While it is still warm, add the dissolved gelatine to the cream mixture. If it should begin to set before it is added to the mixture, reheat again to dissolve.

3. Never add dissolved gelatine to a cream at or under the temperature of 50° F (10° C). The gelatine will set at once and will form lumps and threads. Cream, milk or any other liquid which has been kept in a refrigerator must be warmed a little before mixing with dissolved gelatine.

4. Jellies contain gelatine. This will not set if the room temperature is over 73° F (23° C). Jellies which have already set will begin to liquify if left in too hot a room. So always leave jellies in a cool or cold place, or in a basin of cold water (renew the water frequently) or, best of all, in a refrigerator.

5. Gelatine desserts (jellies) are generally served in individual dishes or glasses. If the jelly is to be turned out, rinse out the container with cold water before filling it with the unset jelly. To turn out, loosen around the edges with a knife and dip the mould up to the rim in hot water for a second. Decorate with chopped jelly, which can be made by pouring a little of the unset jelly onto a flat plate. Sprinkle the chopped jelly over the dish just before serving.

6. Pineapple juice must be boiled for 2 or 3 minutes before being used for jelly.

273

Buttermilk Jelly

1 pint (570 ccm) buttermilk
2–3 oz. (55–85 g) sugar
grated lemon rind
juice of half a lemon
½ bottle Oetker rum flavour
1 packet and 1 level tsp. Oetker
REGINA Gelatine, powdered, white
5 tbsp. cold water

Add to the buttermilk the sugar, the lemon rind, the lemon juice and the rum flavour.

Blend the gelatine with the water and set aside to soak for 10 minutes. Stirring all the time, heat gently until completely dissolved. While the gelatine is still tepid, stir it into the buttermilk. Put the mixture into a large bowl or individual dishes and set aside in a cool place to set. Sour milk may be used instead of buttermilk.

Serve with sauce, made with Oetker Sauce Powder, vanilla flavour.

Yoghurt Jelly

Jelly:
1 packet and 1 level tsp. Oetker
REGINA Gelatine, powdered, white
5 tbsp. cold water
¼ pint (140 ccm) milk
3 well heaped tbsp. (75 g) sugar
1 packet Oetker Vanillin Sugar
juice of half a lemon
grated rind of half a lemon
¾ pint (425 ccm) yoghurt

For Sprinkling:
grated chocolate or chocolate vermicelli

Blend the gelatine with the water and leave it to soak for 10 minutes. Then heat gently over a low heat, stirring all the time, until completely dissolved. Use when lukewarm. Mix the milk, the sugar, the vanillin sugar, the lemon juice and rind and the lukewarm gelatine with the yoghurt. Pour the mixture into a glass bowl and leave to set.

Sprinkle around the edge with chocolate or chocolate vermicelli when set.

Cottage Cheese Jelly

4 level tsp. Oetker REGINA Gelatine,
powdered, white
3 tbsp. cold water
9 oz. (250 g) cottage cheese
2 well heaped tbsp. (50 g) sugar
½ pint (285 ccm) milk
a little lemon juice (optional)

Blend the gelatine with the water, leave to soak for 10 minutes, then heat gently over a low heat, stirring all the time, until completely dissolved.

Rub the cottage cheese through a sieve, add the sugar and beat until creamy. Stir in the milk, then mix in the lukewarm gelatine. Flavour with lemon juice, if desired. Rinse out a mould and fill it with the mixture. Leave to set.

Serve with fruit juice or stewed fruit.

Alternatively, ¼ pint (140 ccm) of fruit juice may be used instead of half the milk quantity.

Grated chocolate may also be added.

Fruit Juice Jelly

1 packet and 1 level tsp. Oetker
REGINA Gelatine, powdered, white
½ pint (285 ccm) cold water

Blend the gelatine with 5 tbsp. of the water and leave to soak for at least 10 minutes. Add the lemon rind to the rest of the water and bring to the boil. Add the soaked gelatine to the hot

274

water and stir until it is completely dissolved. Add the fruit juice, sweeten with sugar if necessary and add the lemon juice, if desired. Pour the mixture into a glass bowl or individual dishes. Leave to set in a cool place for several hours, preferably overnight.

Serve with sauce, made with Oetker Sauce Powder, vanilla flavour.

a piece of lemon rind
½ pint (285 ccm) fruit juice
sugar and lemon juice to taste

Jelly with Fresh Fruit
(Phot. See Page 302)

1 medium-sized apple
1 medium-sized orange
1 banana
1 well-heaped tbsp. sugar
½ pint (285 ccm) water
1 packet Oetker Jelly Powder, lemon flavour
1 well-heaped tbsp. sugar
½ pint (285 ccm) white wine

Peel the Fruit, then cut or slice it finely. Mix with the sugar.

Then put equal amounts of the fruit into 6 small individual dishes.

Make the jelly according to the directions on the packet, but use only half a pint (285 ccm) of water. Leave to set. When the jelly is cold but still liquid, add the wine, pour the mixture over the fruit, and leave to set in a cold place for several hours, preferably overnight.

Serve with sauce, made with Oetker Sauce Powder, vanilla flavour or with whipped cream.

C. CREAMS

General Hints

1. A cream is a semi-solid dessert. It is too soft to be unmoulded, and should be served in a bowl or in individual dishes.

2. Gelatine as well as cornflour may be used as binding agents.

3. Creams prepared with gelatine, beaten egg white or whipped cream, must be of a very good consistency before folding in the beaten egg white or whipped cream.

4. Never whisk or stir a cream dessert in an aluminium saucepan, as this will cause it to discolour.

Pineapple Cream

2 oz. (55 g) Oetker GUSTIN (corn starch powder)
3 well heaped tbsp. (75 g) sugar
1 packet Oetker Vanillin Sugar
tinned pineapple juice made up to 1 pint (570 ccm) with water
2 tbsp. lemon juice
¼–½ pint (140–285 ccm) double cream
7 oz. (200 g) tinned pineapple (3–6 tinned pineapple rings)

Blend the GUSTIN, the sugar and the vanillin sugar with 6 tbsp. of the diluted pineapple juice. Heat the rest of the juice. When it boils, remove from heat and gradually stir in the prepared GUSTIN. Bring again to the boil and cook for a second or so. Leave to cool, stirring occasionally.

When cool but not set, stir in the lemon juice, fold in the whipped cream (reserve some for decorating) and add the pineapple, cut into pieces (reserve some for decorating). Pour the cream into a glass bowl or individual dishes. When set, decorate with a little whipped cream and a few pieces of pineapple.

Orange Cream
(Phot. See Page 232)

1 packet Oetker REGINA Gelatine,
powdered, white
6 tbsp. cold water
3 eggs
4 tbsp. warm water
3½ oz. (100 g) sugar
juice of 2 oranges and half a lemon

Blend the gelatine with the water and leave to soak for at least 10 minutes. Heat slowly, stirring all the time, until it is completely dissolved. Set aside for a time. Whisk the egg yolks and the warm water until frothy and gradually add ⅔ of the sugar. Whip until creamy. Whisk in the orange and lemon juice and add the dissolved gelatine. Set aside to cool.

Whisk the egg whites until stiff and add the rest of the sugar, whisking all the time. As soon as the egg yolk cream begins to thicken, fold in the egg whites. Pour the cream into a glass bowl or individual glasses and chill.

Serve with biscuits.

Coffee Cream with Eggs

1 packet Oetker REGINA Gelatine,
powdered, white
3 tbsp. cold water
¾ pint and 5 tbsp. (500 ccm) milk
2 slightly rounded tsp. powdered coffee
2 eggs
3 well heaped tbsp. (75 g) sugar
1 packet Oetker Vanillin Sugar
1–2 oz. (30–55 g) grated chocolate

Blend the gelatine with the water and leave to soak for at least 10 minutes. Bring the milk to the boil, remove from heat and add the soaked gelatine, stirring all the time, until it is quite dissolved. Add the powdered coffee and set aside to cool.

Beat the egg yolks to a froth with the sugar and the vanillin sugar, add the cold coffee mixture and leave to set. As soon as the mixture begins to thicken, fold in the stiffly beaten egg whites and the grated chocolate.

Nut Cream

1 packet Oetker REGINA Gelatine,
powdered, white
4 tbsp. cold water
1 packet Oetker Sauce Powder,
vanilla flavour
3 well heaped tbsp. (75 g) sugar
1 packet Oetker Vanillin Sugar
2 eggs
1⅓ pint (¾ l) milk
5 oz. (140 g) ground hazelnuts

Blend the gelatine with the water and leave to soak for at least 10 minutes. Mix the sauce powder, the sugar and the vanillin sugar with the egg yolks and 6 tbsp. of the milk. Bring the rest of the milk to the boil, remove from heat, add the sauce powder mixture, return to heat and boil again for a short time. Stir in the soaked gelatine and continue stirring until it is dissolved. Leave to cool.

As soon as the cream begins to set, fold in the hazelnuts and the stiffly beaten egg whites. Pour into a glass bowl or individual glasses.

Serve with sauce, made with Oetker Sauce Powder, orange flavour, or with fruit juice.

Portuguese Cream
(Phot. See Page 162)

3 level tsp. Oetker REGINA Gelatine,
powdered, white
2 tbsp. cold water
2–3 eggs
3 well heaped tbsp. (75 g) sugar
¼ pint (140 ccm) cider
grated rind of half a lemon

Blend the gelatine with the water and leave to soak for at least 10 minutes. Heat slowly, stirring all the time, until it is completely dissolved.

Whisk well together the egg yolks, the sugar, the cider, lemon rind, lemon juice and the dissolved gelatine. Put the mixture into a pan over a very low heat and continue to whisk until thick and bubbly. Fold in the stiffly beaten egg whites and leave to cool.

Then fold in the whipped cream (reserve a little for decorating). Soak the macaroons in the rum flavour, diluted with the 2 tbsp. water and arrange in layers alternately with the cream in a glass bowl or small glasses. Decorate with the macaroons and whipped cream.

juice of half a lemon
¼ pint (140 ccm) double cream
about 2 oz. (55 g) macaroons
½ bottle Oetker rum flavour
2 tbsp. water

Chocolate Cream

Blend the pudding powder, the sugar and the egg yolks with 6 tbsp. of the milk. Whisk the egg whites until stiff. Bring the remaining milk to the boil with the orange peel, remove from heat and stir in the prepared pudding powder. Remove the orange peel, bring again to the boil and cook for a minute or two. Carefully fold in the egg whites while the cream is still hot. Pour into a glass bowl to set.

Serve with sauce, made with Oetker Sauce Powder, vanilla flavour.

Alternatively, 1 oz. (30 g) washed sultanas may be mixed with the cream.

1 packet Oetker Pudding Powder, chocolate flavour with chopped almonds
3½ oz. (100 g) sugar
1–2 egg yolks
1⅓ pint (¾ l) milk
1–2 egg whites
peel of one orange

Vanilla and Cottage Cheese Cream

Blend the pudding powder with the sugar and the 6 tbsp. of the milk. Bring the remaining milk to the boil, remove from heat and stir in the prepared pudding powder. Bring again to the boil for a short time and set aside to cool. Stir occasionally while it is cooling.

Rub the cottage cheese through a fine sieve, add the sugar and the vanillin sugar and lastly the pudding mixture. Add this by the tablespoonful, while it is still warm. Fill into a glass bowl or individual glasses and serve immediately.

Alternatively, pour the cream over about 1⅛ lb. (500 g) of any soft fruit, cleaned and sugared.

1 packet Oetker Pudding Powder, vanilla flavour
1½ oz. (45 g) sugar
1 pint (570 ccm) milk
9 oz. (250 g) cottage cheese
3 slightly heaped tbsp. (60 g) sugar
1 packet Oetker Vanillin Sugar

Wine Cream

Blend the gelatine with the water and leave to soak for at least 10 minutes. Stir over a low heat until completely dissolved. Set aside to cool.

Beat the egg yolks with the wine until very frothy. Gradually add ⅔ of the sugar, continuing to beat until the mixture is thick and creamy. Whisk in the lemon juice and the dissolved gelatine. Set aside to cool.

Whisk the egg whites until stiff, gradually adding the remaining sugar. As soon as the wine mixture begins to thicken, fold in the stiffly beaten egg whites. Fill into a glass bowl or individual glasses and chill.

Serve with biscuits.

1 packet Oetker REGINA Gelatine, powdered, white
4 tbsp. cold water
3 eggs
½ pint (285 ccm) wine
3 well heaped tbsp. (75 g) sugar
2 tbsp. lemon juice

Lemon Cream

1 packet Oetker REGINA Gelatine,
powdered, white
6 tbsp. of cold water
3 eggs
4 tbsp. warm water
3½ oz. (100 g) sugar
juice of 2–2½ lemons

Blend the gelatine with the 6 tbsp. water and leave to soak for at least 10 minutes. Stir over a low heat until completely dissolved. Set aside to cool.

Add the warm water to the egg yolks and beat vigorously until very frothy. Gradually add about ⅔ of the sugar and beat until the mixture is thick and creamy. Whisk in the lemon juice and the dissolved gelatine. Set aside to cool.

Whisk the egg whites until stiff, gradually adding the remaining sugar. As soon as the cream begins to thicken, fold in the stiffly beaten egg whites. Chill until set.

Delicious with biscuits.

Lemon Cream with Milk

1 packet Oetker REGINA Gelatine,
powdered, white
5 tbsp. cold water
2 eggs
1 tbsp. warm water
juice of 2 lemons
3½ oz. (100 g) sugar
1 packet Oetker Vanillin Sugar
the grated rind of half a lemon
(no pith)
⅔ pint (375 ccm) cold milk

Blend the gelatine with the water and leave to soak for at least 10 minutes. Stir over a low heat until completely dissolved.

Beat together the egg yolks, the warm water and the lemon juice until very frothy. Gradually add about ⅔ of the sugar and the vanillin sugar continuing to beat until the mixture is thick and creamy. Add the grated lemon rind, the lukewarm dissolved gelatine and, still whisking, gradually add the cold milk. Set aside to cool.

Whisk the egg whites until stiff and gradually add the remaining sugar. As soon as the cream begins to thicken, fold in the beaten egg whites. Pour into a glass bowl or individual glasses and chill until set.

Rhubarb Cream

1⅛ lb. (500 g) rhubarb
⅔ pint (375 ccm) water
4½ oz. (125 g) sugar
1 packet Oetker Pudding Powder,
vanilla flavour
1 egg and
6 tbsp. water

Wash the rhubarb and cut it up — do not remove the skin. Add the water and bring to the boil with ⅔ of the sugar. Cook until tender.

Blend the pudding powder with the egg yolk and the 6 tbsp. of water and add to the rhubarb, stirring all the time. Bring again to the boil and cook for a second or two. Sweeten to taste with the remaining sugar and fold in the stiffly beaten egg white while the mixture is still hot.

Egg Rice

1 packet Oetker REGINA Gelatine,
powdered, white
8 tbsp. cold water
1⅓ pint (¾ l) milk
¼ pint (140 ccm) water
2 well heaped tbsp. (50 g) sugar

Blend the gelatine with the water and leave to soak for at least 10 minutes. Bring to the boil the milk, the ¼ pint (140 ccm) water, the sugar and the salt. Add the washed rice and simmer gently for about 30 minutes. The rice should be flaky and the grain whole. Remove from heat, stir in the soaked gelatine and continue to stir until the gelatine is dissolved. Set aside to cool.

Beat the egg yolks with the warm water until very frothy and gradually add the sugar and the baking essence. Continue to whisk until the mixture is thick and creamy. Stir in the rice. As soon as this mixture thickens, fold in the stiffly beaten egg whites. Do not beat the egg whites until they are needed.

Fill into a glass bowl or individual glasses and leave to chill until set.

a little salt
4½ oz. (125 g) rice
2–3 eggs
1 tbsp. warm water
2 well heaped tbsp. (50 g) sugar
3–4 drops Oetker Baking Essence, lemon flavour

Chocolate Rice

Sieve the cocoa, mix with the gelatine and the ¼ pint (140 ccm) water and leave to soak. Bring the milk, the ¼ pint (140 ccm) water, the sugar, the vanillin sugar and salt to the boil; add the washed rice and simmer gently for about half an hour. The rice should be flaky and the grain whole.

Stir the soaked gelatine into the cooked rice and set aside to cool.

Beat the egg yolks with the warm water until very frothy and gradually add the sugar. Continue to beat until the mixture is thick and creamy. Stir in the rice. As soon as the mixture begins to thicken, fold in the stiffly beaten egg whites. Do not beat the egg whites until they are needed. Pour the chocolate rice into a glass bowl or individual glasses and chill until set.

Serve with sauce, made with Oetker Sauce Powder, vanilla flavour.

¼ pint (140 ccm) cold water
3 heaped tsp. cocoa
1 packet Oetker REGINA Gelatine, powdered, white
1⅓ pint (¾ l) milk
¼ pint (140 ccm) water
2 well heaped tbsp. (50 g) sugar
1 packet Oetker Vanillin Sugar
a little salt
5 oz. (140 g) rice
2 eggs
1 tbsp. warm water
2 well heaped tbsp. (50 g) sugar

D. ICES AND FROZEN DESSERTS

Ices are one of the most popular sweets, particularly during the summer months and on festive occasions. If you own a refrigerator, making ices is easy, but it is by no means impossible if you have none. The pail-freezer makes excellent ices and even without one ice-cream making is still possible, provided the ice is broken into small pieces and mixed with the right amount of salt.

To make ice cream in a freezer, first break up the block ice into small pieces. Do this by putting the ice into a sack or rough cloth and pounding with a hammer. Then mix it with salt or with a freezing substance. The correct proportion of ice to salt is important; allow four measures of block ice to one measure of coarse rock-salt. Put the container in the middle of the freezer and pack ice and salt in alternate layers around it until the freezer is filled. Make sure the container is spotlessly clean inside, then fill it ⅔ full with the cold mixture, thus allowing for expansion. Turn the cream evenly for 20–30 minutes. Then remove the dasher, but leave the container in the ice for about 30–60 minutes.

If you have no freezer, any pail or basin may be used. Cover the bottom of it with small pieces of block ice, and on top of this put the container of ice cream – any jar or mould will be suitable. Now pack the pail or basin ⅔ full with layers of block ice and salt. Rotate the container from right to left and vice versa. Stir the cream now and again with a wooden spoon, scraping the hard frozen parts from the sides until the cream is evenly frozen.

For ices, made in a refrigerator trays, use a cream mixture of milk and egg yolk, as the refrigerator is not particularly good for making water ices.

Serve ices piled in a glass bowl or in individual glasses. An ordinary spoon or one of the many scoops available may be used. If a bombe, i. e. a cream frozen in a mould, is desired, then press the cream mixture into a cone-shaped mould and freeze in ice for 2 to 3 hours. The ice must cover the mould completely. To prevent icewater from penetrating into the mould, wrap it firmly in plenty of greaseproof paper. Hold the mould in warm water for a second before turning out.

Vanilla Ice Cream I
(Phot. See Page 281)

1 packet Oetker Sauce Powder, vanilla flavour or ½ packet Oetker Pudding Powder, vanilla flavour
3 well heaped tbsp. (75 g) sugar
1 packet Oetker Vanillin Sugar
5 tbsp. cold milk
¾ pint (425 ccm) milk

Blend the sauce powder or pudding powder, the sugar and the vanillin sugar with the milk. Bring the ¾ pint (425 ccm) milk to the boil. Remove from heat and stir in the prepared sauce powder. Bring again to the boil and cook for a second or two. To prevent a skin forming, stir the mixture occasionally as it cools. Pour into the ice container and freeze.

Fruit may be added to the ice cream, if desired. Add about 5 oz. (140 g) of chopped and sweetened fresh or preserved fruit (strawberries, cherries, greengages, Mirabelle plums) to the mixture when it is half frozen.

Vanilla Ice Cream II

1 slightly heaped tbsp. (10 g) Oetker GUSTIN (corn starch powder)
3 well heaped tbsp. (75 g) sugar
2 packets Oetker Vanillin Sugar
2 egg yolks
5 tbsp. cold milk
¾ pint (425 ccm) milk

Blend the GUSTIN, the sugar and the vanillin sugar with the egg yolks and the milk. Bring the ¾ pint (425 ccm) milk to the boil. Remove from heat and stir in the prepared GUSTIN. Bring again to the boil and cook for a second or two. Leave to cool, stirring frequently to prevent a skin forming. Pour into a container and freeze.

Vanilla Ice Cream Recipe See Page 280
Chocolate Ice Cream Recipe See Page 282

Raspberry Ice Cream

½ packet Oetker Pudding Powder,
raspberry flavour
3 well heaped tbsp. (75 g) sugar
5 tbsp. cold milk
¾ pint (425 ccm) milk
4½ oz. (125 g) raspberry jam
or fresh sugared raspberries

Blend the pudding powder and the sugar with the milk. Bring the ¾ pint (425 ccm) milk to the boil, remove from heat and stir in the prepared pudding powder. Bring again to the boil and cook for a second or two. Leave to cool, stirring frequently to prevent a skin forming. Pour into a container and freeze. Add the jam or fruit to the mixture when it is half frozen.

If a pudding powder of a different flavour is desired (lemon, almond, etc.), then vary the fruit or jam accordingly.

Caramel Ice Cream with Nuts

1 slightly heaped tbsp. (10 g) Oetker
GUSTIN (corn starch powder)
2 egg yolks
1 packet Oetker Vanillin Sugar
5 tbsp. cold milk
3½ oz. (100 g) sugar
¾ pint (425 ccm) milk
1 oz. (30 g) ground hazelnuts

Blend the GUSTIN, the egg yolks and the vanillin sugar with the milk. Stirring all the time, heat the sugar until it is light brown. Add the ¾ pint (425 ccm) milk and bring to the boil. Remove from heat and stir in the prepared GUSTIN. Bring again to the boil and cook for a second or two. Add the hazelnuts and leave to cool. Stir frequently while cooling to prevent a skin forming. Pour into a container and freeze.

Chocolate Ice Cream
(Phot. See Page 281)

½ packet Oetker Pudding Powder,
chocolate flavour with chopped
almonds
3½ oz. (100 g) sugar
1 packet Oetker Vanillin Sugar
5 tbsp. cold milk
¾ pint (425 ccm) milk

Blend the Pudding powder, the sugar and the vanillin sugar with the milk. Bring the ¾ pint (425 ccm) milk to the boil, remove from heat and stir in the pudding mixture. Bring again to the boil and cook for a second or two. Leave to cool, stirring frequently to prevent a skin forming. Pour into a container and freeze.

Mocha Ice Cream

½ packet Oetker Pudding Powder,
cream flavour
3½ oz. (100 g) sugar
5 tbsp. cold milk
¾ pint (425 ccm) milk
2 slightly heaped tsp. powdered coffee

Blend the pudding powder and the sugar with the milk. Bring the ¾ pint (425 ccm) of milk to the boil. Remove from heat and stir in the prepared pudding powder. Bring again to the boil and cook for a second or two. Add the powdered coffee and stir until dissolved. While cooling, stir frequently to prevent a skin forming. Pour into a container and freeze.

Cream Puffs with Cherries Recipe See Page 317
Chocolate Cake Recipe See Page 289

CAKE MAKING

Nothing pleases the housewife more than to be complimented by her family and friends on her delicious home-made cakes. There is something especially satisfying about success with cake making, and it is hoped that the recipes which follow will offer valuable guidance and instructions on how this success can be achieved.

Perhaps the most important single element in succes is the baking process itself. A good cake is a well risen cake. And the simplest, easiest, and most familiar raising agent the housewife can use is baking powder. The action of moisture and heat upon baking powder results in the release of carbon dioxide in the form of tiny bubbles. These bubbles raise the cake and give it its spongy texture. The heat of the oven alters the cake's texture, transforming the shapeless dough into a firm set shape, and, of course, giving the cake its crust.

Cherry Tart Recipe See Page 303

These two factors, the raising agent and the oven's heat, have to be correctly balanced against one another in their action on the cake. The oven's heat must not set the cake before it is sufficiently risen, or too dense a mass will result. If the cake rises too quickly, without sufficient heat to set it, it will collapse.

During the baking process the cake's flavour develops. The raw ingredients, as they cook, combine their various qualities to create the special delicious smell and flavour of the good home-made cake.

Oetker Baking Powder BACKIN has been tried and tested by generations of German housewives. Its quality and reliability have made it the most popular baking powder in many parts of Europe. And its packet form (each packet is enough for $1\frac{1}{8}$ lb. (500 g) flour) makes it especially simple to use and ensures accuracy of measurement. Oetker Baking Powder should always be added to the flour and thoroughly mixed and sieved with it right at the beginning of the cake making. This guarantees even texture and raising.

As moisture as well as heat makes the cake rise, always make sure any liquid ingredient is used cold. If the recipe calls for the heating of, say, honey and fat, or as in choux pastry, of flour and water, cool the mixture to blood heat before adding it to flour containing BACKIN.

Always follow the recipe exactly. All the recipes in this book have been chosen to suit the special qualities of BACKIN. All recipes have been carefully tested.

GENERAL HINTS

Tools and Equipment

Ingredients should always be weighed and measured carefully, never guessed at. So a set of accurate scales and a measuring jug or beaker are essential pieces of kitchen equipment.

The mixing bowl should be of china, stoneware, or earthenware, with smooth sides and rounded corners on the inside; not enamel as it chips, and not aluminium as it discolours the cake mixture. Always set the bowl on a wet cloth or in a special holder. This ensures a firm base whilst the cake is being mixed.

An efficient whisk will be needed for sponge mixtures, and, as all cakes turn out better if the flour is sieved, a good sieve will be needed. The tin with removable rim mentioned in several of the recipes is exactly the right size for the cakes. It has a diameter of $10\frac{1}{2}$ inches (26 cm).

All mixture for a baking sheet are calculated for a size "$12\frac{1}{2} \times 18$" (32 cm $\times$ 26 cm) sheet.

Always clean baking tins, sheets, and moulds thoroughly after use, washing and drying them carefully.

The appropriate oven temperature is given for every cake and pastry recipe in this book. A chart of oven temperatures for additional guidance is printed below.

Cake mixtures needing a deep tin, like Sand Cake, Fruit Cake, and Plain Cake may be started in a cold oven. Biscuits, all cakes in shallow tins, pastries, and choux pastries, require a pre-heated oven to keep their shape and to stop them getting too dry.

Baking sheets must be placed quite straight on the shelf. Cake tins should always be put on a rack, never directly onto the bottom of the oven or onto a baking sheet. Tins containing cake mixtures should be placed in the centre of the oven, where there is good even heat, rather than to either side of it. Deep tins should go low in the oven, shallow tins further up, and baking sheets right at the top, or at least well above the middle shelf.

The length of time to allow for cooking a cake depends on oven conditions. Ovens vary, and often have little peculiarities which must be allowed for. Any cake mixture will cook more quickly in a shallow, dark coloured tin than in a deep, light one. Stiff mixtures made by the creaming method take less time than softer ones containing more milk. It is advisable to look into the oven fairly often towards the end of the cooking time to see that all is well. Test cakes made by the creaming method by piercing them in the middle with a wooden cake tester (or long toothpick). If the tester comes away clean, the cake is done.

BAKING IN THE OVEN

Oven Description	Temperatures in C	Temperatures in F	Standard Regulo Mark	Cake Mixture and Type of Tin
Slow	130°-160°	265°-320°	2 or under	Meringues and macaroons.
Moderately hot	170°-200°	340°-390°	2-6	Cakes made by the creaming method in large or medium-sized tins. Medium-sized tins with creamed mixtures and fruit. Sponge mixtures (flans, tarts decorated, sponge sandwiches).
Hot	200°-225°	390°-440°	6-8	Flat cakes (oblong tin or baking sheet) patty tins and biscuits.

Almost all modern ovens are thermostatically controlled. That is to say, once the oven is heated to a certain temperature, it will automatically maintain that temperature. The makers always issue a chart explaining how the dial on the oven works, together with suggested dial settings for the cooking of various foods. In a thermostatically controlled oven, cakes and pastries cook evenly and acquire a good crust. Both gas and electric ovens may be thermostatically controlled. In the chart on page 287 we give Regulo mark readings as well as temperatures in Centigrade and Fahrenheit as a guide to correct oven heating. Whether or not pre-heating is required is indicated in each separate recipe.

CAKES AND BISCUITS

A. CAKES MADE BY THE CREAMING METHOD

I. CAKES IN BAKING TINS

Iced Fruit Cake

Cake Mixture:

7 oz. (200 g) butter or margarine
7 oz. (200 g) sugar
1 packet Oetker Vanillin Sugar
3–4 eggs
½ bottle Oetker Baking Essence, lemon flavour or 1 bottle Oetker rum flavour
1⅛ lb. (500 g) plain flour
1 packet Oetker Baking Powder BACKIN
¼ pint (140 ccm) milk
3½ oz. (100 g) currants
3½ oz. (100 g) raisins
2 oz. (55 g) finely diced candied lemon peel

Icing:

7 oz. (200 g) icing sugar
1 oz. (30 g) cocoa
about 3 tbsp. hot water

For the cake mixture, cream the fat and gradually add the sugar, the vanillin sugar, the eggs and the flavouring. Mix and sieve the flour and the BACKIN and add to the creamed ingredients alternately with just enough milk to give a firm mixture. Finally fold in the washed and drained currants and raisins, and the candied lemon peel. Grease a tube baking tin and dust with breadcrumbs. Fill the mixture into the prepared tin. Place low in the oven.

Oven: moderate.

Baking Time: 50–60 minutes.

For the icing, mix and sieve the icing sugar with the cocoa and stir in enough hot water to give a thick coating consistency. Spread over the cooled cake.

Cream the fat and gradually add the sugar, the vanillin sugar and the eggs. Stir in the mixed and sieved flour, the GUSTIN and the BACKIN, alternately with the milk. The mixture should be firm, so do not use too much milk. Lastly add the chocolate, cut into very small pieces. Grease a tube baking tin and dust with breadcrumbs. Fill the mixture into the prepared tin. Place low in the oven.

Oven: moderate.

Baking Time: 50–60 minutes.

When cold, dust with icing sugar.

Cream the fat and gradually add the sugar, the vanillin sugar, the eggs and the flavouring. Mix and sieve the flour and the BACKIN and stir gradually into the creamed mixture. Add the milk alternately with the flour until a good firm consistency is obtained. Grease a tube or loaf baking tin and dust with breadcrumbs. Fill about ⅔ of the mixture into the prepared tin. Add the cocoa, the sugar and the milk to the remaining mixture. Spread the dark mixture on the light, then draw a fork down and round through both mixtures and swirl the two together. Place low in the oven.

Oven: moderate.

Baking Time: 50–65 minutes.

Cream the fat and gradually add the sugar, the eggs and the flavouring. Stir in the pudding powder, blended with 3 tbsp. of the milk. Mix and sieve the flour and the BACKIN and stir in gradually, alternately with the milk, adding just enough milk to give a firm mixture. Fold in the almonds and the washed and drained raisins. Grease a tube baking tin and dust with breadcrumbs. Fill the mixture into the prepared tin. Place low in the oven.

Oven: moderate.

Baking Time: 50–70 minutes.

When cold, dust with icing sugar.

Chocolate Cake
(Phot. See Page 283)

Cake Mixture:

9 oz. (250 g) butter or margarine
9 oz. (250 g) sugar
1 packet Oetker Vanillin Sugar
3–4 eggs
13 oz. (375 g) plain flour
4½ oz. (125 g) Oetker GUSTIN
  (corn starch powder)
1 packet Oetker Baking Powder
  BACKIN
¼ pint (140 ccm) milk
3½ oz. (100 g) of plain chocolate,
  bitter if possible

For Dusting:

a little icing sugar

Marble Cake

9 oz. (250 g) butter or margarine
9 oz. (250 g) sugar
1 packet Oetker Vanillin Sugar
3–4 eggs
1 bottle Oetker rum flavour
1⅛ lb. (500 g) plain flour
1 packet Oetker Baking Powder
  BACKIN
about ¼ pint (140 ccm) milk
1 oz. (30 g) cocoa
1 well heaped tbsp. (25 g) sugar
2–3 tbsp. milk

Weekend Cake

Cake Mixture:

7 oz. (200 g) butter or margarine
9 oz. (250 g) sugar
3 eggs
½ bottle Oetker Baking Essence,
  lemon flavour
1 packet Oetker Pudding Powder,
  vanilla flavour
about ¼ pint (140 ccm) milk
1 lb. (450 g) plain flour
1 packet Oetker Baking Powder
  BACKIN
2½ oz. (70 g) blanched, chopped
  almonds
2 oz. (55 g) raisins

For Dusting:

a little icing sugar

Ottilia Cake

Cake Mixture:

9 oz. (250 g) butter or margarine
7 oz. (200 g) sugar
1 packet Oetker Vanillin Sugar
4 eggs
½ bottle Oetker rum flavour
7 oz. (200 g) plain flour
2 oz. (55 g) Oetker GUSTIN
(corn starch powder)
1 level tsp. (3 g) Oetker Baking Powder
BACKIN
3½ oz. (100 g) blanched and ground almonds
3 oz. (85 g) plain chocolate, cut into small pieces
2 oz. (55 g) chopped candied lemon peel

For Dusting:

a little icing sugar

Cream the fat and gradually add the sugar, the vanillin sugar, the eggs, and the flavouring. Mix and sieve together the flour, the GUSTIN and the BACKIN, and add by the tablespoonful to the mixture. Lastly fold in the almonds, the chocolate and the candied lemon peel. Grease an oblong cake tin and line it with paper. Fill the mixture into the prepared tin. Place low in the oven.

Oven: moderate.

Baking Time: 65–85 minutes.

When cold, dust with icing sugar.

King's Cake

9 oz. (250 g) butter or margarine
7 oz. (200 g) sugar
1 packet Oetker Vanillin Sugar
4 eggs
½ bottle Oetker Baking Essence, lemon flavour
or 1 bottle Oetker rum flavour
1⅛ lb. (500 g) plain flour
4 level tsp. (12 g) Oetker Baking Powder
BACKIN
5–8 tbsp. milk
9 oz. (250 g) raisins
3½ oz. (100 g) currants
2 oz. (55 g) candied lemon peel
(chopped)

Cream the fat and gradually add the sugar, the vanillin sugar, the eggs and the flavourings. Mix and sieve the flour and the BACKIN and add to the creamed mixture alternately with the milk. The consistency should be firm, so do not use too much milk. Lastly fold in the washed and drained raisins and currants and the candied lemon peel. Grease an oblong cake tin and line with paper. Fill the mixture into the prepared tin. Place low in the oven.

Oven: moderate.

Baking Time: 80–100 minutes.

For the cake mixture, cream the fat and gradually add the sugar, the vanillin sugar, the eggs and the flavourings. Mix and sieve together the flour, the GUSTIN and the BACKIN, and stir in by degrees. Lastly fold in the washed and drained raisins, the almonds and the candied lemon peel. Grease an oblong cake tin and line it with paper. Fill the mixture into the prepared tin. Place low in the oven.

Oven: moderate.

Baking Time: 60–80 minutes.

For the icing, brush the cold cake with the hot melted jelly. Blend the sieved icing sugar and the flavouring with as much hot water as will give a good coating consistency and ice the cake.

English Cake

Cake Mixture:

7 oz. (200 g) butter or margarine
9 oz. (250 g) sugar
1 packet Oetker Vanillin Sugar
4 eggs
1 bottle Oetker rum flavour
4 drops Oetker Baking Essence,
  lemon flavour
9 oz. (250 g) plain flour
4½ oz. (125 g) Oetker GUSTIN
  (corn starch powder)
2 level tsp. (6 g) Oetker Baking Powder
  BACKIN
4½ oz. (125 g) raisins
2 oz. (55 g) almonds
  (blanched and chopped)
3 oz. (85 g) candied lemon peel
  (diced)

Icing:

2 oz. (55 g) redcurrant jelly
5½ oz. (150 g) icing sugar
5 drops Oetker rum flavour
2–3 tbsp. hot water

For the cake mixture, melt the fat, then cool until firm. Add the sugar and the vanillin sugar to the fat and beat together until white and fluffy. Gradually add the eggs and the flavouring. Sieve the GUSTIN and the BACKIN with the flour and stir gradually into the mixture. Grease an oblong cake tin and line with paper. Fill the mixture into the prepared tin. Place low in the oven.

Oven: moderate.

Baking Time: 60–75 minutes.

For the icing, mix together the sieved icing sugar and the cocoa. Add enough hot water to give a good thick coating consistency. Then stir in the melted fat. Spread over the cold cake.

Alternatively, the cake can be baked in a ring tin and coated with chocolate icing.

Sand Cake

Cake Mixture:

9 oz. (250 g) butter or margarine
7 oz. (200 g) castor sugar
1 packet Oetker Vanillin Sugar
4 eggs
½ bottle Oetker rum flavour
4½ oz. (125 g) plain flour
4½ oz. (125 g) Oetker GUSTIN
  (corn starch powder)
½ level tsp. (1½ g) Oetker Baking
  Powder BACKIN

Icing:

4½ oz. (125 g) icing sugar
1 oz. (30 g) cocoa
1–2 tbsp. hot water
1 oz. (30 g) coconut butter (optional)

Frankfurt Ring

Cake Mixture:

3½ oz. (100 g) butter or margarine
5½ oz. (150 g) sugar
3 eggs
4 drops Oetker Baking Essence,
lemon flavour or ½ bottle
Oetker rum flavour
5½ oz. (150 g) plain flour
2 oz. (55 g) Oetker GUSTIN
(corn starch powder)
2 level tsp. (6 g) Oetker Baking Powder
BACKIN

Butter Cream Filling:

1 packet Oetker Pudding Powder,
vanilla flavour
3½ oz. (100 g) sugar
5 tbsp. cold milk
¾ pint (425 ccm) milk
7 oz. (200 g) butter or margarine

Nut Caramel Topping:

1 knob of butter
about 2½ oz. (70 g) sugar
4½ oz. (125 g) blanched and finely
chopped almonds or hazelnuts

For the cake mixture, cream the fat. Gradually add the sugar, the eggs and the flavouring. Mix and sieve together the flour, the GUSTIN and the BACKIN, and stir them in gradually. Fill the mixture into a greased ring tin and bake low in the oven.

Oven: moderate.

Baking Time: 35–45 minutes.

For the filling, blend the pudding powder with the sugar and the 5 tbsp. of milk. Bring the ¾ pint (425 ccm) of the milk to the boil, remove from heat and stir in the prepared pudding powder. Bring to the boil again and cool, stirring fairly frequently to prevent a skin forming. Cream the fat and gradually add the cold pudding. Care should be taken not to let this mixture get too cold otherwise it will curdle.

For the topping, melt the butter and sugar together and stir till the sugar begins to turn a light brown. Add the almonds or nuts and reheat, stirring all the time. When the nut caramel is brown, pour it onto an oiled plate to cool. When cool, break it into small pieces if necessary. Cut the cake twice and spread with the cream filling, saving enough to cover and decorate the outside of the cake. Sandwich together again, spread the remaining cream on the outside of the cake, sprinkle with the nut caramel and decorate with any cream left over.

This cake is best eaten a day after it is made.

Apple Layer Cake

Cake Mixture:

1 packet Oetker Pudding Powder,
vanilla flavour
4 tbsp. milk
5½ oz. (150 g) butter or margarine
5½ oz. (150 g) sugar
2 eggs
9 oz. (250 g) plain flour
3 level tsp. (9 g) Oetker Baking Powder
BACKIN
1 or 2 tbsp. milk if necessary
1⅛ lb. (500 g) apples

For Dusting:

a little icing sugar

Blend the pudding powder with the milk. Cream the fat and gradually add to it the sugar and the eggs. Mix and sieve the flour and the BACKIN and add to the mixture alternately with the prepared pudding powder. If the mixture is too stiff add 1–2 tbsp. of milk. Grease a round cake tin with removable rim, 10½ inches (26 cm) in diameter. Fill in half of the cake mixture, smoothing it across evenly. Then spread over this half of the peeled and sliced apples, then the other half of the mixture and finally the rest of the apples. Place low in the oven and bake till done.

Oven: moderately hot.

Baking Time: 45–60 minutes.

When cold, dust the cake with icing sugar.

Apple Crumble Cake

Cake Mixture:

3½ oz. (100 g) butter or margarine
3½ oz. (100 g) sugar

For the cake mixture, cream the fat and gradually add the sugar, the vanillin sugar, the eggs, and the flavouring. Mix and sieve the flour, the GUSTIN and the BACKIN, and stir them in alternately with the milk. Use only enough milk as to give a heavy dropping consistency. Fill into a greased round cake tin with removable rim, 10½ inches (26 cm) in diameter. Smooth flat with a spoon dipped in water.

For the topping, peel and slice the apples and arrange on the mixture leaving round the edge ⅜ inch (1 cm) free.

For the crumble, sieve the flour into a bowl and mix with the sugar and the vanillin sugar. Cut the fat into small pieces and rub it into form crumbs. Sprinkle evenly over the cake. Put low in the oven and bake till done.

Oven: moderately hot.

Baking Time: about 40 minutes.

Dust with icing sugar before serving.

1 packet Oetker Vanillin Sugar
2 eggs
4 drops Oetker Baking Essence, lemon flavour
5½ oz. (150 g) plain flour
2 oz. (55 g) Oetker GUSTIN
(corn starch powder)
2 level tsp. (6 g) Oetker Baking Powder BACKIN
about 4 tbsp. milk

Topping:
1⅛ lb. (500 g) apples

Crumble:
3½ oz. (100 g) plain flour
2½ oz. (70 g) sugar
1 packet Oetker Vanillin Sugar
2½ oz. (70 g) butter or margarine

For Dusting:
a little icing sugar

"Prinzregenten" Cake

Cake Mixture:
9 oz. (250 g) butter or margarine
9 oz. (250 g) sugar
1 packet Oetker Vanillin Sugar
4 eggs
7 oz. (200 g) plain flour
2 oz. (55 g) Oetker GUSTIN
(corn starch powder)
1 level tsp. (3 g) Oetker Baking Powder BACKIN

For the cake mixture, cream the fat and gradually add the sugar, the vanillin sugar and the eggs. Mix and sieve together the flour, the GUSTIN and the BACKIN, and add by degrees to the creamed mixture. The mixture should be enough for 8 layers, baked separately. Take about 2 tbsp. of the mixture for each layer and spread evenly on a round cake tin with removable rim, 10½ inches (26 cm) in diameter. Remove the ring and use only the base. It is important that the edges should not be spread too thinly as a thin edge may brown too quickly. Bake each layer fairly low in the oven.

Oven: moderately hot.

Baking Time: 8–10 minutes.

For the filling, blend the pudding powder, the cocoa, and the sugar with the 5 tbsp. milk. Bring the ¾ pint (425 ccm) milk to the boil. Remove from heat and stir in the pudding powder mixture. Reheat, stirring all the time. Remove from heat. If coconut butter is used, add this to the hot pudding. Set aside to cool, stirring frequently to prevent a skin forming. Cream the fat and add to it gradually the cold pudding. Care should be taken no to let this mixture get too cold, otherwise it will curdle.

As each layer cools, spread with the filling, cool the next layer, place on top, add further filling, and so on until the eighth layer forms the top of the cake.

For the icing, sieve together the icing sugar and the cocoa and stir in the melted fat, together with enough hot water to make a smooth coating consistency. Ice the cake.

Butter Cream Filling:
1 packet Oetker Gala Pudding Powder, chocolate flavour
1 tbsp. cocoa
3½ oz. (100 g) sugar
5 tbsp. cold milk
¾ pint (425 ccm) milk
2 oz. (55 g) coconut butter (optional)
7 oz. (200 g) butter or margarine

Icing:
5½ oz. (150 g) icing sugar
1 oz. (30 g) cocoa
¾ oz. (20 g) melted butter or coconut butter
2–3 tbsp. hot water

Empress Frederick Cake

Cake Mixture:

9 oz. (250 g) coconut butter
or 10¹/₂ oz. (300 g) margarine
10½ oz. (300 g) sugar
1 packet Oetker Vanillin Sugar
5 eggs
1 egg yolk
¹/₂ egg white
3 drops Oetker Baking Essence,
bitter almond flavour
½ bottle Oetker rum flavour
10½ oz. (300 g) plain flour
2½ oz. (70 g) Oetker GUSTIN
(corn starch powder)
2 level tsp. (6 g) Oetker Baking Powder
BACKIN
4½ oz. (125 g) candied lemon peel
(diced)

Icing:

6 oz. (170 g) icing sugar
½ egg white
about 3 tbsp. lemon juice
2 oz. (55 g) candied lemon peel
(chopped or sliced)

For the cake mixture, melt the fat. Cool it, add the sugar and the vanillin sugar and beat until fluffy. Gradually add the eggs, the egg yolk, and the half egg white, together with the flavourings. Mix and sieve together the flour, the GUSTIN and the BACKIN, and add to the mixture by the tablespoonful. Fold in the candied lemon peel gently. Fill the mixture into a greased round cake tin with a removable rim, diameter 10½ inches (26 cm). Place low in the oven.

Oven: moderate.

Baking Time: 65–75 minutes.

Alternatively, 10½ oz. (300 g) butter or margarine may be used instead of the coconut butter, but should not be melted.

For the icing, sieve the icing sugar and combine with the egg white and enough lemon juice to form a smooth paste. Ice the cake and sprinkle the candied lemon peel over the top as decoration.

II. CAKES ON A BAKING SHEET

Basic Recipe

Cake Mixture I:

3½–5½ oz. (100–150 g) butter
or margarine
5½ oz. (150 g) sugar
1–2 eggs
1⅛ lb. (500 g) plain flour
1 packet Oetker Baking Powder
BACKIN
½ pint (285 ccm) milk

or

Cake Mixture II:

7 oz. (200 g) butter or margarine
7 oz. (200 g) sugar
2 eggs
1⅛ lb. (500 g) plain flour
1 packet Oetker Baking Powder
BACKIN
barely ½ pint (250 ccm) milk

Cream the fat and gradually add the sugar and the egg or eggs. Mix and sieve the flour and the BACKIN and add to the mixture alternately with the milk. Use sufficient milk to obtain a stiff dropping consistency. Fill onto a greased baking sheet and smooth with a palette knife. If the baking sheet has an open end, put a thick fold of greased paper along the edge to prevent cake mixture from running off.

Either flake the fat and distribute it evenly over the cake mixture, or melt it and brush it on. Mix together the sugar, the vanillin sugar and the nuts and sprinkle evenly over the mixture. Place high in the oven and bake till done.

Oven: moderately hot.

Baking Time: 20–25 minutes.

Butter or Sugar Cake

Cake Mixture:
Basic Recipe, Cake Mixture I or II (see page 294)

Topping:
2–4½ oz. (55–125 g) butter or margarine
2½ oz. (70 g) sugar
1 packet Oetker Vanillin Sugar
2 oz. (55 g) sliced or chopped almonds or hazelnuts

Sieve the flour and mix with the sugar, the vanillin sugar and the cinnamon. Rub in the fat by hand or with 2 forks until the mixture resembles breadcrumbs. Spread evenly over the cake mixture and place high in the oven.

Oven: moderately hot.

Baking Time: 20–25 minutes.

Crumble Cake

Cake Mixture:
Basic Recipe, Cake Mixture I or II (see page 294)

Topping:
7 oz. (200 g) plain flour
about 3½–4½ oz. (100–125 g) sugar
1 packet Oetker Vanillin Sugar
a little cinnamon
about 3½–4½ oz. (100–125 g) butter or margarine

Peel the apples and slice into quarters (or, if they are very large, into eighths); or wash and stone the plums. Place the fruit evenly on top of the cake mixture (plums with the skin to the cake mixture). Place high in the oven.

Oven: pre-heat for 5 minutes at very hot, bake at moderately hot.

Baking Time: 30–35 minutes.
When baked, cool and sprinkle with sugar.

Fruit Cake

Cake Mixture:
Basic Recipe, Cake Mixture I (see page 294)

Topping:
about 2¼–3¼ lb. (1–1½ kg) apples or plums

For Sprinkling:
some sugar

American Biscuits

Cake Mixture:

3½ oz. (100 g) butter or margarine
3½ oz. (100 g) sugar
1 packet Oetker Vanillin Sugar
2 eggs
1 packet Oetker Pudding Powder, cream, or almond flavour
3 tbsp. milk
9 oz. (250 g) plain flour
3 level tsp. (9 g) Oetker Baking Powder BACKIN

For Brushing:
a little milk

White Icing:
3½ oz. (100 g) icing sugar
1–2 tbsp. hot water

or

Dark Icing:
3½ oz. (100 g) icing sugar
½ oz. (15 g) cocoa
1–2 tbsp. hot water

For the cake mixture, cream the fat and gradually add the sugar, the vanillin sugar, the eggs and the pudding powder blended with the milk. Mix and sieve the flour and the BACKIN and stir into the mixture, which should be very stiff. Add more flour if it seems at all runny. Spoon the mixture onto the greased baking sheet in medium-sized heaps. Bake fairly low in the oven till golden brown.

Oven: pre-heat at very hot for 5 minutes, bake at moderately hot.

Baking Time: 15–20 minutes.

After about 8 minutes baking, brush the top of the biscuits with milk and continue baking.

For the white icing, combine the sieved icing sugar with enough water to give a smooth coating consistency.

For the dark icing, use the same method but mix the cocoa with the icing sugar before adding the water.

When the biscuits are ready ice them on the underside whilst still hot either with the white or dark icing.

Heidesand Biscuits

10 oz. (280 g) butter
9 oz. (250 g) castor sugar
1 packet Oetker Vanillin Sugar
2 tbsp. milk
13 oz. (375 g) plain flour
1 level tsp. (3 g) Oetker Baking Powder BACKIN

Melt the butter to a fairly dark brown, and cool. Then cream it and gradually add the sugar, the vanillin sugar and the milk. Stir until the mixture is a creamy white. Mix and sieve the flour and the BACKIN. Add about ⅔ of this by degrees to the mixture. Turn out onto a floured board and knead in the remaining flour until smooth. Shape the dough into rolls about 1¼ inch (3 cm) thick and leave to cool until stiff. Cut off slices about ¼ inch (½ cm) thick, place in rows on a greased baking sheet and bake fairly high in the oven till pale yellow.

Oven: pre-heat for 5 minutes at very hot, bake at moderately hot.

Baking Time: 10–15 minutes.

Cream the fat and gradually add the sugar, the vanillin sugar, the eggs and the flavouring. Mix and sieve together the flour, the GUSTIN and the BACKIN, and add to the creamed mixture, alternately with the milk. Add enough milk to give a soft dropping consistency. Pour a little of the mixture onto a very hot greased waffle iron and cook on both sides until golden brown. Dust with icing sugar and serve at once as waffles soften very quickly. They can be reheated for a short time on the iron, if necessary.

Waffles
(Phot. See Page 301)

Mixture:
4½ oz. (125 g) butter or margarine
1–2 oz. (30–55 g) sugar
1 packet Oetker Vanillin Sugar
3 eggs
½ bottle Oetker rum flavour or a few
    drops of Oetker Baking Essence,
    lemon flavour
4½ oz. (125 g) plain flour
4½ oz. (125 g) Oetker GUSTIN
    (corn starch powder)
2 level tsp. (6 g) Oetker Baking Powder
    BACKIN
about ½ pint (285 ccm) milk

For Greasing:
bacon rind or a little oil

For Dusting:
a little icing sugar

Cream the fat and gradually add a little of the sugar, the vanillin sugar, the egg or eggs and lastly, the rest of the sugar. Sieve the flour and stir in alternately with the water, using enough water to give a thin dropping consistency. Pour a little of the mixture into a very hot and well greased Eiser Cake iron and cook on both sides until golden brown. Quickly roll the thin cakes into rolls or cones. They will keep crisp in a firmly closed tin. These cakes can only be made on a special iron.

Eiser Cake
(Phot. See Page 301)

Mixture I:
1 oz. (30 g) butter or margarine
9 oz. (250 g) sugar
1 packet Oetker Vanillin Sugar
1 egg
9 oz. (250 g) plain flour
about ⅔ pint (375 ccm) water
or

Mixture II:
2½ oz. (70 g) butter or margarine
9 oz. (250 g) sugar
1 packet Oetker Vanillin Sugar
2 eggs
9 oz. (250 g) plain flour
about ⅔ pint (375 ccm) water

For Greasing:
bacon rind or a little oil

B. CAKES MADE BY THE KNEADING METHOD

I. BREAD AND CAKES SHAPED BY HAND

Hazelnut Ring

Pastry:

10½ oz. (300 g) plain flour
2 level tsp. (6 g) Oetker Baking Powder BACKIN
3½ oz. (100 g) sugar
1 packet Oetker Vanillin Sugar
1 egg
2 tbsp. milk or water
4½ oz. (125 g) butter or margarine

Filling:

7 oz. (200 g) ground hazelnuts
3½ oz. (100 g) sugar
4–5 drops Oetker Baking Essence, bitter almond flavour
1 egg white
4–5 tbsp. water

For Brushing:

1 egg yolk and
1 tbsp. milk

For the pastry, mix the flour and the BACKIN together and sieve onto a pastry board. Make a well in the middle. Pour the sugar, the vanillin sugar, the egg and the milk or water into the well, and draw in some flour from the side to form a thick paste. Cut the fat, which should be cold, into small pieces on top of the paste. Scoop over this the remainder of the flour and knead with the hands to give a good smooth dough. If the pastry is sticky leave it in a cool place for a little time to stiffen. Roll the pastry out into a rectangle about 14 by 18 inches (35 x 45 cm).

For the filling, mix the hazelnuts, the sugar, the baking essence and the egg white with enough water to give a smooth paste. Spread this smoothly over the rectangle of pastry. Dipping the spatula or knife into water will make this easier. Roll up the rectangle like a Swiss roll, form into a ring, and place onto a greased baking sheet. Brush with the egg yolk mixed with the milk and cut slits across the top about ¼ inch (½ cm) deep at regular intervals. Bake fairly low in the oven.

Oven: moderately hot.

Baking Time: about 45 minutes.

Raisin Plait

Mixture:

7 oz. (200 g) cottage cheese, well pressed out
8 tbsp. milk
8 tbsp. oil
3½ oz. (100 g) sugar
a little salt
14 oz. (400 g) plain flour
1 packet and 2 level tsp. (6 g) Oetker Baking Powder BACKIN
3 oz. (85 g) raisins

For Brushing:

a little milk

Rub the cottage cheese through a fine sieve, stir in the milk, the oil, the sugar and salt, then mix well together. Mix and sieve the flour and the BACKIN and add half of it to the mixture. Knead the raisins, well washed and drained, into the mixture with the rest of the flour. Divide the dough into three, form into rolls about 16 inches (40 cm) long and plait together damping ends to join them. Place on a greased baking sheet, brush thinly with milk and bake fairly low in the oven.

Oven: pre-heat for 5 minutes at very hot, bake at moderately hot.

Baking Time: 25–50 minutes.

For the pastry, sieve the flour onto a pastry board and make a well in the centre. Sprinkle in the salt, then very slowly pour the water and the melted fat or oil into the well and draw in enough flour from the sides to make a thick smooth paste. Cover the paste with more of the flour and start working and kneading the mixture from the centre into a good smooth dough. Boil some water in an enamel saucepan. Empty out the water, then dry the saucepan and whilst it is still hot line it with greaseproof paper. Put the pastry into the saucepan, put on the lid and stand for about half an hour.

For the filling, peel and core the apples, slice thinly and add the flavourings. Mix them well together.

Flour a large white cloth, put the pastry on the cloth and roll out. Brush thinly with a little melted fat and with the hands pull out the pastry to a rectangle about 20 by 28 inches (50 x 70 cm). The pastry should now be transparent.

Cut away the edges if they are thicker than the middle. Again brush the pastry with melted fat, using about ⅔ of it. Sprinkle the breadcrumbs over about ⅔ of the pastry, starting from the long side and leaving about 1¼ inch (3 cm) free of crumbs on the shorter sides. Spread the sliced apples over the breadcrumbs, sprinkle with the sugar, the vanillin sugar, the washed and dried raisins, and the almonds. Turn the 1¼ inch (3 cm) edges of pastry onto the filling and roll up the pastry like a Swiss roll. Press the ends firmly together, place on a greased baking sheet, brush with the rest of the melted fat and place fairly low in the oven.

Oven: pre-heat for 5 minutes at very hot, bake at moderately hot.

Baking Time: 45–55 minutes.

To improve the crust, baste frequently with melted fat during baking.

Alternatively, the pastry may be divided into two, and two smaller strudels made of the same ingredients and baked together on the baking sheet.

Viennese Apple Strudel

Strudel Pastry:

7 oz. (200 g) plain flour
a little salt
5 tbsp. lukewarm water
2 oz. (55 g) melted butter, margarine
  or lard, or 3 tbsp. oil

Filling:

2¼–3¼ lb. (1–1½ kg) apples
1 bottle Oetker rum flavour
3 drops Oetker Baking Essence,
  lemon flavour
2 oz. (55 g) breadcrumbs
3½ oz. (100 g) sugar
1 packet Oetker Vanillin Sugar
2 oz. (55 g) raisins
2 oz. (55 g) almonds
  (blanched and chopped)

For Brushing:

2 oz. (55 g) melted butter or
  margarine

II. PIES AND TARTS BAKED IN A ROUND CAKE TIN

Fruit Flan

Pastry:

6 oz. (170 g) plain flour
½ level tsp. (1½ g) Oetker Baking
Powder BACKIN
2½ oz. (70 g) sugar
1 packet Oetker Vanillin Sugar
1 small egg
2½ oz. (70 g) butter or margarine
1 tbsp. flour for the pastry edges

Filling:

about 1½ lb. (680 g) raw, stewed or
preserved fruit (apples, apricots,
strawberries, cherries, peaches,
gooseberries, etc.)

Glaze:

½ pint (285 ccm) fruit juice
1–1½ oz. (30–45 g) sugar
1 packet Oetker Cake Glaze
transparent

For Decorating:

a few almonds or hazelnuts (sliced)

For the pastry, mix together the flour and the BACKIN and sieve onto a pastry board. Make a well in the centre and pour in the sugar, the vanillin sugar and the egg. Draw in some flour from the sides to form a thick creamy paste. Cut the cold fat into pieces on top of the paste and cover with more of the flour. Starting from the middle, knead all the ingredients well together with the hands till a good smooth dough is formed. Put the pastry aside to cool for a little, if it is sticky. Then roll out about ⅔ of it to fit the bottom of a round cake tin with a removable rim, 10½ inches (26 cm) in diameter. Knead into the remaining pastry the tbsp. of flour, shape into a roll and press it round the sides of the tin, making sure it is also pressed onto the pastry in the bottom of the tin so that the two are sealed together. The rim should be about 1¼ inch (3 cm) high. Prick the pastry with a fork. Bake fairly low in the oven till golden yellow.

Oven: pre-heat for 5 minutes at very hot, bake at moderately hot.

Baking Time: 15–20 minutes.

For the filling, prepare the fruit according to their kind. Raw fruit may be used but should be washed and peeled, if necessary. Stone fruit should have stones and stalks removed. Stewed or bottled fruit should be well drained. Apples should be used peeled and cut in quarters or eighths and carefully stewed in sweetened water. Arrange the fruit on the cooled pastry shell.

The glaze, prepare according to the directions on the packet and pour over the flan.

Decorate with almonds or hazelnuts sprinkled around the rim.

Apple Tart

Pastry:

10½ oz. (300 g) plain flour
2 level tsp. (6 g) Oetker Baking Powder
BACKIN
3½ oz. (100 g) sugar
1 packet Oetker Vanillin Sugar
a little salt
1 egg white
½ egg yolk
1 tbsp. milk
5½ oz. (150 g) butter or margarine

For the pastry, mix together the flour and the BACKIN and sieve onto a pastry board. Make a well in the centre and pour in the sugar, the vanillin sugar, the salt, the egg white, the half egg yolk and the milk. Draw in some of the flour from the sides to mix with these ingredients to form a smooth paste. Add the cold fat, cut into pieces, to the paste, then cover with more of the flour and knead all the ingredients together to a smooth dough, beginning the kneading from the middle. Leave the pastry to cool for a short time, if it seems sticky. When it is ready take half the pastry and roll it out to fit the bottom of a greased round cake tin with a removable rim, diameter 10½ inches (26 cm). Prick with a fork in several places. Bake low in the oven till pale yellow.

300

Waffles Recipe See Page 297 · Eiser Cake Recipe See Page 297
Cream Chocolate Cake Recipe See Page 312

Roll out the pastry about ¼ inch (½ cm) thick and cover a greased baking sheet with it.

For the topping, melt the fat with the sugar, vanillin sugar and milk, mix in the almonds and put aside to cool. When it is cold, spread it evenly onto the pastry on the greased baking sheet. If it is too stiff to spread, thin it down with a little milk. Put the baking sheet fairly high in the oven.

Oven: moderately hot.

Baking Time: about 20 minutes.

Bienenstich

Pastry:
Cottage Cheese Pastry (see page 306)

Topping:
3½ oz. (100 g) butter or margarine
7 oz. (200 g) sugar
1 packet Oetker Vanillin Sugar
2 tbsp. milk
7–9 oz. (200–250 g) blanched almonds, chopped or sliced

Roll out the pastry to ¼ inch (½ cm) thickness and cover a greased baking sheet with it.

For the topping, sieve the flour into a bowl and mix in the sugar, the vanillin sugar, and cinnamon, rub in the cut up fat until the mixture resembles breadcrumbs. Spread it evenly over the pastry. Place the baking sheet fairly high in the oven and bake till done.

Oven: moderately hot.

Baking Time: about 20 minutes.

Cinnamon Crumble Cake

Pastry:
Cottage Cheese Pastry (see page 306)

Topping:
10½ oz. (300 g) plain flour
5½ oz. (150 g) sugar
1 packet Oetker Vanillin Sugar
pinch of cinnamon
5½ oz. (150 g) butter or margarine

IV. BISCUITS AND COOKIES

Mix together the flour, the GUSTIN and the BACKIN, and sieve onto a pastry board. Make a well in the centre and pour in the sugar, the vanillin sugar and the eggs. Drawing flour in from the sides, work to a smooth paste. Cut the cold fat into pieces on top of the paste and, working from the middle, knead all these ingredients together into a smooth dough. Leave it in a cool place, if it is sticky. When it is ready, roll out the pastry to ¼ inch (½ cm) thickness, and cut out round biscuits, diameter about 2 inches (5 cm), put on a greased baking sheet, prick with a fork and bake high in the oven.

Oven: pre-heat for 5 minutes at very hot, bake at moderately hot.

Baking Time: about 10 minutes.

Albert Biscuits

9 oz. (250 g) plain flour
4½ oz. (125 g) Oetker GUSTIN (corn starch powder)
1 level tsp. (3 g) Oetker Baking Powder BACKIN
4½ oz. (125 g) sugar
1 packet Oetker Vanillin Sugar
2 eggs
4½ oz. (125 g) butter or margarine

Ducat Biscuits

Pastry:

9 oz. (250 g) plain flour
1 level tsp. (3 g) Oetker Baking Powder
BACKIN
2½ oz. (70 g) sugar
1 packet Oetker Vanillin Sugar
1 egg
1 tbsp. milk or water
4½ oz. (125 g) butter or margarine

Filling:

4½ oz. (125 g) coconut butter
2½ oz. (70 g) sugar or castor sugar
1 packet Oetker Vanillin Sugar
1 oz. (30 g) cocoa
a few drops Oetker rum flavour
1 egg

Icing:

2 oz. (55 g) icing sugar
½ oz. (15 g) cocoa
1–2 tbsp. hot water
1 tbsp. of melted butter or margarine

For the pastry, mix together the flour and the BACKIN and sieve onto a pastry board. Make a well in the centre and pour in the sugar, the vanillin sugar, the egg and the liquid. Draw in part of the flour from the sides of the well and work to a smooth paste with the other ingredients. Cut the cold fat into pieces on top of the paste, cover with more of the flour and, working from the centre, knead all these ingredients together into a smooth dough. Put the pastry aside in a cool place if it is sticky. Then roll it out very thinly, cut into small rounds and place on a greased baking sheet. Bake high in the oven.

Oven: pre-heat for 5 minutes at very hot, bake at moderately hot.

Baking Time: about 10 minutes.

For the filling, melt the fat and cool it. Put the sugar (sieved, it icing sugar is used), the vanillin sugar, the sieved cocoa and the flavouring into a bowl and gradually stir in the egg and the lukewarm fat. Leave to cool. When it has stiffened, spread on underside of biscuits and sandwich together. Leave to set.

For the icing, mix together the cocoa and the icing sugar, both sieved. Add the fat and the water to the cocoa and sugar, using enough water to give a smooth coating consistency. Ice half of the top of each biscuit and leave to set.

Nut Ducats

13 oz. (375 g) plain flour
4½ oz. (125 g) Oetker GUSTIN
(corn starch powder)
2 level tsp. (6 g) Oetker Baking Powder
BACKIN
9 oz. (250 g) sugar
1 packet Oetker Vanillin Sugar
3 drops Oetker Baking Essence,
bitter almond flavour
2 eggs
9 oz. (250 g) butter or margarine
9 oz. (250 g) hazelnuts

Mix together the flour, the GUSTIN and the BACKIN, and sieve onto a pastry board. Make a well in the centre, add the sugar, the vanillin sugar, the baking essence and the eggs and work to a smooth paste with flour drawn in from the sides of the well. Cut the fat into pieces (it should be quite cold) and roughly chop the hazelnuts. Put the fat and nuts onto the paste, cover with more of the flour and, working from the middle, knead all the ingredients together to a firm dough. Shape the pastry into several rolls about 1 inch (2½ cm) thick and leave them in a cool place to stiffen. Then with a sharp knife cut off slices about ¼ inch (½ cm) thick, place on a baking sheet and bake high in the oven.

Oven: pre-heat for 5 minutes at very hot, bake at moderately hot.

Baking Time: 10–15 minutes.

For the pastry, mix together the flour and the BACKIN and sieve onto a pastry board. Make a well in the centre, pour in the sugar, the vanillin sugar and the egg, and work to a smooth paste with flour drawn in from the sides of the well. Cut the cold fat into pieces on top of the paste, cover with more of the flour and, working from the middle, knead all these ingredients together into a smooth pastry. If the pastry is sticky, add more flour. Divide the pastry in two, then knead in the cocoa and the sugar, blended with the milk, into one half of it. The two pastries may be combined in several different ways.

For a Pinwheel Pattern, roll out two seperate, similar-sized rectangles, brush one thinly with egg white or water, place the other piece of pastry on it and brush it with egg white or water. Then roll up as for a Swiss Roll.

For a Chequered Pattern, roll out the white pastry to ⅜ inch (1 cm) thickness in a rectangle. Cut this into 5 strips, each about ⅜ inch (1 cm) wide and of equal length. Similarly roll out the dark pastry to the same thickness and cut it into 4 strips, each ⅜ inch (1 cm) wide and of the same length as the white. Brush with egg white or water. Arrange the strips of pastry in three layers of three strips each layer, the colours alternating. Wrap the whole in a thin layer of pastry. Leave this in a cool place for a while, then cut into even sized slices, place on a greased baking sheet and bake high in the oven.

The following Black and White Cookies are easier to make: take half of the pastry dough and form a roll about 1¼ inch (3 cm) diameter. Brush with egg white or water. Roll out the other half into an oblong and wrap around the roll. Cut into ¼ inch (½ cm) slices.

Oven: pre-heat for 5 minutes at very hot, bake at moderately hot.

Baking Time: about 10–15 minutes.

Black and White Cookies

White Pastry:
9 oz. (250 g) plain flour
1 level tsp. (3 g) Oetker Baking Powder BACKIN
5½ oz. (150 g) sugar
1 packet Oetker Vanillin Sugar
1 egg
4½ oz. (125 g) butter or margarine

Dark Pastry:
¾ oz. (20 g) cocoa
½ oz. (15 g) sugar
1 tbsp. milk

For Brushing:
a little egg white or water

Mix together the flour, the GUSTIN and the BACKIN and sieve onto a pastry board. Stir in the grated Gruyère. Make a well In the centre, pour in the seasonings, the egg, the egg white, half an egg yolk and the liquid. Drawing in flour from the sides, combine these ingredients together into a smooth paste. Cut the cold fat into pieces on top of the paste, cover with more of the flour and, working from the middle, knead all together into a smooth pastry. Leave in a cool place for a short time if the pastry is sticky. Divide the pastry into 6 equal parts and from it make these 6 different kinds of biscuits:

Mixed Cheese Biscuits

Pastry:
10½ oz. (300 g) plain flour
2½ oz. (70 g) Oetker GUSTIN (corn starch powder)
3 level tsp. (9 g) Baking Powder BACKIN
5½ oz. (150 g) grated Gruyère Cheese, fairly dry
a little paprika
pepper

½ level tsp. salt
1 egg
1 egg white
½ egg yolk
2 tbsp. milk or water
7 oz. (200 g) butter or margarine

For Brushing:
½ egg yolk
1 tbsp. milk or water

For Sprinkling:
some salt, not too fine
caraway seeds
poppy seeds
some grated Parmesan cheese
a little paprika

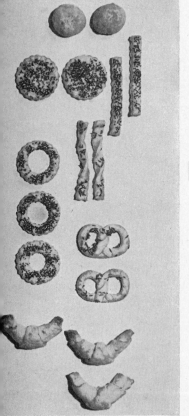

Cheeselets

Roll out the pastry very thinly. Cut into rounds with a small cutter, brush with the whisked egg yolk, prick twice with a fork and sprinkle with salt and caraway seeds. Place on a baking sheet and bake till golden yellow.

Cheese Rings

Roll out the pastry thinly. Cut out rings, brush with whisked egg yolk, prick twice with a fork and sprinkle with poppy seeds. Place on a baking sheet and bake till golden yellow.

Pretzels

Make very thin rolls of pastry — they should be thinner than a pencil and each should be about 6 inches (15 cm) long. Twist into pretzel shape. Brush with whisked egg yolk and place on a baking sheet. Sprinkle some of the pretzels with caraway or poppy seeds.

Cheese Crescents

Roll out the pastry thinly and cut out rounds about 8 inches (20 cm) in diameter (the size of a dessert plate). A pastry wheel could be used for this. Brush with some egg yolk and sprinkle with Parmesan cheese and a little paprika. Cut the rounds four times, first into halves, then into quarters and finally into eighths. Roll up each triangle into a crescent, starting from the long side and curving it slightly, brush with the egg yolk and bake until golden yellow.

Cheese Fingers

Roll out the pastry very thinly. Use a pastry wheel to cut out strips about ⅜ inch (1 cm) wide and 3 inches (8 cm) long. Brush with the whisked egg yolk and sprinkle with caraway seeds. The fingers can be twisted spirally before brushing, one end is twisted to the left the other to the right. Place on a baking sheet and bake till golden yellow.

Cheese Balls

Make rolls about a thumb thick and cut into even-sized pieces. Roll these into balls the size of a cherry. Use a bottle Oetker Baking Essence to make a well in the middle of each ball. Place on a baking sheet, brush with the whisked egg yolk and sprinkle with a little grated Parmesan cheese. Bake very high in the oven till golden yellow.

Oven: pre-heat for 5 minutes at very hot, bake at moderately hot.

Baking Time: 10 minutes.

C. SPONGE MIXTURES (Without Fat)

I. CAKES

For the sponge mixture, separate the yolks from the whites of the eggs and whisk the yolks with the water until frothy. Gradually add ⅔ of the sugar and the vanillin sugar. Beat until the mixture is thick and creamy. In a separate bowl whisk the egg white stiff and add the rest of the sugar, whisking all the time. The whisked egg white should be firm enough to retain the mark made by the blade of a knife. Fill it on top of the egg yolk mixture, sieve the flour, the GUSTIN and the BACKIN on top and gently fold all together. Turn the mixture into a greased and lined round cake tin with a removable rim, 10½ inches (26 cm) in diameter and bake immediately, placing it low in the oven.

Oven: moderately hot.

Baking Time: 25–30 minutes.

This sponge is best made a day before use. Fill it on the day it is to be eaten.

For the filling, stir the pudding powder and the sugar together and combine with the 5 tbsp. of milk. Bring the ¾ pint of milk (425 ccm) to the boil, remove from heat, stir in the pudding powder mixture and bring to the boil again, stirring all the time. Set aside to cool, stirring fairly often to avoid the formation of skin.

Cream the fat and gradually stir in the cooled pudding mixture. Neither the fat nor the pudding mixture should be too cold, otherwise it may curdle.

Cut the cake twice through horizontally, and spread the bottom layer, first with jam and then with about ¼ of the cream filling. Place the second part on top of this and spread with rather less than half of the remaining cream. Put on top layer. Then spread top and sides thinly and evenly with more cream, sprinkle the sides with the almonds or nuts and decorate the top with any remaining cream.

If a Chocolate Butter Cream Cake is preferred, take 1 packet Oetker Pudding Powder, chocolate flavour for the filling instead of the Oetker Pudding Powder, vanilla flavour.

Butter Cream Cake
(Phot. See Page 320)

Sponge Mixture I:
3 eggs
3–4 tbsp. warm water, depending on the size of the eggs
5½ oz. (150 g) sugar
1 packet Oetker Vanillin Sugar
3½ oz. (100 g) plain flour
3½ oz. (100 g) Oetker GUSTIN (corn starch powder)
3 level tsp. (9 g) Oetker Baking Powder BACKIN

Sponge Mixture II:
4 eggs
2 tbsp. warm water
5½ oz. (150 g) sugar
1 packet Oetker Vanillin Sugar
3½ oz. (100 g) plain flour
3½ oz. (100 g) Oetker GUSTIN (corn starch powder)
2 level tsp. (6 g) Oetker Baking Powder BACKIN

Filling:
1. 2–3 tbsp. of red jam

2. Butter Cream:
1 packet Oetker Pudding Powder, vanilla, almond, cream or lemon flavour
3–3½ oz. (85–100 g) sugar
5 tbsp. cold milk for blending
¾ pint (425 ccm) milk
7 oz. (200 g) unsalted butter or margarine

For Decorating:
sliced almonds or hazelnuts

Cream Chocolate Cake
(Phot. See Page 301)

Sponge Mixture:
2 eggs
2–3 tbsp. warm water, depending on
the size of the eggs
3½ oz. (100 g) sugar
2½ oz. (70 g) plain flour
2 oz. (55 g) Oetker GUSTIN
(corn starch powder)
1 level tsp. (3 g) Oetker Baking Powder
BACKIN

Chocolate Icing:
3½ oz. (100 g) icing sugar
½ oz. (15 g) cocoa
about 2 tbsp. hot water
¾ oz. (20 g) hot coconut butter

Cream Filling:
1⅓ pint (¾ l) fresh double cream
3½ oz. (100 g) icing sugar
1 packet Oetker Vanillin Sugar
1 oz. (30 g) cocoa

For Decorating:
1 oz. (30 g) shredded chocolate

For the sponge mixture, separate the yolks from the whites of the eggs and whisk the yolks with the water, gradually adding about ⅔ of the sugar. Beat until the mixture is thick and creamy. In a separate bowl beat the egg white stiff and add the rest of the sugar to it, beating all the time. It must be firm enough to retain the mark of a knife. Add this to the egg yolk mixture, sieve the flour, the GUSTIN and the BACKIN on top and gently fold all together. Turn the mixture into a greased and lined round cake tin with a removable rim, 10½ inches (26 cm) in diameter and bake it immediately, placing it low in the oven.

Oven: moderately hot.

Baking Time: 20–25 minutes.

Bake the cake a day before use. Fill it the day it is to be eaten.

For the icing, sieve together the icing sugar and the cocoa and add the water and the melted fat, using enough water to give a stiff consistency. Turn the cake upside down, cut the cake in two and spread the icing evenly over the top of the bottom half which, because of its even surface, will be the top of the cake.

For the cream filling, whip the cream until stiff. Stir in the sieved icing sugar and the vanillin sugar. Set aside 3 tbsp. of this cream for decoration. Then add the cocoa and set aside 2 tbsp. to coat the sides of the finished cake. Spread the chocolate cream onto the top half of the cake. With a sharp knife, cut the bottom half of the cake (i. e. the half with the chocolate icing) into 12 equal pieces and place them carefully onto the half with the chocolate cream. Coat the sides of the cake with the 2 tbsp. of the chocolate cream. Pipe the 3 tbsp. of the white cream onto the top of the cake in a star decoration, a star on each piece. The chocolate cream around the sides of the cake may be sprinkled with the shredded chocolate, as well as the stars, if desired.

Alternatively, powdered coffee (2 heaped tsp.) may be added to the cream filling instead of the cocoa.

II. ROLLS AND SLICED CAKES

For the sponge mixture, separate the whites from the yolks of the eggs and whisk the yolks with the water. Gradually add ⅔ of the sugar and the vanillin sugar. Beat till the mixture is thick and creamy. In another bowl beat the white stiffly and whisk in the rest of the sugar. The mixture must be stiff enough to retain the mark of a knife blade. Fill onto the egg yolk mixture, sieve on top the GUSTIN, the BACKIN and the flour and gently fold all together. Spread evenly over a baking sheet, greased and lined with paper. Turn the paper up at the open end to prevent the mixture running over. It should be about ⅜ inch (1 cm) thick. Place high in the oven.

Oven: pre-heat for 5 minutes at very hot, bake at moderately hot.

Baking Time: about 10–15 minutes.

When the sponge is baked, quickly turn it out onto a sheet of greaseproof paper sprinkled with sugar. The paper it has been baked on should be wetted quickly with cold water and carefully removed. Then roll the cake with the underneath paper and set aside to cool.

For the filling, stir the sugar into the pudding powder and blend with the 5 tbsp. milk. Bring the ¾ pint (425 ccm) milk to the boil, remove from heat and stir in the pudding powder mixture. Bring to the boil again quickly, stirring all the time. Cool the mixture, stirring it fairly often to prevent a skin forming.

Cream the fat and add the cooled pudding to it by degrees. Do not let either get too cold, or they will curdle. Carefully unroll the cooled sponge and spread the butter cream evenly over it, leaving a little aside for decorating. Roll it up again, spreading the remaining cream over the outside. Use a fork to make ridges on the cream to give the log effect.

Chocolate Log
(Bismarck Oak)

Sponge Mixture:
4 eggs
3–4 tbsp. warm water, depending on
    the size of the eggs
4½ oz. (125 g) sugar
1 packet Oetker Vanillin Sugar
2½ oz. (70 g) plain flour
2 oz. (55 g) Oetker GUSTIN
    (corn starch powder)
a pinch of Oetker Baking Powder
    BACKIN

Butter Cream Filling:
1 packet Oetker GALA Pudding Powder,
    chocolate flavour
3–3½ oz. (85–100 g) sugar
5 tbsp. cold milk
¾ pint (425 ccm) milk
7 oz. (200 g) unsalted butter or
    margarine

Sponge Slices

Sponge Mixture:

3 eggs
5–6 tbsp. warm water, depending on the size of the eggs
5½ oz. (150 g) sugar
1 packet Oetker Vanillin Sugar
3½ oz. (100 g) plain flour
2 oz. (55 g) Oetker GUSTIN (corn starch powder)
1 level tsp. (3 g) Oetker Baking Powder BACKIN

Filling:

1. 2–3 tbsp. jam

2. Butter Cream:
1 packet Oetker Pudding Powder, vanilla flavour
2 oz. (55 g) sugar
5 tbsp. cold milk
¾ pint (425 ccm) milk
3½ oz. (100 g) unsalted butter or margarine

For the sponge mixture, separate the yolks from the whites of the eggs and beat the yolks to a froth with the water. Add about ⅔ of the sugar with the vanillin sugar. Continue to beat until the mixture is thick and creamy. In a separate bowl whisk the egg white stiff, then whisk in gradually the rest of the sugar. The mixture should be stiff enough to retain the mark made by a cut from the blade of a knife. Fill this onto the egg yolk mixture. Sieve together the GUSTIN, the BACKIN and the flour onto this and fold carefully into the mixture. Spread this evenly onto a greased and lined baking sheet. It should be about ⅜ inch (1 cm) thick. Turn up the lining paper at the open end to prevent it running out. Place high in the oven to bake.

Oven: pre-heat at very hot for 5 minutes, bake at moderately hot.

Baking Time: 10–15 minutes.

When the cake is done, turn it out onto a sheet of greaseproof paper, sprinkled with sugar. The lining paper can be removed by wetting it with cold water and quickly but carefully tearing it away.

For the filling, blend the pudding powder with the sugar and the 5 tbsp. of milk. Bring the ¾ pint (425 ccm) milk to the boil, remove from heat and stir in the prepared pudding powder. Bring quickly to the boil again, stirring all the time. Set aside to cool, stirring fairly frequently to prevent a skin forming.

Cut the sponge in two halves, and spread one half with the jam and about half of the pudding mixture. Place the other half of the sponge on top.

Cream the fat and gradually add to it the rest of the pudding mixture, making sure neither is too cold, or they will curdle.

Thinly spread the top of the sponge with this cream, then cut it into slices about 2 inches by 4 inches (5 x 10 cm). Using a forcing bag, decorate the slices with the rest of the butter cream.

Alternatively, the slices can be covered with chocolate icing before being decorated with the butter cream.

To make the icing, sieve together 3 oz. (85 g) icing sugar with 1 heaped tsp. of cocoa and beat in about 1 tbsp. of hot water to get a stiff consistency.

III. SPONGE BISCUITS

Beat the eggs stiffly with a whisk and gradually add the sugar and the vanillin sugar. Continue to beat until the mixture is thick and creamy. This will take about 15 minutes. Sieve together the GUSTIN, the flour, and aniseed and stir into the mixture by degrees. Using 2 teaspoons, put small heaps of the mixture onto a greased and floured baking sheet. Be careful to leave sufficient space between the heaps. Leave them to dry in a warm room overnight. Next day bake high in the oven.

Oven: slow.

Baking Time: 25–35 minutes.

Aniseed Biscuits

3 eggs
7 oz. (200 g) castor sugar
1 packet Oetker Vanillin Sugar
$\frac{1}{2}$ oz. (15 g) ground aniseed
$4\frac{1}{2}$ oz. (125 g) plain flour
$4\frac{1}{2}$ oz. (125 g) Oetker GUSTIN
(corn starch powder)

For the sponge mixture, separate the yolks from the whites of the eggs and beat the yolks with the warm water until frothy. Gradually add about $\frac{2}{3}$ of the sugar with the vanillin sugar. Continue to beat until the mixture is thick and creamy. Whisk the egg white until it is stiff enough to retain the mark made by the blade of a knife. Fill it onto the yolk mixture, sieve the GUSTIN, the BACKIN and flour on top and gently fold all together. Do not stir. Sprinkle a greased baking sheet with flour and, using a forcing bag or 2 teaspoons, drop onto it small heaps of the mixture about 2 inches (5 cm) in diameter placed fairly far apart. Bake high in the oven until golden yellow.

Oven: pre-heat for 5 minutes at very hot, bake at moderate.

Baking Time: 10–15 minutes.

For the filling, blend the pudding powder and the sugar with the 5 tbsp. milk. Bring the $\frac{3}{4}$ pint (425 ccm) of milk to the boil, remove from heat and stir in the prepared pudding powder. Bring to the boil again, stirring all the time. Set aside to cool, stirring frequently to prevent a skin forming. When cool, sandwich the biscuits together in pairs with the mixture.

For the icing, sieve together the icing sugar and the cocoa and add enough hot water to give a stiff consistency. Add the melted fat. Before icing, the cakes should be thinly coated with the apricot jam (the jam must be very hot).

Moors' Heads

Sponge Mixture:

3 eggs
1 tbsp. warm water
$5\frac{1}{2}$ oz. (150 g) sugar
1 packet Oetker Vanillin Sugar
$5\frac{1}{2}$ oz. (150 g) plain flour
2 oz. (55 g) Oetker GUSTIN
(corn starch powder)
1 level tsp. (3 g) Oetker Baking Powder
BACKIN

Filling:

1 packet Oetker Pudding Powder,
vanilla flavour
2 oz. (55 g) sugar
5 tbsp. cold milk
$\frac{3}{4}$ pint (425 ccm) milk

For Coating:

2 tbsp. sieved apricot jam

Icing:

7 oz. (200 g) icing sugar
1 oz. (30 g) cocoa
3–4 tbsp. hot water
1 tbsp. melted butter or margarine,
if desired

Sponge Fingers

2 eggs
2 oz. (55 g) sugar
1 packet Oetker Vanillin Sugar
2 oz. (55 g) plain flour
1 oz. (30 g) Oetker GUSTIN
(corn starch powder)
1 level tsp. (3 g) Oetker Baking Powder
BACKIN

Separate the whites from the yolks of the eggs and beat the yolks with about ⅔ of the sugar and the vanillin sugar. Continue to beat until the mixture is thick and creamy. The white should be beaten separately until it is stiff enough to retain the mark made by the blade of a knife. Fill the egg white onto the yolk mixture, sieve the flour, the GUSTIN and the BACKIN on top and gently fold all together. Do not stir. Dust a greased baking sheet with flour and pipe the mixture onto it in fingerlengths set fairly far apart. Bake high in the oven till golden yellow.

Oven: pre-heat for 5 minutes at very hot, bake at moderate.

Baking Time: about 10 minutes.

Chocolate Eclairs

Choux Mixture:
½ pint (285 ccm) water
2 oz. (55 g) butter, margarine or lard
6 oz. (170 g) plain flour
1 oz. (30 g) Oetker GUSTIN
(corn starch powder)
5–7 eggs
1 level tsp. (3 g) Oetker Baking Powder
BACKIN

Coffee Cream Filling:
1½ level tsp. Oetker Regina gelatine,
powdered, white
1 tbsp. cold water
½ packet Oetker Pudding Powder,
chocolate flavour
1–2 oz. (30–55 g) sugar
⅔ pint (375 ccm) milk
1 well heaped tsp. powdered coffee

Icing:
3½ oz. (100 g) icing sugar
½ bottle Oetker rum flavour
1–2 tbsp. hot water

For the choux mixture, put the water and the fat into a pan (preferably with a long handle) and bring them quickly to the boil. Remove from heat, add the flour, mixed and sieved with the GUSTIN, all at once and stir until a smooth lump is obtained. Return to heat and stir for a further minute. Transfer the hot lump immediately into a bowl and add the eggs one by one. When the mixture is very glossy and of good dropping consistency no more eggs need be added. Set aside to cool, then add the BACKIN. Using a forcing bag with a large nozzle, pipe the mixture onto a greased and floured baking sheet in long éclair shapes. This is best done by piping two fingerlenghts strips side by side on the sheet and close together and then piping a third on top. Repeat for each éclair. Bake low in the oven.

Oven: pre-heat for 5 minutes at very hot, bake at moderate to hot.

Baking Time: about 20 minutes.

Do not open the oven door during the first 15 minutes baking-time or the éclairs will collapse. As soon as they are done, cut them open.

For the filling, mix the gelatine with the water and allow to soak for about 10 minutes. Blend the pudding powder and the sugar with 4 tbsp. of the milk. Bring the rest of the milk to the boil. Remove from heat, stir in the prepared pudding powder, return to the heat again and bring to the boil, stirring constantly. Remove from heat and immediately stir in the coffee and the soaked gelatine. Stir until the gelatine has completely dissolved. Set aside to cool, stirring frequently to prevent a skin forming. Fill the éclairs with the cold cream.

For the icing, sieve the icing sugar, add the flavouring and just enough water to obtain a fairly thick consistency. Spread on the lids of the éclairs.

D. CHOUX PASTRY

For the choux mixture, put the water and the fat into a pan (preferably with a long handle), bring to the boil and remove from heat. Stir in the flour, mixed and sieved with the GUSTIN and stir until a smooth lump is formed. Heat the lump for about a minute, stirring constantly. Transfer the hot lump to a bowl and beat in the eggs one by one. When the mixture is very glossy and of a good dropping consistency, no more eggs need be added. Cool slightly, then add the BACKIN. With 2 spoons or a forcing bag, form the mixture into walnut-sized balls and place on a greased and slightly floured baking sheet. Bake low in the oven.

Oven: pre-heat for 5 minutes at very hot, bake at moderate to hot.

Baking Time: 25–30 minutes.

Do not open the oven door for the first 20 minutes baking-time, or the puffs will collapse. Cut them open immediately they are done.

For the filling, wash and stone the cherries and stir into them 1½ oz. (45 g) sugar. Leave them to soak in this for a short time, then bring them just to boiling point and strain. When both juice and cherries have cooled, take ¼ pint (140 ccm) of the juice (dilute with water if there is not enough) and blend with the GUSTIN. Bring this quickly to the boil, stirring all the time. Remove from heat, stir in the cherries, add sugar to taste and leave to cool.

Fill the puffs with the cold cherries, top with the whipped cream, to which the vanillin sugar and sugar have been added and replace the lid.

Dust with icing sugar.

Cream Puffs with Cherries
(Phot. See Page 283)

Choux Mixture:
½ pint (285 ccm) water
2 oz. (55 g) butter, margarine or lard
6 oz. (170 g) plain flour
1 oz. (30 g) Oetker GUSTIN
(corn starch powder)
5–7 eggs
1 level tsp. (3 g) Oetker Baking Powder BACKIN

Filling:
About 1 lb. (450 g) cherries
1½–2 oz. (45–55 g) sugar
1 oz. (30 g) Oetker GUSTIN
(corn starch powder)
1 pint (570 ccm) fresh double cream
1 packet Oetker Vanillin Sugar
1 tbsp. sugar

For Dusting:
a little icing sugar

317

E. PASTRY FRIED IN DEEP FAT

The success of this pastry largely depends on heating the fat correctly. If the fat is too hot, the outside of the pastry will brown quickly, leaving the inside uncooked. If the fat is not heated enough, the pastry will be sodden. To test whether the fat is heated to the right temperature, dip the handle of a wooden spoon in it. If bubbles form instantly around the stem of the spoon, the fat is just right. It is well worth carrying out this test before putting in the pastry each time.

Eberswalder Pastries

Choux Mixture:
⅓ pint (200 ccm) water
3½ oz. (100 g) butter or margarine
6 oz. (170 g) plain flour
1 oz. (30 g) Oetker GUSTIN (corn starch powder)
1 oz. (30 g) sugar
1 packet Oetker Vanillin Sugar
4–6 eggs
1 slightly heaped tsp. (4 g) Oetker Baking Powder BACKIN

Fat for Frying:
oil, lard, or coconut butter

Icing:
7 oz. (200 g) icing sugar
4 drops Oetker Baking Essence, lemon flavour
about 3 tbsp. hot water

For the choux mixture, put the water into a pan (preferably with a long handle) with the fat and bring quickly to the boil. Remove from the heat and add all at once the flour mixed and sieved with the GUSTIN. Stir until a smooth lump is obtained and reheat for about 1 minute, stirring all the time. Transfer the mixture to a bowl and gradually stir in the sugar, the vanillin sugar and the eggs. When the mixture is glossy and of a good dropping consistency no more eggs are needed. Set aside to cool, then add the BACKIN to the cooled mixture. Using a forcing bag with a large nozzle, pipe the mixture in rings onto a sheet of greaseproof paper greased with margarine. Deep fry immediately in plenty of boiling fat on both sides until golden brown. Remove from fat with a wooden stick or knitting needle and drain well.

For the icing, stir the icing sugar thoroughly with the baking essence and with enough water to make a good coating consistency. Ice the Eberswalder Pastries with the mixture.

Twists

Pastry:
1⅛ lb. (500 g) plain flour
1 level tsp. (3 g) Oetker Baking Powder BACKIN
3½ oz. (100 g) sugar
a few drops of Oetker Baking Essence, lemon flavour
1 bottle Oetker rum flavour
3 eggs
4 tbsp. milk or water
4½ oz. (125 g) butter or margarine

Fat for Frying:
oil, lard or coconut butter

For Dusting:
a little icing sugar

Mix together the flour and the BACKIN and sieve onto a pastry board. Make a well in the centre and into it pour the sugar, the flavourings, the eggs and the liquid. Drawing flour from the sides of the well, mix to a thick paste. On top of this put the cold fat cut into pieces and, bringing in more flour and working from the centre, knead the whole into an even dough. Roll out thinly and cut into strips. Make a slit in the middle of each strip and draw one end through. Fry in plenty of boiling fat till golden brown. Drain well and dust with icing sugar.

Oetker Ice Cream (prepare according to the directions on the packet)

Whisk the egg whites till very stiff and gradually beat in the sieved icing sugar. The mixture should be very stiff, so that it retains the mark of a knife blade. Put aside 2 slightly heaped tbsp. of this mixture for coating. Stir into the remainder the flavourings and spice and about half of the almonds, or hazelnuts. Knead in enough of the remaining almonds (hazelnuts) to make the dough scarcely sticky. Sprinkle a pastry board generously with almonds (hazelnuts) or sieved icing sugar, roll out the dough ¼ inch (½ cm) thick and cut into stars. Arrange on well greased paper on a baking sheet and coat carefully with the stiff egg white saved for the purpose. If the coating does not spread evenly, dilute slightly with water.

Oven: slow.

Baking Time: 30–40 minutes.

The biscuits should still be soft when they are taken out of the oven. Store in an airtight container.

Whip the eggs until frothy, gradually add the sieved icing sugar with the vanillin sugar. Whisk the mixture until it is thick and creamy. This will take about 15 minutes. Mix about ½ lb. (225 g) of the flour with the BACKIN and sieve. Stir as much of this flour into the egg mixture as is needed to make a firm paste. Put the rest of the flour onto a pastry board, put the dough onto it, cover the dough with the flour and knead together till smooth. If the dough is still sticky, flour, up to about further 2 oz. (55 g) may be sieved in. Roll out to about ⅜ inch (1 cm) thick. Flour a springerle board. Press it hard upon the dough to get a good imprint. Separate the squares, place them on a baking sheet, greased and sprinkled with aniseed and permit them to dry for 24 hours in a warm room (do not place sheets on top of each other). Bake high in the oven.

Oven: slow.

Baking Time: 30–35 minutes.

Leave the "Springerle" exposed to the air for few days, and they will become soft. Then store them in a cake tin.

Whisk the egg whites till they are stiff enough to retain the mark of a knife blade. Gradually whisk in the sugar and the vanillin sugar, the cinnamon and the baking essence. Slowly fold in the coconut. Using 2 teaspoons, place the mixture in small heaps on a greased baking sheet and bake high in the oven.

Oven: slow.

Baking Time: 20–25 minutes.

Cinnamon Stars

Mixture:
3 egg whites
9 oz. (250 g) icing sugar
1 packet Oetker Vanillin Sugar
3 drops Oetker Baking Essence,
  bitter almond flavour
1 level tsp. ground cinnamon
10–12 oz. (280–340 g) almonds
  (ground in their skins)
  or hazelnuts, depending on the size
  of the eggs

For Rolling out:
almonds or hazelnuts (ground in their
  skins), or some icing sugar to dust
  the pastry board

"Springerle"

Mixture:
2 eggs
7 oz. (200 g) icing sugar
1 packet Oetker Vanillin Sugar
about 10 oz. (280 g) plain flour
pinch of Oetker Baking Powder
  BACKIN

**For Sprinkling on the
Baking Sheet:**
a little aniseed

Macaroons

4 egg whites
7 oz. (200 g) castor sugar
1 packet Oetker Vanillin Sugar
a pinch of cinnamon
2 drops Oetker Baking Essence,
  bitter almond flavour
7 oz. (200 g) shredded coconut

G. CAKE MAKING WITH YEAST

Baking with yeast is more difficult and takes longer than with Baking Powder BACKIN. Yeast is a living organism and needs special treatment if it is to work properly.

With BACKIN, no special temperature is required, either for the ingredients, except that no hot ingredient may be used or for the room in which they are being prepared. With yeast, the ingredients must be warm, and the room in which they are being prepared should be at the right temperature, 99° F (37 ° C).

Just like any other living organism, yeast requires food if it is to grow. This food is supplied from the other ingredients in the recipe – usually sugar, flour, or starch, i. e. the carbohydrates which are to be found in the dough. When the yeast acts on these they are turned into carbon dioxide and alcohol, both of which are raising agents giving a light textured dough. Sugar is "digested" rapidly by yeast. Flour takes longer because it has to undergo certain chemical changes before it can be "digested". Fat and salt make heavy food for yeast and slow down its growth.

A mixture containing yeast must rise before baking. The moment the yeast comes into contact with the hot oven it "dies" and the dough will not rise any more.

The golden rule for cake making with yeast is that it must never be too hot and never be too cold, nor must the ingredients it touches be hot or cold. To make yeast work really quickly, add a little sugar to the lukewarm milk. Avoid direct contact with fat or salt. The dough should be left to rise in a warm place.

It should almost double its original size.

Always keep to the times given in the recipe. For dried yeast, follow the manufacturer's instructions. All the recipes given are for use with baker's yeast.

Cream the yeast with the 1 tsp. of sugar and 5 tbsp. of the milk. Sieve the flour into a large bowl, make a well in the centre and pour in the yeast. Sprinkle some of the flour over the yeast to about ¼ inch (½ cm) thickness. Put the sugar, the flavouring ingredients, the eggs and the melted fat along the edge of the basin on the flour. They must not be in contact with the yeast.

As soon as the flour covering the yeast shows large cracks, start to mix. Working from the middle, stir all the ingredients together and add enough of the remaining milk to get a dough which drops heavily from the spoon. Beat the dough with a strong wooden spoon until bubbles form. Work in the almonds, the washed and drained raisins, and the candied lemon peel. Leave the dough to rise in a warm oven until it has doubled its size. Stir it thoroughly and put into a well greased ring tin. Put the cake tin low into the pre-heated oven to prove. When it has become about half as big again, bake in the oven.

Oven: moderate.

Baking Time: about 50 minutes.

For the dough, cream the yeast with the 1 tsp. sugar and the 3 tbsp. milk. Sieve ⅔ of the flour into a large bowl, make a well in the centre, pour in the dissolved yeast and cover with about ¼ inch (½ cm) flour. Put the sugar, the flavouring and the melted tepid fat or oil round the edge of the bowl on top of the flour. They must not come into contact with the yeast yet. As soon as the flour covering the yeast shows large cracks, stir all the ingredients together, starting with the yeast and flour and working from the middle. Gradually add the ⅓ pint (200 ccm) milk. Using a large wooden spoon, beat the dough till bubbles rise. Now knead in the remaining flour. If the dough is sticky, add a little flour, but not too much, the dough is meant to be soft. Leave the dough to rise in a pre-heated oven until it has doubled its size. Knead thoroughly again and roll out onto a greased baking sheet. If the baking sheet has an open end, put a border of strong folded paper at the open side to stop the dough running over.

For the topping, cover the dough with the fat – either in flakes or melted. Mix the sugar and the vanillin sugar with the almonds (hazelnuts) and sprinkle evenly over the cake. Leave the dough to rise again in the pre-heated oven until it again doubles its size. Then bake it in the oven.

Oven: pre-heat for 5 minutes at very hot, bake at moderately hot.

Baking Time: about 15 minutes.

Plain Cake with Yeast
(Napfkuchen)

1 oz. (30 g) fresh yeast
1 tsp. sugar
about ⅓ pint (200 ccm) tepid milk
1⅛ lb. (500 g) plain flour
5½ oz. (150 g) sugar
1 packet Oetker Vanillin Sugar
4 drops Oetker Baking Essence,
   lemon flavour
a little salt
2 eggs
4½ oz. (125 g) butter, margarine
   or lard
2 oz. (55 g) blanched and chopped
   almonds
5–6 oz. (140–170 g) raisins
2 oz. (55 g) candied lemon peel
   (chopped)

Butter or Sugar Cake
(On a Baking Sheet)

Dough:
¾ oz. (20 g) fresh yeast
1 tsp. sugar
3 tbsp. tepid milk
1⅛ lb. (500 g) plain flour
3 oz. (85 g) sugar
3 drops Oetker Baking Essence,
   bitter almond flavour
a little salt
2 oz. (55 g) butter, margarine or lard,
   or 3 tbsp. oil
⅓ pint (200 ccm) tepid milk

Topping:
2–4½ oz. (55–125 g) butter
   or margarine
3 oz. (85 g) sugar
1 packet Oetker Vanillin Sugar
2 oz. (55 g) almonds or hazelnuts,
   optional
   (blanched and finely chopped)

Crumble Cake
(Streuselkuchen)

Dough:
¾ oz. (20 g) fresh yeast
1 tsp. sugar
3 tbsp. tepid milk
1⅛ lb. (500 g) plain flour
3 oz. (85 g) sugar
3 drops Oetker Baking Essence,
bitter almond flavour
a little salt
2 oz. (55 g) butter, margarine or lard,
or 3 tbsp. oil
⅓ pint (200 ccm) tepid milk
3–4½ oz. (85–125 g) raisins

Topping:
7 oz. (200 g) plain flour
4 oz. (115 g) sugar
1 packet Oetker Vanillin Sugar
pinch of cinnamon
4 oz. (115 g) butter or margarine

Make the dough as for "Butter or Sugar Cake" (see page 327). Add the washed and drained raisins to the last third of flour and knead them into the dough.

For the topping, sieve the flour into a bowl and stir in the sugar, the vanillin sugar and the cinnamon. Cut the fat into pieces and rub in with the fingers or two forks until the mixture resembles breadcrumbs.

Roll out the dough, place on a baking sheet and sprinkle evenly with the topping.

Oven: pre-heat for 5 minutes at very hot, bake at moderately hot.

Baking Time: 15–25 minutes.

Fruit Cake
(Baked on a Baking Sheet)

Dough:
¾ oz. (20 g) fresh yeast
1 tsp. sugar
⅓ pint (200 ccm) tepid milk
1⅛ lb. (500 g) plain flour
3 oz. (85 g) sugar
1 packet Oetker Vanillin Sugar
a little salt
2 oz. (55 g) butter, margarine or lard,
or 3 tbsp. oil

Topping:
2¼–3¼ lb. (1–1½ kg) apples
or plums

For Sprinkling:
a little sugar

Make the dough as for "Butter or Sugar Cake" (see page 327).

For the topping, peel the apples and slice fairly thickly. If plums are used, wash and stone. Arrange the fruit evenly on the top of the dough (always put plums with the skin to the dough). Leave the dough in a warm place to prove until it has doubled its size, then place in the oven to bake.

Oven: pre-heat for 5 minutes at very hot, bake at moderately hot.

Baking Time: 20–25 minutes.

When it is done, take it from the oven and leave it to cool slightly. Then remove it from the baking sheet and sprinkle with sugar. If a thinner cake crust is preferred, take only ¾ of the quantities given for the dough.

FRUIT AND
VEGETABLE
PRESERVING

When fruit and vegetables are plentiful and cheap in summer and autumn, they should be preserved against the time when they will be scarce and expensive. The outlay of money and time required to carry out preserving is amply repaid when considered in relation to feeding the family over the whole year. Seen in this way, preserving has tremendous advantages, both from the point of view of economy and of variety and nourishment in the family's meals. If you have to work on a strict weekly budget you can, to some extent, lessen the fairly large financial outlay needed, by planning ahead and saving a little each week towards the expense of preserving. Week by week you can set aside a little sugar and other preserving agents, so that when fruit and vegetables are in season, you will be able to take advantage of it. The information in this chapter is based on practical experience, and will help you to fill your store cupboard. These will increase the food value of your meals at times when fresh fruit and vegetables are not so easy to obtain.

Food preserving helps the national larder; it prevents wastage at harvest time, when there is more than enough for the immediate needs of the whole population.

General Hints

1. Only freshly picked fruit and vegetables should be used for preserving. If you have to buy them, shop early, before the heat of the day can ruin the quality of the food.

2. Select firm, sound fruit which is slightly under-ripe and of the best quality. Over-ripe, soft fruit or fruit that is bruised should never be used for preserving.

3. All containers and utensils used for preserving should be kept for this purpose only. It is especially important to prevent their coming into contact with fat. Before use, wash containers and utensils thoroughly in hot water to which a cleansing agent has been added. Then rinse with clean water and place upside down on a clean cloth to drain.

4. Scrupulous cleanliness is essential to success. If the slightest particle of food — even a crumb — falls into the preserves, it will cause fermentation.

5. Label each container with the name of its contents and the date they were made. Use up in rotation, always taking first.

6. Store preserves in a dry, cool, airy place and inspect from time to time to make sure they are in good condition.

A. STERILIZING

To preserve by sterilization is to destroy the bacteria already present by means of heat at boiling temperature; and then to prevent the penetration of fresh bacteria by hermetically sealing the jars. The heat causes the air in the jar to expand, allowing some of it to escape during processing. While cooling, a partial vacuum is created and the pressure of the outside air hermetically seals the jars. For this method special jars with rubber rings and lids, clips or metal screw bands are needed. These jars must be checked and carefully cleaned before use and always kept clean. Never use chipped or cracked jars or lids, or rubber rings that have deteriorated, as they are useless.

The Preparation of Vegetables for Sterilization

Great care must be exercised in preparing vegetables for sterilizing. First cook the vegetables in very little water in an uncovered saucepan. The time required depends on the vegetable, about 5–15 minutes. As soon as the vegetables have cooled, pack them into jars and cover with water. Use either the liquid in which the vegetables have been steamed, or boiled and cooled salted water, or boiled and cooled unsalted water. This depends on the type of water available and on your own experience. Boiled and cooled unsalted water is generally used. Do not pack the jars too tightly, or fill them up too high with water; there must be room enough for the contents of the jars to cook thoroughly. Wet the rubber ring and lid before putting onto the clean rim of the jar and adjust the screw band or clip.

The Preparation of Fruit for Sterilization

Pack the fruit tightly into the jars. Sprinkle in some sugar — 3½–7 oz. (100–200 g) per 2¼ lb. (1 kg) fruit. Alternatively, pour syrup over the fruit. For sweet fruit, the syrup should be made in the proportion of 1¾ pint (1 l) water to 7 oz. (200 g) sugar; for sour fruit, 1¾ pint (1 l) water to about 1 lb. (450 g) sugar. Juicy fruit, like rhubarb and cherries, peaches and plums, need syrup only half way up the jar. Less juicy fruit should be covered with syrup, or it will become discoloured. Wet the rubber ring and the lid, wipe the rim of the jar carefully, put on the ring and the lid — the rubber ring acts as a washer between the jar and the lid—and lastly adjust the metal screw band or clip.

Sterilization in Boiling Water

Special sterilizers are employed for this method. The jars are placed on a rack and the lids are held in position by means of springs. If this type of sterilizer is not available, a large enamel saucepan (fish-kettle, clothes boiler or copper) with a tight-fitting lid, may be used. A good non-conductor of heat (wire rack or slatted wooden rack) should be placed at the bottom of the container to prevent the jars from cracking. If this method is used, the lids must be held in position with clips or band screws. The jars must not touch one another or the sides of the container. Fill the container with water to the height of the jars. The water should have the same temperature as the contents of the jars.

331

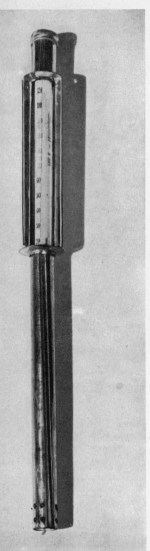

Bring the water almost to the boil, then turn down to a slow heat to sterilize. If a special sterilizer is used, heat the water until the correct temperature is reached, then adjust the heat to maintain the required temperature. The thermometer must be immersed in the water. Detailed directions for the use of a sterilizer are furnished by the manufacturers and should be followed carefully.

The chart below may be referred to when using a special sterilizer, although it may have to be adjusted to meet special conditions.

	Degrees		Minutes	
	C	F		
Apricots	75	167	25– 30	
Pears (soft)	90	194	25– 30	
Pears (hard)	90	194	40– 50	
Strawberries	75	167	20– 25	
Blueberries	80	176	25– 30	
Raspberries	75	167	20– 25	
Currants	90	194	30– 40	
Mirabelles (small yellow plums)	75	167	25– 30	
Peaches (whole fruit)	75	167	35– 45	
Peaches (halves)	75	167	25– 35	Depending on the size of the jars
Damsons or Plums	90	194	25– 30	
Greengages	75	167	25– 30	
Gooseberries (unripe)	75	167	25– 30	
Sweet or sour cherries	80	176	25– 30	
Cauliflower	98	208	90–110	
Beans	98	208	100–130	
Peas	98	208	100–130	
Kohlrabi	98	208	90–110	
Carrots	98	208	90–120	
Mushrooms (cooked)	98	208	60– 75	
Asparagus	98	208	90–120	
Spinach	98	208	90–110	
Tomatoes (whole)	90	194	25– 30	
Tomato purée	90	194	25– 30	

B. BRINED VEGETABLES

This is a practical way to preserve large quantities of vegetables for the winter, being both simple and inexpensive. The vegetables most suitable for brining are French and runner beans, cucumbers and especially successfull, cabbage. "Sauerkraut" (pickled cabbage), the famous German dish, is not only delicious, it also possesses therapeutic qualities and is often included in special diets. Brined vegetables undergo a process of fermentation caused by the presence of yeast and lactic acid bacteria, which transform almost all the carbohydrates into lactic acid, which, like yoghurt and clotted milk, acts on the gastric juices and disinfects the intestines. Uncooked sauerkraut is especially wholesome and if stored in the proper way and not over too long a period will retain its vitamins. If served cooked, increase the vitamin content of the dish by adding to it some uncooked sauerkraut.

The process of fermentation may be speeded up by leaving the jar of vegetables in a warm room for the first few days, then transferring it to a cold place, preferably a cellar.

General Hints

1. Clean all receptacles — stone ware jars or crocks, barrels, etc. — very thoroughly. Scald with hot water and allow to dry in the air.

2. Cabbage and beans should be packed firmly into the container with a wooden presser or by hand, so that the brine covers the vegetables.

3. Cover with a scalded linen cloth.

4. Cover the cloth with a board (not pine) or a plate, preferably of the same diameter as the top of the container; on top of this place a weight (a stone), heavy enough to make the brine come up and wet the cloth.

5. Wash the cloth and board (plate), as well as the stone, every 10–14 days.

6. If during the course of the winter the vegetables need more brine, fill up with cold brine.

7. Always use a **wooden** spoon or fork when you take out some of the vegetables for use.

8. Follow the general hints on preserving (see page 330).

Salted Sauerkraut

11 lb. (5 kg) cabbage
3½ oz. (100 g) salt

Choose very firm and fresh white cabbage. Remove the outer leaves and shred finely. Then pack alternate layers of cabbage and salt into a crock, pressing down firmly so that the juice covers the cabbage. Cover the top layer with cabbage leaves, a board, and then a weight (stone), heavy enough to make the brine come up to the board. Cover the jar with a piece of cloth secured with string and store in a cool place. Time for fermentation, 4–6 weeks.

Alternatively, juniper berries, vine leaves or sliced apples may be put in with the cabbage. Use 1⅛ lb. (500 g) apples to 11 lb. (5 kg) of cabbage.

Salted French or Runner Beans

11 lb. (5 kg) French or runner beans
7 oz. (200 g) salt

Use young beans. Wash, drain well, string and shred, if possible with a special cutter. Mix with the salt and pack as firmly as possible into the crock. Cover with a cloth, place a board on top and then a weight (stone), heavy enough to make the brine come up and wet the cloth. Store covered in a cool place.

Other beans may be salted in the same way. It is advisable to scald the beans for a short while before salting, putting them on a cloth to cool. Then proceed as above.

Salted Cucumbers

Choose sound green cucumbers and allow to soak in cold water for 12–24 hours. Dry and pack firmly into a crock in alternate layers with vine leaves and fresh dill blossoms. Make a brine of 1–1¾ oz. (30–50 g) salt to 1¾ pint (1 l) water; bring to the boil and pour hot over the cucumbers. Cover with a cloth, place a board on top and then a weight (stone), heavy enough to make the brine come up and wet the cloth. Store in a cool place.

Alternatively, layers of bitter cherry leaves, tarragon, bay-leaves or diced horseradish may be put in with the cucumbers.

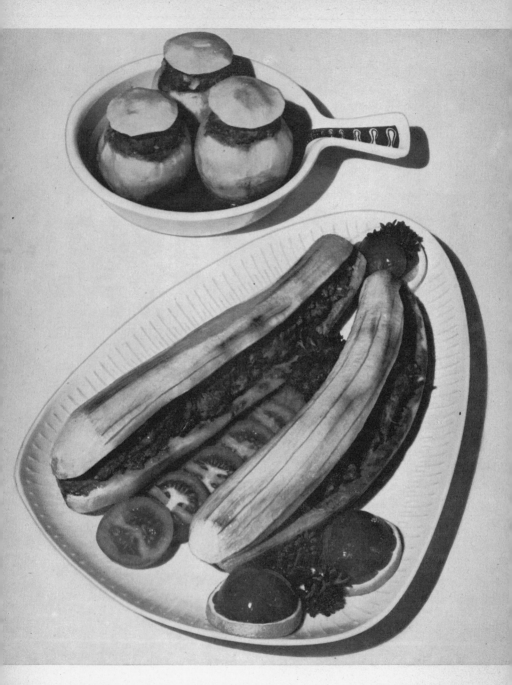

Stuffed Kohlrabi Recipe See Page 165
Stuffed Cucumbers Recipe See Page 164

C. DRYING

The exposure of fruit and vegetables to heat extracts the water from them and so prevents the growth of harmful bacteria, which thrive on moisture. Drying is the oldest known form of food preservation and is still most successfully used, particularly in hot countries. Drying preserves the minerals in the fruit and vegetables and does not spoil their flavour. The method is not only very simple but very cheap as absolutely no preserving agents (vinegar, sugar) are needed. Drying may be done in the open air or in the oven. Wooden racks may be bought or made at home Old wooden picture frames covered with muslin, wire mesh or coarse canvas are excellent for the purpose.

Drying in the Oven

1. Fruit for drying should be perfectly ripe.

General Hints

2. Scald fruit or vegetables for about 5 minutes, drain and spread well spaced out on racks.

3. Before putting the racks into the oven, turn the heat on at the lowest possible temperature.

4. Put one rack on the lowest the other on the highest shelf, then change them around about every hour, so that the fruit or vegetables are evenly dried.

5 Put a wooden spoon between the oven door and the oven, to leave a small gap — this allows moisture to escape. If there is any condensation, the temperature is too high.

6. The drying process is completed when the fruit or vegetables are completely dry to the touch, but not brittle. The fruit should show no sign of juice when broken.

7. After drying in the oven, spread out the fruit, etc., and leave to get quite cold. It should be aired thoroughly for several days.

8. Store in muslin bags and hang the bags in a dry room.

9. All dried fruit and vegetables need soaking for at least 12 hours in water before cooking. They should be boiled in the liquid in which they have soaked, to avoid loss of vitamins.

Apples	Peel, cut into quarters and core. Or remove core and slice into rings.
Pears	Peel. Small pears may be dried whole. Halve large pears. Apples and pears may be strung on strings and air-dried.
Blueberries (Bilberries)	Pick over carefully and spread on packing paper (dried blueberries are good for diarrhoea).
Plums (Damsons)	These should be over-ripe and the skin wrinkly at the stalk end.
Gooseberries	As for blueberries, above (dried gooseberries make a good substitute for raisins).
Rose Hips	Top and tail and, if necessary, remove the seeds. Then dry.
Mushrooms	Clean very carefully, thread on a string or space well out and dry in the sun.
Herbs	These should be gathered before they are in bloom. Dry in small bunches, very slowly, in the sun. Then pulverize and store in air-tight jars.

INDEX